"Will the Third Temple be God's "time bomb?" Chuck Crismier masterfully ties together ancient Bible prophecies and current events. A must read!"

Sid Roth
Host, *It's Supernatural!*

Chuck Crismier's newest book KING OF THE MOUNTAIN is a sweeping, panoramic portrait of God's prophetic plan for mankind. As the world seems to spin hopelessly out of control, KING OF THE MOUNTAIN reminds us that God has an eternal plan that will be accomplished. Every follower of Jesus Christ should read this hope-filled book."

Dr. Robert Jeffress
Pastor, First Baptist Church, Dallas

"This modern commentary on global politics and end time prophecy is one that few could write, but all should read!

"Charles Crismier has aptly portrayed the history of our planet as an attempt to dominate a single mound of ground in the desperate attempt to be "king of the mountain."

"Every despot, like their father the devil, seeks regime change on their terms, but the author proclaims that the great hope of history is the restoration of the rightful rule of Christ as Messiah. It is He who made the mountains and has chosen one at which will be established His long-awaited reign, as it is written, 'I have installed My King Upon My holy mountain' (Psalm 2:6)."

Randall Price, Ph.D.
Distinguished Research Professor
Executive Director, Center for Judaic Studies
Liberty University

The Eternal, Epic,
End-Time
Battle

# KING
## OF THE
# MOUNTAIN

He who rules the Temple Mount rules the world

## CHARLES CRISMIER

*elijah books*
*Richmond, Virginia*

All Scripture quotations are taken from the King James Version of the Bible.

The choice of the King James Version was based upon its continued prominence as the most quoted, read, remembered and published version in the historical life of the Western Church. Emphasis is indicated by bold-faced type to highlight portions of the text for particular focus throughout.

*King of the Mountain*

Copyright © 2013 by Charles Crismier

Published by Elijah Books
P.O. Box 70879
Richmond, VA 23255

Interior design by Pine Hill Graphics
Cover design by Fresh Air Media

Publisher's Cataloging-in-Publication Data
(Provided by Cassidy Cataloguing Services, Inc.)
Crismier, Charles.

    King of the mountain : the eternal, epic, end-time battle-- he who rules the Temple Mount rules the world / Charles Crismier. -- Richmond, Va. : Elijah Books, 2013.
       p. ; cm.

    ISBN: 978-0-9718428-7-8
    Includes bibliographical references.
    Summary: The apex of human history and the culmination of biblical prophecy now loom ominously. What, then, should the inhabitants of this mortal sphere anticipate as history and prophecy become congruent? In order to comprehend the pattern and progress of history, it might best be understood as the battle for "king of the mountain."--Publisher.

    1. History--Biblical teaching.
2. History--Religious aspects--Christianity.
3. End of the world. 4. Bible--Prophecies--Temple of Jerusalem. 5. Eschatology. 6. Kingdom of God--Biblical teaching. 7. Temple Mount (Jerusalem)--Religious aspects--Christianity.
I. Title.

BR115.H5 C75 2013
231.7/6--dc23          1309

**Printed in the United States of America.**

# CONTENTS

# THE TAPESTRY OF HISTORY

*"The time for extracting a lesson from history is ever at hand for those who are wise."*
~Demosthenes

HISTORY IS AN ELUSIVE THING. While the facts and occurrences, places and events of the footsteps of our human forebears are fixed in time and place, recitation of these details, however knowledgeable and seemingly perceptive, reveals little of their individual or collective implication.

On the other hand, we are continually reminded that "the only thing we learn from history is that we don't learn from history." And we are further warned that "those who don't learn from history are doomed to repeat it." What, then, are we to do? How are we to "learn" from history? Are we inevitably "doomed" to repeat it despite persistent warning? And is it the facts of history we are destined to repeat, or is it the patterns driven by underlying forces?

HISTORICAL INTERPRETATION LACKS CERTAINTY. The most insightful efforts to discover and define the driving forces and direction of history, in the final analysis, become little more than informed opinion that becomes de-formed by viewpoints, both individual and cultural, that spin the reality of facts and occurrences into a tapestry portraying the predilections of the philosopher, historian or politician. In our current age, where the doctrines and dogmas of political correctness, multiculturalism and religious pluralism have been granted near absolute authority as the screen through which all reality must be filtered, the task of interpreting history with any measure of intellectual integrity has been rendered nearly impossible. The question then remains, therefore, whether there exists any more hopeful, reliable and even more objective way to study and interpret the last six thousand years of the record of mankind upon our planet. And if so, would it make a shred of difference in the direction, disposition and destiny of the nations and of the world's individual inhabitants? Is there a well-defined and perceptible tapestry of historical truth emerging that might guide us all in this most dangerous time?

**A TAPESTRY OF TRUTH IS EMERGING.** Indeed, the threads of time and the colorful times and events woven therein over sixty centuries last passed are even now revealing an emerging pattern that has been discerned and described by prophets for at least thirty-five centuries. These patterns and their prophetic significance have largely escaped the attention or have been blindly ignored by both the poor and the powerful and by prognosticators even as we teeter on the precipice of global conflagration.

**THIS IS OUR MOMENT OF TRUTH.** The leaders of the nations are trembling. The peoples of our planet are terrified. Nothing seems certain, except chaos. The lust for power and petroleum have catapulted the planet to the precipice of a chasm so sheer as to shake the confidence of the most courageous. Is there any perspective that might shed a ray of hopeful light in the encroaching darkness?

Indeed this is our moment of truth. We are languishing in the valley of decision without genuine direction. Destiny rides in the balance. Please, then, join us on this fascinating journey back through time so as to grasp more effectively the solemnity of our time. Time is short so we must proceed quickly. The prophets of times past will point the way even as we grope in darkness. The picture that will soon emerge will either leave you awash in unprecedented hope or in unfathomable horror. Let us be on our way.

*Part*

# I

# THE CONTEST

IT IS SHOCKING, BUT TRUE! History and biblical prophecy are becoming congruent. The overlap of both ancient and recent history with the foretelling of these events by prophets and bards of the Bible are now converging precisely so as to be nearly indistinguishable from one another to the studied eye.

This unprecedented convergence of prophecy and historical realities is now increasingly revealed in political, economic and religious developments of the decade last passed as well as in the explosive developments flashing daily before our eyes. Like it or not, fear is becoming the norm as terrifying events daily desensitize our minds and hearts to the true issues we face and cauterize our consciences to the consequences.

This first segment of *KING of the Mountain—The Eternal, Epic, End-Time Battle* brings the past into the present so as to better comprehend the greater panoply of this epic and end-time battle with unthinkable eternal import. We must be reminded that, as with the *Titanic*, the *unthinkable* happened to the *unsinkable*. The stage for the end-time expression of this epic battle will here be set with the spiritual furniture upon which the final acts of history will be played out as the harbinger of things to come. The curtain will then be raised for revelation of THE CONTESTANTS in Part 2 and the revelation of THE CONQUEST in Part 3.

*Chapter 1*

# UNCERTAIN TIMES

***"It was the best of times! It was the worst of times."***
~Charles Dickens

THE HEADLINES SCREAM the unprecedented seriousness of our times. Europe is on the verge of collapse. The "Arab Spring" that promised the hopeful rise of democracy has developed into the growing horror of the dictatorial rule of fundamental Islam. Turkey and Iran vie for dominion over the Islamic world—more than a billion people that have no unifying leadership. Will there be a new "Ottoman" empire or a resurrected "Persian" empire? They pursue an Islamic "New World Order" as declared by the "Persian" president, Mahmoud Ahmadinejad. But Islam is not alone.

## PURSUIT OF A NEW ORDER

Leaders of the western world increasingly clamor for clarity and courage to implement a "New World Order," claiming it to be the only hope and salvation for our planet. Russia, China, Britain, Canada.... indeed most of our world, including American leaders, have called for the full implementation of such a new global world order, as did U.S. President George Herbert Walker Bush. His address to Congress in 1991 was the first time any American president had ever publically voiced this global goal.

Even the Vatican, under Pope Benedict XVI, issued a call to implement a new global economic order with a new global currency. Britain's former prime minister, Gordon Brown, former U.S. Secretary of State Henry Kissinger and other leaders strongly suggested the 44th president of the United States was the "anointed one" to lead the way into this new "order of the ages," promising peace and prosperity to a world seemingly in hopeless tumult. Even Germany's respected news magazine, Der Spiegel, titled its cover page "THE MESSIAH FACTOR," in reference to the secularly-promised peacemaker.

Planet earth is not a particularly friendly place at this moment, if indeed it ever was. Perhaps never a more apt description could be given than that of Charles Dickens' in his *Tale of Two Cities*... "It was the best of times, it was the worst of times."

## HOPE AND CHANGE

"Hope and Change" have become an increasingly universal cry throughout the nations. There is an intuitive sense among peoples everywhere that the world cannot continue on with even a remote air of confidence in its current state. Hence the promise of "Change You Can BELIEVE IN" carries immense motivational weight whether or not it is rooted in any meaningful reality.

Is there any hope? Is there anyone we can truly trust? Who can restore order? What promises will tickle our itching ears to promote participation at the ballot box? What good is freedom in the face of enveloping fear? And is there, in reality, any genuine set of principles... or even prophecy... that might shed the light of hope amid the encroaching darkness and enveloping global horror?

Is real hope merely a figment of the imagination? And where does change lead? Change *from* what *to* what? If we are truly living in such a modern and enlightened world and society, why the devastating evidence of rapid deterioration even in the face of exploding technology?

## AN ANSWER YOU CAN BELIEVE IN

Is there any real answer to our dilemma or are we left only with unending and unanswered questions? Must we grope as blind men, hoping upon hope that an exit might be found, that genuine direction be discovered, or that some political savior might appear to usher in a golden age of peace and prosperity?

The answer to these haunting questions lies in an understanding of history—of man's story—from God's viewpoint. History, from God's perspective, has a beginning and an end, and He understands the end from the beginning. The trouble is that we do not, or at least refuse to agree with the plan and purposes of our Creator that are clearly expressed in the Bible, often referred to as "the Scriptures" or "the Word of God."

In the pages that follow, the panoply of history from God's viewpoint as revealed in the Bible will be unfolded in such a way that you will be able to not only capture the grandeur of God's purpose but be able to choose, for yourself, to embrace the only change you will ever be able to totally believe in. A new hope and vision will arise, enabling you to see what lies ahead in this tumultuous time, yet have genuine peace without the terrify-ing fear that will grip our planet.

## KING OF THE MOUNTAIN

In order to understand the great over-arching pattern and "prog-ress" of history, it might best be understood as the battle for "King of the Mountain."

Almost every young boy has played the game. It matters little the cul-ture or geographic location. Boys worldwide battle to become "king of the mountain." Wherever a hill, small or great, may appear, boys will strive to take dominion over the dominate protrusion in the landscape. A mound of snow, a pile of dirt… almost anything will suffice. Each, in turn, may challenge the one currently occupying the hill, striving to pull or push him from his perch. Others may gather, seeking collectively to depose the reign-ing men of the hill, each secretly hoping and conniving to take dominion as "king of the mountain."

It is an inherently violent vocation to pursue kingship of the moun-tain. Blood may be shed as bruises and scrapes begin to appear in the struggle. Whether by political connivery and conspiracy or by the brute force of chariots and horses… or nuclear annihilation… someone will be hurt, lives may be sacrificed, nations may be destroyed in the unfettered pursuit of domination.

"The only difference between men and boys," it is said, "is the price of their toys." And so it is that the only difference between men and boys in the ultimate fleshly struggle for global dominion is the cost or sacrifice in blood, bodies and finances. Similarly, moral and spiritual compromise in pursuit of the prize becomes the fulcrum over which genuine faith is sacrificed in the pursuit of power, fame and fortune.

The greater the hill, the greater the horror and perceived honor. The greater the value placed on the prize, the greater the compromise, con-spiratorial cooperation and carnage.

Such is the nature of our world's final and conclusive battle for "King of the Mountain." It is the war of the ages. It is a no-holds-barred, no-sacrifice-too-great conflict to become ruler of this earth and, yes, "King of the Mountain," exercising global dominion from the most prized and protected "hill" on the planet. It is likewise the eternal epic battle for the souls of men. And the prize awaits the victor.

*Chapter 1*

# PROBING THOUGHTS *for* PROPHETIC TIMES

1. Why is the world pursuing a "New Order?"

2. How is it that the words "Hope and Change" have gained such traction?

3. Do you recall ever playing "King of the Mountain" or "King of the Hill? How would you describe it? Do you see the similarities with events transpiring in our world?

4. Are there any believable answers to the escalating economic, political, and religious confrontations terrorizing our world? Where would you look to find them?

*Chapter 2*

# DESIRE FOR DOMINION

*"And God said... let them have dominion...
over all the earth...."*
Gen. 1:26

DESIRE IS THE DOMINANT FORCE in the history of mankind from Creation to this prophetic, culminating moment of human existence on planet Earth. But *desire* is not a neutral force. Rather, *desire* is a force driven by the nature of man. For that reason, the very nature of man plays the ultimate determining role in the epic and eternal battle for *King of the Mountain*.

## NONE IS EXEMPT

None is exempt from this desire to dominate, whether it be individually, collectively, nationally, regionally or globally. Neither does our political proclivity, religious aspiration, nor social system escape this universal desire to dominate. And there is a reason why this global pursuit of domination has persisted throughout man's sojourn on terra firma.

It is the root of this sometimes pure, yet more often pernicious, desire to dominate that we must first identify. It will yield the clues to unveil the mystery of the epic battle for *King of the Mountain*.

## THE BEGINNING OF THE BATTLE

It all began in the first book of the Bible, the book of beginnings, the Book of Genesis. In fact, it began in Chapter 1.

Without delving more deeply into otherwise provocative issues concerning the origin of man at this moment, the Bible clearly makes some very direct assertions that set the stage for eternal conflict, both geopolitically and spiritually. Please observe and consider these carefully.

Genesis 1:1    "In the beginning God created the heaven and the earth."

Genesis 1:25   "And God made the beast of the earth after his kind…"

Genesis 1:26   "And God said, Let us make man in our image, after our likeness: and **let them have dominion…** over all the earth…."

Genesis 1:27   "So God created man in his own image; … male and female created he them."

Genesis 1:28   "And God blessed them, and God said unto them, Be fruitful, and multiply, and replenish the earth, and **subdue it; and have dominion…."**

Take special notice. Mankind was given dominion over a planet, Earth, that was created by God… in the Beginning. The dominion was delegated. As Creator, the omnipotent God had exclusive authority over His creation and was therefore exclusively qualified and empowered by His own eternal, self-existent power and character as supreme and uncontroverted ruler of the universe to delegate such exclusive authority over a portion of the created universe to the "man" created in His image.

The Psalmist David, declared to be "a man after God's own heart," confirmed this understanding at least 3000 years later. Psalm 8 records his words.

O LORD our Lord, how excellent is thy name in all the earth! Who hath set thy glory above the heavens (vs. 1).

When I consider thy heavens, the work of thy fingers, the moon and the stars, which thou hast ordained: What is man, that thou art mindful of him? And the son of man, that thou visitest him? (vs. 3-4).

For thou hast made him a little lower than "Elohim" [the Supreme God himself] and has crowned him with glory and honor (vs. 5).

**Thou madest him to have dominion** over the works of thy hands; thou hast put all things under his feet (vs. 6).

Mankind was made by God, in God's own image, to exercise dominion over a sphere called Earth. Yet while that authority was exclusive to all other created beings, it was NOT exclusive to the Creator's over-arching authority. Rather, man's authority was to be perpetuated relationally by a humble and loving conformity to the temporal and eternal purposes of the Creator.

*Chapter 2*

# PROBING THOUGHTS *for* PROPHETIC TIMES

1. Is the drive for *dominion* natural or unnatural? Is it good or evil?

2. If the Creator gave Mankind dominion and told him to "have" dominion, how can pursuit of dominion be dangerous... or even damned?

3. In what way was Adam's lawful dominion in the earth usurped? What were the consequences? Do you see the manifestation of these consequences in our world today?

4. Is there any real remedy?

# *Chapter 3*

# "I WILL ASCEND"

—— ⚬⚬⚬ ——

### *"I will ascend…; I will be like the most High."*
Isa. 14:13-14

IT ALL BEGAN IN THE HEAVENS. This is a realm in which we have profoundly limited understanding. Yet our Creator, God, in His kindness and mercy, has, through the Bible, seen fit to give us glimpses of the heavenly realm composed of created spirit beings. These beings, many of whom are referred to as "angels," are not the seed of Adam. They are not of "mankind," and therefore have not been given dominion in the earth.

## HEAVENLY BEINGS

These heavenly, spirit beings well know that their sphere of authority and ministry is limited by their Creator so as to not impair or conflict with man's dominion and authority. In truth, they are "ministering spirits" deputized to do God's bidding (Heb. 1:7). The Scriptures, in fact, make plain that mankind will judge the angels (I Cor. 6:3). It is therefore essential that we take a close look at the very first "angelic" appearance in the Bible. Yet before we visit that first appearance, we need to know some important historical facts revealed to us in the Bible (also known as "The Word of God) about that specific angel described as "the anointed cherub that covereth" (Ezek. 28:14).

## "THE ANOINTED CHERUB"

LUCIFER WAS HIS NAME. He was referred to in the heavens as "the son of the morning" because of his amazing brightness (Isa. 14:12; Ezek. 28:17).

Lucifer was the grandest of all the created heavenly beings, having beauty beyond compare and incomparable wisdom (Ezek. 28:17). So great was his majesty of being that the Word of God describes him as the fulness and summation of wisdom and beauty (Ezek. 28:12). He had a special anointing from his Creator for unequaled authority in the heavens to do the will of God. What more could a created being hope for or desire?

The most desirable place for any created being to be is in the favorable presence of the one who created him. And so it was with Lucifer. Just imagine for a moment. This created angelic being had the greatest favor imaginable in heaven and earth. The prophet Ezekiel described the dramatic presence of Lucifer.

> Thou art the anointed cherub that covereth; and I have set thee so: **thou wast upon the holy mountain** of God, thou hast walked up and down in the midst of the stones of fire.

> Thou wast perfect in thy ways from the day that thou wast created, till iniquity was found in thee (Ezek. 28:14-15).

## "TILL INIQUITY WAS FOUND"

Lucifer was perfect in his ways. He was "perfect" from God's viewpoint... perfect in ALL his ways. Believe it or not, that is the standard that God, yes, Jesus the Messiah, has set for all of us created in His image (Matt. 5:48; II Tim. 3:17).

But Lucifer did not remain perfect. "Iniquity" was found in him. And what was that change of mind, heart and ways in this glorious angel that God saw as iniquity? Consider well the sheer arrogance of this majestic being setting himself as equal to or greater than his Creator.

> For thou has said in thine heart, **I will ascend** into heaven, I will exalt my throne above the stars of God: I will sit also **upon the mount of the congregation**, in the sides of the north:

> **I will ascend** above the heights of the clouds; I will be like the most High (Isa. 14:13-14).

The prophet Ezekiel's description of Lucifer's iniquity piercingly revealed the heart of the matter. Lucifer was in rebellion. He set himself against the authority of His Creator in the boldest and most egregious manner possible. Using the typical metaphor of the "prince of Tyrus," Lucifer was exposed for all time.

> Because thine heart is lifted up, and thou hast said, I am a god, I sit in the seat of God... yet thou art a man, and not God, though thou set thine heart as the heart of God (Ezek. 28:1-2).

22

## CAST FROM THE MOUNT

Iniquity was found. Lucifer, glorious as he was in his created splendor and power, could not be permitted by the Creator to usurp His throne on "the mount of God." The war of the ages had been ignited. A spark of rebellion quickly flamed into a heavenly conflagration. A third of the angels were drawn into the spiritual revolution against the Creator's authority. Hell had broken loose in Heaven.

It was High Treason. Lucifer sought to usurp the authority of God's kingdom rule in the heavens. They could not co-exist on the holy mountain of God. And so the Creator proclaimed judgment on His magnificent created angelic being.

> **I will cast thee as profane out of the mountain of God:** and I will destroy thee, O covering cherub, from the midst of the stones of fire. Thine heart was lifted up because of thy beauty, thou hast corrupted thy wisdom by reason of thy brightness: I will cast thee to the ground, I will lay thee before kings, that they may behold thee (Ezek. 28:16-17).

Lucifer, "son of the morning," was cast to the earth. He is called "the dragon," "the Devil," "The Deceiver," "Satan," and "that old serpent" (Rev. 12:9). No further place was found for him in heaven (Rev. 12:8). So... where would he go? What would Satan do? What would be the nature of his deception? Who would he deceive? And what would be the consequences?

## ENTER EDEN

Eden was on Earth. It was the place where God had placed His man, made in His image, to carry out His dominion and authority. Like Heaven, Eden was a perfect place on earth where God's creative genius and eternal wisdom was manifest. God had said, having concluded His creation, "it was very good." No iniquity was to be found there.

Then "the serpent"... (Gen. 3:1). The serpent was subtil. He was seductive. And he was spiritually rebellious, intent upon depriving the man created in God's image of the delegated dominion given to Adam and his progeny. Satan the Deceiver, disguised as a subtil serpent, would deceptively wage war against mankind's loyalty to his Creator. The Destroyer would gain domination through deception. In fiendish "friendship," the Thief, who was determined to "steal, kill and destroy" (John 10:9-10) in order to declare himself "king," would capture the fealty of man through subterfuge. He would tug at Eve's flesh in order to destroy her faith. He would deceive the woman in order to take dominion over the man to whom the Creator's authority had been delegated.

23

And so the master deceiver promised, "You shall not surely die," as God had warned. Rather, "Ye shall be as gods…" (Gen. 3:4-5). Faith gave place to the lust of the flesh. The promised authority of the Deceiver was embraced by God's man in derogation of God's entrusted dominion.

Satan, the arch enemy of the Creator, through Adam's treasonous shift of trust, became "the god of this world." What Lucifer could not accomplish in the heavenlies, he usurped on earth. He would claim his throne as *king of the mountain*. But it would take time to effectuate total dominion, to ultimately deface and defame the glory of the Creator. It would take 6000 years of progressive deception and seduction to capture the throne upon the holy mount. And that profound moment of the Deceiver's historical program is rapidly nearing its culmination.

Who will be *king of the mountain*? Who will sit upon God's "holy hill?" The psalmist spoke prophetically. He inquired and then responded with the eternal viewpoint of the Creator that echoes to this propitious and prophetic moment of human history.

Who shall ascend into the hill of the LORD? Or who shall stand in his holy place?

He that hath clean hands and a pure heart; who hath not lifted up his soul unto vanity, nor sworn deceitfully (Psa. 24:3-4).

## "I Will Ascend…"

Lucifer had declared, "I will ascend…I will be like the Most High" (Isa. 14:13-14). He was found "in Eden the garden of God" (Ezek. 28:13). Before iniquity was found in him, he had been perfect in his ways (Ezek. 28:15). But because his "heart was lifted up" in pride, he would be "cast to the ground" (Ezek. 28:17). In his diabolical efforts to claim man's dominion in the earth, having "set thine heart as the heart of God," he would transfer his treasonous spirit from heaven to earth. He would declare himself "God" through the man he would deceive to embrace his agenda so as to render the Creator's purposes void and therefore vain, thus disqualifying the Creator as "God."

History would tell the story. The people, having been masterfully deceived, would become "astonished" that this treacherous enemy of their very souls should have seemingly prospered for millennia, craftily corrupting the Creator's cause and loving commitment to mankind (Ezek. 28:19). Much to the agonizing chagrin of the multitudes of earth, Lucifer's diabolical deception to which the peoples have been drawn in opposition to their loving Creator will be revealed. The picture will not be pretty. Satan will lay before kings in order that they will be able to see him for his true and treacherous character (Ezek. 28:17). Shaking their heads in painful disbelief, the peoples of the planet will say...

> Is this the man that made the earth to tremble, that did shake kingdoms; that made the world as a wilderness... (Isa. 14:16-17)?

The world awaits the long-desired ascension of the Deceiver. The day of destiny draws near. Who will be *King of the Mountain*?

*Chapter 3*

# PROBING THOUGHTS *for* PROPHETIC TIMES

1. Might our increasingly dangerous world situation actually have begun in the heavenlies? How?

2. Who was Lucifer? Why is he significant in understanding current global chaos?

3. What was the nature of the *iniquity* that was found in him? Do you see examples of that same "iniquity" as a driving force between individuals, families, tribes and nations today?

4. How was Adam's response to Satan (Lucifer—the Serpent) seen by God, Adam's Creator, as an act of treason, punishable by death?

5. What was Satan's real goal in deceiving Eve?

6. To what point have we come in the biblical history of mankind?

7. Contrasting your own life and decisions with those of Adam and Eve, how would you describe your relationship with your Creator? Is He *"KING of the Mountain"* of your life, or have you ascended to His rightful place?

*Chapter 4*

# THE KINGS VS. THE ANOINTED

***"The kings of the earth set themselves,***
***and the rulers take counsel together...."***
Psa. 2:2

THE TRAJECTORY OF HISTORY has been made plain. The geopolitical developments of today and tomorrow are following the prescribed pattern of divine revelation of yesterday. As we today are enmeshed in persistent developments and even events of potentially great portent "on the ground," it is difficult for us to comprehend the greater picture from God's viewpoint. Yet, in the end, it is the divine perspective alone that truly matters and upon which history truly hinges.

## "KINGS OF THE EARTH"

The Psalmist, 3000 years ago, asked a provocative question that has hovered over all history since David reigned as king over all Israel. That question is the fulcrum over which the premier geopolitical events of history have turned. It is also the foundation upon which our understanding of current and future events can be rightly established. The fate of both people and planet lies largely with "the kings of the earth." That leads us back to the Psalmist's question."

Why do the heathen [nations] rage, and the people imagine a vain thing (Psa. 2:1)?

The simple answer to the question is "The kings of the earth set themselves, and the rulers take counsel together..." (Psa. 2:2). But how is it that the leaders of our world, both historically and presently, could be said to "take counsel together?" With all of the global upheaval, pursuit of power, religious differences, political posturing, wars, dissension and even destruction

27

ravaging this small planet, how could it be remotely suggested, yet alone be a reality, that the leaders of our world are in agreement on anything? Yet it is true now as it was when the Psalmist penned those words.

## TAKING COUNSEL TOGETHER

Indeed, the kings and rulers of planet Earth are in cahoots. There is, in essence, only one issue they agree upon. They are bound together in a virtual conspiracy, always have been and always will be. It is a conspiracy of mutual disdain, inbred hatred and unadulterated rebellion "against the LORD, and against his anointed" (Psa. 2:2).

This is why the nations rage. They are enraged by their collective animus against their Creator. They are governed by the rebel spirit of the "god of this world" to whom Adam treasonously transferred dominion. And, as with their "king" Lucifer, the nations rage against all that represents the Creator's authority in the earth. They rage against, ridicule and seek to reduce to oblivion... yes even annihilation... the Lord's "anointed" (Psa. 2:2).

As we citizens of earth now occupy the general era of the end of 6000 years of human history according to the Scriptures, there is dramatically accumulating evidence that the historical hatred of the world's nations and rulers toward "the LORD, and against his anointed" is coming to culmination. The blatant intensity of open rebellion against God's authority as expressed in the Bible has reached unprecedented proportions. Our world, including Israel and America, has been likened by observant spiritual leaders to the proverbial "Sodom and Gomorrah."

Yet, as always, God has preserved for himself a remnant. Historically, it appears only as a fleshly remnant, yet it will ultimately be manifested as a spiritual remnant. And it is against this remnant that the world rages. It is the Lord's "anointed." It is therefore necessary that we explore this concept of the Lord's "anointed" more fully so that we can better comprehend the unfolding of otherwise unexplained rage the world will witness.

## THE LORD'S ANOINTED

There was in Ur of the Chaldees a distant descendant of Shem, one of the three sons of Noah who survived the Flood of God's judgment upon the earth (Gen. 11). He was born after the building of Babel and was a Shem-ite, part of a Semitic people occupying what is now referred to as the Middle East. His name was Abram, son of Terah, and they relocated from Ur to Haran.

In Haran, God spoke pointedly and perceptibly to Abram with a precise message.

Get thee out of thy country, and from thy kindred, and from thy father's house, unto a land that I will show thee:

And I will make of thee a great nation; and I will bless thee, and make thy name great; and thou shalt be a blessing:

And I will bless them that bless thee, and curse them that curseth thee: and in thee shall all families of the earth be blessed (Gen. 12:1-3).

At seventy-five years of age, "Abram departed as the LORD had spoken unto him," taking his wife Sarai and his nephew, Lot. When Abram came into the land of Canaan, the LORD appeared again to him and said, "Unto thy seed will I give this land" (Gen. 12:6-7).

A grievous famine struck Canaan, compelling Abram to seek food for his family in Egypt. Following his sojourn in Egypt, Abram journeyed back to Canaan. Unfortunately, the immensity of blessing God had outpoured upon this man due to his profound faith and obedience resulted in strife over water and adequate grazing for the combined flocks of Abram and Lot. Abram, desiring peace, gave his nephew first choice of where to settle. Lot's choice of settlement was of historic and spiritual significance as was Abram's resultant choice.

And Lot lifted up his eyes, and beheld all the plain of Jordan, that it was well watered everywhere, before the LORD destroyed Sodom and Gomorrah...

Then Lot chose him all the plain of Jordan: and Lot journeyed east: and they separated themselves the one from the other.

Abram dwelled in the land of Canaan [now generally occupied by the resurrected State of Israel], and Lot dwelled in the cities of the plain, and pitched his tent toward Sodom (Gen. 13:10-12).

Notice carefully the promise reiterated to Abram *after* he separated his family and flock from those of Lot.

And the LORD said to Abram, after that Lot was separated from him, Lift up now thine eyes, and look from the place where thou art northward, and southward, and eastward and westward:

For all the land which thou seest, to thee will I give it, and to thy seed forever (Gen. 13:14-15).

Separation sets the stage for becoming "the Lord's anointed." Abram is now twice separated from earthly loyalties. First, he left his father's house to follow the voice of the heavenly Father. Second, he separated himself from the more fleshly and earthly proclivities of his nephew, Lot, who boldly "pitched his tent toward Sodom" (Gen. 13:12), a place of profound and renowned wickedness (Gen. 13:13).

In Abram's choices for righteous separation we find the first clear demonstration of the progressive "sanctification" or setting apart for holy living required by God of anyone who would truly follow Him in the "fear of the Lord." And God took notice!

"After these things, the word of the LORD came unto Abram in a vision, saying, Fear not Abram: I am thy shield, and thy exceeding great reward" (Gen. 15:1). Abram was concerned because he was childless and well beyond procreative ability as was Sarai, his wife. Yet God promised his seed would be as the stars of heaven, and once again, Abram believed God and God "counted it to him for righteousness" (Gen. 15:2-6). In three distinct tests, Abram displayed his extraordinary trust in the Lord of Creation. And God responded, reiterating His promise of "this land to inherit it" (Gen. 15:6-17).

God entered into profound and permanent covenant with this man on earth who had faithfully demonstrated his trust in his Creator's love, care and character. God would invest in this man the promise of redemption that dominion might be restored under the Creator's authority in the earth. The covenant would be secured by deeded land—promised land—land promised and deeded by the Creator himself.

> And the LORD made a covenant with Abram, saying, Unto thy seed have I given this land, from the river of Egypt unto the great river, the river Euphrates (Gen. 15:18).

## FROM THE LAND TO THE MOUNT

The Creator was not through testing the trust of the one who would be called "the friend of God" (Isa. 41:8; Jam. 2:23). A triumph with God demands a test of trust. Triumph in genuine trust produces a testimony of God's gracious hand.

Unfortunately, when trust is tested, compromise comes knocking at the door to offer an easier way. And so it was with the man of faith, God's "friend" who gave place to his flesh. Just as Eve had seduced Adam to unbelief through the serpent's rationalizing the word of God in the Garden, even so Sarai would, perhaps unwittingly, seek to compromise the clarity of God's prophetic call and promise to Abram, offering him a fleshly alternative to perfect trust, thus forever altering the course of history. The moment of truth of genuine re-established trust would require an extraordinary confrontation between Abram's flesh and spirit on the Mount the Creator would choose.

God had instructed Abram to "Get thee out of thy country... unto a land that I will show thee" (Gen. 12:1-2). He, at the same time, promised this man of growing faith, six things.

1. "I will make of thee a great nation;"
2. "I will bless thee and make thy name great;"
3. "Thou shalt be a blessing;"
4. "I will bless them that bless thee;"
5. I will "curse him that curseth thee;" and
6. "In thee shall all the families of the earth be blessed" (Gen. 12:2-3).

"So Abram departed as the LORD had spoken unto him" (Gen. 12:4). As this amazing man of trusting obedience traveled, "he went out, not knowing whither he went." "By faith he sojourned in the land of promise, as in a strange country... for he looked for a city which hath foundations whose builder and maker is God" (Heb. 11:8-10).

"And the LORD appeared [again] unto Abram, and said, Unto thy seed will I give this land" (Gen. 12:7). Yet Abram had no "seed." He was beyond 75 years of age. To the natural man, the very concept of "seed" was nearly contemptible, nearly impossible to conceive. And so God again appeared to His "friend" to encourage his faith, saying "Fear not, Abram: I am thy shield and thy exceeding great reward." To which Abram responded, "Lord God, what wilt thou give me seeing I go childless..." (Gen. 15:1-3). God re-assured the man who would be sorely tested, "This shall not be thine heir; but he that shall come forth out of thine own bowels shall be thine heir" (Gen. 15:4). Amazingly, "he believed in the LORD; and [the LORD] counted it to him for righteousness," declaring, "I am the LORD that brought thee out of Ur of the Chaldees, to give thee this land to inherit it" (Gen. 15:6-7).

Twelve years passed, yet "Abram's wife bare him no children" (Gen. 16:1). Sarai could not conceive how she, in old age, could conceive seed. But her fleshly mind conceived an alternative plan to purportedly fulfill God's promise. And so she presented her Egyptian handmaid, Hagar, to Abram in the hope of resolving the seemingly impossible test of trust. Ishmael, a surrogate son, was born not of holy promise but of pretense. For thirteen years Ishmael was raised in Abram's house. The tensions between barren Sarai and her Egyptian handmaid were unbearable, and Hagar, together with Ishmael, was banned. What was first intended by Sarai to be a blessing had become a curse, and Abram was profoundly distressed. Hagar and Ishmael were despised by Sarai, yet "the angel of the LORD" found Hagar, who had fled to the wilderness, commanding her to "Return to thy mistress, and submit thyself under her hands" (Gen. 16:1-16). And so it was that the seed of the greatest sibling rivalry of history was sown, having metastasized to global proportions in this final hour of history to determine who shall be "King of the Mountain."

## WHO WOULD BE "ANOINTED"?

To be "anointed" is to be chosen or set apart for a particular role or responsibility. The greater the role or responsibility, the greater the sense of chosenness.

The awareness or very idea of *chosenness*, whether the choosing is by man or God, carries great honor but also great responsibility. It also bears the inevitable brunt of mankind's fleshly or carnal pursuit of power to depose the "chosen" one, thereby claiming the "anointing" with all of the power, perks and position attendant thereto.

Envy is the eternal enemy of genuine anointing. It matters not whether the anointing is from God, or man. Envy is thus the engine that drives the perpetual pursuit to become "king of the mountain," and the engine of envy is fueled by pride and the lust for power.

Given the persistency of human pride and envy since the opening act of history in the Garden of Eden, it then becomes "understandable" that if God, the Creator, should anoint (choose) a man, woman, people group or nation for His unique and particular purpose in history, competitors will soon come knocking, seeking to usurp that role. And so it was—and is—regarding the seed of Abram. Political Correctness has, for man on our planet, replaced Biblical Correctness in order to justify the usurpation of chosenness or anointing, thus enmeshing our world in an end-time battle of sibling rivalry for the ultimate position of anointing as "king of the mountain."

But God, the Creator, has spoken on the issue. He has definitively delineated the terms. As far as He is concerned, there is no question or issue. Israel is His "anointed," and Yeshua (Jesus) is the Mashiach, "The Anointed One," the only truly obedient and faithful Israelite, without whom neither Jew nor Gentile have hope of salvation. This conclusion is boldly and unabashedly stated because these facts are boldly, clearly and unequivocally declared in the Bible, the eternal Word of God. We must therefore briefly re-establish what our Creator, the God of heaven and earth, has spoken concerning His "anointed."

The Psalmist wrote beautifully of giving thanks to the God of Israel. His words deserve particular attention with regard to the matter of *anointing*.

**O ye seed of Abraham his servant, ye children of Jacob his chosen.**

He is the LORD our God: his judgments are in all the earth.

He hath remembered his covenant forever, the word which he commanded to a thousand generations.

**Which covenant he made with Abraham, and his oath unto Isaac;**

**And confirmed the same unto Jacob for a law, and to Israel for an everlasting covenant:**

**Saying, Unto thee will I give the land of Canaan, the lot of your inheritance:**

He suffered no man to do them wrong; yea, he reproved kings for their sakes;

Saying, **Touch not mine anointed,** and do my prophets no harm (Psa. 105: 6-15).

The prophet Isaiah was similarly convinced of Israel's *chosenness.* He further consoled the seed of Jacob (Israel) and warned the world of divine retribution should any seek to trouble or supplant Abraham's promised seed of their anointed place and purpose.

**But thou, Israel, art my servant Jacob whom I have chosen, the seed of Abraham my friend...** I have chosen thee and not cast thee away.

Fear thou not; for I am with thee: be not dismayed; for I am thy God...

Behold, all they that were incensed against thee shall be ashamed and confounded: they shall be as nothing; and they that strive with thee shall perish:

...they that war against thee shall be as nothing, and as a thing of naught.

For I the LORD thy God will hold thy right hand, saying unto thee, Fear not; I will help thee (Isa. 41:8-13).

On what basis could Isaiah, the prophet, be so assured that his prophetic revelation was right? The revelation would have to be rooted in a righteous reality from God's viewpoint. When God the Creator has spoken, the conjured ideas of His creatures, however creative, considered or convincingly presented they might be, are of no consequence. Man's best intentions, however rationalized or justified, will never supersede God's intentions. And God has given us further clarity regarding His intentions. It will lead us to history's most challenging mountain.

*Chapter 4*

# PROBING THOUGHTS *for* PROPHETIC TIMES

1. Do you find it fascinating—credible—that the end-time attitude of world rulers against Israel would be so simply and clearly foretold in Psalm 2 over 3000 years ago?

2. Who are the Lord's "anointed" as clearly described in the Bible? Do you have any reason to disagree? If so, on what authority?

3. Why is Abraham so crucial in the unfolding of God's relationship with Mankind after the fall of Adam?

4. Who are the "chosen people" from God's viewpoint? Why?

5. Do you think the Gentile world and its political and religious leaders consider Israel and the Jewish people today to be "chosen"? Does it matter? If so, why… or why not?

*Chapter 5*

# THE TALE OF TWO SONS

*Mocking set the stage for end-time calamitous confrontation.*

ABRAM WAS IN A QUANDARY. He had listened to the voice of a frustrated wife urging him to bring resolution to the heavenly promise of "seed" that had weighed interminably upon him. Perhaps she had become weary in hearing Abram's persistent lament during the twelve years Abram waited for God to "do something." And so she urged her Egyptian handmaiden to somehow satisfy the expectation of a son.

At eighty-six years of age, Hagar bare Abram a son, and he called his name Ishmael (Gen. 16:15-16). Abram apparently resolved that from Ishmael the promised "seed" would come. But God had a different intention. As fine a human "friend" as Abram was to God, Abram's impatience, like that of so many of us today, actually served to pervert rather than promote the actual divine promise. God, therefore, paid Abram another visit.

## THE PROMISE RE-ITERATED

When Abram was 99 years of age, "the LORD appeared to Abram, and said unto him, I am the Almighty God, walk before me and be thou perfect." "My covenant shall be with thee, and thou shalt be a father of many nations. Neither shall thy name any more be called Abram, but thy name shall be Abraham; for a father of many nations have I made thee" (Gen. 17:1-5).

The world and its' 7 billion denizens should take particular note of the words of God to Abraham during this fourth iteration of the covenant promise, for they make plain the purpose of the Creator in setting the stage for the planet's ultimate redemption. There can be no mistake as to God's viewpoint concerning the promised "seed." And the world and its pastors, priests, popes, presidents, prime ministers and potentates voice their contrary viewpoint to their (and the world's) grave peril. It is grave, indeed, to set one's plans and hopes for peace in direct opposition to the declared purposes of the King of the universe.

## ABRAHAM'S QUANDARY BECOMES OUR QUANDARY

Abraham had an earthly perspective on God's promise, but the Creator had an eternal perspective. By all earthly right and practice, Ishmael, Abraham's firstborn, would be his heir and therefore entitled to stand as the "promised seed" with all of the rights and privileges thereof. Yet God saw things differently.

Ishmael was the product of Abram and Sarai's carnally-conceived plan to pre-empt the divinely-produced seed through a humanly-devised son with Sarai's Egyptian servant. Abram had failed through fleshly weakness. He believed God would fulfill His promise, but through impatience he perverted the purity of the eternal promise God intended.

Now Abraham was faced with a serious dilemma, just as we are today when we have conducted ourselves outside of the perfect will of God. There are earthly (and often enduring) consequences that flow from fleshly-motivated choices and decisions. Thus it was with this otherwise man of faith.

At the age of 99, God appeared to Abram a third time, changing his name to Abraham and his wife's name to Sarah. The change in name was God's imprimatur upon His divine plan to produce a true son of promise.

Abraham was shocked! He laughed in the face of God and said, "Shall a child be born unto him that is an hundred years old? And shall Sarah, that is ninety years old bear" (Gen. 17:17)?

Now what shall be done? Ishmael is Abraham's firstborn. Abraham wanted to do what seemed right in the eyes of man, just as we are so often drawn to do. In his quandary, Abraham argued with God, saying, "O that Ishmael might live before thee" (Gen. 17:18). And that argument persists in the mind of the gentile world to this day, provoking fleshly and carnally-corrupted mankind to the precipice of global destruction in the final desperate efforts of the nations of the world to become *KING of the Mountain*.

God resolved the potential problem, the quandary that haunted Abraham and evolves to the edge of eternity, with a simple, yet unmistakably direct response of His holy view of the matter. Merely acceding in humility to the declared will of the Creator would precipitate the truly divine path to peace on earth as God had intended. The words are unmistakable and incontrovertible, unless one chooses to arrogate his own viewpoint over that of the Creator of the universe. **These words are the hinge of history. Hear and heed.**

And God said, Sarah thy wife shall bear thee a son indeed; and thou shalt call his name Isaac; and I will establish my covenant with him for an everlasting covenant, and with his seed after him.

And as for Ishmael, I have heard thee: behold, I have blessed him, and will make him fruitful… and I will make him a great nation (the Arab nation).

BUT MY COVENANT WILL I ESTABLISH WITH ISAAC, which Sarah shall bear unto thee at this set time next year (Gen. 17:19-21).

## IS ANY THING TOO HARD FOR THE LORD?

Again a fifth time God appeared to Abraham by means of an angelic visit at his tent in Mamre. If you were ninety-nine and your wife ninety, you might just want some heavenly re-assurance concerning the astounding promise by God who would intervene in human history against the very laws of nature.

Abraham ran to provide desert hospitality to these extraordinary visitors, to which they responded:

I will certainly return unto thee according to the time of life; and lo, Sarah thy wife shall have a son (Gen. 18:1-10).

Sarah heard the prophetic words and laughed within herself, since "it ceased to be with Sarah after the manner of women." But the heavenly visitor pressed on to challenge Sarah's faith, asking a question that has reverberated throughout history, hinging the birth of the first "son of promise," Isaac, to the birth of Yeshua (Jesus) who would be the culminating "promised Son of God," full of grace and truth. It is a question first uttered by an angel to Abraham and resolved in holy declaration by an angel announcing the soon-to-be-born only begotten son of God, "the son of Abraham" by faith (Matt. 1:1). This question and its answer in the life of each person on this planet will determine destiny.

IS ANY THING TOO HARD FOR GOD (Gen. 18:14)?

The angelic visitor that arrested a young virgin's attention, announcing the anticipated birth of the Messiah, the long-expected One, resolved the dilemma of faith for Abraham, for Sarah, for Mary and Joseph, and for all who would truly believe, in spirit and in truth….

WITH GOD NOTHING SHALL BE IMPOSSIBLE (Luke 1:37).

The seemingly "impossible" becomes both possible and prophetic when God has spoken. When God speaks, both heaven and earth respond in the fulness of time to fulfill His purposes, despite the contrary words, ways and will of mankind, otherwise made spiritually in His image. And so

His story continues to unfold today, progressively revealing that which had been hidden, to the ultimate honor of His name in the earth. Therefore the tale of the two sons continues today, awaiting the final chapter to be written in the ongoing saga of sin and salvation.

## THE SON OF PROMISE

"And the LORD visited Sarah as he had said, and the LORD did unto Sarah as he had spoken. For Sarah conceived and bare Abraham a son in his old age, at the set time of which God had spoken to him" (Gen. 21:1-7).

"And Abraham called the name of his son that was born unto him, whom Sarah bare to him, Isaac. And Abraham circumcised his son Isaac being eight days old, as God had commanded him. And Abraham was an hundred years old, when his son Isaac was born unto him. And the child grew, and was weaned: and Abraham made a great feast the same day Isaac was weaned" (Gen. 21:3-8).

That *weaning* issued a *warning* to the world. A bitter rivalry of consuming envy would envelope Ishmael and his descendants, breeding a hatred increasingly calculated to consume the Creator's holy promise, thus destroying God's redemptive plan. As it is written, "Looking diligently lest any man fail of the grace of God; lest any root of bitterness springing up trouble you, and thereby many be defiled" (Heb. 12:15).

Consider carefully. "And Sarah saw the son of Hagar the Egyptian which she had born unto Abraham, mocking. Wherefore she said unto Abraham, Cast out this bondwoman and her son: for the son of the bondwoman shall not be heir with my son, even with Isaac. And the thing was very grievous in Abraham's sight because of his son [Ishmael]" (Gen. 21:9-11).

Sarah could not countenance the unfolding consequences of her fleshly conniving to fulfill God's promise of a son to Abraham. Abraham, like most of us today, felt caught in a quandary issuing from his own decision to pre-empt God's promise through a carnal scheme borne of impatience. What should he do? Should he preserve the status of heirship for Ishmael, his firstborn, thus ensuring a divided household of chaos and confusion? Should Hagar's ongoing presence be protected, causing a perpetual "thorn-in-the-flesh" with his wife, Sarah? On these issues it might be said that "reasonable minds might differ." The deciding difference, however, is that God had spoken. The Lord of Creation had already declared His holy purpose for a "son of promise" through whom He alone understood the redemptive hope of the earth should come. And can we not all, born of woman, understand viscerally the choice Abraham had to make? How many times have we elevated human reasoning in difficult decisions over God's declared and written will, only to suffer the echoing and otherwise unnecessary consequences?

God understood the heart-rending choice Abraham faced, for God himself would eventually face an even greater choice for the sake of all mankind.

> And God said unto Abraham, Let it not be grievous in thy sight because of the lad [Ishmael] and because of thy bondwoman; in all that Sarah hath said unto thee, hearken unto her voice; for **in Isaac shall thy seed be called** (Gen. 21:12).

"And also the son of the bondwoman will I make a nation; because he is thy seed" (Gen. 21:13). Thus began what is commonly called "The Arab Nation."

Mocking set the stage for end-time calamitous confrontation. And the citizens of all nations now formulate their final choices as to which side of the envious breach to embrace. All of us stand, in a very real sense, with Abraham. He neither hated nor rejected his firstborn son, but his own choices had created the dilemma. His choice is our choice. Abraham was faced with the same choice Adam and Eve had faced in the Garden. It is the ultimate question of all history... "Hath God said...?"

Faith versus feelings is the fulcrum of such choices. When God has spoken, will I agree with God and rest, or will I resort to my own feelings as the final arbiter of truth? Will I birth "Ishmaels" that haunt and taunt persistently and perpetually because I ignore what God hath said by resorting to the "authority" of my flesh? Or will I see "Isaacs," "sons of promise" come forth to bless because I made the difficult choice in the crucial hour to trust what God has clearly said?

So what did God say? The future of our world hinges upon our honest answer. Will we follow our feelings, fickle as they are, and wherever they may lead? Or will we trust God, rest in His plan and purposes, and be blessed with faithful Abraham? Let us again be clear as to the Creator's intent.

> God said, Sarah thy wife shall bear thee a son indeed; and thou shalt call his name Isaac; and I will establish my covenant with him to an everlasting covenant, and with his seed after him (Gen. 17:19).

> But my covenant will I establish with Isaac... (Gen. 17:21).

> And God said unto Abraham...in Isaac shall thy seed be called (Gen. 21:12).

What do you say? As the clouds of war and eternal envy gather over our planet, each of us—every man and woman, yes even children—are forced by the mocking voice of history to make our choice. A global "March on Jerusalem" to embrace "Ishmaelites" and to reject the descendants of Isaac revealed the choreographed choices of clamoring inhabitants of our planet even as this chapter was penned. Where do you stand? In your heart, are you joining forces with the multitudes driven by ever-intensifying feelings to "march on Jerusalem," or are you humbly yielding, by faith, to the eternal and unchanging declared viewpoint of the Lord of Nations, sojourning as a pilgrim with the physical seed of Abraham, Isaac and Jacob to Mount Zion?

*Chapter 5*

# PROBING THOUGHTS *for* PROPHETIC TIMES

1. Abraham had two sons—Ishmael and Isaac. With which son do you most closely identify? Why?

2. Do you agree or disagree with God's clear choice in Genesis 17, designating Isaac as the "son of promise" through which the blessings promised to Abraham and his seed would advance in the earth? Why?

3. In what way or ways does your attitude on this issue affect your outlook on our world today?

4. In what way have popular notions of multiculturalism, religious pluralism and political correctness caused many (even professing Christians) to rise up against God's clear word on the matter and to register their disagreement? Does it matter? Why… or why not?

5. Abraham was severely tested on Mt. Moriah. Why is that significant for our world today? Are you being tested in your trust of God's Word, the Bible, perhaps even now? How will you resolve the conflict? Will you be "King of the Mountain," or will God?

*Chapter 6*

# TESTING ON THE MOUNT

**"In thy seed shall all the nations of the earth be blessed...."**
Gen. 22:18

A LIFE *TEST* IS ALWAYS REQUIRED FOR A LIFE *TESTIMONY*. The greater the needed testimony to the ages, the greater the test demanded in the present. And so it was with Abraham.

"After these things," (all that had transpired for twenty-five years from the original promise until the birth of the son of promise and the separation from Ishmael), God did tempt [test] Abraham. And he said,

> Take now thy son, thine only son [of promise] Isaac, whom thou lovest, and get thee unto the land of Moriah; and offer him there for a burnt offering **upon one of the mountains** that I will tell thee of.

> And Abraham rose up early in the morning, and saddled his donkey, and took... Isaac his son... and went to the place of which God had told him (Gen. 22:1-3).

## IT WAS A SPECIFIC PLACE

Notice carefully! Abraham acted immediately. He, unlike most of us, did not equivocate with the clear instruction from God. He did not argue, neither did he seek to substitute his own finite reasoning for what his Creator required. Note further. Abraham "went unto the place of which God had told him." It was a specific place for a yet-to-be-disclosed specific and prophetic purpose of which we have no record of having ever been revealed to this man of faith. Rather, absolute trust was the measuring rod of the supreme test of Abraham's faith.

Then on the third day Abraham lifted up his eyes, and saw the place afar off (Gen. 22:4).

Note again. Abraham saw a specific place, not just any convenient place. It was "the" place he recognized as having been described by God. And so he told the young men accompanying him to wait with the donkey. "I and the lad [Isaac] will go yonder and worship, and come again to you soon," said Abraham (Gen. 22:5).

The time of testing was approaching the ultimate moment of truth. Would Abraham truly trust the God of promise who had miraculously given him a "son of promise?" History would hinge upon his faith-born hope. And when Isaac reasonably questioned the circumstances—the fire, the wood, but no lamb for the sacrifice—Abraham grasped again the promise, almost incredibly declaring, "God will provide Himself a lamb…" (Gen. 22:8).

Never did a righteous man face a greater test of his trust. History would report the heart-wrenching decision and the resulting direction of man's' destiny.

And they came to **the place** which God had told him of; and Abraham built an altar there, and laid the wood in order, and bound Isaac his son, and laid him on the altar upon the wood.

And Abraham stretched forth his hand, and took the knife to slay his son [Isaac] (Gen. 22:9-10).

## DESTINY WAS RIDING IN THE BALANCE

Destiny now rides in the balance. Abraham believed that God was able to raise his son even from the dead to fulfill God's promise.

By faith Abraham, when he was tried, offered up Isaac… his only begotten son, of whom it was said, That in Isaac shall thy seed be called:

Accounting that God was able to raise him up, even from the dead… (Heb. 11:17-19).

To this visceral test on the mount, God, as "Jehovah-Jireh," responded as mankind's ultimate true provider. The angel of the Lord [the pre-incarnate Messiah] called out, "Abraham, Abraham… lay not thine hand upon the lad… for now I know that thou fearest God, seeing thou hast not withheld thy son, thine only son from me" (Gen. 22:11-12). A ram in a thicket became the temporal salvation for the son of promise until the propitious moment when history, prophecy and divine purpose should intersect in the fulness of time and God would truly "provide Himself a lamb," the Messiah, who would be offered up as God's eternal sacrifice upon that very mount.

> By myself have I sworn, saith the LORD, for because thou hast... not withheld thy son, thine only son [of promise, Isaac]:
>
> That in blessing I will bless thee... And in thy seed [through Isaac] shall all the nations of the earth be blessed; because thou has obeyed my voice (Gen. 22:16-18).

## THE MOUNT AND THE FINAL MOMENT

The test at the mount was complete. Abraham triumphed in humble faith in the God who had called him from Ur of the Chaldees to the Mount of God. Faith was made complete in profound trust revealed in absolute obedience. The stage of divinely ordained-history was thus set by faithful Abraham. Now, the very God of history would provide Himself a Lamb in the fulness of time. His "only begotten Son," Yeshua, would give Himself as a ransom for many on that very mount of triumphant testing, becoming "obedient unto death, even the death of the cross" (Phil. 2:8).

> Wherefore God also hath highly exalted him [Yeshua HaMashiach—the Messiah—the "Anointed One"], and given him a name which is above every name:
>
> That at the name of Jesus [Yeshua] every knee should bow... and that every tongue should confess that Jesus Christ is Lord, to the glory of God the Father (Phil. 2:9-11).

The battle lines of history were thus drawn. Who would be "Lord?" Would men's traditions triumph over the Creator's Truth? Would mankind accept, by faith with faithful Abraham, the clearly declared and determined will of God? Or would the creature exalt his or her will over that of the Creator of all things in heaven and earth? Who would be "king of the mountain?" Who would, when the last jot and tittle of history has been written, reign upon the mountain of men's hearts? That ultimate moment of human engagement upon planet earth is soon coming to its final act in the divine drama. On which side of HIS STORY will you stand?

*Chapter 6*

# PROBING THOUGHTS *for* PROPHETIC TIMES

1. Why does a legitimate *TESTIMONY* always require a *TEST*?

2. Why do you think God instructed Abraham to go to a specific place to sacrifice his son rather than allowing Abraham to choose just any place?

3. In what way did Abraham "set the stage" of divinely-ordained history?

4. Abraham's faith was defined by obediently submitting to God's will regardless of his contrary feelings of the flesh. Do you have such faith? If not, how is your "faith" defined and displayed?

5. How may the great end-time battle for *KING of the Mountain* be both geopolitical and spiritual?

# Chapter 7

# WHY DO THE NATIONS RAGE?

*"Proclaim this among the Gentiles; Prepare war."*
Joel 3:9

THE NATIONS ARE DETERMINING DESTINY. Even now, the drum roll announcing the opening of the final curtain on the divine drama of human history is fading, revealing the spectacular conflict soon to take center stage.

The nations are raging. The geopolitical lines and historical alliances once deemed destined to endure the ravages of time have shifted dramatically in a single decade. Arch enemies have baffled the world, becoming end-time friends. Friends have become implacable foes. Betrayal has bereaved the world of ancient trusts, leaving leaders bewildered at the shocking events unfolding rapidly before their terrified eyes.

Indeed, the nations are being stirred in unprecedented rage. But for the student of the Bible, these circumstances were long-expected and clearly foretold three thousand years ago. They were foretold from the very mount of God... Mount Zion. It behooves us, then, to take a journey back to that ancient and, for many, long-forgotten time.

## INDEED THEY RAGE

The ancient Psalmist asked a provocative question that echoes to our prophetic moment poised on the edge of eternity... "Why do the heathen rage..." (Psa. 2:1)? The word translated *heathen* in the King James Version is the Hebrew word "gowy" or more commonly "goy." It is a term or word used to identify any people or nation other than the physical descendants of Abraham, Isaac and Jacob. It refers generally to all Gentiles. Therefore, the Psalmist's question is more timely translated, "Why do the Gentiles or gentile nations rage?"

Before we can explore "why" the gentile nations rage, perhaps it would be helpful to more fully establish "that" the gentile nations are raging. Indeed they rage. And that rage is intensifying. So great is the intensifying of rage against any and all things Jewish or related to Israel that a virtual global boycott has been declared against all direct or even incidental investment in Israel. Choreographed hatred by those to whom we have entrusted our youth for higher learning has metastasized throughout our colleges and universities, resulting in a pandemic and vicious virus of anti-Semitism sweeping all Western nations. And the institutions of "higher learning" are not alone in this rising rage.

Business, multinational corporations and even our churches have become partners in the irrational rage against Jews, Jerusalem and Israel. "Political correctness" choreographs the anti-Semitic carnage, leaving a world-wide wake of destructive bitterness that is defiling the entire Gentile world.

Political and so-called NGO's or "non-governmental organizations" further institutionalize the tsunamic rage sweeping the earth. The United Nations have, in effect, assumed the seemingly ultimate objective of uniting the "goyim" or Gentile nations in a final end-time opposition to the State of Israel, daring the nascent state to endure their collective disdain.

Many churches and pastors have followed suit. Resurgent "Replacement Theology" has enabled a rapidly growing number of arm-chair theologians to hitch their star to the politically-correct wave of cultural and global animus toward Israel. These pastors seek to wrap a robe of pseudo-righteousness around their cultural rebellion against the very clear and unadulterated words of the God they claim to serve, who proclaimed His eternal covenant both to the people and to the land deeded by the Lord of Nations to the physical descendants of Abraham, Isaac and Jacob [Israel].

## JUDICIAL NOTICE

Pastors, priests, presidents, popes and prime ministers would do well to take judicial notice from the God of Heaven and Earth.

> When I shall have gathered the house of Israel from the people among whom they are scattered, and shall be sanctified in them in the sight of the heathen [goyim, Gentile nations], then shall they dwell in their land that I have given to my servant Jacob.

> And they shall dwell safely therein, and shall build houses, and plant vineyards; yea, they shall dwell with confidence, when I have executed judgments upon all them that despise them round about them; and they shall know that I am the LORD their God (Ezek. 28:25-26).

For **in mine holy mountain, in the mountain of the height of Israel,** saith the LORD God, there shall all the house of Israel, all of them in the land serve me.

And ye shall know that I am the LORD, when I shall bring you into the land of Israel, into the country for which I lifted up mine hand to give it to your fathers (Ezek. 20:40-42).

Interestingly, it is not the Arab or Muslim nations or peoples alone who rage against Israel. It is a global phenomenon that grows geometrically, month by month, year by year. So where will it all end? Will there be a culmination? Will the collective animus of the gentile world against the Jewish people result in a calamitous confrontation with the Lord of Nations? Will even the Christian Church betray her trust to bless the seed of Abraham, Isaac and Israel? For indeed it is written:

I will bless them that bless thee, and curse him that curseth thee (Gen. 12:3).

## WHY THEN DO THE NATIONS RAGE?

The rage of the nations is rationally irrational. It is borne of a fundamental flaw that has been the driving force throughout history and now is culminating in uncontrollable rage. Just as there is a certain perverse "rationality" to what has been called "road rage," even so the rage of the nations is driven by a decidedly perverse rationality rooted in a collective malignancy of mind and heart.

It is uncertain why the Psalmist inquired: "Why do the heathen [nations] rage" (Psa. 2:1)? Was he truly making inquiry, lacking knowledge and insight into the prophesied future flailings of the world? Or, was the prophetic Psalmist totally baffled by the apparent bullish blindness of the end-time Gentile nations, as "the people imagine a vain thing" (Psa. 2:1)?

The "vanity," sheer foolishness and arrogance of the rage was directed "against the LORD, and against his anointed" (Psa. 2:2). The Psalmist prophetically observed that mere man, a creature, had the temerity or *chutzpah* to set himself against the Creator of the universe and to defy His clearly designated will for the physical descendants of Abraham, Isaac and Jacob [Israel].

The overwhelming pride of earthly power shaking its collective fist against the God of ultimate power and might, who had created the very worlds by the breath of His mouth (Psa. 33:6) so that "the worlds were framed by the word of God" (Heb. 11:3), was seemingly beyond the imagination of the Psalmist to comprehend.

Yet "the kings of the earth set themselves, and the rulers take counsel together, against the LORD, and against his anointed" (Psa. 2:2). The power brokers of this planet collectivize their animus against God and His choice to sanctify or "set apart" Israel as a "chosen people." In one culminating thrust, they purpose to punish, even to pulverize this historical "thorn in the flesh" that now festers in their faithless hearts. They conspire, united in vitriol, against Israel. They set aside their historic differences in order to destroy what God has declared, driven by the Devil to whose service they have given themselves. In mutual rage that animates this shocking confrontation, the rulers of earth, moved by ageless and accelerating envy, set their violent course, declaring: "Let us break their bands asunder, and cast away their cords from us" (Psa. 2:3).

Unrestrained envy, coupled with rebellion against the God of Israel, gives perverse "rationality" to their rage. The nations, venting their historic hatred and envy against the people once delivered from the bondage of Egypt, join with Pharaoh of old, echoing his perversity, "Who is the LORD, that I should obey his voice to let Israel go? I know not the LORD, neither will I let Israel go" (Ex. 5:2).

Just as "pride goeth before destruction and an haughty spirit before a fall" (Prov. 16:18), so the nations and their prideful potentates will soon face their moment of truth with the "only Potentate, the King of kings, and Lord of lords" (I Tim. 6:15). And the picture will not be pretty.

"He that sitteth in the heavens shall laugh," declared the Psalmist. "The LORD shall have them in derision" (Psa. 2:4). The God who declared Israel to be "the apple of his eye" (Deut. 32:10) has lost His patience with the potentates, people, presidents, prime ministers and pastors who have set themselves against Him by setting themselves against "his anointed."

> For I, saith the LORD, will be unto her [Jerusalem] a wall of fire round about, and will be the glory in the midst of her.

> For thus saith the LORD of hosts; After the glory hath he sent me unto the nations which spoiled you: for he that toucheth you toucheth the apple of his eye (Zech. 2:5, 8).

## "MY HOLY HILL"

The kings and rulers of the earth have set themselves, confederating against the LORD and His anointed, Israel (Psa. 2:2). They are unrighteously enraged. "Political correctness" has become a devious and deceptive device to mask the underlying motivations of men and their institutions maligning the sons of Jacob. But the Lord of Nations is not deceived. Man may look on the outward appearance of the matter, but God looks to the heart motivations. And "He that sitteth in the heavens shall laugh" at their disingenuousness in their dogged efforts to destroy Israel while pretending to do "righteousness."

Then shall He [God] speak unto them [the nations and their rulers] in his wrath, and vex them in his sore displeasure.

The Lord of Nations and God of Israel is not happy. On the contrary, He is "sore displeased" (Psa. 2:5). And it is not wise to knowingly, intentionally and egregiously displease the Lord who made heaven and earth. Therefore God has set the record of history straight. Despite the arrogant conspiracy of the world's leaders to dispossess Israel and therefore rule from the Mount, God has made His purpose plain.

**Yet have I set my king upon my holy hill of Zion** (Psa. 2:6).

"I will declare the decree," said the Lord. "Thou art my Son [Messiah—Anointed One]; this day have I begotten thee. Ask of me, and I will give thee the heathen [gentile nations] for thine inheritance.... And thou shalt dash them in pieces like a potter's vessel" (Psa. 2:7-9).

The prophet Joel puts it differently, yet no less poignantly. "For, behold, in those days, and in that time, when I shall bring again the captivity of Judah and Jerusalem [return the Jews to their Promised Land] I will also gather all nations, and will bring them down into the valley of Jehoshaphat [Valley of Megiddo] and will plead with them there for my people and for my heritage Israel, whom they have scattered among the nations, and parted my land" (Joel 3:1-2).

## "PREPARE WAR"

"Proclaim this among the Gentiles," says the LORD. "Prepare war" (Joel 3:9). "Beat your plowshares into swords and your pruning hooks into spears." "Assemble yourselves, and come all ye heathen [Gentile nations]..." (Joel 3:10-12).

"Let the heathen [Gentile nations] be wakened, and come up to the valley of Jehoshaphat: for there will I judge all the heathen [nations] round about. Put ye in the sickle, for the harvest is ripe... for their wickedness is great." "Multitudes, multitudes in the valley of decision: for the day of the LORD is near in the valley of decision" (Joel 3:12-14).

"The LORD also shall roar out of Zion, and utter his voice from Jerusalem; and the heavens and the earth shall shake: but the LORD will be the hope of his people, and the strength of the children of Israel" (Joel 3:16).

So shall ye know that **I am the LORD your God dwelling in Zion, my holy mountain** (Joel 3:17).

## "THE HOLY MOUNTAIN"

God means business. He has declared destiny with passion and determination. The machinations of men will not prevail contrary to His plan and purpose. And so... again... comes the word of the Lord.

Thus saith the LORD of hosts; I was jealous for Zion with great jealousy, and I was jealous for her with great fury.

Thus saith the LORD; I am returned unto Zion, and will dwell in the midst of Jerusalem: and Jerusalem shall be called a city of truth; and **the mountain of the LORD of hosts the holy mountain** (Zech. 8:1-3).

In the latter days, "Thus saith the LORD of hosts; Behold, I will save my people from the east country, and from the west country; and I will bring them, and they shall dwell in the midst of Jerusalem: and they [the seed of Abraham, Isaac and Israel] shall be my people, and I will be their God, in truth and in righteousness" (Zech. 8:7-8).

## "IN THE LAST DAYS"

The "last days" have become our days. The words of the ancient prophets are being fulfilled breathtakingly before our eyes. History's moment of truth is on our doorstep. All prophecy will soon be history. So we must ask ourselves, How will the rage of the nations be resolved? *How will the eternal battle for king of the holy mountain end?* To these questions, the Word of God has given precise answer. "Yet have I set my king upon my holy hill" (Psa. 2:6), said the LORD.

And it shall come to pass in the last days, that the mountain of the LORD's house shall be established on the top of the mountains, and shall be exalted above the hills, and all nations shall flow unto it.

And many people shall go and say, Come up, and let us go up to the mountain of the LORD, to the house of the God of Jacob; and he will teach us of his ways, and we will walk in his paths: for out of Zion shall go forth the law, and the word of the LORD from Jerusalem.

And he shall judge among the nations, and shall rebuke many people: and they shall beat their swords into plowshares....

And the loftiness of man shall be bowed down, and the haughtiness of men shall be made low: and the LORD alone shall be exalted in that day (Isa. 2; Micah 4:1-3).

*Chapter 7*

# PROBING THOUGHTS *for* PROPHETIC TIMES

1. Why DO the "heathen" or gentile nations have such historic and growing animus toward Jews and Israel?

2. How does collective bitterness and covetousness affect our supposed "national" thinking?

3. What is meant by the term "Judicial Notice?"

4. Why might Judicial Notice be seriously warranted to the gentile nations and their rulers?

5. Would God really declare war on the nations that come against Israel politically, economically or militarily? Why does the prophet Joel, speaking for God, declare "Prepare war" to gentile nations?

6. Is mankind setting himself up against the God of Jacob for an open and destiny-daring confrontation? Do we, do you, dare risk the outcome of such *chutzpah*?

*Chapter 8*

# GOING UP

*"Be wise, therefore, O Kings: be instructed,*
*ye judges of the earth."*
Psa. 2:10

"LET US GO UP TO THE MOUNTAIN OF THE LORD, to the house of the God of Jacob…," declared the prophet Isaiah (Isa. 2:3). The prophet Micah reiterated the call, expanding it clearly to Gentile followers of the LORD who became grafted into Israel. "Many nations shall come," prophesied Micah, and say, "Come, and let us go up to the mountain of the LORD, and to the house of the God of Jacob… for the law shall go forth of Zion, and the word of the LORD from Jerusalem" (Micah 4:2). Micah made clear this shall happen "in the last days" (Micah 4:1).

It has been the historic aspiration of the physical descendants of Jacob [Israel] to "go up" to Jerusalem and to the house of the LORD on the holy mount. Jerusalem, in a physical sense, is elevated above all the surrounding topography in the "Promised Land." Although it gives no competition to the great peaks of the earth that draw climbers worldwide to their summits, from the Creator's perspective, Jerusalem, crowned by His holy mount, is the center of the globe and symbolically stands as the height of the holy presence of the God of Israel, Lord of Nations, who woos all men unto Himself.

Even as Jerusalem and the Temple Mount represent the presence of God who made Himself manifest through Messiah in the flesh, so it also represents the power of the Lord of the Universe. That a rebellious mankind should perversely long to displace the holy presence with a carnal counterfeit striving to rule and reign from this place of prominence, purporting to merge religious and secular power, should come as no surprise to the student of Scripture or to those truly seeking a savior.

## ALIYAH

Jewish people throughout the nations, from the North to the South, and from East to West, are being drawn by the Spirit of the God of Jacob to "go up." Millions have followed the call to "go up," to return, to make permanent pilgrimage back to the "Promised Land" exemplified by Jerusalem and magnified by the anticipated glory of God to once again display Jehovah's presence from the Temple. They are making "Aliyah," which means "to go up." Gentile believers also are being drawn, all as declared over two millennia past by the prophets. Some are drawn to join the Jewish *Aliyah* physically; others are moved in spirit by the Holy Spirit (Ruach HaKodesh) to assist in this final "exodus" of the Jews from "Egypt" and "Babylon" back to the land of promise. "We will go with you," they say, "for we have heard that God is with you" (Zech. 8:22-23).

Others, the majority of the inhabitants of earth, have a contrary heart and hope. Their hope is rooted not in the God of Heaven but in the governments of earth. They seek not the power and purifying presence of a holy God but rather a pervasive, providing presence of a global government promising an elusive "peace on earth." And therefore the final stage of the historic battle for "king of the mountain" is nearing its cosmic conclusion. Will conquest rest in Christ, the "Anointed One," or in His earthly counterfeit empowered by the arch enemy of our Creator?

The kings of the earth, caught in this ultimate pursuit of conquest, not only conspire as mutual enemies against Israel, but also surreptitiously seek, each for their own purposes and driven by their own camouflaged agendas, to rule and reign over the earth from "the mount," the "holy mountain," God's "holy hill." It is this oft-undisclosed set of intentions that the God of Heaven has decisively discerned, such that, "He that sitteth in the heavens shall laugh: the LORD shall have them [the rulers and nations of earth] in derision" (Psa. 2:4).

## FROM RAGE TO RIGHTEOUSNESS

Even as the kings of the earth rebel against the authority of their Creator and set themselves against His anointed, the King of kings extends His scepter of righteousness, calling the rulers and inhabitants of earth to repentance. The King of Creation passionately urges, through prophetic warning, that the rebels against His divine rule humble themselves in agreement with His declared purposes and plans as disclosed so clearly in His holy Word. To this end, the Psalmist prophet pleas:

Be wise now therefore, O kings: be instructed, ye judges of the earth.

Serve the LORD with fear, and rejoice with trembling.

Kiss the Son [restore the humble relationship with Yeshua, Christ, as Messiah] lest he be angry, and ye perish from the way, when his wrath is kindled but a little. Blessed are all they that put their trust in him (Psa. 2:10-12).

## THE KING AND HIS HILL

History will reveal the fulness and finality of His Story. The plans and purposes of the Lord of Nations and of the God of Jacob as revealed by the holy prophets are soon to be completed. A final confrontation between the kings of earth and the King of glory will consume the peoples of this planet in a holy conflagration. This moment of truth is even now being staged in the "valley of decision" (Joel 3:14). Hear the Word of the LORD, ye kings!

Behold, the day of the LORD cometh, and thy spoil shall be divided in the midst of thee.

For I will gather all nations against Jerusalem to battle;

Then shall the LORD go forth, and fight against those nations...

And the LORD shall be king over all the earth: in that day shall there be one LORD, and his name one.

And it shall come to pass, that every one that is left of all the nations which come against Jerusalem shall even go up from year to year to worship the King, the LORD of hosts, and to keep the feast of tabernacles (Zech. 14:1-16).

"Multitudes, multitudes in the valley of decision: for the day of the LORD is near in the valley of decision" (Joel 3:14).

*Chapter 8*

# PROBING THOUGHTS *for* PROPHETIC TIMES

1. Other than direct fulfillment of Biblical prophecy, why do you suppose that over 6 million Jews have returned to the abandoned "Promised Land" over the last generations; after having been dispersed for two thousand years throughout the nations?

2. If Jerusalem and the Temple Mount represent the presence and power of God, can you see why the godless governors and governments of earth would be surreptitiously setting themselves to gain dominion from the "Holy Mount?"

3. Do you think that the power brokers of this present age will heed and hear the clear and profound warnings of the ancient prophets speaking for the God of history as to His declared ultimate governance by His Messiah, Yeshua Ha Mashiach, over His world from the Temple Mount? Why, or Why not?

*Chapter 9*

# THE TEMPLE MOUNT

***He who rules the Temple Mount rules the world.***

"THE HOLIEST PLACE IN THE WORLD" is how the Temple Institute in Jerusalem describes the Temple Mount, this ancient site where Abraham, by faith, offered up his only "son of promise" Isaac. After 2000 years, that "son of promise" who gave birth through Jacob to the nation of Israel was ultimately replaced, for all eternity, by the Creator Himself offering up His "only begotten son," Yeshua, the Lamb of God, who would offer redemption to all who would receive Him.

In the fulness of time, God became flesh in the form of man, giving Himself as a ransom to Jew and Gentile who, by the same faith as ancient Abraham, would humble themselves in repentance, obedience and righteousness to become "the sons of God" in these end times (I Jn. 3:1-3).

It was this "Anointed One," Yeshua HaMashiach, Jesus of Nazareth, Y'shuah ben Yoseph (Joseph), born of a virgin young woman by the very power of the Highest, the Spirit of God, who was not only crucified as God's sacrificial Lamb upon Mount Moriah, but would one day, from that very place, reign supreme as "King of kings" over the kings and peoples of the earth as promised by the prophet. As the Psalmist declared, "Yet have I set my king upon my holy hill" (Psa. 2:6; John 1:1-14, 3:16; Luke 2:26-35:3; Gal. 4:4).

It has now been two thousand years since the crucifixion and resurrection of Yeshua the Messiah, "the Holy One of Israel," making a total of some four thousand years since the birth of Isaac, the "son of promise." And the world awaits, with accelerating birth pangs, the cataclysmic events ushering in the promised "Second Coming" of the "Anointed One," Jesus the Christ, to rule and reign from Mount Zion, the Temple Mount.

## VOLATILE, YET VITAL

The Temple Mount has been called not only "the holiest place in the world" but also "the most *volatile* acreage on earth." Yet the study of the

Temple that once, then twice, graced that mountain has been said to be "one of the most *vital* activities for faith and worship." That is the continuing, perhaps growing, viewpoint of both Jews and Christians. For them, the Temple is *vital*, but for Muslims and most of the physical descendants of Ishmael (Abraham's first son), the very thought of the Temple produces *visceral volatility*. In a later chapter we must further explore the issue of "The Temple," but for now our eyes remain fixed upon the real estate.

Realtors, the marketers of real property (buildings and land), use a commonly-quoted phrase in describing variations in value of property. That phrase is: "LOCATION, LOCATION, LOCATION." The clear conclusion to be drawn is that the more desirable the property due to its location, the greater will be its value. On this basis of valuation, the 37 acres comprising the Temple Mount are, beyond all comparison, the most *valuable* acres on the planet; therefore the most *volatile*.

That value cannot be reduced to dollars and cents or to any economic measure. These acres are truly invaluable by every possible measure, whether economic, religious, social, national, global or political. These 37 acres truly define the destiny of our world. It is a prophetic landmark that now emerges as the centerpiece of the planet. It is a lodestone irresistibly drawing the kings and rulers of earth to vie for ultimate dominion.

Lurking within the purported political and religious machinations of men for world peace is the undisclosed, yet dominating desire to rule the world. Although seldom said openly, behind closed doors it is a universally-believed truth that, in the end, "He who rules the Temple Mount rules the world."

Hence, the battle is on. The battle for "king of the mountain" has, in many respects, only just begun. This war will not be waged primarily with weapons of mass destruction but rather with the new-found weapons of mass global persuasion. Religious and political chicanery will be rampant, demonstrating that deception remains one of the most effective tools of warfare. Israel, herself, will be dramatically deceived, threatening her destiny (Isa. 28:14-18).

The pernicious promises of a counterfeit Messiah will lure, through the ostensible pursuit of peace, the unsuspecting seed of Jacob into a terrifying trap. It will necessitate annulment of her "covenant with death" and direct intervention by the returning Messiah. This will transpire "in the latter time" when "transgressors are come to a full" and "a king of fierce countenance and understanding dark sentences shall stand up." "Through his policy also he shall cause craft to prosper" and "by [pursuit of] peace shall destroy many" (Dan. 8:19-25).

## THE CHOSEN MOUNT

What exactly is it about this 37 acre site known as the *Temple Mount* that makes it so desirable? What would cause the power brokers of this world to invest their highest hopes in controlling, and therefore governing, the globe from this historic plot of land? The further answers to those questions will reveal the otherwise hidden motivations and machinations of the great and competing powers of the planet in their final and desperate decisions that will determine our world's destiny, culminating in an unprecedented arrogant and dictatorial display of global dominion.

To understand the panoply of the greater global picture, including divine purpose, we must again look back over the shoulder of history, which, as it turns out, is God's story in the earth. Whether or not one agrees with the ultimate implications for our unique moment in history, a truly honest observer must admit to the historical facts.

The present state of political, "politically-correct," religious and "religiously-correct" stances concerning the Temple Mount appear clear, at least on the surface, based upon either historical evidence or hysterical claims. What seems certain, at present, is that since the days of Abraham, his descendants through Isaac (Israelites and/or Jews) claim exclusive historical right to the Temple Mount as the holiest site in Judaism, the place to which all Jews turn daily during prayer. Gentile Christians make claim to the Mount as spiritual heirs of Abraham, Isaac and Jacob, but only through the primary and first claim of the physical descendants. For most Christians, their claims do not compete with, but rather complement the Jewish exclusive claim to the Mount, except where political power seeks to ride upon the back of religion in order to achieve indirectly what it cannot achieve directly, i.e., global domination.

The third claimant is the Muslim world. Among Sunni Muslims, the Mount is widely considered to be "the third holiest site in Islam," reserved as the "Noble Sanctuary," claimed to be the location of Mohammed's journey to Jerusalem and ascent to heaven upon his horse. After the Muslim conquest of Jerusalem in 637 AD, Umayyad caliph Abd al-Malik commissioned the construction of the al-Aqsa Mosque and Dome of the Rock on the site. The Dome was completed in 692 AD, making it one of the oldest Islamic structures in the world. The Dome sits in the middle of the site, near where the physical descendants of Isaac, the "son of promise," believe God expects them to rebuild the Temple in the last days.

It is no mystery that the Temple Mount is the most contested religious site in the world. It is the three monotheistic religions that openly and clearly lay claim to the prize. Yet, lurking in the background are other contenders who will (and even now) seek the ultimate place of political power so as to set their throne upon the Mount. The contest, through religious and political "chess" movements, is approaching the claim of "check mate." It therefore behooves all truly Christian believers and believing Jews to be on alert to the political and religious chicanery coupled with countermanding threat of force that will soon engulf an unsuspecting world in the most monstrous deception ever perpetrated upon the planet.

The prize is without measurable price. No realtor's appraisal could approach setting a value upon this 37 acre parcel. It is deemed "priceless" and therefore worthy of all risk in pursuing its possession. Again, you may ask, "But why?" And the simple answer remains that it was "chosen." It is the very essence and nature of this "chosenness" that undergirds its value to all contenders.

## MORIAH

The Mount in contest was originally called *Mount Moriah*. We visit that name again because we first encountered it as the place where Abraham offered up Isaac, his "son of promise," and where Jehovah God redemptively provided a ram as a substitute sacrifice (Gen. 22). In recognition of the profound significance of that place that God had specified to be the precise place of sacrifice (Gen. 22:2), Abraham, in overwhelming gratitude, "called the name of that place *Jehovah-Jireh*."

This name is a composite of the unspoken name of God and the Hebrew word conveying "provision." Hence, in real terms today, Abraham called Mount Moriah… "the place of God's provision." Because God, in a practical way as touching man in the earth, had to be present in the miraculous provision of the substitute sacrifice given to Abraham just as he prepared to take the life of Isaac, this unusual place came to be more greatly understood not only as the place of God's *provision*, but even more importantly, the place of God's very *presence*.

If, indeed, Mount Moriah is the place where God, the Creator of all flesh, chose to uniquely manifest His presence, the location begins to take on monumental significance both for the descendants of Abraham, Isaac and Jacob as well as for all other persons on the planet. The full spiritual significance of this matter of *presence* is more clearly comprehended by believing Jews and Christians, but when processed by the secular mind or through other religious filters, it is not valued so much as the place of God's *presence* but rather as an ultimate prize in the pursuit of false *peace* on the road to global *power*.

It is in the valley between these two overriding viewpoints that the respective contestants arrive, or their surrogates, longing to seize dominion of this world's premier prize, juxtaposing their forces, whether military or "diplomatic," for the final conquest. It is indeed fascinating to watch the sometimes-dramatic and often subtle geopolitical positioning taking place before observant eyes, setting the final stage for history's most decisive confrontation, a winner-take-all battle that will determine world destiny.

The oft-missing piece in this profound puzzle is the failure to consciously recognize and humbly admit that Mount Moriah, the Temple Mount, is "the" place that God, Jehovah, the Creator, the Lord of Heaven and Earth chose. It would seem simple enough that if God makes a choice, it would be in mankind's best interest to conform. But history only proves that a rebellious heart and attitude not only perverts judgment but also the ability to assess the consequences of arrogantly choosing contrary to the express will of the Creator. And so the nations continue their ever-escalating rage.

"Moriah" is an interesting word. It is composed of two parts—"Mori" and "Yah." The word (or suffix in this case) *Yah* is the word for Jehovah God. The word or prefix *Mori* carries the sense of "selection," as in a place "seen by" and "chosen" by God for a purpose. Distilling these definitions and uniting them in clearest comprehension, we see Mount Moriah as "the hill God has selected or chosen." If that be true, it is of supreme significance, echoing even to this tenuous and increasingly terrifying time of human history.

## POSSESSION VS. PROMISE

"Possession is nine-tenths of the law" is a common phrase or legal aphorism. It distills, in a simple expression, what is commonly understood in a practical sense, i.e., that regardless of the truth or contention of "legal" claims to a property, he who holds the property in *possession* has the upper hand in a battle for or claim of ownership. This concept is inbred in the English Common Law and has been codified in many, if not most, places, at least in the Western world, under the term: "The Law of Adverse Possession." This phrase, in practical terms, simply means that the longer a person holds and exercises possession of property against the rights of the true owner, the more likely the "adverse" possessor will ultimately, in a dispute, be afforded permanent possession and ownership.

This is a point upon which "reasonable minds may differ," as a court might say, thus relying for equitable determination based upon the given set of facts. Sometimes a specific period of time of "adverse possession" may be codified as a "presumption" of ownership to be overcome only by a "preponderance" of (or overwhelming "clear and convincing") evidence to the contrary, thus overcoming the presumption.

This concept, although not usually framed in this fashion regarding claims to the Temple Mount, is nonetheless operative in world thinking and is deemed by many to be politically persuasive. The point is that whosoever may have at one time claimed ownership, subsequent possession by another supersedes the claims of an earlier possessor. As should be readily seen, this thinking is actually nothing more nor less than a battle for "king of the mountain." In other words "If I can gain possession against the rightful possession and ownership of my predecessor, and if I can hold that possession openly and notoriously long enough, I can now (under color of law) claim permanent ownership of the hill or mountain.

While this rationale may carry sway in the general affairs of men, is it persuasive with our Creator if He has indeed previously spoken on the matter? The obvious answer to the rhetorical question is a resounding "NO!" To affirm the concept of adverse possession as against the decreed or spoken will of the Creator is to elevate the word and will of the creature over his Creator. To avoid this dilemma, men have cleverly "created" an alternative explanation for "Creation," calling it "Evolution."

If humankind has merely "evolved" rather than being "created," he has no moral need to submit to the will of a Creator, and therefore he becomes "the sole master of his fate," "the captain of his soul," and the prize goes only to "the fittest" or to "the most powerful at the moment." It is for this reason the United Nations has decreed that the most important thing the U.N. must do is to globally decree the dogma of evolution. The Creator must not be given "a foot in the door."

This has profound implications for the status of Mount Moriah, the Temple Mount, in our time. The reality is that God, Jehovah Jireh, has spoken. If, in deed and truth, He is God, Creator of all things in heaven and earth as stated in the Scriptures (the Bible) that all three monotheistic faiths profess to be true, then what God has said should be determinative among reasonable and humble representatives of humankind on this planet.

God made a promise, and He is not a man that He should lie (Numb. 23:19). He is God, and there is no other (Isa. 45:5). Jehovah promised Abraham that he would have a "son of promise" in his old age. "My covenant," He said, "I will establish with Isaac..." (Gen. 17:21). "I will establish my covenant between me and thee and thy seed after thee in their generations for an everlasting covenant...." "And I will give unto thee and to thy seed after thee... all the land of Canaan, for an everlasting possession; and I will be their God" (Gen. 17: 7-8). God then pointed Abraham to the place of His choosing, Mount Moriah, the Temple Mount, where the God of creation chose to reveal His eternal presence and provision to the man to whom the promise was made.

And so each of us must now decide. Every man and woman must decide. Every president, prime minister, politician, pastor, pope and priest must decide. To decide is to determine destiny. Will the eternal promise of the Creator hold determinative sway in our politics and polemics, or will the ephemeral feelings of fickle men placing their hope upon evolutionary progress be the deciding factor?

These choices are mutually exclusive. The Lord of Nations and God of Abraham, Isaac and Jacob awaits our decision. In that day, the God of Heaven and Earth declared to Abraham:

By myself have I sworn, saith the LORD...

And in thy seed shall all the nations be blessed; because thou hast obeyed my voice" (Gen. 22:16-18).

*Chapter 9*

# PROBING THOUGHTS *for* PROPHETIC TIMES

1. What is it that makes the Temple Mount such a magnet for mankind and the world's rulers?

2. Do you think there is any substance to the claim that "He who rules the Temple Mount rules the world?" Why, or why not?

3. Can you see why the very thought that the Temple Mount may be "chosen" by God would provide a perverse, yet powerful, motivation to religious and secular leaders to gain dominion and authority over that prized piece of real estate?

4. If something is deemed to be a "priceless prize," to what ends might power thirsty presidents and prime ministers—or even popes—go to claim dominion over the prize?

5. In what way has the teaching of *evolution* been used as a not-so-subtle effort to evade or avoid the authority of a Creator God? Is it working in the ways and thinking of the peoples of the world? Might such rebellion against a Creator's authority actually precipitate the greatest human calamity in history in the unfettered pursuit to become *KING of the Mountain*?

# Chapter 10

# THE POWER OF POSSESSION

## *Is the Temple Mount God's Time Bomb?*

POSSESSION OF THIS most prominent square mile on our planet, both past and present, will afford some perspective on the historical problem of the Temple Mount. While "the devil may be in the details," a brief overview should suffice and will be surprisingly revealing.

### HOW ISRAEL GAINED POSSESSION

At least four religions are known to have used the Temple Mount: Judaism, Christianity, Islam and Roman paganism. Yet preceding all of these was God's covenant with Abraham to be established through Isaac and to be confirmed in Jacob whose name was changed by God to *Israel* (Gen. 32:28; 35:9-12). Regardless of all other historically-recorded uses and occupations of the Temple Mount, the Mount and all of the surrounding land was deeded by God through immutable covenant to Abraham and his seed through God's chosen "son of promise," Isaac (Gen. 15:18-21; Gen. 17:7-8, 18-21; Gen. 26:1-5; Gen. 28:1-4, 13-15; Gen. 35: 9-12; Gen. 37:1).

The hill we now identify as the *Temple Mount* is believed to have been inhabited since perhaps the 4th millennium BC. Its southern section identified as the biblical *Mount Zion* is believed to have been walled around 1850 BC by Canaanites who established a settlement in the vicinity called *Jebus*. Biblical scholars have identified this place with Mount Moriah, where Abraham bound Isaac.

According to the Hebrew Bible, the *Tanakh*, Mount Moriah became a threshing floor owned by Araunah the Jebusite. The prophet Gad advised King David, the second king of Israel under whom the northern and southern kingdoms (Ephraim and Judah) were united, to erect an altar to YHWH [YHVH]—יהוה (commonly known as Yahweh or Jehovah), on this threshing floor, since it was on that spot that a destroying angel was standing when God stopped a plague of judgment that had destroyed 70,000 men in Jerusalem. David then bought the property from Araunah for fifty pieces of silver, thereby becoming its owner. There he built an altar, and later established plans for the building of the first Temple on that very site to replace the traveling Tabernacle of God's presence.

To the less informed, these may appear bland, extraneous or even irrelevant details in light of the world's current dilemma regarding the Temple Mount. In reality, however, these historical facts form the very foundation of Israel's claim to the Mount, long preceding any interest or claim by further challengers.

It is of pre-eminent significance, seldom publicly recognized, that this same David, the King of Israel who united the descendants of Abraham, Isaac and Jacob into what scholars call "The United Kingdom," was given a specific and far-reaching covenant by יהוה (YHWH), the God of Abraham and Israel. This covenant is of monumental consequence, since it once again expresses God's viewpoint regarding the eternal and epic battle for *KING of the Mountain.*

The "word of the LORD came unto Nathan" the prophet for David, saying… "And thine house **AND THY KINGDOM** shall be established for ever before thee: thy throne shall be established for ever" (II Sam. 7:4, 16). God's throne or rulership was to be fulfilled in and through David forever. Isaiah, the prophet, confirmed this covenant centuries later in commonly-quoted words concerning the promised Messiah, words reiterated in the renowned *Messiah* by George Frederick Handel. These prophetic words must and will define God's determination concerning the end-time battle for *KING of the Mountain.*

> For every battle of the warrior is with confused noise, and garments rolled in blood; but this shall be with burning and fuel of fire.

> For unto us a child is born, unto us a son is given: and **the government shall be upon his shoulder:** and his name shall be called Wonderful, Counselor, The Mighty God, the Everlasting Father, The Prince of Peace.

> Of **the increase of his government** and peace there shall be no end, **upon the throne of David,** and upon his kingdom, to order it, and to establish it with judgment and with justice from henceforth **even forever.** The zeal of the LORD of hosts will perform this (Isa. 9:5-7).

If this be true, it is little wonder that the nations rage, for the very thought that a descendant of David should rule and reign over the earth from the Temple Mount is untenable. It is anathema, not only to Muslims but to the many who yearn to be "king," not only of the earth but of their own personal "kingdoms."

Contenders for personal and global dominion would do well, also, to consider the opening words of the New Covenant:

> The book of the generation of Jesus Christ, the son of David [by lineage], the son of Abraham [by faithful obedience] (Matt. 1:1).

In light of the supreme biblical role of King David and God's eternal covenant that His promised Messiah would one day sit "on the throne of David," it should come as no surprise that unbelieving scientists and archeologists should have waged a continued campaign to debunk any legitimacy to an historical king of Israel named *David* or even to such a kingdom. Once again, however, the multiplying archeological finds of recent years have not only confirmed David's historical reality but also the reality of his kingdom. It should be clear that, in the mind of a humanistic cynic or dis-believer, the debunking of David is paramount to hiding from the reality of the promised King of kings who would rule over the earth from the Temple Mount on the throne of David. To them, such a thought is untenable, for they, in their hearts, declare, "We will not have this King to reign over us!"

## FROM ISRAEL TO BABYLON / PERSIA

For nearly 500 years, Israel had and exercised exclusive possession and dominion over the Temple Mount. It was the centerpiece of Jewish life and culture. From King David to Judah's final king, Zedekiah, the Temple Mount defined and was the pre-eminent expression of Jewish existence. When Babylon, under Nebuchadnezzar, conquered Judah in divine discipline of the increasingly apostate southern remnant of Israel, the first Temple, built by David's son, Solomon, was destroyed. This was the ultimate expression a foreign power could communicate to demean and dislocate the very soul of the Jewish people.

After 70 years in captivity, as promised by the prophets, Israel's corrective spiritual "spanking" by the God of Abraham, Isaac and Jacob was complete. God then used Persia as His arm of justice to bring judgment upon Babylon for bringing the curse of destruction upon Israel/Judah, as had been promised to Abraham, saying, "I will bless them that bless thee, and curse him that curseth thee…" (Gen. 12:3). The spirit of the LORD moved upon Cyrus the Great, King of Persia, to restore Judah to the land promised to Abraham. Incredibly, this Persian king not only permitted but provided for the Jews to return to their homeland, and personally secured and promised all necessary provisions for the rebuilding of the Temple (Ezra 1:1-4).

Interestingly, the prophet Isaiah referred to Cyrus as God's "anointed." "Thus saith the LORD to his anointed, to Cyrus, whose right hand I have holden, to subdue nations before him... I will go before thee, and make the crooked places straight.... For Jacob my servant's sake, and Israel mine elect, I have even called thee by thy name: I have surnamed thee, though thou hast not known me" (Isa. 45:1-6).

Here lies one of the conundrums of history. A great Persian king is used by the God of Jacob (Israel) to rebuild the Temple and to restore Israel to her God-deeded homeland. So great was this king's favor and grace toward God's "elect" that he was described as God's "anointed," language that clearly identified him, from God's viewpoint, as a "type" of Israel's Messiah that was to come, who would bring final and ultimate restoration and rebuild the Temple. And why is this such an historical paradox? It is because nearly 2500 years later, in 1935, Persia became Iran. Through a new "king," Iran's recent President Mahmoud Ahmadinejad and Supreme spiritual leader Ayatollah Khomeini, Persia/Iran has now decreed Israel's annihilation, as did the wicked Persian Haman in the Book of Esther, forbidding Jews, through their Persian proxies, the "Palestinians," Hamas and Hezbollah, from even entering the Temple Mount. This, to any reasonable mind, must be a catastrophic choice with enormous consequences in these end-times. For it is written, "Behold, he that keepeth Israel shall neither slumber nor sleep" (Psa. 121:4).

## From Persia to Greek "Hellenism"

The whirlwind campaign of Alexander the Great for global dominion from the Adriatic Sea to the Indus River, from 336 B.C. to 323 B.C., ushered in a change for Israel from Persian favor to Greek or Hellenistic fervor. Hellenism became the politically-correct culture of the realm and was profoundly pagan. As the pompous Antiochus Epiphanes swept into power under the Seleucid expression of Hellenism when Alexander's Empire was divided between his four generals, the profound paganism of Hellenism came into dramatic conflict with Jewish principle and practice. It was explosive.

Antiochus took dominion of the Temple Mount in order to dominate Judaism with Hellenism. Swine were sacrificed upon the sacred altar. The divine sanctuary was desecrated with unholy, demonic delight. The Jews rebelled through the Maccabean Revolt, resulting in a short-lived victory, cleansing of the Temple and the celebration of the miraculous enduring light of the Menorah which gave birth to the "Feast of Lights" or Hanukkah.

Such rejoicing among the righteous in divine victory was intolerable to the demonically-driven Antiochus. He determined that hell should break forth among the Jews to perpetuate the pagan Hellenism that now governed the global culture. And so he determined to destroy the Jews and bring ultimate and final desecration to their Temple, declaring himself "God" on the sacred Mount, a counterfeit of the Messiah or "anointed one" that was to come. Thus, just as Cyrus had been a "type" of the Messiah or Christ to come, so Antiochus was a "type" of the Anti-Christ, the counterfeit, pre-emptive, "Messiah" who would, in these end-times, declare himself "God" in a rebuilt Temple on that very Mount.

## FROM GREEK HELLENISM TO ROME

By 146 BC, the "global empire of Alexander the Great (which had been divided among his four generals) was also increasingly divided, resulting in the gradual waning of Hellenism or Greek culture. Since, as has been said, *Nature abhors a vacuum*, Rome was now poised to fill the void and began its quest for global dominion through its legendary legions and the "Internet" of the day—Roman roads—which facilitated expeditions and unprecedented communication and therefore control.

The city of Aelia Capitolina was built in 130 BC by the emperor Hadrian at the site of Jerusalem. Aelia came from Hadrian's cognomen (family name), while Capitolina meant that the new city was dedicated to Jupiter Capitolinus. A temple was built to Jupiter on the very site where the first and second Temples once stood on the Temple Mount.

It had been Hadrian's purported intent that the new city be a gift to the Jews. However, he had erected a giant statue of himself in front of the Temple of Jupiter, and the Temple of Jupiter had a huge statue of Jupiter inside of it. There were now two massive "graven images" on the Temple Mount in direct and open conflict with the commandment, "Thou shalt not make unto thee any graven image... for I the LORD am a jealous God..." (Exod. 20:4-5).

To "add insult to injury," Hellenistic religious practitioners sacrificed swine to their deities, a practice despicably offensive to any true Jew. Hadrian had also forbidden the Jews to practice circumcision which God had, through Moses, commanded them to do as a physical demonstration of being separated unto God. Collectively, these were seen by the Jews as a new "abomination of desolation," a repeat of the defiant and diabolical decrees of Antiochus Epiphanes, effectively pushing the thumb of earthly power into the eye of the Creator who had decreed Israel to be the "apple of His eye" (Zech. 2:8).

Thus was launched the Bar Kochba rebellion, the Third Jewish Revolt, resulting in a devastating response from Rome. All Jews were prohibited, on pain of death, from even entering Jerusalem, and thus were utterly prevented from coming within proximity to the Temple Mount. It now appears, in our generation, that history has nearly repeated itself. The "helix of history" is approaching its culminating moment when "Rome" once again viciously asserts dominion, preparing to place her "king" on the Holy Mount.

## CHRISTIAN / BYZANTINE PRESENCE

The earliest followers of Yeshua, Jesus, were all Jewish. Jesus was a Jew, all of his original disciples were Jews, and the earliest followers were all Jews, known as "followers of the Way." They were admonished by their Lord to "go into all the world and preach the gospel…" (Mark 16:15; Matt. 28:18-20).

By the early fourth century AD, the gospel (good news) of salvation through the "anointed one," Yeshua HaMashiach, had spread throughout the gentile or Greek and Roman world. Gentile followers began to rapidly outnumber Jewish believers. Because of overt Roman bias, even belligerence, against all things Jewish, Gentile believers increasingly rejected their Jewish roots, ultimately distancing themselves from any and all practices remotely related to Jewish belief and culture.

By 323 AD, Gentile believers in Jesus Christ had become of such influence throughout Rome that the culture began to be strongly affected, although powerful tensions persisted as the pervasive paganism of Roman culture came into conflict with "Christians" who refused both to bow to pagan shrines and to the emperor who claimed to be divine. And so it was a profound moment in modern history when the Emperor Constantine had his proclaimed "Vision of the Cross," and soon declared Christianity to be the official religion of the Roman realm.

But Rome had been divided. Maximian ruled at Rome and Constantine ruled in the alternate capitol at Constantinople in Turkey, then called Byzantium. Conflict was constant. In rather simple terms, with an environment rife with political chicanery and pursuit of power, the ultimate conflict might well be framed as "pagan Rome vs. the person of Jesus Christ." Who would reign supreme? Who would be Lord, the emperor, or Christ? And that eternal question remains to be answered in the minds of "Roman" citizens throughout the earth today. Each of us, in our own way, is even now making that decision. Thus, the "eternal, epic" battle is being waged in these end-times in the heart and mind of every man and woman.

About 325 AD, it is commonly believed that Constantine's mother, Helena, built a small church on the Temple Mount, calling it the Church of St. Cyrus and St. John. It was later enlarged and called The Church of the Holy Wisdom.

In AD 363, Emperor Julian, an opponent of Christianity, granted the Jews permission to begin rebuilding the Temple. The destroyed Temple, as seen by gentile Christians, had been a symbol of Christianity's triumph over Judaism. Rebuilding was halted, however, by a great Galilean earthquake in AD 363.

Archaeological evidence establishes an elaborate Byzantine church, monastery or other religious building on the Temple Mount during Byzantine times, believed to be the Church of the Holy Wisdom, since it is known that Helena ordered the Temple of Venus to the west of the Temple Mount to be torn down so as to construct the church. That church was later destroyed, and on its ruins the Dome of the Rock was built.

## THE STRUGGLE FOR POSSESSION PERSISTS

History, when distilled, makes clear that the battle for *KING of the Mountain* is indeed epic.

In 610 AD, the Sassanid Empire (the last great Persian Empire before Muslim conquest and adoption of Islam) drove the Byzantine Empire out of the Middle East. This, remarkably, gave the Jews possession of Jerusalem for the first time in centuries. They soon resumed animal sacrifice on the Mount for the first time since the Second Temple. The Byzantines re-took the area about five years later, but just before that took place, the Persians (notably) gave control to the Christians, who tore down the partially-built temple and turned it into a garbage dump. Enter, the Muslims.

## MUSLIMS BUILD THE "FURTHEST MOSQUE"

Sometime in the decade of the 630's AD, the Muslim Caliph Omar took the City of Jerusalem. Upon capture of Jerusalem, Omar headed immediately to the Temple Mount in order to find the holy site of the "Furthest Mosque" which was mentioned in the Koran but specified in the Hadith as being in Jerusalem. Reportedly, a former Jewish rabbi who had converted to Islam advised Caliph Omar to build the Dome of the Rock monument on the Temple Mount, contending the site must be where Mohammed ascended to heaven on his horse. A wooden building was constructed.

In 1691, Caliph Abd al-Malik constructed an octagonal Islamic building topped by a dome. The shrine became known as the Dome of the Rock, and was later covered in gold in 1920. The term al-Haram al-Sharif or "Noble Sanctuary" describes the entire surrounding area of the rock central to the Temple Mount.

For Muslims, the significance of both the Dome of the Rock and the al-Aqsa Mosque makes Jerusalem the third most holy city after Mecca and Medina.

Interestingly, a Jewish synagogue was built on the Temple Mount during a period of apparently favorable relations between the Islamic rulers and the

Jewish subjugants, but that structure was later destroyed by the Crusaders who, in 1099 AD, conquered the city, massacring both Jews and Muslims, curiously and falsely in the name of Christ, under Pope Urban II (the "Vicar of Christ") while pursuing dominion of the Mount.

The Dome of the Rock was turned into a place of Christian worship and renamed Templum Domini, meaning "the temple of the Lord." The al-Aqsa Mosque became a palace for Crusader kings and later headquarters of the Knights Templar. After nearly a century of Christian rule, the Muslim Sultan Saladin laid siege to Jerusalem, defeating the Crusaders in 1187 AD. He tore down the cross, replacing it with the Islamic Crescent.

## OTTOMAN / TURKISH DOMINION

The epic, eternal quest for dominion of the Temple Mount is not restricted to nation vs. nation or to religion vs. religion. It is a prize that inexorably draws all comers, whether individually or collectively. Hence, the Ottoman Empire now appears on the scene.

Following the Ottoman (Turkish) conquest of Palestine in 1516 AD under "Suleiman the Magnificent," Ottoman authorities continued prohibiting non-Muslims from setting foot on the Temple Mount. Thus, the Muslim Turks gained dominion over the world's ultimate prize, in effect claiming absolute dominion for 400 years in derogation of the rest of the Muslim world, while preserving Islamic authority until the end of World War I.

Of special interest at this advancing moment of geopolitical maneuvers is that Turkey has now increasing fashioned itself under President Erdogan as a resurrecting Ottoman Empire while a resurrecting Persia (Iran) sets itself in hot pursuit of global Islamic leadership. Each now strives to become "king of the Islamic mountain" so as to establish global dominion under the planet's world-wide caliphate.

The tectonic geopolitical and religious forces pressing increasingly upon the Temple Mount will soon cause cataclysmic eruption; precipitating a tsunami of violence unprecedented in the history of man.

The British Mandate ultimately deprived the Ottoman Turks of Temple Mount dominion, allowing Arab control under Jordan, during which time all Jews were deprived of access even after the rebirth of Israel in 1948.

## ISRAEL'S TENUOUS CONTROL

The year 1967 was shocking to Arab, Muslim and world sensibilities. The impossible became the inevitable. Israel, on the precipice of utter annihilation by confederate Arab forces under military finance and facilitation by Russia, miraculously turned the tide, dramatically winning the Six-Day War. The world powers were stunned, but none so much as Russia and her Arab proxies.

Israel not only survived but regained territory once promised to Abraham, Isaac and Jacob as a result of the Six-Day War. Israel captured the Temple Mount with all of East Jerusalem (biblical Jerusalem) from Jordan, which had controlled it since Israel's astonishing and historically-unprecedented rebirth in 1948, all in fulfillment of Isaiah's prophecy in a question:

> Who hath heard such things? Who hath seen such things? Shall the earth be made to bring forth in one day? Or shall a nation be born at once? For as soon as Zion travailed, she brought forth her children.
>
> Shall I bring to the birth, and not cease to bring forth? saith the LORD (Isa. 66:8-9).

Perhaps most astonishing of all, causing many to shake their heads in disbelief, is the picture of the bold and brash Israeli General, Moshe Dayan, almost immediately turning over administrative control of the Temple Mount to the Islamic Waqf, granting the Muslim world the power of possession, leaving only formal or technical authority in the hands of Israel.

How could such a thing be? How could this military hero of Israel compromise possession of Israel's greatest prize in a desperate ploy for peace? The answer is actually quite simple. For at that time and in this continuing season, the majority of Jews have, like ancient Israel and Judah, abandoned their roots and the God of Abraham, Isaac and Jacob. While seeming to prosper for a season in the flesh, they flounder in the spirit. In desperate striving to be like all other nations, they have rejected their spiritual DNA. They clamor again for a king to reign over them while declaring of the promised "anointed one" who offered himself as the sacrificial Lamb of God upon the Mount, "We will not have this man reign over us" (Luke 19:14), for "We have no king but Caesar" (John 19:15).

Israel, in hot pursuit of adolescent-like acceptance among the goyim (gentile nations), has, like much of the global gentile Christian church, abandoned the fear of the Lord to please men. Having abandoned trust in the God who made, preserved and restored her as a nation, she has cast her claim of hope upon godless goyim and Christ-less culture, pandering to every whim of a feckless and faithless world that despises her very claim to destiny.

Fear of man, be it Islamic hatred, European Union rejection or United Nations isolation, has engendered a paralysis and perversion of purpose leading to faithless foolishness in policy and in practical politics in the land of Jacob. As it is written, truly, "The fear of the LORD is the beginning of wisdom..." (Psa. 111:10), but "The fear of man bringeth a snare" (Prov.

29:25). For "The secret of the Lord," for both Jew and Gentile, "is with them who fear him, and to them [and them only] will he shew [reveal, manifest, make operationally effective] his covenant" (Psa. 25:14).

This is *Tikvat Israel* (the Hope of Israel) as revealed in Yeshua, and why, as "the Word made flesh" He, as the final sacrificial Lamb of God, had to make a "quick understanding in the fear of the LORD" (Isa. 11:3). Thus, in both deed and truth, the "rod out of the stem of Jesse [David's father]" should become the surviving "Branch" of Israel so that it might be said of Him:

> The spirit of the LORD shall rest upon him, the spirit of wisdom and understanding, the spirit of counsel and might, the spirit of knowledge and of the fear of the LORD (Isa. 11:1-2).

Therefore it is written in the "Deuteronomy" of the New Covenant:

> Though he [Yeshua, Jesus Christ] were a Son, yet learned He obedience by the things which He suffered;

> And being made perfect, He became the author of eternal salvation [for both Jew and Gentile] unto all them that obey Him (Heb. 5:8-9).

Therefore, as was recorded in the Torah [the first five books of Moses in the Bible], "Thou art a priest forever after the order of Melchizedek" (Heb. 7:17). "For this Melchizedek, king of Salem, priest of the most High God, who met Abraham, ... and blessed him: To whom also Abraham gave a tenth part of all [a tithe]; first being by interpretation King of righteousness, and after that also King of Salem, which is King of peace... made like unto the Son of God; abideth a priest continually" (Gen. 14:18-20; Heb. 7:1-3).

Both Jew and Gentile are thus brought to the further choice of historical revelation concerning the Mount of God's presence. Yet, you say, "How is that?"

This Melchizedek was "King of Salem," a shortened form of Jerusalem or "city of peace." He was also "King of righteousness" and only after that fact of absolute righteousness, "also King of Salem, which is King of peace"... "without descent, having neither beginning of days, nor end of life; but being made like unto the Son of God; abideth a priest continually" (Gen. 14:18-20; Heb. 7:1-4).

## THE END-TIME BATTLE LIES DEAD AHEAD

The rulers and peoples of our planet must now, in this propitious moment of history, humbly come to grips with this spiritual reality if there is to be true "peace on earth" and genuine "good will toward men" (Luke 2:14). This, by all rights, should begin first with the Jew (the physical descendants of Abraham, Isaac and Jacob) to whom the oracles of God were first given and to which the humble Gentile will gravitate.

> For behold, the darkness shall cover the earth, and gross darkness the people; but the LORD shall arise upon thee, and his glory shall be seen upon thee.

> And the Gentiles shall come to thy light, and kings to the brightness of thy rising.

> Surely the isles shall wait for me… to bring thy sons from far, their silver and their gold with them, unto the name of the LORD thy God, and to the Holy One of Israel, because he hath glorified thee.

> And the sons of strangers shall build up thy walls, and their kings shall minister unto thee: for in my wrath I smote thee, but in my favor have I had mercy on thee.

> For the nation and kingdom that will not serve thee [Israel and Zion] shall perish; yea, those nations shall be utterly wasted (Isa. 60).

This "Melchizedek," as "King of righteousness" and as "King of peace" was none other than a pre-incarnate manifestation of the Messiah who was to come, and was declared to be "King" of the mountain. "Before Abraham was," declared Yeshua to His Jewish brethren, "I AM" (John 8:58). For "your father Abraham rejoiced to see my day: and he saw it and was glad" (John 8:56).

Melchizedek, as "King of Salem" [Peace and the city of peace Jerusalem] was a "type" of Messiah, an appearance of the "Anointed One" to Abraham, the father of the faith, before Yeshua layed down His life on the very Mount upon which He would be declared "King." Again, as it is written: "And they crucified him… and set up over his head his accusation written as recorded in Matthew 27:37:

THIS IS JESUS THE KING OF THE JEWS.

The eternal record is clear as spoken by the prophets. The epic battle for *KING of the Mountain* will advance with escalating vengeance as time and eternity come ever closer to ultimate confrontation on the Temple Mount. The rulers of earth will rage in envy for ultimate dominion, power and glory, blinded by their blazing pride.

Yet the choice remains clear. For the prophet well stated: "He that putteth his trust in me [God the Father as revealed in His Son, Yeshua] shall possess the land, and shall inherit my holy mountain (Isa. 57:13). For "I dwell in the high and holy place, with him also that is of a contrite and humble spirit, to revive the spirit of the humble, and to revive the heart of the contrite ones" (Isa. 57:15).

Israel, even the more so, has a clear choice, for to him were the oracles of God first given. Jacob's tenuous hold on the Temple Mount will become increasingly troubling, indeed terrifying, as Jerusalem becomes "a cup of trembling" and "a burdensome stone," drawing all the peoples of earth to "be gathered together against it" (Zech. 12:2-3). The "time of Jacob's trouble" draws near. It stands now knocking at history's door (Dan. 12:1; Jer. 30:7). Yet the Lord of Nations and the God of Israel cries out still: "Today, if you will hear his voice, harden not your hearts..." (Psa. 95: 7-8; Heb. 3:6-15). "Repent ye: for the kingdom of heaven is at hand."

> Behold, the day of the LORD cometh.... For I will gather all nations against Jerusalem to battle.
>
> Then shall the LORD go forth, and fight against those nations... (Zech. 14:1-3).
>
> And his feet shall stand in that day upon the Mount of Olives, which is before Jerusalem on the east [the very place from which Yeshua ascended back to the Father after His resurrection and where angels foretold His return (Acts 1:9-11)], and the Mount of Olives shall cleave in the midst thereof... (Zech. 14:4).

"In that day shall the LORD defend the inhabitants of Jeru-salem; and he that is feeble among them at that day shall be as David: and the house of David shall be as God [through Yeshua, the "son of David" by lineage]". "And it shall come to pass in that day, that I will seek to destroy all nations that come against Jerusalem [which includes the Temple Mount]. And I will pour upon the house of David [through Yeshua Ben Joseph, Jesus the Messiah], and upon the inhabitants of Jerusalem, the spirit of grace and of supplications: and they [the physical descendants of Abraham, Isaac and Jacob as well as of David] shall look upon me [Yeshua] whom they have pierced...." "And there shall be a great mourning in Jerusalem." And "they shall mourn for him [Yeshua HaMashiach], as one mourneth for his only son..." (Zech. 12:8-14).

From that moment, the troubling and terrifying trials of Jacob shall turn to victorious rejoicing. Israel will cry, in bitter remorse yet emerging glory, "Baruch HaBa B'Shem Adonai – Blessed is He who cometh in the name of the LORD" (Psa. 118:26; Matt. 21:9; 23:37-39). "And the LORD their God shall save them in that day…" (Zech. 9:14-16).

As it is written, "Rejoice greatly, O daughter of Zion; shout, O daughter of Jerusalem: behold, thy King cometh unto thee: he is just, and having salvation;" "And his dominion shall be from sea even to sea, and from the river to the ends of the earth" (Zech. 9:9-10).

Bow the knee, ye kings of the earth! Humble yourselves in the sight of the Lord, and He shall lift you up (Jam. 4:10). Give glory to the God of Israel, worship Him that made heaven and earth. "Prepare to meet thy God" (Amos 4:12). If not, "… the day of the LORD is great and very terrible; who can abide it" (Joel 2:11)? "Blow the trumpet in Zion, and sound an alarm on my holy mountain, for the day of the LORD cometh, for it is nigh at hand" (Joel 2:1).

"Proclaim ye this among the Gentiles; Prepare war…. Beat your plowshares into swords… Multitudes, multitudes in the valley of decision: for the day of the LORD is near in the valley of decision" (Joel 3:9-14).

"The LORD shall roar out of Zion, and utter his voice from Jerusalem; and the heavens and the earth shall shake: but the LORD will be the hope of his people, and the strength of the children of Israel. So shall ye know that I am the LORD your God dwelling in Zion, my holy mountain (Joel 3:16-17). "For the LORD is our defense; and the Holy One of Israel is our king" (Psa. 89:18).

Take heed to yourselves, ye rulers, who deign to lift up the sword against the LORD and against His anointed. Dare you imagine yourselves to be a match for the LORD of hosts? For it is written:

The LORD shall be king over all the earth: in that day shall there be one LORD, and His name one (Zech. 14:9).

Indeed, the Temple Mount looms as "God's time bomb." It is ready now to explode, engulfing the world in unprecedented war. Will a rebuilt Temple be the fuse, causing the planet to burst into a flaming conflagration? The epic, end-time battle lies dead ahead.

*Chapter 10*

# PROBING THOUGHTS *for* PROPHETIC TIMES

1. How far back in history did Israel, through King David, gain possession of the Temple Mount?

2. Do you think that the fact that Abraham (4000 years ago) offered his "son of promise" Isaac upon Mt. Moriah, now called the Temple Mount, is of any historical or prophetic significance? In what ways?

3. Why would historians want to debunk the existence of King David and his kingdom? How might such persistent attitudes designed to debunk the prophetic promise of God in the Bible actually undergird a defiant end-time enterprise to place a counterfeit "prince of peace" on the Temple Mount to govern the world?

4. In what ways might the Temple Mount be God's "time bomb" to effectuate His prophesied purposes?

5. Have you struggled with your own attitude on these matters? On what basis will you resolve your struggle?

# *Chapter 11*

# THE TEMPLE AND JACOB'S TROUBLE

### *The eternal, epic and end-time battle for*
### *KING of the Mountain lies straight ahead.*

**PROPHECY IS BECOMING HISTORY** at a breathtaking pace. The span of time between prophecy becoming history is no longer measured in millennia or centuries but in days and weeks. History's final moments may well be knocking at the door of time. And no issue brings greater, more intense focus to this unique moment in time than the call for a rebuilt Temple. Yet despite the growing intensity of expectation among the descendants of Abraham, Isaac and Jacob for a Temple to once again complete Jewish identity, will it become the catalyst for the prophesied "time of Jacob's trouble" (Jer. 30:7)? Will the *inconceivable* become the *inevitable*?

## THE CENTER OF TIME

Time is no longer seeming to *stand still.* The world's inhabitants, whether religious or secular, are increasingly coming to the conviction, however subtle, solemn or secularly-wrapped, that time is inexorably marching toward a moment of truth unprecedented in the annals of recorded history.

The renowned physicist and mathematician, Sir Isaac Newton, was also a profound biblical thinker. He, with amazing intellect, also had an extraordinary understanding of Hebrew and Christian Scripture, with particular fascination focused on biblical prophecy. Newton was convinced that a code was encrypted that, when deciphered, would reveal deeper truths concerning future times. The key, he believed, was the Temple of Solomon, Israel's First Temple, that would reveal the template for our times. Further focus on this concept is made clear in a recent globally-encompassing view of the Temple.

> The description of Jerusalem as a terrestrial center point, situated in the center of the world, is found in Philo's Legatio ad Gaium.

The world is like a human eyeball. The white of the eye is the ocean surrounding the world, the iris is the continent, the pupil is Jerusalem, and the image is the Holy Temple.[1]

The all-encompassing conclusion is that just as Zion is "the apple of [God's] eye" (Zech. 2:8; Deut. 32:10; Lam. 2:18), even the more so, the Temple stands as the "Temple at the Center of Time."[2] If the Temple Mount is figuratively "God's time bomb," is the Temple, then, God's triggering time clock?

## FROM TABERNACLE TO TEMPLE

While Israel well understood in truth that "the Most High dwelleth not in temples made with hands" (Isa. 66:1-2; Acts 7:48-49), God had made plain to Moses that, to practically demonstrate His presence and glory to terrestrial-bound mankind, Moses was to build a tabernacle [dwelling] where the presence of the Lord would tangibly rest among the people delivered from the bondage of Egypt as they traversed the wilderness on their way to the Promised Land (Exod. 25). "And Moses took the tabernacle, and pitched it *without the camp*, afar off from the camp, and called it the Tabernacle of the Congregation." "…every one which sought the LORD went out unto the tabernacle of the congregation, which was *without the camp*" (Exod. 33:7).

In requiring Israel to come to Him "without the camp," God made abundantly clear that He was holy, and that Israel must discern the difference between "the holy and the profane," between "the clean and the unclean" (Ezek. 44:23). The manifestation of the glory of God's presence would be predicated on the purity of their presentation before Him.

To further that end, the Lord commanded Moses to build an "ark" which He called "the Ark of the Testimony." Inside the ark was to be placed "the Testimony" or Ten Commandments defining the relationship between the people and HaShem (God) and the relationship among the "called out" ones, the Children of Israel, who had been delivered from the dominion of Pharaoh so as to live freely by faith in the Creator's care.

Realizing that, despite good intentions, the "chosen people" would fall short of His covenant commands, the Lord instructed Moses to make a *mercy seat* of pure gold and to place it above the ark. "And there," said the Lord, "I will meet with thee, and I will commune with thee from above the mercy seat…" (Exod. 25:10-22). The Ark of the Testimony and Mercy Seat were to be placed in "the most holy place" or "Holy of Holies," the innermost chamber of the tabernacle, separated from all other by a veil, through which the High Priest might pass only once per year for the purification of the people (Exod. 26: 33-34; 28:29-43).

Upon dedication of the Tabernacle, God, by fire and cloud, visibly displayed His glory (Lev. 9:23-24; Exod. 40:38). With holy fire, HaShem wooed the people He had called by His name to faith, calling them to set themselves apart from the fleshly ways of a faithless world, for "ye shall be holy; for I am holy." "I am the LORD that bringeth you out of the land of Egypt, to be your God: ye shall therefore be holy, for I am holy" (Lev. 11:44-45). "Thou shalt make no covenant with them [the unbelieving, pagan inhabitants of the land] nor with their gods. They shall not dwell in thy land, lest they make thee sin against me" (Exod. 23:32-33).

This "Tabernacle of the Congregation" served as the epicenter of worship for centuries, following the pattern given by God. But when the northern and southern kingdoms of Israel were united under King David, "a man after God's own heart" (Acts 13:22; I Sam. 13:13-14), this David (whose very existence has been vigorously sought to be denied by those desperate to debunk God's promise of a Messiah to reign on the throne of David), sought to build a permanent sanctuary or Temple.

## A TALE OF TWO TEMPLES

It is impossible for anyone honestly hoping for understanding of the direction and destiny of the inhabitants of earth to disconnect that direction and ultimate destiny from the Temple Mount and, more particularly, from the Temple itself. It may, indeed and in a profound sense, be God's time piece, both historically and prophetically. We then must move from the transportable Tabernacle to the tale of two "permanent" Temples.

### THE FIRST TEMPLE

Blinded by the pursuit of temporal power, perks and position, the multiplied kings and priests of this present world, from Creation to this crucial moment, have steadfastly turned their gaze from God's eternal plan to their own personal ambitions. Yet now, in this propitious place in time, as history and prophecy merge in a moment, it behooves us all to, with everything that in us lies, seek to comprehend and embrace God's timeless purposes. We, of necessity, turn then to the First Temple.

King David, again, becomes the figure of destiny. Israel had rejected HaShem (God) as her king, demanding a king like all other nations. To the prophet Samuel, the Lord painfully pronounced: "Hearken unto the voice of the people... for they have not rejected thee, but they have rejected me, that I should not reign over them (I Sam. 8:7). From Samuel to the sacrifice of Yeshua, this issue has defined Israel's ultimate dilemma and remains so to this day. As was declared by parable and priests before Pontius Pilate, "We will not have this man to reign over us" (Luke 19:14).

"We have no king but Caesar" (John 19:15). But what about the "son of David" (Matt.1:1)?

This choice between Caesar and Christ [Yeshua HaMashiach] has haunted Israel since the days of Moses. This greatest of the Hebrew prophets had centuries earlier foretold: "The LORD thy God will raise up unto thee a Prophet from the midst of thee, of thy brethren like unto me; unto him ye shall hearken" (Deut. 18:15).

Israel has not yet "hearkened" but continues to search after an earthly "king" as deliverer, for a temporal "savior" to deliver her from the encroaching "Romans" and other enveloping powers of earth that threaten her in our time. Such pursuit remains permanently elusive, yet persistently sought.

But what of this King David? The world cannot comprehend its current crisis without first concerning itself with this second king of Israel who, rather than rebelling against God as did Israel's first king (Saul), did repent and humbly walk in obedience before the Lord. To this king David, the "King of kings" to come (Rev. 19:16) did liken Himself for a visual demonstration among the chosen people.

This King David, who purchased the Temple Mount, yearned to build "a house" for the Lord that would no longer relegate His presence to a traveling tent. He desired that God's place of presence be made permanent as fitting for His glory. God's response, through Nathan the prophet, set the eternal stage, now the backdrop, for the final ACT of the divine drama unfolding before us on this near edge of the seventh millennium. David, himself, would not be permitted, as a warrior, to build this "house," but…

The LORD telleth thee that he will make thee a house.

I will set up thy seed after thee, which shall proceed out of thy bowels, and I will establish his kingdom. He shall build a house for my name, and I will establish the throne of his kingdom forever.

And thine house and thy kingdom shall be established forever before thee: thy throne shall be established forever (II Sam. 7:11-16).

This *Davidic Covenant* included two promises. God would bless David's son, Solomon, to build an earthly *house* or Temple, and God would, in turn, build Himself a *house* and kingdom through David and his descendants, that would endure forever. Both Israel and the Gentile world continue, even now, to live in this *forever*.

Thus, Solomon, who peacefully reigned over the united kingdom of Israel and Judah in and over the land promised to Abraham, Isaac and

Jacob, built the First Temple "in Mount Moriah, where the LORD appeared unto David his father…" (II Chron. 3:1). At the dedication of this magnificent Temple, Solomon declared to the Lord, "I have built an house of habitation for thee, and a place for thy dwelling forever" (II Chron. 6:2). He then repeated God's covenant with David for His people: "But I have chosen Jerusalem, that my name might be there; and have chosen David to be ruler over my people Israel" (II Chron. 6:6). When Solomon had finished praying in dedication, "the fire came down from heaven… and the glory [cloud] of the LORD filled the house" (II Chron. 7:1-2).

## THE SECOND TEMPLE

For nearly 500 years the glory of God graced Solomon's Temple on the holy Mount. God had been faithful to His covenant with the seed of Jacob, but Israel was not. The glory had long before departed (I Sam. 4:21-22), to be restored only in David.

Now, the ten northern tribes, in rebellion, declared, "What portion have we in David? To your tents, O Israel…see to thine own house, David." "So Israel rebelled against the house of David to this day. And it came to pass when all Israel heard that Jeroboam was come again, that they sent… and made him king over all Israel: there was none that followed the house of David, but the tribe of Judah only" (I Kings 12:16-20). What, then, would be the implication for the promised king who, as the seed of David, was to reign upon the throne of David forever? The answer resided in the last words of Jacob as he gathered his sons, the "children of Israel," before his death to prophesy to them what "shall befall you **in the last days**" (Gen. 49:1). The following words, in particular, have powerful and prophetic significance for not only Israel's and Judah's ensuing future but for the future of the entire world. Such words should not be lightly dismissed.

Judah, thou art he whom thy brethren shall praise; thy father's children shall bow down before thee.

The sceptre [symbol and solemn promise of God's eternal government] shall not depart from Judah, nor a lawgiver from between his feet, until Shiloh come [the Messiah]; and unto him shall the gathering of the people be" (Gen. 49:8-10).

Through persistent, unremitting and idolatrous rebellion, the ten northern tribes experienced the progressive withdrawal of God's providing and protecting hand. "The LORD testified against Israel, and against Judah, by all the prophets… saying, Turn ye from your evil ways, and keep my commandments." "Notwithstanding they [like America, the West and Israel today] would not hear, but hardened their necks...." "Therefore the LORD was very angry with Israel, and removed them out of his sight [to Assyria—the first great dispersion]: There was none left but the tribe of Judah only" (II Kings 17:5-18).

Due to the dramatically divided kingdom, the ten northern tribes had, for centuries, substituted golden calves for the golden altar of the Temple. Judah, alone, had access to the uniting and cleansing sacrificial Temple culture in Jerusalem. Yet Judah, also, "kept not the commandments of the LORD their God" (II Kings 17:19). Just as HaShem "rent Israel from the house of David" (II Kings 17:21), even so 135 years later, would he rend Judah from access to His holy Temple.

Their king rebelled. "Moreover, all the chief priests, and the people transgressed... and polluted the house of the LORD..." (II Chron. 36:13-14). "And the LORD God of their fathers sent to them by his messengers [the prophets wooing and warning]; because he had compassion on his people, and on his dwelling place [the Temple]: but they mocked the messengers of God, and despised his words [Just as Jew and Gentile, including many professing Christians do today] and misused his prophets, until the wrath of the LORD arose against this people, till there was no remedy" (II Chron. 36:12-16).

The God of Israel and Judah therefore employed the services of a pagan king, Nebuchadnezzar, as "my servant" (Jer. 25:9; 27:6) to carry the people away to Babylon, there to remember and keep their unkept Sabbaths for seventy years until the reign should shift from Babylon to Persia (II Chron. 36:20-21). Nebuchadnezzar promptly dispatched the glorious Temple of Solomon, which had served as the epicenter of Jewish identity for half a millennium, to utter ruin.

It has been said that the God of Israel is "the God of second chances." The proof of this postulate is the restoration of Judah to Jerusalem and of the fickle bearers of HaShem's truth to the Temple Mount and a rebuilt Temple.

In the first year of Cyrus, king of Persia, "the LORD stirred up the spirit of Cyrus" causing him to make a proclamation that would cause revulsion to the 21st century Islamic occupiers of the Persian realm. "Thus saith Cyrus king of Persia, All kingdoms of the earth hath the God of heaven given me; and he hath charged me to build him an house in Jerusalem, which is in Judah" (II Chron. 36:22-23).

Thus was built the Second Temple, beginning in approximately 536 BC, facilitated and financed by Cyrus the Great, King of Persia, who restored also the priceless Temple vessels of gold and silver taken captive by Nebuchadnezzar. So Israel/Judah rebuilt the Temple and the wondrous walls of Jerusalem, much to the consternation of surrounding competitors.

The people prospered in building through the prophesying of Haggai and Zechariah which anchored the elders and administrators, Ezra, Nehemiah, Zerubbabel and Joshua. But of special import is noted: "For Ezra had prepared his heart to seek the law of the LORD, and to do it, and to teach in Israel statutes and judgments" (Ezra 7:10).

When the builders lay the foundation of the Temple, the people, priests and Levites praised the Lord "after the ordinance of David king of Israel" (Ezra 3:10). Many "who were ancient men that had seen the first house… wept with a loud voice and many shouted aloud for joy" (Ezra 3:12). And so the Lord restored to Israel, through the instrumentality of Persian kings, Cyrus, Darius and Artaxerxes (Ahasuerus), the place of God's presence among His people (Ezra 1:1-4; 6:1-12; 7:11-23).

## WILL THERE BE A THIRD TEMPLE?

If the God of Israel is "the God of second chances," will Israel have a third chance, or would that be too much of a chance for re-born Israel to contemplate in the face of international consternation and condemnation? That is the ultimate existential question confronting the seed of Abraham and David at this precise moment of history now poised on the cusp of the seventh millennium.

The Second Temple endured for another nearly five centuries until, after having been dramatically expanded by Herod the Great, it was destroyed by the Romans, intent on absolute rule of the world. The Emperor could not countenance a Temple on Moriah representing an alternative kingship, and so he dispatched his son, General Titus, to again destroy the Temple, demolish the walls of Jerusalem, and disperse the people in the third great dispersion from which the Jews have not yet fully recovered… but will.

The Temple has always, or at least always eventually, spelled trouble for the Jews. That which more than any other symbolized and solidified national identity also, eventually, became the symbolic expression of Israel's destruction. The incredible connection seems to have largely escaped Jewish consciousness, despite the annual lament of *Tisha B'Av*.

Yet the trials of the Temple were not, in truth, merely persistent and recurring tribulation of the Jews as Jews, but were rather the collective effect of their recurring and progressive abandonment of allegiance to the God of Abraham and David. A covenant God could not continue to manifest His favored presence among a people who persistently and rebelliously stiffed His Holy Spirit of grace, thus paralyzing His mercy that had been promised only to them who fear and obey Him. As Miriam, the earthly mother of "the son of David" upon whose shoulders all God's government should ultimately rest (Isa. 9:6-7), said, "…his mercy is on them that fear him from generation to generation" (Luke 1:50).

When Israel's fear of the Lord revealed in faithful covenantal obedience waned, so did God's Shekinah glory dissipate and depart from among the people, leaving His Temple desolate and open for destruction. Whether by the ruthless hand of Babylon's Nebuchadnezzar, Syria's despotic Antiochus Epiphanes or Rome's deified Pontifex Maximus, Temple trouble became a time of Jacob's trouble.

It should not, then, have been surprising to the disciples of Yeshua, nor to the dominating Jewish leaders of the day, that, upon departing from the Temple two days before His crucifixion, while they were marveling at the magnificence of the Temple, Jesus said, "Verily I say unto you, There shall not be left here one stone upon another that shall not be thrown down" (Matt. 24:1-2). For judgment had already been rendered. As Yeshua crossed the Kidron Valley from the Mount of Olives on His historic and prophetic presentation to Israel as her Priest/King in accordance with the prophecy of Zechariah (Zech. 9:9; Matt. 21:4-9), the multitude cried out "Baruch Ha Ba BaShem Adonai" (Blessed is he that cometh in the name of the Lord), upon which Jesus went into the Temple of God. After casting out the money changers, He pronounced:

> It is written, My house shall be called the house of prayer; but ye
> have made it a den of thieves (Matt. 21:12-13; Isa. 56:7).

When the children cried out in the Temple, "Hosanna to the son of David," the chief priests and scribes "were sore displeased" (Matt. 21:15). They would have none of a king, even if he be the very Son of God, who would threaten their position as kings of the holy mountain, depriving them of their precious power, perks and position (John 11:47-48; Matt. 27:18).

"Your house is left unto you desolate," declared Yeshua. "For I say unto you, Ye shall not see me henceforth, till ye shall say, Blessed is he that cometh in the name of the Lord" (Matt. 23:38-39).

Jesus then told His disciples privately concerning "what shall be the sign of thy coming and the end of the world?" (Matt.24). He minced no words. Not only were the Romans to destroy the Temple that was now spiritually desolate, but a more desperate time was coming at "the end of the world."

> When ye therefore shall see the abomination of desolation spoken
> of by Daniel the prophet, stand in the holy place [the Temple],

Then let them which be in Judea flee into the mountains:

For then shall be great tribulation, such as was not since the beginning of the world to this time, no, nor ever shall be (Matt. 24:15-21).

When the Temple of God's presence is desolate, trouble is on the way. The greater the spiritual desolation, whether in the physical Temple or in a nation or in an individual, the greater the anticipated destruction in the epic battle for *KING of the Mountain.*

The great prophet Malachi made perfectly clear that, "the LORD... shall suddenly come to his temple...." He will be "like a refiner's fire" to purge and purify. "But who may abide [endure] the day of his coming? and who shall stand when he appeareth" (Mal. 3:1-3)?

There will yet be another Temple. With it will come the *promise* of peace but ultimately the terrifying *power* of the sword. It will be "the time of Jacob's trouble" (Jer. 30:7) but will strike terror among the nations. For Yeshua so poignantly declared, "Except those days should be shortened, there should no flesh be saved" (Matt. 24:22).

The eternal, epic and end-time battle for *KING of the Mountain* lies straight ahead.

*Chapter 11*

# PROBING THOUGHTS *for* PROPHETIC TIMES

1. Why do you suppose the Temple to be such a critical factor in the life and times of Israel and the Jewish people?

2. Why was the Temple on the Temple Mount the focus for destruction of the Babylonians and Romans?

3. What toll do you think the absence of the Temple for 2000 years has taken on the Jewish identity and hope?

4. Why did Jesus (Yeshua the Messiah) declare to Israel and the Jews (His own people) "Your house is left unto you desolate"?

5. Do you see how the issue of a third temple may become dominant in the geopolitics of our time?

*Chapter 12*

# THE END-TIME TEMPLE

*On June 5, 1967, time and eternity shook hands,
and the world would never again be the same.*

IS THIS THE TIME? Is it "Time for a New Temple?" inquired the headline of *TIME* in its October 16, 1989, edition. And, indeed, if this is "THE" time, what time is it?

The French have a phrase that every purported student of the language must process and be prepared to present to *le professeur*. That phrase will now be engraved upon the membranes of every reader's mind for future and necessary reference. The simple, yet profoundly memorable phrase is… "Quelle heure est-il?" And it simply means, "What time is it?" And so, in terms of the merging of history and prophecy after (according to the famous Archbishop Ussher) 6000 years of history, what time is it? Are we nearing the culmination of the biblical story as foretold by Hebrew prophets from Moses through Yeshua, and if so, what are the implications for our world, and more specifically, the Temple Mount? Will there be a Third Temple, and if so, is this the time?

## THE SIGNIFICANCE OF 1967

It is called *The Six Day War*. It was a war begun by the surprise attack of four surrounding Arab/Islamic nations to finally and forever annihilate the Jews and destroy once and for all the hope of their promised eternal homeland. The Arab nations, under the clandestine tutelage and financing of Russia, clearly had the upper hand. Portending doom swept the Land of Promise. Destruction was at hand. But miraculously the tide began to turn.

Those who had been marked by the on-looking nations as the *vanquished* soon, to global shock, emerged the *victors*. And Israel, for the first time in nearly 2000 years, regained possession of East Jerusalem (biblical Jerusalem) and the Temple Mount. On June 5, 1967, time and eternity shook hands, and the world would never again be the same. If September 11, 2001, was earthshaking, June 5-10, 1967, was heaven-shaking. As it is written, "Yet once, it is a little while, and I will shake the heavens, and the earth, and the sea, and the dry land;

> And I will shake all nations, and the desire of all nations shall come: and I will fill this house with glory, saith the LORD of hosts.

> The glory of this latter house shall be greater than the former... and in this place will I give peace, saith the LORD of hosts (Hag. 2:6-9).

## THE TEMPLE TIME-TABLE

If, indeed, the time has come to rebuild the Temple, we should expect to see the convergence of ancient prophecy and geopolitical events pointing to such an historic moment, supported perhaps also by polls and priestly prognostications.

Perhaps Isaiah, in his prophecy, sets the broader time table. His words, written over 2700 years ago, give fascinating perspective, "concerning Judah and Jerusalem."

> And it shall come to pass *in the last days*, that the mountain of the LORD's house shall be established in the top of the mountains, and shall be exalted above the hills; and all nations shall flow unto it.

> And many people shall go and say, Come ye, and let us go up to the mountain of the LORD, and to the house of the God of Jacob... (Isa. 2:1-3).

## ARE THESE THE "LAST DAYS?"

Are these "the last days?" According to the Apostle Peter, *the last days* began on the Hebrew feast of Shavuot or Pentecost, fifty days after the resurrection of Jesus. Quoting the Hebrew prophet Joel, Peter boldly declared of the striking and unprecedented outpouring of the Holy Spirit (Ruach HaKodesh) that amazed the Jewish multitudes gathered for the feast, "This is that which was spoken by the prophet Joel; And it shall come to pass **in the last days** saith God, I will pour out my spirit upon all flesh..." (Acts 2:16-40; Joel 2:28-30).

For nearly 2000 years we have thus lived in *the last days*. But there is yet another biblical period referred to as "the end of the age" or "the end of the world" more commonly called "the end times" (Matt. 24:3), which concludes the *last days*. The *end times* are finally fulfilled in a shorter, climactic moment known as "the day of the Lord" or "the day of Christ" (II Thess. 2:2; Mal. 4:5).

Might our times be the *end times*? Yeshua (Jesus) likened the end times to the fig tree. Two days before His crucifixion, while on the Mount of Olives overlooking the Eastern Gate of Jerusalem, He spoke privately with His disciples, knowing His time was near. "Now learn the parable of the fig tree," He said. "When the branch is yet tender, and putteth forth leaves, ye know that summer is nigh: So likewise ye, when ye shall see all these things, know that it is near, even at the doors (Matt. 24:32-33).

Jesus then made a puzzling, yet powerful statement to which we might well pay particular attention.

Verily, I say unto you, This generation shall not pass, till all these things be fulfilled.

But of that day and hour knoweth no man, no, not the angels of heaven, but my Father only (Matt. 24:34-36).

## IS THIS THE GENERATION?

What did Jesus mean? Was He referring to that generation then living or to a future generation? Were all of the things He warned of fulfilled during the lifetime of those disciples present? Although some may argue the point, the clear reality is that not all those items spoken of or declared by Jesus in Matthew 24 were fulfilled by the time of the Roman destruction of the Temple in AD 70. How might we then reasonably define Jesus' term, "This generation?"

Most scholars seem to have resolved this question in favor of the conclusion that Jesus must have been referring to the end times in which the final fulfillment would be consummated. What, then, is a *generation*? When would "this" generation commence and conclude? Arguably, a generation might be the general number of years between one's birth and the beginning of a new marital family (perhaps 25 years). A further alternative might be a period of 40 years from a person's birth to the beginning of "middle age." The third alternative would appear, however, to be the most compelling—a period of "three-score and ten years," the biblically-allotted years of a man's life (Ps. 90:10).

If, indeed, a period of 70 years reflects the "generation" of which Yeshua spoke, when did (or does) that *generation* begin? The answer to that question would seem to be of immense import for all inhabiting this mortal sphere called earth.

The miraculous and prophesied rebirth of Israel in 1948 is an historic and prophetic line of demarcation comparative only in the Jewish mind and memory to the great deliverance from Egypt some thirty-three centuries earlier. It defines the period from deliverance to the Promised

Land under Moses to restoration of the Promised Land under David Ben Gurion. Might the seventy year period beginning in 1948 be the prophesied "this generation?" Seventy years, the period of Hebrew captivity in Babylon, would then conclude in approximately AD 2018.

Nineteen years following the rebirth of Israel came the restoration of biblical (East) Jerusalem to Jewish control in 1967. The Temple Mount also was restored to Hebrew hands after 1897 years (although soon released to Islamic administration in the hope of peace). These are historic and prophetic landmarks, all within a generation following the prophesied rebirth.

"Israel shall blossom and bud," foretold Isaiah, "and fill the face of the world with fruit" (Isa. 27:6). "The desert shall rejoice, and blossom as the rose" (Isa. 35:1). Yet in the mid 1800's, Mark Twain, upon visiting the land, had deemed it barren and a malaria-infested swampland, unfit for human habitation. What happened? The God of Israel had spoken. In the fulness of time, His time, "It shall blossom abundantly, and rejoice… they shall see the glory of the LORD and the excellency of our God" (Isa. 35:2).

Isaiah exhorted to hope and preparation. "Strengthen ye the weak hands…. Say to them that are of a fearful heart, Be strong, fear not: behold your God will come with vengeance… He will come and save you. Then shall the eyes of the blind be opened… for in the wilderness shall waters break out, and streams in the desert. And an highway shall be there… and it shall be called the way of holiness.

> And the ransomed of the LORD shall return, and come to Zion with songs and everlasting joy upon their heads: they shall obtain joy and gladness, and sorrow and sighing shall flee away (Isa. 35:3-10).

All of this has, and is continuing to, come to pass in "this generation"… our generation. We must take heed, therefore, that what happened to Israel in the wilderness coming Out of Egypt does not happen to us in the "wilderness" of our time on the near edge of the ultimate "Promised Land," for all those things happened to them for our warning examples, "and they are written for our admonition, upon whom the ends of the world are come. Wherefore, let him that thinketh he standeth take heed lest he fall" (I Cor. 10:11-12).

The re-gathering of the dispersed physical seed of Jacob from the corners of the earth point also to "this generation." How and when, throughout history, have a people who have been violently dispersed for up to 2500 years been re-gathered and restored to a reborn nation? It is breathtaking to watch the seemingly impossible become a prophetic reality—in our time—just as many of the Hebrew prophets had foretold.

Behold, the days come, saith the LORD, that it shall no more be said, The LORD liveth, that brought up the children of Israel out of the land of Egypt;

But, The LORD liveth that brought up the children of Israel from the land of the north, and from the lands whither he had driven them: and I will bring them again into their land that I gave unto their fathers.

The Gentiles shall come unto thee from the ends of the earth, and shall say, Surely our fathers have inherited lies… things wherein there is no profit (Jer. 16:14-19).

"Aliyah" has become a global phenomenon. *Aliyah* means to go up, and for the Jew, to *go up* is to head toward Jerusalem and ultimately to the Temple Mount in anticipation of the restoration of HaShem's presence in a rebuilt Temple.

Nearly forty-five percent of all Jews throughout the world now make their home in *the land of promise*. They came first from the land of the North, a million strong. They have fled and continue to flee from the South and make their way from the East. The West is now giving up their Jewish inhabitants to *Aliyah*, particularly as anti-semitism and political and economic circumstances create increasingly uncomfortable and inhospitable environments. As Zechariah had so powerfully proclaimed, "Thus saith the LORD of hosts;

Behold, I will save my people from the east country, and from the west country;

And I will bring them, and they shall dwell in the midst of Jerusalem: and they shall be my people, and I will be their God, in truth and in righteousness.

Yea, many people and strong nations shall come to seek the LORD of hosts in Jerusalem, and to pray before the LORD (Zech. 8:7-23).

## "IS IT TIME FOR THE TEMPLE?"

The question of whether or not it is "Time for the Temple?" has been recurring, now, with increasing frequency and intensity over the past quarter century.

As earlier indicated, *TIME* asked the question in October 1989. In 1993, there was a great controversy between the former Chief Sephardic

Rabbi Mordechai Eliahu and Rabbi Yisrael Ariel who headed the Temple Institute, concerning whether it is the responsibility of the Jews to build a Third Temple or whether the Temple will be brought down from heaven when the Messiah comes. Rabbi Ariel argued that it was a biblical obligation of every Jewish man and woman to rebuild the Temple. Maimonides (AD 1135-1204) listed the necessity of a rebuilt Temple as one of the 613 commandments of the Torah. The debate still rages on among Orthodox Jews whether a rebuilt temple will precede, or be brought about by, the coming Messiah.

One thing, however, seems certain. A rebuilt Temple is increasingly anticipated, desired and even demanded. A 1983 newspaper poll showed a surprising 18.3% of Israelis thought it was time to rebuild; a mere 3% wanted to wait for the Messiah.[3] According to a Ynet-Gesher survey, by 2009, nearly two-thirds (64%) of Israelis said "the time is right to rebuild the Jerusalem Temple." Even half of non-religious Jews favored rebuilding the Holy Temple, an idea politically unthinkable just 10 or 20 years earlier. The poll was taken on Tisha B'Av (the 9th day of the Hebrew month of Av), the very day on which both the First and Second Temples had been destroyed.[4] Israel's National News confirmed the secular sentiment with the headline "Seculars Want Temple…."[5]

Evangelical Christian followers of Yeshua as "the Messiah" seem to embrace the same sentiments, indeed growing convictions, of their Israeli counterparts. In 1992 Randall Price and Thomas Ice penned *Ready to Rebuild*, the first in the American evangelical world to introduce the growing temple movement in Israel. By 2005, the question was repeated with increasing conviction. "Is It Time for the Temple?"[6] Thomas Ice reiterated the astounding developments that had transpired since 1992, concluding, "In spite of contemporary turmoil, Israel's third temple will one day be rebuilt." "There will be a rebuilt Temple by the middle of the seven-year Tribulation in order to facilitate the fulfillment of Bible prophecy."[7]

Just as this pronouncement was made in the publication *MIDNIGHT CALL*, so the prophetic clock ticks toward midnight. It is time, therefore, for all persons on the planet to prepare their hearts and minds for the transforming and terrifying events that lie just ahead. It is for this precise reason that this epistle was penned. For the Savior of the world, the long-expected "Anointed One" will soon come as KING, not only of the Jews, but as KING of kings and Lord of lords. As it is written, He "shall suddenly come to his temple…" (Mal. 3:1-3). It is time, not just for a temple made with hands but for the "temple" of God's Spirit in our individual hearts to be prepared. The time is NOW (Isa. 40:3; Matt. 3:3; Heb. 3:6-19)!

## PREPARATION, PROPHECY
## AND A PROPITIOUS MOMENT

If this is *THE* time for a third Temple, the test may well be persistent and practical preparations. If this is the *propitious moment*, prophecy and preparation will merge as one. The facts on the ground increasingly reveal the reality that this is not only "THE" time but is also the "propitious moment," notwithstanding seeming insurmountable obstacles. A brief overview will suffice to prove that the end-time stage has been set for the Third Temple "made with hands."

"No group," declared TIME, in 1989, "is more zealous than the Temple Institute, whose spiritual leader... Rabbi Israel Ariel, was one of the first Israeli paratroupers to reach the Mount in 1967." "Our task," stated the American—born director, Zev Golom, "is to advance the cause of the Temple and to prepare for its establishment, not just talk about it."[8] Those preparations have been significant... no, phenomenal!

### THE CORNERSTONE

Every significant building begins with a select cornerstone. Even though it is declared of Yeshua (understood by Gentile followers as the Messiah) that He was to be the "chief cornerstone" of God's ultimate temple "not made with hands" (Isa. 28:16; I Pet. 2:5-8; Eph. 2:19-22), nevertheless a physical temple requires a physical cornerstone. Even though, in a spiritual sense, "the stone which the builders refused (Yeshua) is become the head stone of the corner" (Psa. 118:22-23; Matt. 21:42-46), nevertheless a rebuilt physical structure will require a selected stone upon which to begin construction of the Third Temple.

Marvelously, perhaps even miraculously, that cornerstone has not only been prepared but is ready for placement on the Mount. "History is made" was the headline August 6, 2003, in *Israel National News*. Israeli police had grudgingly agreed to a Court-requested compromise, allowing the Temple Mount Faithful to hold a special cornerstone-laying ceremony on Tisha B'Av, the day the two previous temples were destroyed. Gershon Solomon, the group's leader spoke excitedly of the historic nature of the event. "This has tremendous significance, it is a real revolution—the crown jewel of the People of Israel in the Land of Israel"[9]

Six years earlier, October 20, 1997, "In an historical event, a cornerstone for the Third Temple was brought to the gates of the Temple Mount and the City of King David in Jerusalem...." Said the Temple Mount Faithful: "Every part of the life of Israel will be affected by this and a new era will be opened in the life of Israel and all mankind. Israel is now living in the time of prophetic redemption and fulfillment of all G-d's end-time promises."

"A new era will be opened in the life of all the world and Mashiach benDavid (Messiah son of David) will come and be King of Israel and all mankind."[10] The date was Sukkot, the Feast of Tabernacles, the culminating of Israel's seven annual *Feasts of the Lord.*

As early as 1989, the Associated Press reported an effort to lay a cornerstone for the new Jewish temple. Each year to the present, some effort has been made to place the cornerstone, either actually or symbolically.

Again during Sukkot 1998, in commemoration of the date King David brought the Ark of the Covenant from the City of David to the Temple Mount, a further cornerstone placement ceremony took place. The cornerstone of 4.5 tons or 13,000 pounds brought from the desert of Israel near Mt. Sinai, was carried by truck to circle the Temple Mount seven times just as Joshua had done at Jericho. Shofars were blown, the cornerstone was allowed to stand briefly before the Eastern Gate of the Temple Mount (the Golden Gate), where prayers were offered that the gate (now sealed) would soon be opened and the Messiah would enter therein to take up His prophesied rule "upon the throne of David" (Isa. 9:6-7). Once again the Temple Mount Faithful proclaimed, "We shall do everything to open the Eastern Gate for Mashiach ben David and He will be king of Israel and of all the world." "We trust in G-d that this godly end-time vision will soon be a reality in our lifetime...."[11]

By October 2000, violence in the Middle East had progressively escalated. When again the Temple Mount Faithful sought to lay a cornerstone in an anointing ceremony, backlash from the Arab world exploded. The Arab-American community called it a "very grave provocation." "Some thought that all-out war was imminent."

But the process of annual presentation of the cornerstone has continued unabated. In July 2001, *Rensa.com* reported "a historic decision, of the highest importance." Israel's Supreme Court ruled that despite the threat of Arab reaction, the Temple Mount Faithful could plant a symbolic cornerstone for the "third temple in Jerusalem's Old City" but not on the Mount itself. Again in 2008 the Temple Mount Faithful made a further effort, declaring:

> This great occasion was one of the most exciting and major events that Israel has experienced during this special end-time age.

> We knew that soon G-d will resume leadership over all the earth from His Holy Temple on Mount Moriah in Jerusalem.

> Everyone is called at this historical godly moment to actively... help the Temple Mount and Land of Israel Faithful Movement...

to build the Temple of G-d and to bring to pass all of G-d's end-time prophetic expectations and plans for Israel and the entire world.[12]

On Jerusalem Day, May 21, 2009, the cornerstone was again transported along the walls of the Old City and presented to the people of Israel and the world. The report stated:

> Since 1967, Jerusalem Day has become one of the most important holidays in Israel. It commemorates the liberation of the Temple Mount, the biblical city of Jerusalem, the City of David and the biblically significant areas of Judea, Samaria, Gaza, the Golan Heights and the Sinai Peninsula. All of this happened in the Six Day War of 1967. It was then that God returned the Temple Mount in Jerusalem to His people Israel so that they would immediately rebuild His Holy Temple in order to renew biblical worship there.[13]

Professor Hillel Weiss, October 25, 2009, declared, "The third temple must be built now." Chief Rabbi Dov Lior made clear, "Reclaiming our sovereignty over the Temple Mount will bring redemption closer."[14]

## SACRIFICIAL ALTAR CONSTRUCTION

The rebuilt Third Temple must have the requisite sacrificial altar for Temple worship as God commanded Moses:

> And there you shall build an altar unto HaShem your God, an altar of stones: you shall lift up no iron tool upon them. You shall build the altar of HaShem your G-d of unhewn stones.
> (D'varim/Deut. 27:5, 6)

As reported by *Arutz Sheva*, Israel National News, that command has again been accomplished in anticipation of the Temple soon to come. A model, relatively small—one cubit wide, one cubit deep, and three cubits high—was built. The rocks were collected from the Dead Sea. Material for filling the cracks between the stones was collected with a gold-plated shovel so as to prevent any contact with the iron.[15]

The building of the actual sacrificial altar began on Tisha B'Av, 2009, the day Jews annually mourn the destruction of the First and Second Temples. The rebuilt altar is of minimum size, since it had to be rebuilt off site from the Temple Mount and be transportable. The rocks, gathered from the Dead Sea, were individually wrapped so as not to be touched by metal.[16]

## PRIESTLY GARB

The Temple Institute announced, "High Priest's Crown is Ready!" The Tzitz—the High Priest's headplate—is made of pure gold, engraved with the words "Holy for G-d" in accordance with Exodus 28:36, and was completed by December, 2007.[17]

Two years earlier (2005), Rabbi Chaim Richman, international director of the Temple Institute, declared that "After much hard work and research, the Techelet (azure blue) robe of the High Priest has been completed... and it is hoped to be fit to be worn in the Third Temple." "The completion of this sacred garment marks a great step forward towards the renewal of the Divine service in the Holy Temple."[18] This historic robe, woven of blue, purple and scarlet wool, joined the already completed *ephod* and *choshen* (breastplate) featuring 12 precious stones representing the twelve tribes of Israel.[19]

Next came the 120 sets of white garments for the "regular" priests (not the High Priest), which required special thread from India. These will be worn by "Every *Kohen* (descendent of Aaron) from all over the world," who may register to serve in the rebuilt Temple, according to Rabbi Chaim Richman.[20] The *JERUSALEM POST* reported on July 1, 2008, "Third Temple preparations begin with priestly garb." "Years of diligent research was needed to create the garments in accordance with Jewish law." Rabbi Yehuda Glick, then director of the Temple Institute said, "The Temple is not a message [just for] the Jewish people." "All the prophets say that at the End Times all the nations will be coming to Jerusalem and take part of building [the Temple]."[21]

## WORSHIP VESSELS

It was shocking, yet confirming. Such was the news that on the last day of Sukkot (the Feast of Tabernacles) in October 2007, "a 34-person delegation from West Papua presented a large amount of gold to be used in the building of the Holy Temple." The delegation from the southwestern Pacific Gentile nation "explained that they study the Bible regularly and recently came upon a verse in Zechariah 6:16 reading 'And the distant ones will come and build the Temple of G-d.' They... decided that their faith obligates them to fulfill the verse." "The group presented a kilogram (2.2 pounds) of gold and a large sum of money. They requested that the gold be used to construct vessels for the temple...."[22]

The Temple Institute, established twenty-five years ago, "has prepared more than 70 of the gold, silver and copper vessels needed for Temple service." These include "the golden menorah, the show-bread table, the golden altar, Levitical musical instruments" and "a large 'King David's Lyre.'"[23]

Of considerable interest is the politically-subliminal conflict between Israel and the Vatican over Temple vessels. A report titled "Let My Temple Artifacts Go!" in 2003, recounted a then-recent visit by Moshe Katsav, then President of Israel, to the Secretary of State of the Vatican, Cardinal Angelo Sodano. Mr. Katsav asked the Vatican Secretary to "prepare a list of all the treasures, vessels and Judaica that are being held by the Vatican." Of "major importance… is the fact that the Vatican holds the Temple Menorah of pure gold which, together with other holy vessels from the Temple, was stolen by the Romans and taken to Rome in 70 CE."[24] More will be said later regarding the growing conflict between Israel and the Vatican that will spill over into the accelerating global conflict over Jerusalem and the Temple Mount.

## TEMPLE OF PEACE… OR PROVOCATION?

"Is this how World War III Begins?" That was the question concluding a *World Net Daily* article titled "A cornerstone for 3rd Temple?"[25] Yet there are substantial, conflicting claims that, rather than precipitating war, a rebuilt Temple is the only hope for peace. And interestingly, "a large portion of the financial support for the Temple Institute actually comes from evangelical Christians," according to executive director, Yehuda Glick.[26] Why? Because many (if not most) evangelical Christians are convinced, on the authority of the Scriptures, that Yeshua the Messiah (Jesus Christ) will soon return and rule the earth as "Prince of Peace" for a thousand years (Millennium), bringing true justice and genuine peace on earth, good will toward men (Isa. 9:6-7; Psa. 22:28; Isa. 16:5; Isa. 61:1-11; Luke 2:1-14; Rev. 20:1-4; Rev. 19:5-16).

### THE REVIVED SANHEDRIN

One of the most significant events in the last century did not register a report or notice from the media throughout the world, except in Israel. It was the re-launching or revival of the Sanhedrin, the highest Jewish-legal tribunal in the land of Israel.

On October 13, 2004, *Israel National News* proclaimed, "A unique ceremony—probably only the 2nd of its kind in the last 1600 years—took place in Tiberias today."[27] On February 9, 2005, just a few months after 71 rabbis from across the Jewish spectrum received special ordination; another enormously important event took place. The religious sages began to consider and plan for the actual rebuilding of the Temple and reinstitution of ancient annual sacrifices as prescribed by the law of Moses. Having rejected the "Chief Cornerstone" of the living Temple "not made with hands" two thousand years ago, a new physical temple must be built to fulfill the Law. Having condemned and crucified the "Lamb of glory" who would "once for all" save and sanctify sinners, both Jew and Gentile, the same Jewish body that once cried, "Crucify him," is now compelled to reinstate the practice of persistent animal sacrifice that can neither purge the heart nor the conscience of sin, being only "a shadow" of that which was to come in Yeshua HaMashiach (Isa. 26:18; Isa. 52:15; Isa. 53:4-12; Jn. 1:29,36; Jn. 19:13-22; Acts 2:16-40; Heb. 9:1-28, 10:1-16).

In an interesting twist, the same group of sages that once "knew not the time of their visitation" in rejecting God's proffered Messiah is now charged, in this propitious moment of history, with "authenticating a Messiah when he comes" (Hos. 9:1-17; Luke 19:41-44). In this regard one might reasonably inquire, *How will they know Him?* How will they identify this "Prince of Peace" and distinguish Him from the satanic counterfeit that will soon confront them with an enticing covenant of proffered "peace" at an existential price (Isa. 9:6-7, 28:18; Dan. 8:19-25, 9:26-27, 11:20-45; II Thess. 2:1-12)?

The first task of the re-constituted Sanhedrin was to determine the exact location of the former Temple's foundation. The Sanhedrin determined there are only two possible alternatives—(1) that the Temple stood on the same site on which the Muslim Dome of the Rock was built; or (2) that the Temple was built on that portion of the platform just north of the Dome of the Rock that lies directly in an east-west centerline passing through the Golden Gate, now situated directly over the ancient Eastern Gate that has been sealed since antiquity awaiting the coming Messiah. What does that mean? Perhaps, although repugnant to the ultra-orthodox, the Temple might actually be buildable without disturbing any Muslim monument on the Mount. Would that preserve or foster peace... or provoke war? Regardless, a Temple will be built.

### THE SANHEDRIN'S PEACE INITIATIVE

Prepare for two profound shocks! On May 2, 2007, *YnetNews.com* presented the historic headline, "The Sanhedrin's peace initiative." How might the re-established Sanhedrin, dedicated to rebuild the Temple on the Temple Mount, present a plan for global peace amid such seeming provocation?

The Jewish sages drafted a letter, "translated into 70 languages and sent to all government institutions in the world, including the sons of Esau and Ishmael...." "In the letter, the rabbis of the... Sanhedrin warn that the world is nearing a catastrophe." They write that "the only way to bring peace among nations, states, and religions is by building a house for God, where Jews will worship, pray and offer up sacrifice, according to the vision of the prophets." "The rabbis also call on non-Jews to help the people of Israel fulfill their destiny and build the Temple, in order to prevent bloodshed across the globe."

A renowned prophecy teacher, surveying the seeming shocking announcement of the reborn Sanhedrin, declared:

> The fact that a re-established Sanhedrin is now considering the rebuilding of the Temple after 2000 years is extremely important to students of Bible prophecy. I believe that we are very near the final climactic events that end with the Second Coming of Christ.[28]

## MUSLIM LEADER WANTS TEMPLE REBUILT

Given the explosive volatility of the global religious and political scene, a proposal… no… a request and expectation by the Sanhedrin that the nations of the world participate in the rebuilding of the Temple in pursuit of peace may, on the surface, border on the absurd. What, then, should the leaders of the world conclude when prominent Muslims propose a rebuilt Temple? Consider two such recent instances.

Adnan Oktar, who uses the pen name Harun Yahya, is a controversial but highly influential Muslim intellectual and author with more than 65 million of his books in circulation worldwide. Oktar, in 2009, met with three representatives of the re-established Sanhedrin to discuss how religious Muslims, Jews and Christians might embrace a rebuilding of the Temple. Oktar refers to the Temple as "Masjid (Mosque)" or the "Palace of Solomon."

Oktar stated that the Temple of Solomon "will be rebuilt and all believers will worship there in tranquility." During his meeting with the rabbis, he further stated his belief as to how long it might take to rebuild.

> It could be done in a year at most. It could be built to the same perfection and beauty. The Torah says it was built in 13 years, if I remember correctly. It could be rebuilt in a year in its perfect form.[29]

Sheikh Prof. Abdul Hadi Palazzi, the leader of the Italian Muslim Assembly, paid a surprise visit to the Temple Institute's Exhibition of the Holy Temple Vessels in Jerusalem on December 30, 2009. Although the Sheikh is highly controversial, he is nevertheless "widely respected as one of the leading Moslem experts today." As reported, "Sheikh Palazzi believes that the authentic teachings of Mohammed as expressed in the Qur'an and the Hadith instruct Moslems to support the return of the Jewish nation to its historic homeland in Israel, and the rebuilding of the Holy Temple in Jerusalem."[30]

## DOES THE WORLD NEED THE TEMPLE?

It could not have been stated more boldly nor more dramatically. The International edition of the *Jerusalem Post* (July 13-19, 2007) declared:

### The World Needs The Temple[31]

The article is explicit in explaining, from the Jewish perspective, why the entire world needs the Temple. "The Temple is cardinal to Israel's purpose as a holy nation and a kingdom of priest-teachers through whom all the families of the earth are to be blessed."

> The people of Israel were entrusted to teach the world that because God created every human being in His image, each must be free and inviolable, and that our God of love and morality wants a world of peace and security for all.

> The place from which this message must emanate is Jerusalem, the City of Peace; and the Temple is to be the beacon from which this message goes forth… to usher in the time when 'nation shall not lift up sword against nation and humanity will not train for war anymore' (Isa. 2, Micah 4, Zech. 7, 8, 9).

> Only a Temple teaching absolute morality in the City of Peace can secure the future of freedom in our global village.[32]

## THE DEVIL STILL LIES IN THE DETAILS

The 19th chapter of Numbers requires that a *red heifer* be sacrificed on the Mount of Olives and the ashes be used to cleanse the Temple site. The amazingly rare red heifer vanished for two thousand years, but there are those now who claim a red heifer, or several, to be available.[33] Regardless of whether or not a red heifer has made its appearance, there remains much "smoke," and therefore "fire" with respect to the rebuilding of the Temple.

The progressive history of developments recorded herein clearly marks the inexorable march of time and eternity toward a rebuilt Temple. Yet, many questions remain.

> When would such a Temple be built? Does the world truly need the Temple? Who will build the Temple, and under what auspices?

Will it be a purely Jewish endeavor? Will it be a religious partnership? Will the United Nations join the nations in partnership? Will the Vatican seek to gain oversight? Does the end justify the means? Will this be a "house of prayer for all nations" to worship the God of Abraham, Isaac and Jacob? Or will this be a multi-faith project where all religious faiths purport to worship their respective gods as they please?

The real question yet remains. Who will be *KING of the Mountain*? Who will rule and reign from Mt. Zion? Whose glory will be displayed throughout the earth? Will it be that of Mashiach ben David? Or will it be a shared glory by all faiths, whether or not they embrace Yahweh as God and Yeshua as Messiah?

Will a deceptive counterfeit promising a false peace gain global dominion and Sanhedrin embrace as the long-awaited "Anointed One," promising a Temple in time while desecrating the Truth? Will Israel and her leaders recognize the "time of her visitation" and salvation from Father God, or be deceived once again by the "father of lies" to receive "another who should come in his own name" (John 5:39-43) with a "covenant with death" (Isa. 28:18)?

Multitudes, multitudes are in the valley of decision (Joel 3:14). Who will be *KING of the Mountain*?

*Chapter 12*

# PROBING THOUGHTS *for* PROPHETIC TIMES

1. Will there be a Third Temple? If so, is this the time?

2. How did *The Six Day War* in 1967 merge history and prophecy as related to the possibility of a Third Temple?

3. Are these the "end times" of which biblical prophecy speaks? On what authority do you base your opinion?

4. What significance do you attribute to the amazing restoration of Israel in the "Promised Land" in this generation? Is it a series of mere happenstances, or is it more likely fulfillment of multiplied and ancient biblical prophecies?

5. How important are the multiplied, specific preparations of the last twenty-five years toward the rebuilding of the Temple?

6. Does the world need a rebuilt Temple, despite the potential provocation?

7. Does a rebuilt Temple relate to an expected coming of the Messiah? If so, how?

# Chapter 13

# GLOBAL-ISM VS. GOD

*As with ancient Rome, the resurrecting end-time*
*'Rome' will brook no opposition once enthroned.*

"WE SHALL HAVE WORLD GOVERNMENT, whether or not
we like it," declared James Paul Warburg on February 17, 1950, speaking before the United States Senate. "The only question is whether World
Government will be achieved by conquest or consent." In this chapter, we
surgically explore the hidden depths of the final battle for dominion.

## MEN'S DREAM OF DOMINION

World government has been the dream and dominion of men throughout the ages to this present age. From the Tower of Babel in Genesis 11 to
the trumpeting of the New World Order in our generation, mankind and
his various kingdoms and rulers have sought to govern the then-known
world in power and glory. Inevitably, man's lust for power and glory seeks
to eclipse, escape, or even defy the power and glory of the Creator.

The problem with pursuit of global government is not in the nature
of government itself, for God has ordained government as "the minister
of God to thee for good," to protect against evil and praise that which is
good (Rom. 13:1-4). Civil government among mankind is to be conducted
under the overarching fear of the God of the Bible and His governance.
When humans forsake the fear of the Lord, God's ways of government
and covenantal oversight and revelation are no longer available (Ps. 25:14).
Man thus devises his own ways, seeking inevitably to create a utopian
world order promising peace on earth.

The promise and hope of a global order ushering in world peace
is profoundly alluring to the natural mind. After all, who in their right
mind would not yearn for peace to avert a nuclear holocaust? Those under
thirty years of age today have haunting fears that their lives or the lives of

their children will be cut short in a worldwide conflagration. The aura of fear with empty promises of peace recalls the oft-repeated phrase, "Peace, peace; when there is no peace" (Jer. 6:14, 8:11).

In this chapter we will briefly explore the advanced stage of preparation in every major sphere of man's endeavor for a One World government and a new global order. We will unveil the massive deceptions paving the way and why these are of potential eternal consequence to you and the world's inhabitants in the epic battle for *KING of the Mountain*.

## Daniel's Dominion Dream

While the prophet Daniel was captive in Babylon, God gave him a prophetic dream (Dan. 7). In that dream, he saw four great beasts representing the existing and future great powers of the earth that would rule until the "latter days" and the great "time of trouble." These kingdoms have been commonly interpreted as:

FIRST:    A Lion- Babylon
SECOND:  A Bear- Medo-Persia
THIRD     A Leopard- Greece
FOURTH  An "Exceedingly Dreadful Beast"- Rome

The fourth beast, "dreadful and terrible," "exceedingly strong," was different from all the others. It had ten horns representing governing powers. The book of Revelation describes this same beast as having "seven heads and ten horns" with "ten crowns" (Rev. 13:1). These ten horns are further described as to "receive power one hour with the beast. These have one mind, and shall give their power and strength to the beast." These ten kings or powers "shall make war with the Lamb..." (Rev. 17:12-14).

This great and fearsome fourth beast that "shall devour the whole earth, and shall tread it down, and break it in pieces" (Dan. 7:23) is generally understood to be a resurrected or revived Roman Empire. Ancient Rome, a democratic republic, was diverse in government from the monarchies that preceded it. Rome governed the then-known world with an iron fist through its legendary legions, amassing great wealth, ushering in the *Pax Romana* or "Roman Peace" even as Christ, the Prince of Peace was being born.

Rome declared the government of the world to be upon its shoulder, even as the King of kings was sent by God to re-introduce God's governance in the world.

Isaiah had prophesied:

For unto us a child is born, unto us a son is given: and the government shall be upon his shoulder:

Of the increase of his government and peace there shall be no end, upon the throne of David [not Rome], and upon his kingdom, to order it, and to establish it with judgment and with justice from henceforth even forever (Isa. 9:6-7).

The battle lines for dominion were drawn. God had promised His "Prince of Peace" (Isa. 9:6), and Satan, the dragon, would empower His counterfeit "prince" with a global government promising peace on earth. That final world government would be a composite of the previous world powers, blending the best man had to offer to blasphemously compete with the Christ of God.

And the beast which I saw was like unto a leopard, and his feet were as the feet of a bear, and his mouth the mouth of a lion: and the dragon gave him his power, and his seat, and great authority."

And they worshiped the beast, saying, Who is able to make war with him?

And he opened his mouth in blasphemy against God... (Rev. 13:2-6).

## THE BATTLE FOR DOMINION

The battle for dominion rages. The great dragon (Satan) is determined to dominate the planet to satisfy his personal vendetta against God. He is marshaling every tool at his disposal, and he knows destiny is in the balance. His determination is to "deceive the whole world" (Rev. 12:9). He is convinced his spiritual cunning and clever seduction will draw the vast majority into his final global conspiracy against the Christ of God through a counterfeit christ. That is why Yeshua (Jesus) warned us in his final words before his crucifixion, "Take heed that no man deceive you" (Matt. 24:4).

How will such diabolical deception take place? Why will the vast majority be deceived? What is the Deceiver's scheme or *modus operandi*? What is wrong with globalization? Will you be able to discern the difference between truth and deception?

## THE MOMENT TO BE SEIZED

The date was September 11, 1990. U.S. President George Herbert Walker Bush stood before a joint session of Congress, a fresh wind of patriotism blowing across the country. Consider closely the words of the 41st president.

The crisis in the Persian Gulf, as grave as it is, also offers a rare opportunity to move toward an historic period of cooperation.

> Out of these troubled times… a new world order can emerge: a new era—freer from the threat of terror, stronger in the pursuit of justice, and more secure in the quest for peace.[34]

That "new world," declared President George H.W. Bush, "is struggling to be born." The "opportunity" that he so eagerly desired to seize, was the building of a "new-world order." Over 200 times, the senior President Bush declared this "new world order" during his administration. It was historic. It was as if the world had become pregnant and the president of its reigning superpower was deputized to announce the conception long-thought to be but the rantings of conspiracy theorists. But the gestation period was not given. The birth would come in the "fulness of time"… heaven's prophetic time and Satan's false-gospel hour to seduce the world.

It would be man's glorious gospel of self-salvation, of utopian peace and of global safety without the God of Creation and of biblical revelation. A substitute god would be prepared, designed democratically, without dogma or doctrine offensive to a multicultural, religiously pluralistic world intent on global unity. The Scriptures had warned, "when they shall say, Peace and safety; then sudden destruction cometh upon them, as travail upon a woman with child; and they shall not escape" (I Thess. 5:3). But such warnings, however dire, are deemed unworthy in the face of such lofty ambitions as a global order of unprecedented peace and prosperity.

Eleven years later, the Prime Minister of Britain could not contain his enthusiasm. Two weeks after the infamous Islamic attack on the World Trade Center Towers and the United States Pentagon, Tony Blair delivered "the most powerful speech of his career," causing one member of Parliament to remark, "He spoke as if he were President of the World." Note well his words.

> This is the moment to seize. The kaleidoscope has been shaken… let us reorder this world around us. Today, humankind has the technology to destroy itself or to provide prosperity to all. Yet science can't make that choice for us. Only the moral power of a world acting as a community can."[35]

The very concept of a grand global order almost defies the imagination. For thousands of years, the world, its people and nations, being inherently sinful and selfish, have sought self-gain by grinding others into submission. Europe is a classic study. It's various nations and peoples have been in almost perpetual warfare from the purported fall of Rome to the end of World War II. So, what is so unusual about this moment of history? Will the world now become "one"? Since the failure of Charlemagne's

"Holy Roman Empire," what "gospel" will now gather and what glue will now bond the world into a bold new order of the ages?

## UNITY FEVER

The pressure for and toward world unity, at every level, is unprecedented. This pressure has reached a fever pitch. The flames of global fever are fanned by fear of global conflagration and by a utopian vision for a global peace and prosperity that has heretofore escaped mans' grasp.

The great and growing river of unity gradually becoming a global sea is fed by the confluence of many streams and tributaries, both religious and secular. Neither time nor space here permit detailed delineation of the vast and pervasive scope of this movement. We must therefore limit our latitude of observation to that which enables us to bring into focus the emerging sculpture of a global order being forged as mans' ultimate achievement and salvation.

This emerging global-ism is being forged out of the multitude of prevalent isms in our world, the most significant of which we can broadly distill as the "science isms," "social-isms," "political-isms" and "religious-isms," with the ultimate goal of unprecedented material-ism. While seemingly separate in their respective disciplines, upon closer inspection one cannot escape the merging and synergetic interaction of these various broad categories of isms, each reinforcing the other and developing a kind of "magnetic" attraction, chasing each other ever closer into an uncanny bond now universally defined as *global-ism*. While jointly and severally becoming mutually interdependent, it is the religious isms that globalists increasingly, although often reluctantly, acknowledge as the ultimate catalyst to bind the world in the final thrust for global unity.

It is fascinating to watch the threads of the emerging global tapestry being woven into a discernible pattern through the unprecedented pursuit of unity. One can easily be trapped in its seductive web of deception, especially because of the sheer weight of the supposed "authorities" and their massing majorities embracing global-ism as a veritable new "gospel."

## EMERGING "ONENESS"

The year was 1630 AD. John Winthrop, a godly English attorney, was preparing to settle four boatloads of Puritans seeking "Promised Land" in the "New Canaan" called America. Before landing, he penned *A Model of Christian Charity*, setting forth the vision of biblical unity that would bind this "New Israel" in their "errand into the wilderness" to establish that "City upon a hill" Jesus had spoken about that "could not be hid" (Matt. 5:14). Winthrop wrote:

...we are a company professing ourselves fellow members of Christ.... We ought to account ourselves knitted together by this bond of love, and live in the exercise of it, if we would have the comfort of being in Christ.

We must delight in each other, make others conditions our own, rejoice together, mourn together, labor and suffer together, always having before our eyes, our community, as members of the same body.[36]

## BIBLICAL ONENESS

Note the oneness of purpose and practice in Winthrop's early declaration. This oneness was rooted in righteous relationships which were rooted and grounded in Jesus Christ and His truth. There was no desire, direction or decision to achieve earthly unity apart from the Scriptures which bound them into the commonality of the Messiah who declared himself to be "the way, the truth and the life (John 14:6).

So great was that unifying holy purpose and practice that 200 years later, the secular French philosopher and observer, Alexis de Tocqueville, noted with amazement in his *Democracy in America*:

In the United States the sovereign authority is religious, ...there is no country in the world where the Christian religion retains greater influence over the souls of men than in America, and there can be no greater proof of its utility... than that its influence is powerfully felt over the most enlightened and free nation of the earth.[37]

## EVOLUTIONARY ONENESS

Just 29 years after de Tocqueville penned *Democracy in America*, Charles Darwin released *The Origin of Species* in 1859, sowing the spiritual seeds of an alternative unity, defying the Creator and denying that man was made in God's image. Scientists embraced this alternative unity in Naturalism, lending to it an aura of authenticity to persuade the unsuspecting masses. Evolution thus became the unifying "creation doctrine" of the developing global alternative gospel.

"The survival of the fittest was quickly interpreted as an ethical precept that sanctioned cutthroat, economic competition, embraced by the most ruthless capitalist giants to justify their practices. Andrew Carnegie said in his autobiography that evolution came in like a light, because it not only eliminated the need for God, but it justified him in his business practices."[38] A century later, the same "survival of the fittest" philosophy had grown into massive multi-national corporations functioning as quasi world and regional governments, globalizing a new business bond, unifying the world in material "oneness."

Evolution became the unseen bond, facilitating the emerging world unity in virtually every sphere, whether political, scientific, social or religious... even material and legal.

## SOCIAL ONENESS

Into the growing spiritual vacuum of the soul, sweeping like a plague throughout the western world, as evolution sucked the god-image from man, came a new unifying alternative to the Creator's gospel of the soul. Freud's war against God meshed well with man having been cut loose from his Creator through evolution.

Humankind needed a new bond to unify socially. A new "acceptable" version of love was needed—SELF love. Through Freudian psychology, feelings replaced biblical faith and human experience replaced biblical truth. Eros and phileo love supplanted the selfless agape love of Scripture. Oneness of *feelings* now progressively replaces oneness in biblical *faith* as experience trumps truth even in our churches. Psychology had become the unifying ethos of an emerging global social order where increasingly godless men could embrace *feelings* as lord and *SELF* as king.

The church divorced the God of mercy from the God of truth, abandoning the fear of the Lord for the fear of man, thus baptizing the new psychologized "gospel" with the aura of a man-centered faith. Few can resist the universal secularization of feelings. The spirit of the faith "once delivered to the saints" has been suffocated, replaced by a soulish "sacrifice" of ever-evolving feelings to be offered on the altar of world peace to usher in the enticing era of global oneness. Unity born of feelings has been deemed vastly preferable in the emerging global culture to the "divisive" unity that sets people apart as followers of an exclusive truth in Messiah Yeshua that alone will make and keep men free (Jn. 8:31-32, Jn. 17:17-19).

## POLITICAL ONENESS

Just as Israel, the "apple of God's eye" (Zech 2:8), was entering the prophetic birth canal to be re-born as a nation, the Deceiver sought to pre-empt the divine drama with an equally dramatic birth.

### Pursuit of Peace and Prosperity

World War II had shaken the world. Germany had decimated the Jews. The nations were in despair and Europe was destroyed. And so the United Nations was founded to provide "world peace and security." Interestingly, the Hebrew word "Shalom" might be best translated "peace and security" or "security and prosperity." The divine plan was to send forth His anointed One, the Prince of Peace, to unify the "Israel of God," genuine believing Jews and Gentiles, into "one new man" in Christ," "so making peace" (Rom. 2:28-29, Rom. 9:4-8, Rom. 11:25-26, Eph. 2:12-22).

### Satan's Counterfeit

But Satan seduced the nations with his own alternative peace plan. Unite the nations, contrary to God's express command, and let them build a global "tower" system that will reach heaven, or at least create man's best heaven on earth, thus "saving" the earth from the inevitable consequence of sinful rebellion. Unwittingly, history would repeat itself. The God-dispersed tower of Babel of Genesis 11 would now become global. The world would become one, under the Deceiver's direction, until its final destruction.

The United Nations was thus founded in 1945. One of its earliest official acts was to partition the land of Palestine, which God had eternally deeded to Israel, into two nations, one for the Jews and one for Arabs. The partition was to transpire in 1948. The Deceiver was deft in his direction: Divide Israel, which God decreed to be united as one, and unite the nations which God had commanded to separate. The divine penalty would be severe... ultimate divine judgment (Joel 3:1-2, Zech. 12:8-9). Israel was re-born May 14, 1948, and the world has been haunted for its division to this day, and will repeat that debacle.

Just as God would breathe life into the house of Israel (Ezek. 37:1-5), so Satan would breathe life into the unifying of the Gentile nations. Satan's counterfeit is nearing completion. Let us further trace Satan's historical tracks in our time and his deceptive plan for global dominion.

### A Global Phenomenon

From the ruins of World War II, a global phenomenon began. Just as Israel began its phenomenal resurrection from historical obscurity in fulfillment of biblical prophecy on May 14, 1948, so Europe began a breathtaking rise to world prominence in 1951 with the establishment of the European Coal and Steel Community or "Common Market." Established by the Treaties of Rome in 1957 and 1958, the declared aim was to give Western Europe greater influence in world trade and economic affairs. By 1999, a single European currency, the Euro, was created, and now competes with the dollar for global acceptance.

The Maastrict Treaty of 1993 established the political entity known as the European Union. The renowned Roman Empire of antiquity faded into diverse peoples and countries from the Mediterranean to the Baltic and North Seas for 2000 years. As the curtain is drawn on the "church age," the countries now clamour to be included in the spectacular "resurrection" of "Rome." Twenty-seven nations, historically at enmity, now embrace as political "friends," all in pursuit of *security* and *prosperity* (shalom).

Never before in history has a nation, obliterated from its roots and dispersed to the four winds for two thousand years, been resurrected in its own land, as has Israel, against all social, political and economic odds. By contrast, never before in history have so many countries and peoples, now nearing 500 million, voluntarily come together in time of peace, as has the European Union. Said Jacques Delos, former head of the resurrecting "Rome," "We must hurry. History is waiting."

Prophecy is not waiting, but rather surging inexorably toward the Second Coming of Christ, God's promised "Prince of Shalom" (Isa. 9:6). In less than a generation of seventy years, the world has witnessed the rebirth of Israel, the "apple of God's eye," and the rebirth of "Rome," the Deceiver's counterfeit, merging the spirit of Egypt, the spirit of Babylon and the spirit of Rome into one global enterprise destined to declare dominion over the souls of men. Babel of Babylon (Gen. 11) is being rebuilt in men's hearts as "Mystery Babylon" (Rev. 17:5), just as the Kingdom of God, through the "Israel of God," is being given life through the hearts of men as the "Mystery of God" (Rev. 10:7).

## The Reviving Roman Empire

The two kingdoms are coming into mortal and eternal conflict. Satan, as the "god of this world" (II Cor. 4:4), is drawing the peoples of this planet into godless oneness. In drafting the historic Treaty of Lisbon as the constitution for the reviving Roman Empire, the European Union elite refused even to recognize God, having embraced the godless antipathy of the French Revolution. Rather, this expanding union chose to declare its rebellion against the Creator by adopting symbols to set itself blatantly against Christ's coming kingdom.

The twelve stars of the European Union flag set themselves against Christ's twelve disciples and the twelve tribes of Israel. The Tower of Babel, through a variety of European posters and other depictions, displays open contempt for oneness in Christ, boldly declaring man's intent to unify for his own salvation. The European Parliament in Strasburg is even architecturally designed to visually replicate, with a modern flair, the ancient Tower of Babel.

## A "Radical New Dream"

But the political rebuilding of "Rome" is not yet complete. The nations, observing the seeming phenomenal success of the European Union in such historically short order, are seeking to create similar regional unions throughout the world, all for *security* and *prosperity*. The goal is "global consciousness." The first transnational political entity in history, the "United States of Europe," represents "the rise of a new ideal that could eclipse the United States as focus for the world's yearnings for well-being and prosperity [shalom], declared Jeremy Rifkin in a profound editorial analysis.[39] Rifkin noted, as an American, "Yet our country is largely unaware of and unprepared for the vast changes that are quickly transforming the Old World and giving birth to the new European Dream." His words should grip the heart and soul of every Christian believer worldwide.

> The European Dream, with its emphasis on inclusivity, diversity, sustainable development, and interconnectedness is **the world's first attempt at creating global consciousness.**

Interestingly, it is precisely Barack Obama's open embrace of this vision that connected him so powerfully with America's youth and ingratiated him as a veritable "rock star" throughout the European continent, earning him the moniker of "messiah" by *Der Spiegel*, a German magazine.[40] Oprah Winfrey announced the Obama election as "a change in global consciousness." His presidential campaigning counterpart, John McCain, also embraced the new global vision, calling for creation of a new "League of Democracies" which its boosters argue, "would have not only the moral legitimacy but also the will to right the world's wrongs effectively"…[41] a utopian vision.

Columnist Jeremy Rifkin reveals the cataclysmic "change" that is enervating the vision of global-ism modeled by the New "European Dream," replacing the American Dream whose life support has been nearly severed from its original Godly roots. Europe now represents *peace* and *prosperity* to the world.

- Europe has the largest internal market in the world.
- The Euro has vied for superiority with the dollar.
- Europeans are the world's bankers, claiming 14 of the world's 20 largest commercial banks.
- Sixty-one of the 140 biggest companies on the Global Fortune 500 are European, while only 50 are U.S. Companies.
- The American homicide rate is four times that of Europe.
- Europeans provide 47 percent of the world's humanitarian assistance, the United States contributes 36 percent.

"Utopian as it sounds," notes Rifkin, "remember that 200 years ago, America's Founders created a new dream for humanity that transformed the world. Today, a new generation of Europeans is creating a radical new dream." "Romano Prodi, the President of the European Commission, has admitted that the EU's goal is to establish 'a superpower on the European continent that stands equal to the United States.'" When Prodi was asked to explain what he meant, Rifkin notes, "he spoke of the European vision as one of a new type of power... a new kind of superpower based on **waging peace**."[42]

## IMITATION AS FLATTERY

It is said that imitation is the ultimate flattery. If that be so, the European Union, the resurrecting bones of the Roman Empire, stands profoundly flattered, for the entire world is in hot pursuit of "waging peace" to achieve *security* and *prosperity* (Shalom) by forming regional unions.

Most prominent, perhaps, has been the "Security and Prosperity Partnership" or SPP signed in secrecy by U.S. President George W. Bush with Mexican President Vincente Fox and Canadian Prime Minister Paul Martin in Waco, Texas on March 25, 2005. Although long publically denied, the North American Union to merge the United States, Mexico and Canada is well under way to emulate the European pursuit of *security* and *prosperity*, all without act of Congress. It has been continued, under cover, by President Barack Obama, emerging now once again from the shadows into the supposed glorious light of globalism.

On April 30, 2008, President George W. Bush signed the "Transatlantic Economic Integration" agreement between the U.S. and the European Union, citing the same ostensible economic purpose to which the rise of the European Union was attributed. Co-signatories included German Chancellor Angela Merkel, president of the European Council, and European Commission President José Manuel Barroso. The United States became committed to a Transatlantic Common Market between the U.S. and the European Union by 2015, a period of seven years, without ratification of a treaty or act of Congress.[43]

This plan, being implemented by the White House with the aid of six U.S. senators and 49 congressmen as advisors, appears to follow a plan written in 1939 by a world government advocate who sought to create a Transatlantic Union as an international governing body. An economist from the World Bank agreed in print that the foundation of this Transatlantic Common Market "is designed to follow the blueprint of Jean Monnet, a key intellectual architect of the European Union," who admitted the true purposes of the Common Market were intentionally not disclosed to Europeans, intending rather that it lead inevitably from economic integration to political integration and a European superstate.[44]

Where will this process now end, and what are its implications not only for the world but for Israel and for those who profess ultimate allegiance to Jesus Christ?

On February 1, 1992, then President Herbert Walker Bush, having over 200 times announced the coming New World Order, declared:

> It is the sacred principles enshrined in the UN Charter to which we will henceforth pledge our allegiance."

In 1993, President William Jefferson Clinton pushed congressional approval of NAFTA, the North American Free Trade Agreement and in 1995, CAFTA, the Central American Free Trade Agreement. These laid the foundation for George W. Bush's North American Union and an ultimate merger with the European Union.

The echo of these events continues to circle the earth. The Mediterranean Union has now been declared, established July 13, 2008, to "form a bridge between Europe, North Africa and the Middle East." It was the brainchild of French President Nicholos Sarkozy, composed of 43 member nations. The Union committed to "peace, stability and security" (Shalom), was formed "to ensure the region's people could love each other instead of making war," emulating the European Union. Announcement was timed to coincide with the French presidency of the European Union. As *The Guardian* in Britain noted, "Sarkozy's big idea is to use imperial Rome's centre of the world as a unifying factor, linking 44 countries that are home to 800 million people."[45]

Now established or in process are the following global unions, some with overlapping nations:

| | | |
|---|---|---|
| European Union | 27 nations | Actual |
| Mediterranean Union | 43 nations | Actual |
| North American Union | 3 nations | Formative |
| Trans Atlantic Union | 30 nations | Formative |
| South American Union | 12 nations | Actual |
| Central American Union | 8 nations | Actual |
| Pacific Union | 13 nations | Formative |
| Russia and Belarus Union | 2 nations | Actual |
| Indian Union | 25 states | Actual |
| African Union | 53 nations | Actual |
| Central Asian Union | 5 nations | Formative |
| South Asian Union | 44 nations | Formative |

## The Anti-Gospel

Global governance is not a conspiracy theory but a confrontive truth. The "gospel" of global government and the unification of the world is secularly described as global-ism. Its spiritual roots draw life not from trusting God's wisdom, grace and power but rather from mans' desire to sever dependence on his Creator and to depend upon mankind's "good nature" to do the right thing for the "common good," and hence save himself. It is the "anti-gospel" precisely because it denies mans' fundamental sinful condition necessitating a savior other than himself, shifting ultimate trust to the "arm of flesh," which brings a curse. (Jer. 17:5).

Israel, continuing her search to be like all the other nations (I Sam. 8:5-7), and to be included among them despite God's declaration they "shall not be reckoned among the nations" (Numb. 23:9), now seeks inclusion in the European Union and has been received into the Mediterranean Union. Having rejected her Messiah, she continues to proclaim, "We have no king but Caesar" (Jn. 19:15), trusting the proffered *shalom* (security and prosperity) of man's systems rather than her Savior's sacrifice. And so a European Commissioner wrote in one of Israel's key daily newspapers, "We will also work with Israel to promote and uphold the values we share and which we believe hold the key to prosperity in Europe and everywhere else in the world."[46]

America, as a Gentile "New Canaan," has followed the path of Israel. Having progressively abandoned the God of her fathers and the fear of the Lord, she now fears man. Having lost actual trust in the Creator, she desperately clings to a motto, *In God We Trust*, that has become little more than a faded symbol and an empty mantra. The God who "made and preserved her a nation" had set her apart from all other nations, yet now, in growing fear, she seeks to wed herself to their pagan global enterprise for *shalom* (security and prosperity).

## The Unbelief of False Trust

Both Jew and Gentile, "God has concluded them all in unbelief…" (Rom. 11:32). The rabbis of the Supreme Judicial Court of the Jewish People, the Sanhedrin, reconstituted in 2004 after nearly 2000 years of dispersion, have presented their "peace initiative." In a letter drafted in 70 languages to "all government institutions of the world," the rabbis warn that "the world is nearing a catastrophe" and that the "only way to bring peace among nations, states and religions is by building a house for God." The rabbis, having little seeming trust in God as their "I AM," call on "non-Jews to help the people of Israel fulfill their destiny and build the Temple, in order to prevent bloodshed across the globe."[47]

Nature abhors a vacuum. When our genuine trust in God and His Word wanes, Satan is quick to interject an alternative, inevitably shifting our focus from authentic faith to a fleshly counterfeit. Israel, as with the West and the western Gentile church, suffers from acute spiritual anemia. We are wide open for Satan's final spiritual deception. It has been well designed to entrap both Jew and Gentile, and its final manifestation is soon to be revealed for those who have an eye to see.

For the Jew, the Temple may well be the perfect trap, diverting trust from God's "Anointed One" to Satan's appointed one, the "Son of Perdition" who makes ingratiating promises as "the little horn" emerging from the "ten horns" of the resurrecting Roman Empire (Dan. 7:7-8). He will "speak great words against the most High, and shall even wear out the saints…", both Jew and Gentile (Dan. 7:19-25), once he gains power. The mere flattering promise of security and prosperity will be sufficient bait to ensnare and co-opt the trust of most Gentiles, for by the pursuit of peace this imposter will destroy many (Dan. 8:23-25).

Yet, for this latter-time trader in trust to gain global dominion so as to invite men to sacrifice their eternal souls for the promise of temporal peace and prosperity, Satan's global governmental "gospel" must become nearly universally embraced. Shockingly, even now, "Anyone Who Resists the EU Is A Terrorist" according to Italian President Giorgio Napolitano at a news conference. The German President, Horst Kohler, also present at the Siena conference, nodded in agreement.[48] But those broadly labeled "terrorist" today will be deemed "traitor" tomorrow. Just as with ancient Rome, the resurrecting end-time "Rome" will brook no opposition once enthroned.

How will such universal acceptance be achieved? What will win the mind and heart of the world to passionately embrace global-ism as the ultimate "gospel" for "peace on earth, goodwill toward man" (Luke 2:14)?

Will you recognize Satan's duplicity in the hour of deception? Or will you dance with the Deceiver, seduced by his offer of counterfeit *shalom*, packaged alluringly in religious robes calculated to convince all but those who "keep the commandments of God, and the faith of Jesus" (Rev. 14:12)? Is it not time to "prepare the way of the Lord" in your life and in the life of those in your sphere of influence so that you "may be able to withstand in the evil day" (Eph. 6:13)?

## RELIGIOUS ONENESS

Massive spiritual deception is mounting as the final bridge, bidding politicians pastors, priests, parishioners and parachurch leaders to cross over a worldly "Jordan" into a counterfeit "Promised Land" of global *security* and *prosperity* (Shalom). The rivers and rivulets of the world's religious isms are now combining to propel even professing Christians and Jews in the powerful currents of global "oneness" into the counterfeit Christ's new global order. As Jesus well warned, "if it were possible, they shall deceive the very elect" (Matt. 24:24). Globalism is, in reality, the "Anti-Gospel," choreographing an increasingly faithless, feeling-driven world in a final collective rebellion against God in the battle for *KING of the Mountain.*

We will pull back the curtain from what may be the final acts of this deceptive drama in the next chapter. Please prepare your mind and heart in an attitude of profound humility and prayer, for of necessity we must hereafter increasingly delve into delicate issues of doctrine and tradition that potentially impact destiny.

*Chapter 13*

# PROBING THOUGHTS *for* PROPHETIC TIMES

1. Why do you think mankind has repeatedly sought to form global government despite God's command to disperse throughout the earth and despite His obvious displeasure with those at the Tower of Babel?

2. What, according to Daniel's prophecy, will be the final world government before the Messiah returns?

3. What is it about this time in history that is so unique as to cause Tony Blair to declare, "This is the moment to be seized?" What did President H. W. Bush mean when he boldly stated, "The new world is struggling to be born?"

4. How has the press for unity, both locally and globally, unwittingly caused rabbis, pastors, priests and people to play into the ungodly spirit of the emerging counterfeit satanic government, economy and religion?

5. Are you able to discern the difference between genuine oneness in Yeshua the Messiah and the emerging counterfeit "oneness" movement?

6. Can you see how the promise of the New "European Dream" actually vied dramatically, luring the American heart in the Presidential election campaign of 2008, seducing vast numbers of American citizens into the waiting arms of socialistic globalism, deftly offered to satisfy a longing hope for governmental salvation?

7. Why is *global-ism* the anti-gospel?

8. What is God's goal for ultimate government bringing "peace on earth?"

# Chapter 14

# THE DREAM OF DOMINION

*This great and fearsome fourth beast "shall devour
The whole earth, and shall tread it down, and break
it in pieces."*
Dan. 7:23

**FROM THE BEGINNING OF TIME,** mankind has pursued and practiced *dominion*. From Creation to the Cross, and from the Cross to this Century, the first in the seventh millennium of biblical history, humankind has delivered dramatically and doggedly (albeit perversely) on the Creator's instruction to "have dominion" (Gen. 1:26-31).

## "TAKE" DOMINION OR "HAVE" DOMINION?

Interestingly, the Creator's command was not to *take* dominion but to "have" dominion (Gen. 1:26, 28). But man inevitably twists the truth to suit his own designs. Therefore, the design of the Designer becomes perverted, distorted and ultimately destructive. This has been the Devil's ploy from the beginning... to deceitfully ask, "Hath God said...?" and then to seductively insert mans' *whim* as a satisfactory surrogate for God's *will*.

Thus, from the moment of Cain exercising "dominion" in bringing about the death of his righteous brother, Abel (Gen. 4), mankind, in pursuit of dominion over his fellow creatures made in the Creator's image, has brought death and destruction to the earth, fulfilling the arch–Deceiver's modus operandi to "steal, kill and destroy," John 10:10, thus inevitably to frustrate God's salvation of mankind through His Deliverer, Mashiach ben David. Cain was cursed. "And Cain went out from the presence of the LORD..." crying, "My punishment is greater than I can bear" (Gen. 4:13-16). Mankind, separated from the face and Spirit of God, thus diabolically extends his dominion from the sphere allocated by his Creator (the beasts and plant life of the earth—Gen. 1:26-30) to the very beings created in

God's image (Gen. 1:26-27). A pernicious theory of "evolution" is then conceived, in these latter days, to further sever, in the name of "science," the man from his Creator, rendering him but a *beast*. The Deceiver has thus prepared the way for the final "beast" empire.

## THE DREAM OF DOMINION

The dream of man's dominion over man has persisted since the Fall of Man from selfless service to sinful selfishness. Refusal to submit to the Creator as Lord birthed in mankind the perverse premise that he was to be "lord" of his fellow man... to exercise dominion, whether by force or threat of force. The God who was King of Creation was displaced by the creature's pursuit of kingship over his fellows. It is clear that such was never God's intent as revealed in His dealings with Israel, His chosen people, who insisted upon having a king like all of the surrounding nations, much to the prophet Samuel's despair (I Sam. 8).

"Give us a king to judge us," they cried. But the LORD responded to Samuel,

> Hearken unto the voice of the people in all that they say unto thee, for they have not rejected thee, but they have rejected me, that I should not reign over them.

Samuel spoke all of the words of the Lord to the people. He declared explicitly the nature of what a man exercising dominion over his fellows would look like... the progressive taxation, oppression, loss of freedom, and enforced service. "And ye shall cry out in that day because of your king which ye shall have chosen; and the LORD will not hear you," warned the prophet.

> Nevertheless the people refused to obey the voice of Samuel; and they said, Nay; but we will have a king over us;

> That we also may be like all the nations; that our king may judge us, and go out before us, and fight our battles.

"And the LORD said to Samuel, Hearken unto their voice, and make them a king." Israel got her king. Indeed several of the books of the Tanakh, the Old Testament, are historical reminders of the troubles and triumphs of Israel's kings, their most frequent godlessness and painful dominion over the people God had delivered from the bondage of Egypt. They despised the promise of the "Promised Land."

## RESTORING DOMINION

After a thousand years of rebellion, prophetic rebuke, a divided kingdom and ultimate exile, God, in His compassion for the "people of promise," again sent them a Deliverer to restore the years the locust had eaten and to provide for the promised "Hope of Israel." The Deliverer would restore the dominion of the Creator among a people chosen to be a light to the world. He would be the very incarnation of God Himself, in human flesh, son of David by lineage and son of Abraham by faithful obedience (Matt. 1:1). His very name, Yeshua, would declare his holy purpose... "Yahweh saves."

But again, He came unto His own (Israel) but His own received Him not (John 1:11). He was "despised and rejected," again, as Israel's king, but the Jews "esteemed him not..." (Isa. 53:3). In the crucible of all history, the chief priests "cried out, saying Crucify him, crucify him" (John 19:6). When a pagan governor sought to spare Him, saying, "Behold your King," they cried out, "Away with him. We have no king but Caesar" (John 19:14-15). As Yeshua had already made clear by parable, the Jewish leaders would declare, in effect, "We will not have this man to reign over us" (Luke 19:14).

## WHO WILL HAVE DOMINION?

A thousand years of the demeaning and enslaving dominion of earthly kings had not yet revealed the devilish nature of man's dominion, despite any ameliorating good intentions. Israel would have Caesar, however despised, as opposed to the Creator's chosen Anointed One, Yeshua HaMashiach. And so, again, for two thousand years God, spurned by His own chosen people, gave them over to their hearts' desire. "Caesar you desire, Caesar you shall have."

Even now, "Caesar" is emerging once again to claim global dominion. Will a resurrected "Rome," exercising ruthless dominion, wield a heavy hand again over Israel, seeking to sit in pontifical glory upon the Temple Mount. Will the physical descendants of Abraham, Isaac and Jacob hear again the words, "Behold your king?" Will a counterfeit Messiah present himself to a resurrected Sanhedrin for history's final question; "Will you have this man to reign over you?"

Both Israel and the Gentile world must prepare for this question. History and prophecy are now converging with breathtaking speed. The final "beast" empire foretold by the prophet Daniel is preparing to exercise global dominion (Dan. 7). And the centerpiece, the ultimate prize, is Jerusalem, the Temple Mount and ultimately the Temple.

There are many contestants for the prize. Some will come in their perceived individual capacity while others will confederate to augment their power for the final battle for *KING of the Mountain.* The battle is epic and eternal. It began before Creation and continues to the soon Culmination.

Who will have dominion? Will it be China, Russia, Turkey, Iran, The United Nations, the North American Union, the European Union, Islam, the Vatican, Israel, or the God of Abraham, Isaac and Jacob?

The *dream of dominion* will soon become a global nightmare as the people of planet earth choose sides. Who will have dominion... over you? Choose carefully!

*Chapter 14*

# PROBING THOUGHTS *for* PROPHETIC TIMES

1. Why is mankind's persistent effort to dominate others made in God's image a pernicious, deceptive device of Satan to destroy God's human creation?

2. At what point does the accelerating goal of global dominion reach the "tipping point" leading to global destruction?

3. If indeed Satan, the enemy of your Creator and your soul, is the driving and diabolical force compelling the world toward a totalitarian globalized dominion, what consequences might we rightly anticipate? Order… or chaos? Freedom… or bondage? Joy… or oppression? Peace… or panic? Love… or war? Fulfillment… or desperate finality?

4. What have been the prevailing consequences over the past 2000 years of Israel's choice of "Caesar" over "Christ"—Yeshua HaMashiach? How long will those consequences continue?

5. What would the consequences be to a Gentile or gentile nation that persists in choosing "Caesar" over Christ as "king"?

*Part*

# II

# The Contestants

THE BATTLE FOR *King of the Mountain* is neither unilateral, bilateral, linear nor waged on a single plane. Rather, this battle of the ages is multi-tiered, multi-national and multi-dimensional. While global in scope, it is also uniquely provincial as to geographic regions and some nations. The battle lines are not clearly drawn "on the ground," as yet, thus masking true underlying intentions. Adding to the geopolitical complexity is a multi-tiered religious overlay.

In this section we will seek to explore the historical and recent geopolitical and religious dominions and developments that, in the last generation (indeed this last decade), are revealing the final stage being set for this mother-of-all battles—the battle for *King of the Mountain*.

This is neither the time nor place for interposing political correctness in order to obscure both political and religious realities. Rather, if ever there was a time to set aside our propensities to protect our favorite agendas and to genuinely seek a truth that, to a truly rational mind, would lead us to embrace the time-tested and increasingly proven biblically-prophetic outlook, it is now. In relative terms, few tomorrows remain to pridefully or stubbornly fumble around with dire matters of both temporal and eternal destiny.

We begin by mounting our chariots for a ride into the ancient past, resorting then, to more familiar modern conveyances. Our journey will take us to places and ideas already visited, to be explored in greater depth, as well as to new venues, "hidden" alliances, and even provocative revelations that may truly trouble preconceived notions or beliefs. Perhaps an open heart will be of greater value than merely an open mind as we begin.

Mount your chariot!

# Chapter 15

# THE BEAST OF BLASPHEMY

———— ∞ ————

*"The angel said... I will tell thee the mystery of the woman, and of the beast that carrieth her...."*
Rev. 17:7

THE "PROPHET OF HOPE" is the unusual title ascribed to Dr. Robert Muller, former Assistant Secretary General of the United Nations. Dr. Muller has made it clear that world unity cannot be achieved simply through political unions and alliances. Such unity, according to Muller, requires a one-world religion.[49]

## A COUNTERFEIT BODY

In his book, *New Genesis: Shaping a Global Spirituality*, Robert Muller reflects: "I would never have thought that I would discover spirituality in the United Nations...! Perhaps spirituality is a such a fundamental human need that it always reappears in one form or another in life and throughout history and we are about to witness now its renaissance in a global, planetary context."[50] In 1993, Dr. Muller delivered the historic Parliament of World Religion's first keynote address, calling for a "permanent institution" dedicated to pursuing religious unity.[51]

Dr. Muller believed we were entering "a new period of spiritual evolution," a period of rising planetary consciousness and global living which is expected to result in the perfect unity of the human family. Central to his theology are views of "a divine United Nations" and a "cosmic Christ." "If Christ came back to earth, his first visit would be to the United Nations to see if his dream of human oneness and brotherhood had come true," wrote Muller. "I often visualize," said Dr. Muller, "of a United Nations which would be the body of Christ."[52]

In every chapter of *New Genesis*, writes Gary H. Kah in his *The New World Religion*, Robert Muller calls for a U.N.-based world government and a new world religion "as the only answers to mankind's problems." "Through it all," notes Kah, "Muller maintains his status as a Catholic Christian," ultimately linking the U.N.'s mission to Roman Catholicism. Note well his passionate pseudo prophecy.

> Pope John Paul II said that we were the stone cutters and artisans of a cathedral which we might never see in its finished beauty.

> All this is part of one of the most prodigious pages of evolution. It will require the detachment and objectivity of future historians to appraise... the real significance of the United Nations.[53]

## THE DE CHARDIN CONNECTION

Pierre Teilhard de Chardin was born in France in 1881. Evolution was the passion of his life. As a Jesuit priest of the Catholic Church, Teilhard pursued his first love—blending the physical and spiritual worlds under the banner of evolution.[54] The "Christ" of de Chardin was not the Christ of the Gospels. For him, Christ had to fit into the theory of evolution. According to Teilhard's concept of evolution, God had not previously evolved enough to express himself through human consciousness. Chardin's process of evolution concludes with man becoming conscious of who he is—"God."[55]

"Christ is above all the God of Evolution," wrote de Chardin. "He is the supreme summit of the evolutionary movement... evolving into a Super-Christ. Humanity is the highest phase so far of evolution... beginning to change into a Super-Humanity... the Omega Point."[56] He is the most widely-read author of the New Age movement, and his ideas "gained acceptance among many Catholic leaders, including Pope John Paul II."[57]

Father Teilhard de Chardin influenced most of the prominent United Nations leaders of his day. Norman Cousins, former president of the World Federalist Association, made the connection, writing in the Forward to Robert Muller's autobiography...

> Whatever the uncertainties of the future may be... oncoming generations will need living examples of the conspiracy of love that Teilhard de Chardin has said will be essential to man's salvation. Robert Muller is involved in such a conspiracy."[58]

Muller, in *New Era Magazine*, made the final connection, saying, "It is necessary that we have a World Government centered on the United Nations." ... we can credit the coming World Government to the 'influence of the writings of Tielhard de Chardin.'"[59]

Bringing all the world's religions into cooperation with the United Nations was Robert Muller's top priority. "My great personal dream," he explained, "is to get a tremendous alliance between all the major religions and the U.N.". Muller, in 1997, exulted, "... during the 50th Anniversary of the United Nations... we launched again the idea of United Religions... and a meeting... to draft and give birth to a United Religions.... I will be the father of the United Religions."[60]

## THE MARCH OF INTER-FAITH ECUMENISM

Even as the vision for uniting the nations through a common religion advances through the United Nations, the systemic spirit of inter-faithism and ecumenism is marching lock step to the spiritual drumbeat of a deceptive "unity" movement worldwide. The cry of "UNITY" in our churches, cities and throughout the various religious expressions globally, as well as through a variety of governmental and (NGO) Non-governmental yet quasi-governmental structures, is in itself becoming a common voice and unifying mantra.

It is profoundly seductive, for who, in the current market of politically-correct ideas, desires or even dares to resist the tide. And where is the deceptive danger?

Exchanging trust in the truth of God's revealed Word, the Bible, for trust in man's experience and relationships is becoming the new model of "Christian" ecumenism. It is subtle and it is seductive. To break down walls of division, the new approach is to ignore divine proposition in favor of personal testimony. As Cecil "Mel" Robeck of Fuller Seminary, an Assemblies of God minister said, "We will not get embroiled in disputes involving scripture or homosexuality because it "would have the potential to derail our effort."[61]

Cecil Robeck is on a 12-member committee for Global Christian Forum. The *Christian Century* reported, "After keeping a low profile for several years, advocates of a fresh approach to ecumenism are going public...." "About 240 leaders from the Vatican, World Evangelical Alliance, Orthodox Churches, historic Anglican and Protestant communions, and Pentecostal and independent churches" gathered November 6-9, 2007, for the Global Christian Forum, to advance the new approach based on "personal testimony." Just one month earlier, Catholic Cardinal Avery Dulles admitted the potential for harmonizing doctrines was exhausted, necessitating "an ecumenism of mutual enrichment by means of personal testimony."[62]

"How then can Christian unity be envisaged?" asked Cardinal Dulles. Testimony must trump truth so as to build trust in man. As Dulles declared,

"Our words, they may find, carry the trademark of truth."[63] We would do well to remember the warning of the Psalmist.

It is better to trust in the LORD than to put confidence in man.

It is better to trust in the LORD than to put confidence in princes [pastors, priests, popes and presidents] (Ps. 118:8-9).

Once again, this false unity movement requires that you spiritually dance with the devil, the very Deceiver himself. Remember, there is a great eternal battle between Satan and God for the souls of men, to become *"KING of the Mountain"*... of your heart. Satan seeks to seduce your soul away from the faithful trust and allegiance in HaShem, the one true God, and His Son, *Yeshua*, Jesus Christ.

Yeshua, the "Anointed One," the Mashiach, the Holy one of Israel, is the "express image" of God's person, "upholding all things by the word of his power." He declared, "I and my Father are one" (Jn. 10:30). He said, "He that hath seen me hath seen the Father" (Jn. 14:9). And Yeshua also said, "I am the way, the truth, and the life: no man cometh to the Father but by me" (Jn. 14:6). Jesus made clear that the only true unity pleasing to God was that which is the fruit of being *sanctified* or set apart through God's truth as found in the Scriptures. It was this unity "through the truth" that would cause the rest of the world to "believe that thou has sent me" and would display God's glory as true followers of Yeshua (Christ) became "one" even as Yeshua was one with the Father (Jn. 17:16-23). Never forget! It is our trust in the truth of God's Word, the Bible, that binds us in biblical oneness. Anything else is a counterfeit, however attractive it may appear and however broadly it may be embraced. We, whether Jew or Gentile, are *in* the world, but not *of* it, if we truly love the God of Creation, as revealed in Messiah.

Yet interfaith-ism and ecumenism march on to a louder and more incessant drumbeat. The Third Parliament of the World's Religions met in December, 1999, in South Africa, with 6000 delegates from more than 200 different religious groups. Catholic theologian, Hans Küng, said he maintains a "horizon of hope" that the 21st century might witness "unity among churches, peace among religions, and community among nations."[64]

The most ambitious organization in today's interfaith movement has been the United Religions Initiative (URI), founded by William Swing, the Episcopal bishop of California. Although this movement is little known to the public, "it now provides a spiritual face for globalization, the economic and political forces leading from nationalism to a one-world system," says Lee Penn, an investigative reporter. The interfaith movement "is no longer… a coterie of little-heeded religious idealists…" he says. "The URI's proponents range from billionaire George Soros to President George W. Bush, from the far-right the late Rev. Sun Myung Moon to liberal Catholic theologian Hans Küng, and from the Dalai Lama to the leaders of governmental-approved Protestant churches in China."[65] Penn warns in his *False Dawn* that the United Religions Initiative and the interfaith movement are poised to become the spiritual foundation of the New World Order—the "new civilization" now proposed by Mikhail Gorbachev, the last leader of the Soviet Union.[66]

## A GEO-POLITICAL STRUGGLE

We dare not lose sight of the global context in which the accelerating move toward ecumenism and interfaith-ism is taking place. To do so is to run the risk of being assimilated into a compromised faith system that is sucking an unsuspecting and naive world into a deception from which few will be delivered. What is truly at stake is a massive geo-political struggle for governance of the earth in which religious faith is but a pawn. Again, it is mankind's rebellious pursuit of a counterfeit peace or *shalom* outside of the true claims of Yeshua, Jesus the Messiah.

Illustrative of this geo-political struggle is the historic battle between the Vatican and Russia, in which Russia symbolizes a *secular* vision and the Vatican a *spiritual* vision for a New World Order. Each, however, utilizes the counterpart, whether spiritual or secular, to achieve its long-term objective of global dominance.

Under Vladimir Putin, the Russian Orthodox Church was exalted to near unprecedented favor, with Putin having to kiss the ring of the reigning archbishop. Secular power embraced religious power in pursuit of global dominance. Moscow, thus empowered and supported by massive petrol dollars, signaled its "place in the new world order."[67]

Seeking global influence, Vladimir Putin declared Russia "Defender of the Islamic World," thus uniting the world's greatest concentration of oil and gas production and reserves in an embrace of Islam, the goal of which is world domination.[68]

The Vatican had earlier moved to neutralize the clearly growing wedding of Russian Orthodoxy to Russian nationalism being parlayed into global power. Pope John Paul II, seeing Russia as the greatest opposition to ultimate Vatican objectives, did everything he could to romance the Russian Orthodox Church back into the fold of Rome after a 1000 year schism. As of July, 2008, the Archbishop of Moscow said to Pope Benedict XVI, "the right conditions do not yet exist for Pope Benedict to visit Russia." "He needs an explicit invitation."[69]

Looking back to the time of the fall of the Iron Curtain and the dissolution of the Soviet Union by Mikhail Gorbachev, Vatican insider, Malachi Martin, noted that "These two men [Gorbachev and John Paul II] are the only two among world leaders who not only head geopolitical institutions but have geopolitical aims. Geopolitics is their business." But, observed Martin, "for the vast majority of onlookers and for many in government... the gargantuan change being effected in the shifting ground escapes them." Malachi Martin called Gorbachev and Pope John Paul II "Forces of the 'New Order': The Two Models of a Geopolitical House."[70]

## THE VATICAN—"A GEOPOLITICAL HOUSE"

"The newest game in the City of Man," declared Vatican insider Malachi Martin in *The Keys of This Blood*, "is the building of a geopolitical structure. Everyone who is anyone in terms of sociopolitical and economic power is engaging in it... and ultimately... all nations, great and small, will be involved. It is the millennium endgame." But where does the Vatican fit? Why would a Vatican insider be talking so seriously about geopolitics? Most people undoubtedly think of religion when they hear words like *Vatican* and *Pope*. What then is the geo-political connection?

According to Malachi Martin, since the start of his pontificate in October 1978, Pope John Paul II was a consummate geopolitician. "He heralds a new and as yet unrecognized force in the geopolitics of nations, a force that he actually claims, will be the ultimate and decisive factor determining the new world order." He further notes, "... there are no other feasible ways of rationalizing this Pope's performance on the world stage." "His Holiness has assiduously carved out for himself an international profile" which "no pope ever did on a like scale. Nor has any human being known in history attempted it."[71]

During his Pontificate, John Paul II visited 130 countries, establishing personal relationships with governmental leaders in most of them. He invited representatives of 100 of the world's largest religions to join him in Italy for the ultimate multicultural, religious-pluralistic prayer meeting, directing prayers to over 300 million gods. He was the most traveled Pope in history. He even re-established relations with Israel after 2000 years of rejection, resulting in the first official visit by an Israeli head of state to the Vatican seat of Roman Catholicism.

Vatican City is not just the locus of Roman Catholicism but is an independent state. The Vatican is "considered among the nations" whereas God declared Israel "shall not be reckoned among the nations" (Num. 23:9) and that true followers of Christ would be as "strangers and pilgrims" on the earth (I Pet. 2:11).

The Vatican lies within Rome, Italy, and is the world's smallest state, having no commerce of its own. As a sovereign state, it has its own flag, currency and postal system. It has diplomatic relations with most of the nations of the earth. The Pope, as "Bishop of Rome" known as the "VICAR of Christ," has absolute legislative, executive and judicial power, the ultimate merger of church and state. He resides in the largest and grandest palace in the world with 1400 rooms, while Christ himself had no place to lay his head (Matt. 8:20).

John Paul II was the first Pope in history to actually call for a New World Order. A CNN news release from VATICAN CITY January 1, 2004, is instructive.

> Pope John Paul II rang in the New Year with a renewed call for peace… and the **creation of a new world order** based on respect for the dignity of man and equality among nations…. He stressed that to bring about peace, there needs to be a new respect for international law and the **creation of a "new international order" based on the goals of the United Nations.**[72]

It should come as no surprise that upon the death of Pope John Paul II, 4 million pilgrims and 100 heads of state gathered in Rome to mourn, surrounding hundreds of scarlet-clad cardinals and bishops shown surrounding a golden, crucified Christ. He had ingratiated himself and the smallest of all states to the world for a generation, wooing all faiths and political powers to come under papal authority.

But why did Pope John Paul II wait for 25 years before announcing his clear embrace of a "New World Order?" Perhaps the only real answer why John Paul II took this opportune moment to declare the New World Order as his objective is that the world stands at the threshold of the appearance of the first "beast" of Revelation, a beast "having seven heads and ten horns… and upon his heads the name of blasphemy" (Rev. 13:1-8).

## RISE OF THE BEAST

The Scripture makes clear that a "beast," as used metaphorically in both Old and New Testaments, refers to a political kingdom or power. The Prophet Daniel's great vision of the world's kingdoms portrayed them as "four great beasts." The fourth and last beast was "dreadful and terrible, and strong exceedingly… it was diverse (different) from all the beasts that were before it; and it had ten horns." Out of these ten horns or governing powers came a "little horn" that would rule through the others, using their consolidated global power. This "little horn" had "eyes like a man," "a mouth speaking great (pompous) things," and will ultimately speak blasphemous things about God and Yeshua, His Son, wearing out the true saints, and even changing divine times and laws (Dan 7). These "ten horns" envisioned by Daniel would appear to be the same "ten horns" described in Revelation 13:1-8 and Revelation 17. Scholars have almost universally identified that fourth and final "beast" in Daniel's vision as the Roman Empire.

## RESURRECTING THE *PAX ROMANA*

The Roman Empire never fully "died." Just as with Israel, in its prosperity it was greatly weakened and decayed internally, incapable of resisting its enemies. Its citizens were, in effect, dispersed (as it was with Israel) throughout the then-known world, having largely lost their Roman identity. But the emergence of "Rom-ance" languages and Roman-esque laws, and culture and architecture over the centuries that spread throughout the European continent revealed the Roman root.

Eventually that Roman root spread across the Atlantic and Pacific to the Americas, revealed largely in laws, government, language and culture… and even in religious practices. The *Pax Romana* or "Roman Peace" was, two millennia later, identified as the *Pax Americana*. English became the lingua franca (common language) of the western world, indeed of the entire earth. America, with her glorious eagle wings spread, had become the reigning "Roman" superpower with a Roman capital and a Roman government seeking to export a Roman democracy to an ever-expanding Roman world to bring a Roman "peace on earth." Yet in her prosperity, she also progressively abandoned the Prince of Peace, the only true source of **shalom** (security and prosperity). And as with ancient Israel and Rome, she also began a precipitous internal decay. As her moral and spiritual foundations crumble, fear and fragmentation grow even as her citizens and "caesars" pump their chests in Roman pride. And so America's President, George W. Bush, in the waning days of his presidency, reached for security and prosperity from the new and rising Roman star, the European Union,[73] envisioned as the pulpit from which the new counterfeit gospel of Satan's false Roman peace will be preached as "man's last best hope of earth."

## PLEA for PROPHETIC PERSPECTIVE

A bird's-eye view or heavenly top-view perspective on earthly history reveals valuable prophetic insights not otherwise apparent on this plane of casual life experience. By analogy, it may appear like a chess game being played in three or even four dimensions at once. That may already have become apparent, but if not, it is necessary to point out that in the "end game" of geopolitics compounded by religious objectives, the actual significance or prophetic connection of historical events may not be superficially apparent or even recognizable for centuries. Deception for many arises in failure or refusal to "connect the dots" biblically.

As we complete this chapter, our difficulty, in very limited space, will be to translate, in distilled fashion, the vast historical and more recent information available in an attempt to convey the convergence of geo-politics in pursuit of a new Roman global government with the pursuit of a unified global religion that is preparing to usher in and undergird the New World Order that will set itself "against the LORD, and against his anointed" (Ps. 2:2).

Many, without prophetic perspective, will be seduced to swim in the surging stream of global-ism and of interfaith-ism, caught up in its politically-correct euphoria, unaware that deception is leading them to destruction. But those who are truly "looking for that blessed hope, and the glorious appearing of the great God and our Savior Jesus Christ" will "purify themselves even as he is pure" (Tit. 2:13; I Jn. 3:3).

## E PLURIBUS UNUM

*E Pluribus Unum* is a Latin phrase out of ancient Rome meaning "Out of Many, One." It was proposed by Franklin, Jefferson and Adams in 1776 as a motto for the United States. It first appeared on the Great Seal of the U.S. in 1782 and has continually appeared on America's coins. However, the official motto of the United States is "In God We Trust."

The original settlers on American shores sought to display the kingdom of God as described in the Bible in living color. What Israel had failed to do, they intended to complete for God's glory until Christ's return in the "New Canaan." Many were joined together from the European continent for one holy purpose—to spread the gospel of Jesus the Messiah across the seven seas and seven continents, as described in their founding documents. That spiritual vision gave rise to a secular dream... the American Dream, magnetizing mankind everywhere. As prosperity multiplied, trust in God waned. Discipling people to obey the commands of the Master was exchanged for an increasingly godless democracy worshiping at the feet of the Market. For the last generation, America has exported to the world the salvation power of democracy bowing to the Market. Lamentably, that model has become our global legacy, as the Market has become "lord."

As with Israel, God called America to be separate for His glory, and blessed her with power and prosperity. But as with Israel's abandonment of obedience to God in her prosperity, so it is with America. She now joins the world system with vigor and vengeance and is preparing to pass the baton to the new rising star modeling unity for the emerging global order.

"The POST-AMERICAN WORLD" was *NEWSWEEK's* shocking cover story May 12, 2008. "Over the last 20 years, globalism has been gaining depth and breadth," wrote Fareed Zakaria. "To bring others into the world, the United States needs to make its own commitment to the system clear." "For America to continue to lead the world, we will have to first join it," he notes. He closed the article with this painful observation: "... when historians write about these times, they might note that by the turn of the 21st century, the United States had succeeded in its great, historical vision— globalizing the world."[74] Having abandoned our unity "Under God," we have sown the seeds of a false trust. We have exchanged our divine call of globally preaching the "Great Commission" for a mess of globalizing material "pottage." The baton of leadership is being passed.

The European Union now models the new global mantra. "Unity in diversity" is the motto of the European Union. According to the EU website, the motto means that Europeans are "united in working together for peace and prosperity."

Notice the continual recurrence of the words "peace and prosperity" or "security and prosperity." These have become the marketing mantra for the coalescing of nations in pursuit of global government. God desires that we enjoy *peace and prosperity* in pursuit of Him. When we seek the fruit without the root of righteousness in Christ, it becomes idolatrous... and insidiously dangerous.

When men or nations collectivize themselves in idolatrous pursuit, rejecting God's governance, God rejects them and despises their efforts as open and notorious violation of the first three of the Ten Commandments. That is what brought God's judgment on the builders of Babel and what will bring His judgment on Europe's end-time effort to "union-ize" the world into a godless democracy.

Godless unionizing of the world is an act of collective rebellion against the rule of the Creator. And that is why the European Union, in establishing its constitution, refused to even give God a polite "goodbye" or "au revoir", refusing even to recognize His name in a historical sense or to acknowledge Him or the Christian faith in historically "Christian" Europe.

## FROM CONSTANTINE TO CHARLEMAGNE

In order to understand the European Union's prophetic role today, it is necessary to recall Europe's papal past. This becomes a sensitive matter for those raised within or currently embracing the Roman Catholic Church and its Vatican governance through absolute papal authority and the "Holy See." Yet to remain pure and escape the seductive snare being laid for your soul, it cannot be avoided. Please read prayerfully rather than through the lens either of tradition or of political correctness. We are about to pull back the curtain, beginning the final ACT of an unfolding historical drama that will reveal the Deceiver's choreography of a masterful counterfeit to deceive the nations and consign the seduced masses to eternal perdition. It will lead us to solve the "Mystery of the Woman."

We begin this final dramatic ACT by looking back over the shoulder of history to the ancient Roman Empire. But before we begin this fascinating journey, we can gain perspective by re-visiting a most recent dramatic and historic event—the founding of the Mediterranean Union July 13, 2008.

Nicolas Sarkozy, the French president who conceived the concept for the Mediterranean Union in the womb of his Roman mind, declared its birth just as he began his presidency of the European Union, hosting an "unprecedented gathering of leaders from Europe and all sides of the Mediterranean."[75] The summit's participants committed themselves to "peace, stability and security" with "the same goal and the same method" as the European Union.[76] *The Guardian* from Britain noted: "Sarkozy's big idea is to use imperial Rome's centre of the world as a unifying factor linking 44 countries that are home to 800 million people."[77]

Let us now fasten the seat belts of our chariots and return to ancient Rome whose *Pax Romana* promised peace, stability and security (shalom) to the world just as God's "Prince of Peace" was being born.

In 63BC, Julius Caesar, who had been elected *Pontifex Maximus*, became emperor of Rome and vested the governmental office of Roman emperor with ultimate priestly powers. From that time forward, the title *Pontifex Maximus*, which had been used solely among the pagan priesthood, was appropriated by the Roman Caesars. The Caesars not only merged the role of supreme governmental ruler with that of supreme religious leader (Pontiff), but also claimed to be deity or god in the flesh and were worshiped as such.

In 376 AD, Gratian became the first Roman Emperor to refuse the idolatrous title of *Pontifex Maximus* and presented that role to the Bishop of Rome. By this time, Roman bishops had gleaned substantial political power, and in 378 AD, Bishop Damasus was elected *Pontifex Maximus*, the first pope in history to bear the title. All the pomp and ceremony that had characterized Rome's pagan worship was imported into the Roman version of Christianity.

Historian Will Durant in *Caesar and Christ* succinctly describes the transfer of the power of Rome's decaying government to the increasingly politically powerful Roman version of the Christian Church.

> The Roman See increased its power…. Its wealth and ecumenical charities exalted its prestige.

By the middle of the third century, the position and resources of the papacy were so strong that Decius vowed he would rather have a rival emperor at Rome than a pope. The capitol of the Empire became the capitol of the [Roman Catholic] Church.

Rome absorbed a dozen rival faiths and entered into Christian synthesis. It was not merely that the Church took over some religious customs and forms common in pre-Christian Rome—the stole and other vestments of pagan priests, the use of incense and holy water, the burning of candles... the worship of the saints... the law of Rome as the basis of canon law, the title of *Pontifex Maximus* for the Supreme Pontiff, and... the Latin language as the enduring vehicle of Catholic ritual.[78]

Durant, in concluding his history of the growth of the Roman Catholic Church, makes secular observations that have had profound spiritual implications echoing down to this fulcrum moment of world history. He notes that "as secular failed," Roman government "became the structure of ecclesiastical rule." Consider well his concluding remark and its implications for our time.

The Roman Church followed in the footsteps of the Roman state; it conquered the provinces, established discipline and unity from frontier to frontier. Rome died in giving birth to the [Roman Catholic] Church; the Church... inheriting and accepting the responsibilities of Rome.[79]

The prophetic pattern emerging from the merger of political and spiritual authority in the pope is best captured in the lives of two emperors, Constantine and Charlemagne.

Constantine is credited with declaring Christianity to be the official religion of the Roman realm. In the Edict of Milan, he granted toleration to all religions and increasingly showed favor to Christians, "But as the Roman Empire became Christian, Christianity in turn became imperially Roman."[80]

Despite his ostensible "conversion" to Christianity, Constantine was a consummate politician deeply rooted in a pervasively pagan empire. "He treated the bishops as his political aides; he summoned them, presided over their councils, and agreed to enforce whatever opinion their majority should formulate." Observed Will Durant, "A real believer would have been a Christian first and a statesman afterward; with Constantine it was the reverse. Christianity was to him a means, not an end." "Constantine's support of Christianity was worth a dozen legions to him…."[81]

"Constantine aspired to an absolute monarchy; such a government would profit from religious support," noted Durant in *Caesar and Christ*. "Perhaps that marvelous organization of bishops and priests could become an instrument of pacification, unification and rule."[82] Perhaps, as we await the return of Christ, the visionaries of global government will again utilize the power of the Roman church to gain and authenticate power for a resurrected "Rome." Constantine, while claiming to be a "Christian," maintained the pagan title of *Pontifex Maximus*. His coins were inscribed: "SOL INVICTO COMITI" (Committed to the Invisible Sun). During his reign, Constantine blended pagan worship with worship of the Creator, ordering the Roman realm and the Roman Church to change the biblical Sabbath of the Fourth Commandment so that all would worship "on the venerable day of the Sun," Sunday.

In a powerful sense, surrounded by a profound aura of mystery, Rome never truly expired in 476 AD as often written in the obituaries of nations. Rather, Rome was revived in 800 AD when Pope Leo III, in desperation, fled to Charlemagne for protection. On Christmas Day, with Charlemagne at Rome, Pope Leo III crowned Charlemagne emperor of the Holy Roman Empire. He was the first in a line of emperors that continued for the next one thousand years. But if Leo conferred a great honor on Charles that Christmas morning, he conferred a still greater honor on himself: the right to appoint, and to invest with crown and sceptre, the Emperor of the Romans. Here was something new, even revolutionary. No pontiff had ever before claimed for himself such a privilege—not only establishing the imperial crown as his own personal gift, but simultaneously granting himself implicit superiority over the emperor whom he had created.[83]

Take note, ye leaders of this leasehold of mankind on earth. That dominion which was sown under Constantine and consolidated by the papacy under Charlemagne is about to be claimed in a culminating act of dominion by this world's ultimate consolidation of church and state, the Vatican. In exercise of this papal precedent of power to anoint and appoint the Emperor to govern the state, so the pope, claiming to be "Christ in the flesh," will assert his "lordship" to anoint, appoint and affirm the one who shortly will grant the sceptre to rule over the world's ultimate and final global order. Consider well.

The reaction in Constantinople to the news of Charles's (Charlemagne) coronation can easily be imagined. To any right-thinking Greek it was an act not only of breathtaking arrogance but also of sacrilege. The Byzantine Empire (eastern half of the Roman Empire) was built on a dual foundation: on the one hand, the Roman power; on the other, the Christian faith. The two had first come together in the person of Constantine the Great, Emperor of Rome and Equal of the Apostles, and this nuptial union continued through all his legitimate successors. It followed that, just as there was only one God in Heaven, so there would be but one supreme ruler on Earth; all other claimants to such a title were imposters and blasphemers as well.[84]

From then on, the power of the Papacy steadily grew, and before long it was generally agreed that every new emperor must be anointed by the pope personally, in Rome.[85]

And that vision was revived under Pope John Paul II, the "geopolitical" pope, throughout his papacy from 1978 to his death in 2005 AD. The world's near universal obeisance and adulation at his Vatican state funeral by Protestant, Catholic, Hindu, Buddhist and a hundred other faiths revealed that the scarlet-robed bishops led by the *Pontifiex Maximus* ruled a global "Roman" world. As the *BBC News* noted, it was "history's largest funeral," attended by millions and broadcast worldwide to billions. The then leader of the free world, George W. Bush, eulogized the pope as "a hero of the ages."

Indeed, as Nigel Rodgers notes in *Roman Empire,* "The Catholic Church, with its hierarchy and universalist ambitions, is the most obvious inheritor of ancient Rome."[86]

## ALL ROADS LEAD TO ROME

A British newspaper headline read, "Pope declares EC (European Community) heaven sent." In 2004 AD, Pope John Paul II began the process of canonization for Konrad Adenauer, Alaide de Gasperi and Robert Schuman, founders of the European Union. Indeed it is "extraordinary" for a politician to be canonized, declared the Catholic newspaper, *The Tablet. The Daily Telegraph* quoted one attending the canonization synod as saying, "The European Union is a design not only of human beings but of God." He added that the canonization of the politicians would show that the European Union was "built on a rock,"[87] the very biblical words used to describe the pre-figured Messiah of God.

Why the historical and accelerating role of the Roman Catholic Church in global political matters? Why did Pope John Paul II make history with his journeys to 130 nations and the building of connections with heads of state worldwide. What are the goals of the smallest nation-state, the

146

Vatican, and its *Pontifex Maximus*, increasingly seeking to merge the religious role with political power? Indeed, it appears that all roads are leading inexorably to Rome, setting the stage for the great apocalyptic showdown between a prostituted religious power and the global political powers that pimp her for personal gain until she is cast away in disdain. The great contestants claiming "KING of the Mountain" are showing their colors.

The Treaty of Rome in 1957 established the European Economic Community now known as the European Union. In 2004, the European Parliament presented to the member states of the EU the text of a proposed constitution to be ratified. EU leaders agreed in Brussels that the constitution should be officially adopted in Rome in November 2004; if ratified by all member countries, it would replace the Treaty of Rome (1957).

Also in 2004, the Vatican received additional political power as a representative of the United Nations. Rome now has the right to be heard at the UN General Assembly.

The Vatican sees its role in the United Nations as essential to fulfill its geopolitical ambitions. The UN sees the pope as the world's greatest "moral leader" to persuade global citizens of the glories of the New World Order. Each needs the other. The matter of religion in the global scheme is taking "front row-center." In his final address before the U.N. General Assembly September 21, 2006, Secretary General Kofi Annan warned of a "new war of religion on a global scale" and declared only the United Nations can solve the world's problems.

Israel has become complicit. President Moshe Katsav visited Pope Benedict XVI at the Vatican on November 17, 2005. It was the first official visit by an Israeli head of state to the seat of Roman Catholicism after John Paul II had recognized Israel for the first time in history. Israel, as with the world's nations, fears catastrophe and seeks global religious union. On February 19, 2006, *Arutz Sheva*, Israeli National News, delivered this news brief:

> Israel's Ashkenazi chief rabbi, Yonah Metzger, meeting with the Dalai Lama, a Buddhist monk… suggested that representatives of the world's religions establish a United Nations in Jerusalem, representing religions instead of nations, like the UN currently based in New York.

> "Instead of planning for nuclear war… it will invest in peace," Metzger said.

> Also at the meeting was Chief Sephardic Rabbi Shlomo Amar, Rabbi David Rosen of the American Jewish Committee (who is on

good terms with the Roman Catholic Church), Rabbi Menachem Froman of Tekoa, Ethiopian rabbis and various Islamic sheikhs."[88]

## The Woman Rides the Beast

In the 1990's, unusual biblical symbolism began to appear throughout Europe. Britain issued a stamp to commemorate the European Parliamentary elections. The stamp depicted a woman riding a beast. Paintings and statues of the woman and the beast appeared in official Brussels' circles and on a poster. A mural of the woman and the beast even decorated the Brussels' airport lounge.

"The woman on the beast is now the official picture of the EU," according to Rev. Dr. Ian Paisley, a Northern Ireland minister who was also a member of both the Westminster and European parliaments. He said that when the multibillion dollar new parliament building in Brussels, Belgium, was completed, at the end of where the parliament meets is a dome. On the dome is a colossal painting, three times life size, of the woman riding the beast.

In Strasburg, France, the rival new headquarters of the parliament, designed like the Tower of Babel, is a painting of a naked woman riding the beast. When designs for the new Euro coin were unveiled, there was the woman riding the beast on the back of the Greek euro-coin. In 1992 a German ECU coin was issued showing Europa and the beast. In the new Brussels building of the Council of Europe is a bronze statue of the woman riding the beast.

A United Airlines' seat-pocket magazine contained this headline in German, "Good morning, Europe." The article began with these words.

This May, a daring picture appeared on the cover of *Der Spiegel*, one of Europe's most prestigious news magazines: a pitch black bull, horns lowered, charging straight at the reader. On its back sat a young woman draped in dark blue cloth and waving the blue flag of a United Europe. The cover was a delight for European readers since the woman was the very popular French supermodel Laetitia Casto, who had also recently been selected as the "Marianne 2000" in France—the feminine personification of the French Revolution...[89]

According to tradition, Europa is the Great Goddess, mother of the European continent. According to mythology, Zeus, also known in Rome as Jupiter, fell in love with Europa, the beautiful daughter of a Phoenician king. He seduced her attention by assuming the form of a white bull. When she sat on his back he whisked her away, returned to his normal form, and she bore him three sons. This supreme deity of mythology also bore other names including *Pater* (father) and *Soter* (Savior).

All this may be fascinating history, but why should we be concerned about mythological figures even if they have been adopted for the identity of the resurrecting Roman Empire? The reason is simple. The Bible gives specific description and warning concerning a woman sitting upon such a beast which figuratively depicts the merging of religious power and political power ushering in the grand finale of Satan's deceptive drama of the ages. Shockingly, the final ACT of this drama is now happening before our eyes, and most, whether rich or poor, and regardless of status, race, color or religion, are predisposed to embrace the coming counterfeit salvation offered by a false "Christ" bearing false promises of *security* and *prosperity*. What, then, has God said concerning this mystery woman? The answers are found in the book of Revelation, chapter 17.

## MYSTERY OF THE WOMAN

Revelation 17 and 18 are perhaps the most explicit prophetic chapters of Scripture. They may also be the most dramatic. The sheer scope of their historical applications and prophetic implications is breathtaking as well as heart-rending.

God despises "whoredom." God actually "hated" Esau because he prostituted his birthright for a mess of temporal pottage (Mal. 1:1-6; Rom. 9:13; Gen. 27, 28:1-9). He ultimately dispersed Israel, the "apple of his eye," throughout the nations because of her spiritual whoredoms (Jer. 3:1-3). Our Creator is pure and holy. He despises those who, for personal or institutional gain, will compromise their principles. He hates those who will exchange eternal favor and power with God for temporal favor and power with man. Consequently, when the Scripture speaks of a great "whore," we should universally take notice.

## THE GREAT WHORE

According to Revelation 17:1-2, this *whore* is like no other in the spiritual monstrosity of her prostitution. She is a "great" whore! And she sits on "many waters." The sheer magnitude of her influence and those with whom she has prostituted herself are global. Both the kings and political power brokers of earth as well as the world's common inhabitants are dramatically affected by her spiritual fornication and have become, in one way or another, complicit in it.

## A WOMAN of SCARLET and PURPLE

The great whore of Revelation 17 is "arrayed in purple and scarlet" and "decked with gold and precious stones…," "having a golden cup in her hand." The cup is "full of abominations and filthiness of her fornication" (vs. 4).

## MOTHER of HARLOTS

This "great whore" is not content with her own prostituted life and ways but seeks to birth others who will likewise prostitute themselves as she, so that she can bring them in under her mothering wings, claiming them as her own. She is "THE MOTHER OF HARLOTS." Her home is also the seedbed, supply center, and seductive cover of "ABOMINATIONS OF THE EARTH," all under the cover of "sainthood" (vs. 5).

## PERSECUTOR of TRUE SAINTS

The "Mother of Harlots" fiercely protects her global prostitution ring and will brook no opposition. True saints cannot be tolerated, since the true gospel light of their lives shines into the dark corner, revealing the shocking spiritual debauchery characterizing the "Great Whore's" prostitution system. Persecution of true saints is inevitable for the Mother of Harlots to maintain the global spiritual brothel that decks her with "gold and precious stones" and vast wealth. Throughout history, she has become "drunken with the blood of the [true] saints, and with the blood of the martyrs of Jesus" (vs. 6).

She is a great mystery. The political leaders and peoples of the planet stand in amazement, "with great admiration" at her immense earthly power and glory (vs. 6). They seek her influence, long for her prosperity and lust for her power, The Whore needs them, but they need her. Can this brothel relationship persist indefinitely, or will one prevail?

# THE WOMAN AND THE BEAST

The Great Whore sits upon "a scarlet colored beast, full of the names of blasphemy, having seven heads and ten horns" (vs. 3). These ten horns or powers would appear to be the same "ten horns" spoken of by the prophet Daniel in describing the "fourth beast" and final world empire, Rome (Daniel 7:7-25). Just as Rome seemed to rise triumphant, fall into obscurity, and now resurrect with astonishing vitality, so the world is wondering with amazement at the dramatic rise of the European Union now merged with the Mediterranean Union which the nations now regionally strive to emulate. It is "the beast that was, and is not, and yet is" (Rev. 17:8).

Here is "the mystery of the woman, and of the beast that carrieth her" (Rev. 17:7). This "mystery" is made historically and prophetically manifest to those with an eye to see; an ear to hear; and with a mind, heart and will to understand. Please contemplate with conviction of heart and conscience the inherent warning of this prophetic passage:

> …they that dwell on the earth shall wonder, whose names were not written in the book of life from the foundation of the world, when they behold the beast that was, and is not, and yet is (Rev. 17:8).

## THE BEAST

The beast that carries the woman is something to behold. It will captivate the entire world, the overwhelming majority of the earth's population. It is a global political or governmental system "which hath seven heads and ten horns" (verse 7). The "ten horns" are component governmental powers that give global governing power to "the beast" which is the fourth and final world empire (Dan. 7:16-25). The ten horns are "ten kings" (governing authorities) which have not had ongoing historical existence but rise throughout the earth in the final season ushering in the end of the age, and they receive power one hour (a short time) with the beast." "These have one mind, and shall give their power and strength to the beast" (Rev. 17:12-13).

The spirit and purpose of this beast that carries the woman is not only secular but in serious rebellion against God, having declared evolution as the "creator" so as to vacate all vestiges of divine dominion. All who truly submit to the God of Creation, in obedience to His Word and commandments, and who walk faithfully in the spirit and truth of Jesus, Yeshua the Messiah, will be seriously persecuted, as they were in ancient Rome, in the beast's "war with the Lamb" (Rev. 17:14, 14:12, Dan. 7:21). But "he that shall endure unto the end, the same shall be saved" (Matt. 24:13).

The mushrooming power of "the beast" and of the "ten horns," from whence it receives power, are inadequate, by themselves, to fully convince the world's citizens of the great glory and authenticity of their enterprise. Once again, as with ancient Rome, so it is with the final emerging global "Rome." The power of the secular is seen as insufficient. A religious power must be embraced. They will accomplish global dominion together. The woman "drunken with the blood of the saints" will ride the beast (Rev. 17:6-7), out of which partnership each hopes to gain preeminence to become *KING of the Mountain.*

## THE WHORISH WOMAN

The "kings of the earth have committed fornication" with the "great whore" that rides the beast (Rev. 17:1-2). Each has, historically, and will, prophetically, use the other for illicit self gain. That is the nature of prostitution. Each seeks to gain through geopolitical intercourse the perceived power and favor of the other so as to gain ultimate power and favor with the people.

The beast is described as having "seven heads and ten horns" (Rev. 17:7). The "horns," we have seen, are political governing powers. The "seven heads," however, are "seven mountains on which the woman sitteth" (Rev. 17:9). This woman that rides the beast into global power "sitteth on many waters" (vs. 1). The "waters" are "peoples, and multitudes, and nations and tongues" (vs. 15). The whore's influence is vast, multicultural and perceived as the most globally influential religious power.

The "beast," despising the God of Creation, determines to use the "woman," and her feigned and prostituted faith, to establish the beast's global authority, until she is no longer needed. The "ten horns," then, "shall hate the whore," and "shall make her desolate and naked," and "shall eat her flesh," and "shall burn her with fire" for "God hath put in their hearts to fulfill his will" (Rev. 17:16-17).

We must now establish the woman's identity. Her identity is established geographically and geopolitically. God makes her identity historically recognizable so that no one of honest heart, "keeping God's commandments" AND "having the faith of Jesus" (Rev. 14:12), could mistake His message. The identification is an implicit warning to beware and not participate overtly or covertly in the whore's deception.

The woman which thou sawest is that great city, which reigneth over the kings of the earth" (Rev. 17:18).

The seven heads are seven mountains [hills] on which the woman sits" (Rev. 17:9).

The "great whore" is also symbolically described as "Babylon the great" (Rev. 18:2). Many of the same descriptions given of the "woman" that rides the beast in Revelation 17 are given of "Babylon the great" in Revelation 18. "The kings of the earth, who have committed fornication and lived deliciously with her, shall bewail her, and lament for her, when they shall see the smoke of her burning... saying, Alas, alas, that great city Babylon, that mighty city, for in one hour is thy judgment come" (Rev. 18:9-10).

The global merchants that have participated with the beast in prostitution with the "great whore" shall weep and wail, saying, "Alas, alas, that great city, that was clothed in fine linen, purple and scarlet, and decked with gold and precious stones...! They "cried when they saw the smoke of her burning, saying, What city is like unto this great city" (Rev. 18:15-18).

## THE "GREAT CITY"

The rhetorical question of Revelation 18 echoes to our time... "What city is like unto this great city?" Is there any historical and continuing city on earth that matches the geopolitical and religious descriptions of Revelation 17 and 18?

There is only one city on earth that for more than 2000 years has been known and identified globally as the city on seven hills. That city is Rome.

And the Bible unambiguously declares that the "great whore," the woman that rides the geopolitical "beast," is "that great city, which reigneth over the kings of the earth" (Rom. 17:18). She has prostituted eternal truth for temporal power and prosperity,[90] becoming the wealthiest institution on earth. Much of her wealth has been acquired through the sale of salvation. Under her proclaimed power to mediate heaven and hell, millions gave untold billions, thinking they could purchase heaven on the installment plan, not by the free grace of God but by the forceful merchandising of a false gospel by "His grace," the Pope.

There is only one city in history that could be characterized globally as fornicating with the kings of the earth, mixing the persuasive power of religion with the power of politics to gain dominion over the world's people. It is Vatican City. *The Catholic Encyclopedia* states: "It is within the city of Rome, called the city of seven hills, that the entire area of Vatican State proper is now confined."[91] The words *Vatican* and *Rome* are used interchangeably. When one speaks of *Rome*, the most common reference is to the hierarchy that rules the Roman Catholic Church.

The Pope, claiming to be the "Vicar of Christ" (in essence, "Christ in the flesh") has absolute monarchal rulership over Vatican State, the world's smallest political state, yet "reigning over the kings of the earth" (Rev. 17:18). Popes have claimed dominion over kings and kingdoms throughout history and claim their word and that of the Roman Catholic Church, which the Pope mediates, has authority over and supersedes the authority of the Scriptures. And now, at the end of the age, the Vatican seeks to bring the entire "Christian" and pagan world under its whorish motherhood.

The Scriptures describe her as "MYSTERY, BABYLON THE GREAT, THE MOTHER OF HARLOTS..." (Rev. 17:5). The Roman Catholic Church describes herself as "The Mother Church." But having prostituted herself for earthly wealth and power with political suitors, she became the "MOTHER OF HARLOTS." She presents herself as a great "MYSTERY" to the world, claiming global moral authority while committing global fornication; claiming to be a bearer of the truth while embracing treachery in her heart. Her prostituted power reigns supreme through threat of political blackmail. Hell hath no fury like the "great whore's" scorn mediated by the *Pontifex Maximus*.

The Pope has become the most powerful ruler on earth today. Ambassadors from every major country come to the Vatican to do obeisance to "His Holiness." As Pope Gregory IX thundered, the pope was lord and master of everyone and everything. As one historian noted, the papacy in Rome is "a single spiritual and temporal authority exercising powers which, in the end, exceed those that had ever lain within the grasp of the Roman Emperor."[92] One historian has called the papacy "*ABSOLUTE MONARCHY*."[93]

## USURPATION OF AUTHORITY

In the name of Christ, the Roman Catholic Church has, in effect, usurped God's authority in the earth. With blasphemy of the highest order, the Pope, claiming to be "The Holy Father," has declared his pontifications to be co-equal with or superseding the very Word of God. The Scriptures admonish: "Ye shall be holy: for I the LORD your God am holy" (Lev. 19:1-2). But the Pope claims the title, "YOUR HOLINESS." Jesus Christ is declared "King of kings and Lord of lords" (Rev. 19:16), yet the Pope is coronated, with the accolade: "Father of princes and kings, Ruler of the world...."

The Deceiver's culminating act to defy God's authority in the earth is to exalt his counterfeit as "Father of princes and kings, Ruler of the world," bringing every tongue, tribe and nation under his dominion and authority in religious defiance of what God hath said. The Roman *Pontifex Maximus* is about to proclaim that authority and dominion as the woman rides the beast into global glory and power. It has begun in Europe.

## RELIGION—THE NEW POLITICS

A veteran European journalist wrote: "what is emerging in Europe is a Holy European Empire, an attempt to rebuild the old empire united under the pope. This is becoming blatant: The stained glass window of the Council of Europe at Strasbourg Cathedral features the Virgin Mary under a halo of twelve stars, the same stars you see on the EU flag. The Vatican is playing a major role in the creation of a new Holy European Empire." "The pope repeatedly called for religious unity in Europe. This means a united Catholic Europe, which was consecrated to Mary by the Vatican in 1309 AD."[94]

Otto von Habsburg, head of the house of Habsburg, whose family dominated Europe for centuries as the continent's leading Catholic layman, wrote in *The Social Order of Tomorrow*:

> Now we do possess **a European symbol which belongs to all nations** equally. This is the crown of **the Holy Roman Empire**, which embodies the tradition of Charlemagne, the ruler of a united occident....[95]

How then does this "European symbol which belongs to all nations" extend the "Holy European Empire" to become a global "Holy Roman Empire?"

On May 29, 2008, the former British Prime Minister, Tony Blair, declared, "I'll dedicate the rest of my life to uniting the world's religions." "Faith is part of our future... an essential part of making globalization work." He said faith could be a "civilizing force in globalization."[96]

In December 2007, Tony Blair converted to Catholicism, after meeting numerous times in private with the pope. On May 30, 2008, Mr. Blair formally announced the Tony Blair Faith Foundation. He declared, "Into this new world, comes the force of religious faith." His goal is to bring the six leading faiths together: Christian, Muslim, Hindu, Buddhist, Sikh and Jewish. "Religion is the new politics," declared the new Catholic convertee. "Religious faith will be of the same significance to the 21st century as political ideology was to the 20th century."[97]

Blair, who serves also as Middle East peacemaker—the official emissary of the United States, the European Union, the United Nations and Russia—told *TIME* he "converted to Catholicism to fully share his family's faith. But he plainly enjoys being part of a worldwide community with shared value, traditions and rituals." "In a sense," observed *TIME*, ***"The Catholic Church has long embodied the attributes of globalization*** that now engage Blair."[98]

The rising spirit of globalism is compelling and profoundly deceptive. It is drawing business and corporate leaders, political leaders and spiritual leaders, yes, even professed Christian leaders and Protestants of every stripe. It has become the "IN" thing, a mark of modern savvy and of market and ministry success, but the Master becomes little more than a mascot in pursuit of secondary agendas that wed the world in counterfeit unity or oneness.

A classic, but by no means exclusive, example of this global fever is the cover story of *TIME*, August 18, 2008. The cover title reveals the globalizing spirit: "THE PURPOSE DRIVEN PASTOR—RICK WARREN—America's most powerful religious leader takes on the world." But the title of the feature article goes straight to the heart of the matter: "The Global Ambition of Rick Warren."[99] In the seeming righteous pursuit of ridding the world of material poverty, an unrighteous wedding, "unequal yoking," of religious pluralism is embraced to accomplish the secondary agenda (II Cor. 6:14). The *purity* of the faith once delivered to the saints is inevitably compromised. The apparent "goodness" of the global agenda becomes a subtle substitute for the God who commands us to care for the poor. We may be "purpose driven" but not "purity and principle—driven." The *good* has seductively replaced *God* in the pursuit of a compromised and more universally acceptable *global gospel...* all in the name of Christ. It lures world leaders, not to the foot of the Cross, but to a counterfeit faith rooted in false unity. Might this explain how Rick Warren joined Tony Blair's Faith Foundaion?

As Tony Blair declared, "Religion is the new politics." The global spirit uniting religion and politics is also politically uniting Protestants under the *Pontifex Maximus*. The British *TIMESONLINE* reported "Churches back plan to unite under Pope."[100] These efforts are well under way as the report set forth.

> Radical proposals to reunite Anglicans with the Roman Catholic Church under the leadership of the pope were published… and have been agreed by senior bishops of both churches. In a 42 page statement prepared by an international commission of both churches, Anglicans and Roman Catholics are urged to explore how they might reunite under the Pope.

> Rome has already shown itself willing to be flexible [on doctrinal issues]. In England and Wales, the Catholic Church is set to over-take Anglicanism as the predominant Christian denomination for the first time since the Reformation….

The document titled *Growing Together in Unity and Mission* significantly reported:

> The Roman Catholic Church teaches that the ministry of the Bishop of Rome [the Pope] as a universal primate is in accor-dance with Christ's will for the Church and an essential element of maintaining unity and truth.

> We urge Anglicans and Roman Catholics to explore together how the ministry of the Bishop of Rome might be offered and received in order to assist our Communions to grow towards full, ecclesial communion.[101]

Reports throughout the Protestant and Charismatic world show a similar pattern of pastor, priest and people drifting toward and embracing the catholicism of Rome, ultimately leading to papal primacy and submis-sion to the *Pontifex Maximus* who embodies both the spirit and substance of the resurrecting Roman Empire, leading the Roman Church to ride the Roman political beast to world domination and ultimate destruction. The Deceiver's seductive system is clever but will prove cataclysmic.

## "COME OUT OF HER"

The "King of kings and Lord of lords," Jesus Christ, Yeshua HaMashiach, will not countenance a counterfeit that seeks to usurp both His glory and His authority. He will not tolerate those who trifle with His truth. He cannot and will not bless those who blasphemously claim authority to change His eternal Word for political or pontifical gain or to arrogate themselves to change even His Ten Commandments, proudly declaring the papal magesterium's authority to change the very "times and laws" God hath put in His own hand (Dan. 2:21, 7:25).

The "great whore" is seducing kings and kingdoms, both political and religious. Her bed is spread with "purple and scarlet, and decked with precious stones… having a golden cup in her hand full of abominations and filthiness of her fornication" (Rev. 17:4). As she lures many into her lair, she becomes "THE MOTHER OF HARLOTS" (Rev. 17:5). She has gathered to herself the very colors worn by Roman Caesars and with which Christ was mockingly clothed. *The Catholic Encyclopedia* declares her golden chalice "the most important of the sacred vessels… of gold or silver… and the inside surfaced with gold."[102]

For more than fifteen hundred years, the Roman Catholic Church, under the *Pontifex Maximus,* exercised both religious and civil control over Rome. The Pope abolished the Roman Senate and placed all authority under his hand. The *Curia Romana* that once governed Rome was adopted by the Roman Catholic Church as the "Roman Curia" that is now "the whole ensemble of administrative and judicial offices through which the Pope directs the operations of the Catholic Church."[103] That usurped authority is once again being merged as the "woman" rides the "beast" of a resurrecting global Roman empire. Her symbolic name is "Babylon." "Catholic apologist Karl Keating admits that Rome has long been known as *Babylon.* Keating claims that Peter's statement 'The church here in Babylon… sends you her greeting' (from I Peter 5:13) proves that Peter was writing from Rome. He further explains, "Babylon is a code word for Rome."[104]

To all, whether Catholic or Protestant, or of whatever religious or political persuasion, the God of Creation warns from heaven…

> "COME OUT OF HER, MY PEOPLE, that ye be not partakers of her sins, and that ye receive not of her plagues. For her sins have reached unto heaven, and God hath remembered her iniquities" (Rev. 18:4-5).

He that hath an ear to hear, let him hear what the spirit saith to professing Christians, Jews and Gentiles across this shrinking globe.

*Chapter 15*

# PROBING THOUGHTS *for* PROPHETIC TIMES

1. What do you think is the significance of the "United Religions" campaign under the United Nations?

2. How is the continual call to "unity" propelling the world into a "spiritual force for globalism?"

3. Did you know that Pope John Paul II called for "the creation of a new world order" based "on the goals of the United Nations?" How does that reflect upon a *geopolitical* role for the Vatican as opposed to a *spiritual* role?

4. Can you see how the political and spiritual history of Rome and of the Vatican connects the prophecies of Daniel and Revelation? Does this history reveal the nature of the final "beast" empire? In what ways?

5. Historian Nigel Rodgers noted, "The Catholic Church, with its hierarchy and universalist ambitions, is the most obvious inheritor of ancient Rome." How does this provide foundation for massive deception, particularly among Roman Catholics?

6. In what ways do you think Tony Blair was right in declaring: "Religion is the new politics?"

7. Does it appear to you that the promoters of global government and the Roman Catholic Church (The Vatican) are working in concert, each for their own purposes of global dominion?

8. What should be the attitude and response of true followers of Christ? Of Jews? Of the Gentile World?

# Chapter 16

# MOHAMMED VS. THE POPE

———— ✦ ————

*"Jerusalem is the 'holy grail' of Jihad. It is the symbol of Islam's triumph over the world… to establish an Islamic throne upon the Temple Mount."*

"THE EFFECT WAS CATACLYSMIC!"[105] No one truly expected the turn of history 1300 years ago that would resurrect with a cry of "victory" over the earth in our generation. And so the epic battle for *KING of the Mountain* continues, yet now with a profound and palpable sense of finality.

## THE RISE OF ISLAM

Early in the seventh century, a new people and a new faith appeared on the world stage. In September 622 AD, the Prophet Mohammed fled from the hostile city of Mecca to Medina. This event, known as Al-Hajira or Al-Hegira, marked the beginning of what might be called "the Muslim era." Within only eleven years, the followers of Mohammed exploded out of Arabia and began a brutal military pursuit of domination of the then-known world. Within ten years, the Arab Muslims not only defeated the Byzantine Empire (Eastern Rome), but also controlled Damascus and Jerusalem. Within twenty years, they controlled Syria, Palestine, Egypt and the Persian Empire. Amazingly, their advance to control all of Europe was stopped short in 732 AD by Charles Martel, only 150 miles from Paris.

Three of the pope's five historic patriarchies—Alexandria, Antioch and Jerusalem—were decimated. All the great Catholic churches of North Africa disappeared, except for the Copts of Egypt. The lands which had seen the origins of Christianity were all lost, never to this day to be truly recovered. The eastern Roman Empire was "hideously maimed." "As the Belgian historian Henri Pirenne suggested, it was Mohammed who made Charlemagne possible."[106]

## TWO EMPIRES COLLIDE

The threat of the rapidly-advancing Muslims was of great moment to the papacy of Rome. That threat was augmented by perpetual political assaults throughout Europe on the pope's power. Hence, when Charlemagne reached Rome in 800 AD to be anointed by Pope Leo with the crown and sceptre as "Emperor of the Romans" to reign over a "Holy Roman Empire," the battle lines were clearly drawn between the colliding empires of papal Rome and the ever-pressing and growing power of Islam. There was no true truce, only the biding of time. Which of the contestants for world dominion would gain the upper hand in history?

Who can truly and definitively explain the hidden whys and wherefores of historical development? What historian would or could have foretold, with particularity, the geopolitical developments and religious dogmas that would direct the course of history, that would lie dormant and then rise with a vengeance in this culminating moment of man's sojourn on earth?

## THE NATURE OF ISLAM

Apart from the Christian faith, Islam is arguably the most influential religion in the world, with approximately 1.2 billion followers. *Islam* is the correct name for the religion of Mohammed, while *Muslim* describes a follower of Islam. Islam dominates over 50% of the countries on three continents.

Mohammed (570-632 AD) claimed to have received visions or supernatural revelations from God (Allah) through the angel Gabriel. These revelations were compiled into a book called the *Koran* or *Al-Qur'an*. There are two principal schools of Islam. The majority of Muslims are *Sunnis* (±90%) and the minority are *Shi'ite* (±10%). There are also millions of Muslim mystics called *Sufis*. The overtly belligerent black Muslim movement (i.e.– Nation of Islam) has dominated in America, although in the past ten years, more traditional Islam has grown rather significantly to perhaps six percent of the population. It claims to be the fastest growing religion in the world.

The meaning, heart and soul, of Islam is *submission*. It is this defining term and the full implications thereof that the western world fails to grasp, either knowingly or negligently, either intentionally or through the massive interpretive deception born of political correctness, religious pluralism and multiculturalism. It is as if the West has voluntarily blindfolded itself to the religious, political and indeed global implications and intent woven into Mohammedan "submission."

It is neither our intention nor desire to present here a theological treatise on the religion of Mohammed and his vast adherents. Rather, our purpose is to distill from the details an understanding sufficient to honestly, justly and practically discern the grave dangers lurking in the ominous clouds gathering across the world. Indeed, lightening is about to strike, and when it does, a global conflagration will be ignited. It will be a winner-take-all battle for *KING of the Mountain.*

Muslims believe that there is only one true God and that his name is *Allah.* "There is no God but Allah, and Mohammed is his prophet," recites the creed. Unlike the Christian faith, however, Islam does not rely upon personal conviction leading one to conversion of heart and voluntary submission to our Creator through Jesus Christ. Instead, Islam *demands* submission to Allah. The world and its people will either voluntarily "submit" to Sharia law, the governing code of Islam, or do so by force or threat of force at the point of a sword... or of a nuclear weapon.

When George W. Bush, as America's president, declared following the infamous September 11, 2001, attack on the World Trade Center Towers, the U.S. Pentagon, and the Capitol that Islam is a "peaceful" religion that was "hijacked" by terrorist extremists, he either knowingly or negligently misstated the truth. When Britain's then Prime Minister, Tony Blair, catering to the West's dominating deception of political correctness, religious pluralism and multiculturalism, said that when anyone thinks of Islam, their first thoughts should be of "peace, tolerance and a force for good," he blatantly blinded his fellow Brits to reality. In an interview with Muslim News, the Prime Minister boasted he had "no truck at all" with those who suggest that conflict is inevitable between Islam and the West. He said he wants the Muslim community to feel "fully accepted and catered for in Britain...."[107] And so Mr. Blair assures the world, as the founder of the Faith Foundation, dedicated to unite the religions of the world so as to undergird the emerging "New World Order," that he reads his *Koran* (as a good Roman Catholic) every day.[108]

The world and its leaders must quickly face and admit an unspeakable reality—Islam, at its very core, is mandated by Mohammed, his Koran, and the supporting Hadiths, to rule the world and to bring every nation, every religion and every person inhabiting the planet under the rulership of a global Caliphate that will, quite un-democratically, impose Sharia law with impunity under the expected Mahdi, the Islamic "Messiah." The unvarnished warning truth is knocking loudly and insistently at the door of every president, prime minister, pastor, priest... and yes, the pope. One can hear the deafening "Clash of Cultures" now in near final-formation for a battle beyond the belief of the Tony Blairs, George Bushes and Barack Obamas of the world. But it is coming. Listen!

## THE CALL TO JIHAD

It is nothing more than sanctified hatred. The sixth mandate on the head and heart of every true Muslim follower of Mohammed under authority of the *Qur'an* and the *Hadiths* is the unequivocal, inescapable call to global *jihad* or holy war.

Under Islamic law, there are only two types of nations—a nation that is of the "house of Islam" or a nation that is of the "house of war." "The true Muslim believes that the whole world is his home and that he is commanded to submit the world to the authority of Islam."[109] Therefore, all nations and peoples who have not submitted to Islam and Sharia law are subject to the vengeance of holy war or *jihad*. This is neither a joke nor information to be received with jocularity. It is *jihad*, and it is deadly serious, as the world is just beginning to discover, albeit sheepishly and reluctantly due to the paralyzing constraints of the "unholy trinity" of political correctness, multiculturalism and religious pluralism.

"The focus of jihad is to overcome people who do not accept Islam."[110] Let the Qur'an speak for itself.

> Those who reject Islam must be killed. If they turn back [from Islam], take them and kill them wherever you find them...
> -Surah 4:89, *The Noble Qur'an*

> So, when you meet those who disbelieve [Islamic teaching], smite [their] necks till when you have killed and wounded many of them, then bind a bond firmly [take them as captives].
> -Surah 47:4, *The Noble Qur'an*

> O you who believe! Fight those of the disbelievers who are close to you, and let them find harshness in you...
> -Surah 9:123, *The Noble Qur'an*

This discussion is not herein intended to be an attack on the Muslim faith but rather an open revelation of fact as it reflects upon the nature and nurture of that system of belief as it bears upon the emerging global battle for *KING of the Mountain*. Background and belief form the basis for the battle. They are inseparable.

## JIHAD AND JURISDICTION

For the true Muslim, "There is only one way to guarantee entrance into Paradise.... The only way to know for sure that you will get into Paradise is to die in *jihad*—to die while fighting the enemy." "Jihad simply means that Muslims must fight the enemy of Allah until the enemies die or the Muslims die."[111] All who are not Muslim are "infidels" or the "enemy."

This understanding is critical for all non-Muslims to comprehend and accept at face value from the viewpoint of Islam. It is, indeed, the Islamic "missionary" method. If they will not submit as "conquered," they must die, for Allah will not countenance any resistance… even the resistance of conscience. This understanding of jihad has even been defined in legal terms by Islamic *fiqh*. Consider.

[Jihad] is fighting anybody who stands in the way of spreading Islam. Or fighting anyone who refuses to enter Islam (based on Surrah 8:39 of the Qur'an)[112]

Interestingly, "Islam is not just a religion; it is a government, too." "Islam teaches that Allah is the only authority; therefore, political systems must be based on Allah's teaching and nothing else." "People fighting jihad consider themselves to have succeeded when a nation declares Islam as both their religion and their form of government."[113] Because of this belief system, Islam gains jurisdiction over the nations and the world through *jihad*. For a genuine Muslim, therefore, Allah gains supreme jurisdiction over the planet and its peoples when…

-The worship of Allah is universal, with no residual resistance;
-The rule of Sharia law is universal, with no residual resistance.

Thus, the very concept of democracy or a truly democratic republic as a form of government is fundamentally inconsistent with the Islamic belief/governmental way of existence. It should not, therefore, be a mystery that a genuine democratic form of government can neither thrive nor survive wherever Islam has become deeply rooted. Only brutal dictators have been able to restrain the insurgent violent force of those who employ jihad to advance and enforce true Islamic life and jurisdiction. Western dreams of such democratic freedoms are an illusion driven either be ignorance or intentional rejection of reality due to the thought-paralyzing constraints of "political correctness." To persist in embracing such hopes is not only irrational and irreconcilable with Islamic belief but is profoundly pernicious for the rest of the planet. Hence, the battle for *KING of the Mountain* will soon be fully engaged.

## WHY SEEMING INCONSISTENCIES?

Why is there such apparent divergent expression in the Qur'an regarding attitude and approach toward Jews and Christians, the other two claimants to monotheistic faith? How can there be such seemingly positive and affirmative verses in the Qur'an speaking favorably of Jews and Christians as "People of the Book," yet such dramatically dire and vicious passages calling for the demise and destruction of the same? The answer, in actuality, is quite simple.

The Prophet Mohammed's life in Mecca was mostly about prayer and meditation. Thus, the verses of the Qur'an written or "revealed" in Mecca talk of peace and cooperation. But in Medina, the mandate of Mohammed changed dramatically. In Medina Mohammed became militant and reverted to violence and invasion as the means to propagate his "prophetic" purpose and exemplify his power. *Jihad* was thus born. "Sixty percent of the Quranic verses talk about jihad, which stands to reason because Mohammed 'received' most of the Qur'an after he left Mecca. Jihad became the basic power and driving force of Islam."[114]

Unfortunately to the average reader, the surahs in the Qur'an are not organized chronologically as to which were prompted or penned in Mecca and which were inspired or written in Medina. While there are some versions of the Qur'an which identify each verse as to where it was revealed, whether in Mecca or Medina, the reader must normally consult more scholarly Islamic references in order to know those elements of timing. Such knowledge, however, is crucial to honest comprehension and application of Mohammed's message, for it is radically contradictive moving from Mecca to Medina. Religious pluralists and multiculturalists bound by political correctness invariably invoke the peaceful platitudes of Mecca, utterly ignoring the far greater and later vitriolic and violent provocations coming from Medina.

How, then, are these vast differences resolved and rationalized within Islam? How did the Jew and the Christian, the other "People of the Book," become transformed from *friend* to *foe* so as to become the implacable and eternal enemies of the Muslim, destined to be eradicated from the earth? Islamic scholars bridged the disconnect. This was accomplished by the principle of *naskh*.[115] To resolve contradictions, new revelations would be deemed to override previous revelations.

"There are at least 114 verses in the Qur'an that speak of love, peace and forgiveness, especially in the surah titled 'The Heifer' (Surah 2:62, 109). But when Surah 9:5 was revealed later, it cancelled out those previous verses."[116] Consider carefully the global implications of this verse in the context of the epic battle for *KING of the Mountain*.

> Fight and slay Pagans [non-Muslims] wherever you find them, and seize them, beleaguer them, and lie in wait for them in every stratagem [of war];
>
> ALI TRANSLATION

"This is known as the verse of the sword, and it explains that Muslims must fight anyone who chooses not to convert to Islam. It is considered to represent the final development of jihad in Islam."[117] "The principle of *naskh* is very strong. If a verse is *nasikh*, or overridden, it is as if that verse doesn't even exist."[118] Jihad thus became "the basic power and driving force" of Islam.[119]

## TRUE MUSLIMS

Are all Muslims truly "Muslim?" We might just as well ask, "Are all Jews truly 'Jewish,' or are all professing Christians truly 'Christian'?" The answer in each case is ultimately, "NO," for there are some very precise foundational beliefs and corresponding actions required in each of these monotheistic religious faiths that must define anyone who would claim to be a true, dedicated and sincere adherent.

It is without question by any reasonable observer within or without these respective faiths that the largest proportion, if not the majority, of professed adherents are what would be called *secular*. This is certainly true for Jews and Christians. A further large group of adherents to these faiths might be best identified as *traditionalists*. These persons clearly identify with the particular persuasion, practice many of the usual rituals or activities customarily defining the religion, but for a variety of reasons choose not to be fully persuaded by all of the tenets, dogmas, doctrines or practices required under the Bible or other governing documents. One might refer to such as a peripheral "believer," desiring the identification with the faith but refusing to be bound by its burdens. Lastly, there are the "true" believers. These are those who not only identify with the faith and follow many of its practices but who seek to conduct their lives in strict conformity to the words and ways of Yahweh (God) and the prophets. These have a genuine fervor for the faith and believe its precepts as "fundamental" to life and practice.

These same distinctions are clearly seen within the broader scope of those who profess to be *Muslim*. Secular Muslims "believe in the nice parts of Islam, but they reject the call to jihad. They take on the cultural trappings of the message, but they are not living it out completely. These Muslims may be very dedicated to their system of thought, even though it does not represent true Islam (just as it is with many Christians and Jews). The majority of Muslims around the world—both in the East and in the West—fall into this category (at least at present)."[120]

Traditional Muslims are more consistent in both the study and practice of Islam, but have a struggle when it comes to jihad. Some consider jihad to be only a spiritual battle, rejecting the vitriol and violence. Others actually believe in jihad, that it requires fighting non-Muslims, but they take little or no action (at least at present) for fear of what might happen to them or their families, preferring a nice life on earth to the promise of Paradise by dying for the cause.

Then there are the true believers. These are the smaller group who take their faith seriously, even to death. They not only *believe* the Qur'an, but also *behave* as if they believe. "Their goal is to practice Islam as Mohammed did. Though we call them *radicals*, they are practicing true Islam"[121] They believe and practice the fundamentals of Islamic faith. They, together with many traditionalists, will carry the Muslim banner to claim dominion over the Mount of God and thereby dominion over the earth.

## JIHAD AND JERUSALEM

Regardless of the prevailing views of the Western world bound by the chains by religious pluralism, multiculturalism and political correctness, the realities "on the ground" present other than a pleasant and peaceful face. These "realities" are defined and declared by true believers and must therefore be carefully considered, for it is these which will determine the destiny of every nation, every people group and religious group on the planet. All others are merely parenthetical to the "holy war" of jihad.

Jerusalem is the "holy grail" of jihad. It is the symbol of Islam's ultimate triumph over the world, opening the gate of glory to establish an Islamic throne upon the Temple Mount. "Jerusalem will be Muslim Forever" declared the Al-Aqsa Sheikh on July 20, 2012. What underlying viewpoint precipitated such a provocational pronouncement to Israel and the world?

Sheikh Yusuf Salameh, a preacher at Al-Aqsa Mosque on the Temple Mount denounced a statement by Israel's Attorney General that Israeli law must be applied to the Al-Aqsa Mosque complex in Jerusalem. The Attorney General, Yehuda Weinstein, said that the Temple Mount in Jerusalem is part of Israeli territory so Israeli law applies there. That is a fact of law and was stated factually. So how is the rest of the world to comprehend the explosive response by Sheikh Salameh? Listen... and ponder... the words of a "true" Muslim believer.

Sheikh Salameh said that "Al-Quds [the Arabic name of Jerusalem] is an Islamic city, as determined by the creator of the world and as indicated in the Koran.

He said that no decision by one person or another will be able to change this reality, stressing that "Al-Quds" will remain Islamic until the end of time.[122]

## THE POPE AND THE PROPHET

The battle is engaged. Political posturing and false hopes of genuine peace are coming to a screeching halt amid absolute claims of Mohammed and his followers to Jerusalem and the Temple Mount while the Vatican itself has been positioning for similar claims. The Pope and the Prophet are about to engage in the only global gladiatorial religious battle in history. Who will be *KING of the Mountain*? Israel, for now, becomes a virtual bystander, providing the venue for this cataclysmic confrontation that will spread its napalm fire throughout the earth.

Even as the "Vatican and Israel joust over Jerusalem,"[123] Islam declares "Jerusalem will be Muslim Forever."[124] Even as the Roman Catholic Church seeks to regain dominion over sacred sites on Mt. Zion, the Al-Aqsa Sheikh declared Al-Quds (Jerusalem) an Islamic city. Just as the papacy pontificates from the "Holy City" of Rome claiming jurisdiction over Jerusalem, God's biblically-determined Holy City where He chose to place His name, so Sheikh Salameh pronounced Jerusalem "an Islamic city, as determined by the creator of the world and as indicated in the Koran." Which is correct? Are either correct? Yet the Palestinian Authority National Assembly called for Jerusalem "to become the capital of the world."[125]

Iran, claiming the role of global Islamic leader, the "vanguard of the Islamic Revolution," boasts, "THERE WILL BE WAR—AND WE'LL WIN."[126] Even as the Vatican strives to extend its pontificate across the planet, so Muslims boldly strike—"Christianity should be destroyed and wiped from the face of the earth.[127]

There can be no doubt. The pope and the Prophet Mohammed's religious progeny are preparing for the mother of all battles. We must therefore explore the role of the papacy with greater particularity, or we will likely miss the point of prophetic implications. For as Iran's supreme leader, Ayatollah Ali Khamenei declared in July 2012, "We must prepare for war and the 'End of Times,'" so as to prepare the world for the coming of the Islamic messiah.[128] To accomplish that preparatory task for the coming of the Mahdi, the twelfth Imam, the Islamic messiah, the Ayatollah's message could not be more clearly stated. For on February 5, 2012, he pronounced on the website proxy for the Iranian government: "Kill all the Jews and annihilate Israel...."[129]

The Iranian secret documentary, "The Coming Is UPON US," unmistakably states the Islamic viewpoint that the destruction of Israel will trigger the coming of the Islamic messiah, and that even Jesus Christ will come and convert to Islam, acting as the Mahdi's deputy, praying to Allah as he enforces the will of the 12th Imam.[130] To this end, the Ayatollah's strategy specialist, Alireza Forghani, made clear that both Israel and America must not only be defeated but annihilated.[131]

To understand the geopolitical machinations leading to this "mother of all battles" looming on the near horizon, we must pay a further visit to the Vatican.

*Chapter 16*

# PROBING THOUGHTS *for* PROPHETIC TIMES

1. Both Islam and the Vatican each represent dramatically opposing geopolitical claims for world dominion combined with religion. Can you see how they are poised for more open, even violent confrontation, each currently claiming nearly the same number of adherents?

2. In what way did Mohammad make Charlemagne possible, to be papally appointed as emperor to the "Holy Roman Empire?"

3. What teaching or characteristic of Islam has virtually guaranteed open and violent conflict with Rome and even the rest of the world?

4. What is the difference between passages of the *Koran* penned in Mecca versus those later written or "revealed" in Medina? Should that make a difference in how non- Muslims view the Muslim faith and the implications for Islam throughout the world?

5. Why do you think the western world, including presidents and prime ministers, have been so willing to ignore or deny the true nature of Islamic jihad as clearly defined by Mohammed? Is it ignorance? Is it malignant negligence? Is it blinders borne of political correctness, multiculturalism and religious pluralism? What are the implications for you, your country and our world?

*Chapter 17*

# "ETERNAL CITY" VS. HOLY CITY

### *"Vatican demands Temple Mount to be placed under Pope rule."*

THE TWO CITIES ARE IN CONSUMMATE CONFLICT. And that conflict is rapidly nearing consummation. Charles Dickens made famous his *Tale of Two Cities*, but we now must grapple with a politically explosive and religiously troubling tale of the two most prominent cities on the planet, symbols of an eternal, spiritual conflict now nearing its culmination. The cities are Rome and Jerusalem—Rome, euphemistically referred to as the "Eternal City," and Jerusalem, reverently described as the "Holy City."

It is impossible to comprehend the greater panoply of history or of God's prophetic Word without delving into this dangerous, even diabolical, tale pitting these two great, famous (or infamous) cities against each other in a drama unprecedented in the history of man. The delicate discussion demands a monumental effort to set aside all pre-conceived notions and "politically-correct" processing so as to see emerging from the minutiae of history the greater and monumental spiritual scope of developments over the two thousand years last past and their dire implications that are now destined to define the course of the closing hours of this earthly drama. We begin first with a brief overview of these cities as they are generally perceived.

## THE "ETERNAL CITY"

Rome, "La Citta Eterna—The Eternal City," has developed her reputation upon the planet for over 3000 years. From those within her borders, she is described as "unquestionably the most magnificent city in the world… stealing your senses one by one and hastening your return."[132] "No city in the world reflects the history of man's endeavors quite as much as Rome."[133] "...everywhere there is evidence of timelessness."[134] "This is the essence of the Eternal City."[135]

The city of Rome lies between the hills and the sea, encompassing approximately 420 square miles. It was originally built on the famous "Seven hills" that still form part of the city. According to legend, Rome was founded in 753 BC by the mythical Romulus, who—along with his twin brother Remus—was son of the god Mars. After the young boys were abandoned on the Palatine Hill, they were suckled (as the story goes) by a she-wolf. Romulus, thereafter, founded Rome atop the Palatine Hill, naming it after himself. Today, the she-wolf remains the symbol of Rome. In 510 BC, the Romans rose up against the oppressing Etruscans to establish a republic.[136]

Why, then, would a city established on such a mythical foundation assume both the aura and mystical authority of an "Eternal City"? Men usually attribute powers and authority to persons, objects or political institutions based upon human values and perceptions. These accrued and amalgamated viewpoints often take upon themselves a life greater than their sum, eventually defining and even determining destiny. And so it is with Rome.

## THE LONGEVITY OF HISTORY

"It is hard to stand anywhere in Rome and not be taken aback by the magnitude of her history." Indeed, the city is "layered in nearly three millennia." Within the scope of recorded human occupation of the planet, Rome has been a deciding factor geopolitically for nearly half of that recorded history, at least as set forth in the pages of the Bible.

## THE LINGERING PROPHET

It was the biblical prophet Daniel who, in interpreting the famous and terrifying dream of Babylon's Nebuchadnezzar, declared the fourth and last great kingdom to rule the world would be "as strong as iron," "part of iron and part of clay." In a further vision of his own in Babylon, this same prophet saw "four great beasts." The fourth beast was "dreadful and terrible" and "was diverse from all the beasts that were before it."[137] Most scholars have interpreted that fourth beast to be Rome, existing not only from at least 510 BC to the time of Christ, but existing in mutated form to this very day.

## THE LONGSTANDING MYSTERY

Rome is shrouded in an enticing mystery that pervades her history, from her mythical founding to the papal magisterium that governs a city within the city, and through that mystery she holds court over the world, its people and its politicians. As one has said, "The Eternal City exudes a magic and richness that is hard to define." "Rome will overwhelm you... welcome you with her infinite charms."[138] Rome, ultimately, through the independent Vatican city-state, became and remains the hierarchal head of the Roman Catholic Church worldwide, the home of the reigning popes claiming descent from St. Peter and authority as "VICAR of Christ" on earth.

## LONG-AWAITED RESURRECTION

Although Rome stands as the capital of Italy, she was once the capital seat of the Roman Empire, "the most powerful, largest and longest lasting empire of the classical Western civilization."[139]

The slow decline of the Roman Empire, together with the rise of power within the bishops of the Roman Catholic Church, ultimately resulted in the official shift of the title *Pontifex Maximus* from the deified emperor to a soon-to-be deified pope. Thus the empire shifted power from "Augustus" to an august spiritual ruler wielding ever-sought political power and dominion.

Although many efforts have been made to enforce papal rule through evil rulers (i.e., kings and counts), a true "Holy Roman Empire" eluded popes, presidents and kings. But such an ultimate wedding of pope and politician now looms upon the horizon, thus fulfilling the long-delayed prophecy of Daniel describing ten horns (powers) out of which one "little horn" shall emerge to accomplish the ultimate uniting of church and state for global domination. It is this seeming "Utopian" fulfillment of political and papal power for global rule that will ultimately set the "Eternal City" in direct and open conflict with the "Holy City," Jerusalem.

# THE "HOLY CITY"

Its very name means "City of Peace," yet Jerusalem has been commonly known, either affectionately or with mocking disdain, as "The Holy City." Indeed, according to the Bible, The LORD God made plain beyond dispute, "I have chosen Jerusalem, that my name might be there." Furthermore, the Lord of Nations and God of all Creation declared his chosen rulership over Jerusalem as capital of Israel "to be over my people Israel." "I have chosen David," declared the eternal Word of the LORD (II Chron. 6:6).

Mankind, throughout history and in arrogant expression of his free-will, has consistently chosen to disagree, both in precept and in practice, with the declared will of God regarding Jerusalem. The entire Gentile world has persistently and consistently sought, over the course of history, to claim dominion over "The Holy City." Yet despite the political pontifications and military maneuvers of the power brokers of earth claiming dominion, depriving the "Holy City" of its peace, the God of Creation and Lord of Nations will once again step over the threshold of human history to claim and effectuate ultimate dominion over this truly "eternal" city where God himself chose to place His name. The world and papal powers would do well to gravely consider the ancient words of the Lord expressed through the pen of Zechariah the prophet.

> Thus saith the LORD; I am returned unto Zion, and will dwell in the midst of Jerusalem: and Jerusalem shall be called a city of truth; and the mountain of the LORD of hosts the holy mountain (Zech. 8:3).

Thus, the "Holy City" is the global magnet drawing the peoples of this earthly plane either to embrace the Lord and His anointed, Israel, or to oppose the Divine will. In ultimate terms, dominion over earthly Jerusalem is not primarily a matter to be decided by practical politics of religious pluralism, multiculturalism and political correctness, but rather by Divinely-declared purpose as revealed in Biblical prophecy. To ignore this ultimate reality is to tempt Divine wrath in judgment of human pride and defiance of holy purpose.

Again, the Biblical message could not be more clearly stated.

> Thus saith the LORD of hosts; Behold I will save my people [Israel and Judah] from the east country and from the west country;
>
> And I will bring them, and they shall dwell in the midst of Jerusalem: and they shall be my people, and I will be their God, in truth and in righteousness.
>
> And it shall come to pass, that as ye were a curse among the heathen [Gentile nations], O house of Judah, and house of Israel; so will I save you, and ye shall be a blessing; fear not, but let your hands be strong (Zech. 8:7-8, 13).

Jerusalem is the vortex of mankind's violent rebellion against God and His chosen people, Israel. It is both a *sacred* city and a *symbolic* city. Similarly, and set in a fascinating juxtaposition to the "Holy City," is the "Eternal City," for it also is "sacred" and "symbolic." And therein lies the inherent conflict between these cities and those who express their allegiance thereto. A brief further look at earthly Jerusalem may therefore be helpful to comprehend the contrast and conflict.

No city on earth excites such passion as Jerusalem. But why? Why has it stood as the world's ultimate prize demanding its ultimate passion and ultimate pursuit? The "Eternal City" has pursued men for power and influence, but the "Holy City" has drawn men like a magnet to its almost ethereal majesty and reflected glory, notwithstanding its embattled walls oft breached by the would-be power brokers of the earth. And for the Jews, it is the glorious "home where the heart is," hence the ageless world-wide call at Passover and Yom Kippur, "Next year in Jerusalem."

We do well, then, to consider the root of Jerusalem's passion, regardless of her unholy stance before a righteous and holy God at major junctions of her 3000 year history as the capital, first of Israel and then of Judah.

## "THE CITY OF OUR GOD"

The Psalmist, in glorifying the greatness of the God of Israel, declared that He was worthy to be praised "in the city of our God," "in the mountain of His holiness" (Psa. 48:1). If for no other reason, the epic battle for *KING of the Mountain* is predicated on these two claims of assertions establishing the presence and power of God as directly connected for eternity to this place often called "The HOLY CITY." Perhaps unwittingly and without full comprehension of the claim, *U.S. News and World Report* boldly proclaimed by its cover to the world that Jerusalem is truly "God's City."[140]

## "THE CITY OF THE GREAT KING"

What ambitious earthly king or leader obsessed with the pursuit of power and glory would not be drawn, in fleshly or carnal pursuit, to depose from power the "King of Glory," the "Great King?" "The pretext for such pursuit of power is again made clear by the Psalmist in reference to Jerusalem as "the city of the great King" (Psa. 48:2). The arch-enemy of the "Great King," Satan himself, desires and determines nothing less than to supplant that "Great King" in His own city and to enthrone himself on the "holy mountain" by means of a ready and willing human surrogate.

## "THE JOY OF THE WHOLE EARTH"

If the desire is "peace on earth," the practical manifestation of that heavenly peace must be joy. It is little wonder, then, that the Psalmist declares Jerusalem to be "the joy of the whole earth" (Psa. 48:2). Yet the same Psalmist writes that the kings of the earth assemble themselves around the glorious city of joy, "they were troubled," and "Fear took hold of them there…" (Psa. 48: 5-6).

## "NOT A MERE CITY"

Jerusalem, wrote historian Martin Gilbert, is not a "mere" city. "It holds the central spiritual and physical place in the history of the Jews as a people."[141] "Even during the diaspora of 2000 years, Jews have called Jerusalem their ancestral home."[142]

## CENTER OF THE WORLD

"Location, location, location" is the commanding cry of the purveyors of land and properties worldwide. For political, practical and principled purposes, Jerusalem continually, throughout history, ultimately emerges as the centerfold of the earth, despite her divinely-permitted destructions. As Ezekiel prophesied long before the birth of Christ,

> Thus said the LORD God; This is Jerusalem: I have set it in the midst of the nations and countries that are round about her (Ezek. 5:5).

This is Jerusalem, the "center of the world" from the God's-eye view. In the messianic moment rapidly approaching, "all nations shall flow to it." As Isaiah prophesied nearly eight centuries before "the coming of the Just One," in the "last days... the mountain of the LORD's house shall be established in the top of the mountain [Temple Mount]...." "And many people shall go and say, Come ye, and let us go up to the mountain of the LORD, to the house of the God of Jacob... for out of Zion shall go forth the law [for the entire world] and the word of the LORD from Jerusalem" (Isa. 2:1-3).

## SEAT OF JUDGMENT

Even as "the law shall go forth out of Zion," so the judgment seat of the God of Abraham, Isaac and Jacob, Lord of Creation, shall rest upon God's holy hill (The Temple Mount) in the midst of Jerusalem. For Isaiah prophetically proclaimed:

> And he [the Messiah] shall judge among the nations, and shall rebuke many people (Isa. 2:4).

Only then will this planet experience genuine "peace on earth, good-will toward men" as proclaimed by the angels to shepherds in the Judean Hills announcing the birth of Israel's Hope and Redeemer (Luke 2:9-14). Only then will the peoples striving for mastery as *KING of the Mountain* "beat their swords into plowshares..." so that "nation shall not lift up sword against nation; neither shall they learn war anymore" (Isa. 2:4).

## POPE VS. HIGH PRIEST

The discussion now turns delicate, dicey at best and indescribably dangerous at worst. But history has a way of repeating itself, sometimes in the light but more often in the shadows. From a biblical and prophetic perspective, viewed not from a temporal vantage point but rather from the eternal, a series of types and anti-types emerges to plot the trajectory of divine design and mankind's incessant pattern of perverting that design and holy purpose. It is tragically unfortunate that untold millions become trapped in the never-ending battle between the holy and the profane as the world careens violently toward the ultimate battle for *KING of the Mountain*.

The twenty-plus years last past have pulled back the curtain of hidden Vatican intentions that have long persisted but without public proclamation. The curtain having been pulled back, the stage upon which one of the final ACTS of history will be played out has now been fully set. The global actors in this end-time drama of—"The Pope vs. The High Priest"—are gradually making their debut on stage as the astounding plot unfolds in the epic, eternal battle for *KING of the Mountain*.

Consider the unabashed, brazen headline taken from the translated content of an article that appeared in March 1998, in Kreuztal, Germany.

**Vatican Plans To Establish Jerusalem As The Capital of the World.**

According to the will of the Vatican, Jerusalem could become the capital of the world. The one-sided claim by Israel does not justify the equality of Muslims and Christians and their claim to the Holy City, according to the Secretary of the Cardinals, Angelo Sodano.

In a press release, the pope invited all people to create conditions in which Jerusalem should fulfill its calling as a city of peace to the honor of God. The Vatican is willing to supply the finances for such an undertaking.

According to Catholic dogma, Jerusalem is the most important city universally for the 900 million Catholics on planet Earth.[143]

This proclamation is nothing short of breathtaking, both in boldness and in breadth. Yet the truth and trajectory of this long-sought Vatican triumph is revealed in the increasingly transparent diplomatic actions no longer shrouded in mystery but glorified in a proposed mission of peace on the planet. Neither space nor time permit a full exposé of the historic thrust of the Vatican's efforts to gain dominion over both the Holy City and the Temple Mount, and so we are limited to brief distillations that give credibility to the pressing conflict between the Pope and the "High Priest."

## "VATICAN WANTS TO LAY ITS HANDS ON JERUSALEM"

"Peace negotiations in the Middle East must tackle the issue of the status of the holy sites of Jerusalem," declared Cardinal Jean-Tauran, head of the Vatican's Council for Interreligious Dialogue, from Rome, December 15, 2011. Tauron further stated, "There will not be peace if the question of the holy sites is not adequately resolved." "The part of Jerusalem within the walls [Old Jerusalem/ Biblical Jerusalem]—with the holy sites of the three religions—is humanity's heritage. The sacred and unique character of the area must be safeguarded and it can only be done with a special, internationally-guaranteed statute."[144]

"A major voice for the Vatican's plan is Hanna Siniora, the elder states-man of Palestinian 'peace' activists, whose office is in the Vatican's Tantur Institute for Ecumenical Studies in Jerusalem." "The site known as King David's Tomb is the major target in the Vatican's plan." "The Vatican wants Israel relinquishing sovereignty at the Western Wall and the Temple Mount. The Holy See uses the expression 'Holy Basin,' which refers to the area of the Temple Mount, the Mount of Olives, Mount Zion and a variety of Christian holy sites" to be administered under a "special regime."[145]

## VATICAN DEMANDS TEMPLE MOUNT UNDER POPE

Dominion over the City of David and the Temple Mount is the Vatican's definition of ultimate global victory. The undisclosed purpose is to place, as a final ACT in the soon-closing drama of history, a pope on the seat of ultimate global religious and political power for universal rule of the Roman Catholic Church through the political chicanery of the Vatican. The epic effort now nears completion.

On December 15, 2011, the world was presented with a gripping head-line for all who would hear and heed.

*Vatican demands Temple Mount*
*to be placed under Pope rule.*

The article subsumed under this eye-popping headline referred again to the public disclosure of Vatican intentions by Cardinal Jean-Louis Tauran, head of the Vatican's Council for Interreligious Dialogue. "The Vatican's former foreign minister asked [Israel} to place some Israeli holy places under Vatican authority."[146]

"The Israeli government and the Vatican are deadlocked in discussions...," declared the article. "Vatican officials are now reiterating their demand for control over the religious sites in the ancient and holy city founded by King David as the capital of ancient Israel and now the capital of the reestablished Jewish state." "In the last weeks, the Roman Catholic Church's authorities increased their political initiatives for Catholic control...." In fact, "The Vatican's former archbishop in Jerusalem, Michael Sabbah, just promoted an appeal to the European Union and United States to 'stop the Hebraization of Jerusalem.'"[147]

## ISRAEL'S CONTROL OF MT. ZION IN DANGER

A lamentation went forth throughout Israel and around the world in April 2009. *Arutz Sheva* carried the story.

"Ten-year-long negotiations between Israel and the Vatican appear to be drawing to a close, with concerns rising that Israel will cede control of the building housing King David's Tomb in Jerusalem." "A team of negotiators representing Israel and the Vatican—released an upbeat press release... speaking of 'meaningful progress,' 'great cordiality,' and a mutual commitment to reaching a final agreement 'as soon as possible.'" "The two states [Vatican and Israel] have been negotiating a treaty since March 1999...."

Now, "In addition, the Vatican is claiming areas around Lake Kinneret [Sea of Galilee], as well as in Caesarea and Jerusalem."[148] In more precise terms, the Vatican is pursuing control and dominion over every significant place and step where Jesus, God's "High Priest forever after the order of Melchizedek" placed His foot, performed a miracle or promised salvation. What more might the Pope demand but the Kingdom of God itself? Will the Pope, indeed, attempt to walk the footsteps of Christ in a final bid, as "VICAR of Christ," to declare himself "Prince of Peace" and the surrogate savior of the world in promulgating a new global order of the ages? Will the papacy become nothing but a pompous, carnal subterfuge to deceive and enslave unsuspecting billions in a false hope securing a disastrous eternal destiny?

On Israel's behalf, the Diaspora Yeshiva which has run the Mt. Zion compound since the Six-Day War in 1967, warned "of the catastrophic implications for Israel and the Jewish People" if the deal went through.[149]

## VATICAN SIGNS AGREEMENT WITH ARAB LEAGUE

It is shocking, but true. "While the Vatican representatives were talking [negotiating] with Israel, they signed an agreement with the Arab League that ostensibly is intended to promote "peace, security and stability." But what might such generalized pontification actually mean? "Are they dividing up the spoils of the Vatican agreement with Israel—or perhaps they are preparing for the next Arab war with Israel?"

Professor Hillel Weiss of Bar Ilan University presciently noted: "This new agreement with the Arab League renders the Vatican, most gravely, an invested party in the Israeli-Arab dispute."[150] It may be a "conflict of interest" yet surprising not a conflict in self-interested purposes. For both Arabs and the Vatican seek dominion over Israel and Israeli control, each for their own agendas, and each is politically-manipulating the other to achieve their nefarious ends.

## PERES PRESSES FOR CAVE-IN TO VATICAN?

Even as Pope Benedict XVI was preparing for his historic visit to Israel in the Spring 2009, Israel's President Shimon Peres was "urging the government to yield control of Christian holy sites to the Vatican."[151] [152] He was concerned that the longstanding dispute would "cast a pall" over the Pope's visit. Ever the peace-nik, and without any personal spiritual commitment to or understanding of Israel's spiritual past and God-declared future, Mr. Peres urged the blithe abandonment of sacred sites, ever willing to sacrifice them on the glorious altar of world peace promised by the Pope.

## A SEAT FOR THE POPE

The saga continues. On February 1, 2013, *Israel National News* announced: "Exclusive: A Seat for the Pope at King David's Tomb."[153] The subtitle is more telling: "Israel seems to have sold Jerusalem to the Vatican."

The excerpts that follow resoundingly confirm the contentions expressed herein that have undoubtedly troubled many of whatever persuasion. Allow the facts concerning this momentous news to pierce the protective armour you may have donned to insulate from the impact of shocking and world-shattering revelations.

An historic agreement has been drafted between Israel and the Vatican. The Israeli authorities have granted the Pope an official seat in the room where the Last Supper is believed to have taken place, on Mount Zion in Jerusalem, where David and Solomon, Jewish kings of Judea, are considered by some researchers to be buried.

It is the culmination of a long campaign by the Catholic Church....
The Catholic Church has long wanted control over part of the area

on Mt. Zion.... Now, after the Muslim Waqf authority expelled the Christians from the Temple Mount and turned it into a mosque, it's the turn of the Vatican to lay its hands on the Jewish Jerusalem.

The Vatican is also asking that Israel hand over to the Vatican's control dozens of sites, 19 in Judea and Samaria [the West Bank] and 28 in Jerusalem. The Vatican wants the Jews out of the Old City.

Sovereignty over Mount Zion is politics, not only religion. The day after the Pope celebrated mass on Mt. Zion in 2000, he went to Yasser Arafat's headquarters to support the Palestinian's right of return. A few months later, the Oslo war began. And Jews were sacrificed again on the altar of "peace." It was figuratively their "last supper."

## THE VATICAN'S LAST CRUSADE

The Crusades of history past have been both glorified and vilified. Regardless of multiplied arguments and interpretations of that dramatic and violent period of history on our planet, the overarching and simple truth is that the Roman Catholic Church and her popes urgently sought dominion over the Holy City. The "Eternal City" was expendable to gain the Holy City of Jerusalem.

Such battles are now, in this "enlightened" era, not fought primarily by the point of a sword but by the "sword" of the pen. It is the persuasion and prolific chicanery in intended purpose that now defines the battle for *KING of the Mountain* under the rubric of "diplomacy." Yet it is equally dangerous.

Papal power, exercised through the state diplomacy of the Vatican, is making its final bid, its "last crusade" for rulership of the world from the Temple Mount. The mystery has passed and the moment of ultimate truth now presses the aorta of the world, and especially Israel, until she finally relents in a desperate gasp for relief. Pandering to Islamic interests against Israel not only carries favor with the Vatican's arch competitor for dominion on the Mount, but also increases pressure on Israel to embrace a false hope for peace.

Islam, from the perspective of the religion-merging, interfaith espousing and syncretizing theological expansions of the Roman Catholic Church, is of little ultimate consequence, since Muslims will gladly assimilate (the bishops believe) into the greater global religion of peace. It is Israel's claim as "heirs according to the promise" to Abraham that stands in the way of papal supremacy. It is Israel's standing in the Holy Land, the Holy City, and the Holy Mountain that must be desiccated, diminished and destroyed, lest the Messiah come and claim His place in His city and on His Mount.

## THE FINAL ACT OF MANS' ARROGANCE

The final ACT of man's arrogance to supersede the rule of the Lord of Creation in the person of the returning Messiah as King of kings and Lord of lords, is nearing consummation. Will it be Messiah, the Anointed One, the Holy One of Israel who will rule and reign from God's "Holy Hill," or will it be an imposter? Will it be the "VICAR of Christ" or the "VICTOR over death and the grave?" Will it be the Pope, or will it be God's ordained and eternal "High Priest (Heb. 6:20, 7:1-28)?

It is not just for history to decide the outcome. Each of us will decide for ourselves, for God's Holy Mountain is not found just on the Temple Mount but in the heart of every man, whether Jew or Gentile, whether male or female, whether bond or free. All will stand before the Judge of the earth. Will the Judge be the Pontiff or God's only Eternal Potentate, the King of kings and Lord of lords (I Tim. 6:15), Yeshua the Christ? Viewpoint determines destiny.

*Chapter 17*

# PROBING THOUGHTS *for* PROPHETIC TIMES

1. In what ways do Rome and Jerusalem represent opposing sides in the epic and eternal battle for *KING of the Mountain*?

2. Can you see how the Pope of Rome, in many ways, is set contrary to Jesus (Yeshua) as the eternal "High Priest"?

3. Why has the Vatican been in a full-court-press for the last twenty-five years to "lay its hands on Jerusalem?"

4. How do you explain the December 15, 2011, headline, "Vatican demands Temple Mount to be placed under Pope rule?"

5. What perhaps shocking or troubling inferences emerge in light of the *Israel National News* article of February 1, 2013, titled: "A Seat for the Pope at King David's Tomb" with the provocative subtitle: "Israel seems to have sold Jerusalem to the Vatican"?

# Chapter 18

# THE BEAR VS. THE POPE

*"Few who strive for KING of the Mountain believe such dominion can be achieved without a religious component, however disingenuous it may be."*

"HOLY VLADIMIR, PRAY FOR US."[154] This shocking and seemingly incongruous headline from the online version of *Der Spiegel*, one of Europe's most respected news magazines, grabs immediate attention, if not wonderment. Why would a rising trend in Russia lead people to pray to Vladimir Putin, honoring the ex-KGB "once and future president as a reincarnation of St. Paul?" Yet it is true, and it reflects a moral, spiritual, social and nationalist yearning in Russia to regain global glory, regardless of the cost.

## PUTIN AND THE "PREPARATION"

Members of this Russian Orthodox sect hike up a hill near the Volga to what is called the "Chapel of Russia's Resurrection," where they spread out prayer rugs and pray to their patron saint; Vladimir Putin whom, they believe, is a "reincarnation of St. Paul." Their leader says she "proclaims what God has revealed to me." Just as Saul persecuted Christians before his conversion to St. Paul, she believes Putin once persecuted the faithful as a Soviet KGB officer. "The Soviets blew up churches, or replaced them with swimming pools," she said, "but when he [Putin] became president, the Holy Ghost came to him." Since then, Putin leads his flock "wisely, just as the Apostle did."[155]

Try to enter the Russian bosom, broken-hearted and laden with despair since the Bolshevik Revolution a century ago. Hopes have been crushed, faith dismembered, existing as a moral vacuum from which has been virtually sucked all vestiges of spiritual life and direction for four generations. Then along comes one, a seeming champion, in whom those devoid of direction can suddenly and vicariously live out their hopes and dreams for a resurrection of Russian glory—that is Vladimir Putin.

"Across Russia, popular affection for Putin has started turning to religious worship." Indeed, the country's top Jewish rabbi, Berel Lazar, swooned that Russians had "every reason to ask God to bless you... you save hundreds and thousands of worlds." Vladislav Surkow, the influential deputy chief of the Kremlin administration, sees in Putin "a man whom fate and the Lord sent to Russia."[156] So how broadly are these or similar sentiments weighing in the minds and hearts of long-downtrodden people aspiring to a return of national glory on the world stage?

Polls show 57 percent of Russians notice "signs of a Putin cult" and "52 percent believe it's a positive trend." But just how deeply do these dramatically-shifted sentiments residing now in Putin present in the popular and governmental imagination? In St. Petersburg, posters proliferate, picturing Putin as an angel. Crowning the city's Peter and Paul Cathedral, Putin's face is mounted on a photo of cherubim. "He has the spirit of a czar in him," says Mother Fotina. "Every day we've prayed for him to return to the Kremlin."[157]

Prayerful pleas did not go unheard, at least to the 11,000 delegates and party members of the "United Russia." At a party congress to usher Putin in as president, they "cheered like true believers in Moscow's Ice Palace, at what amounted to a Coronation Mass." Regardless of the glowing and growing public worship, Mother Fotina believes the people have no real choice. Why? Because "God has appointed Putin to Russia to prepare for the coming of Jesus Christ," she says.[158]

## BID TO DOMINATE

The relevancy of ideas and imaginations that resonate in the minds and hearts of Russians is not found in validating the ultimate truths of their beliefs and assertions but rather in the deeply-rooted nature of those beliefs. It is those beliefs or viewpoints that unite the people in common purpose, regardless of their underlying validity. And it is those viewpoints that, collectively, have ensconced Vladimir Putin on a nearly-divine pedestal, thus supplanting the earlier godless glorification of Lenin and Stalin with a more worthy recipient of nationalized worship, now wrapped in the robe of prophetic expectation—even the preparation for the Second Coming of Christ.

Now, by analogy woven with the thread of nationalistic faith and fervor, when many Russians see the take-charge boldness of Vladimir Putin against all comers, foreign and domestic, they see a "spiritual" power akin to "the boldness of Peter and John" against the rebel-rulers of the Temple in the Book of Acts of the Apostles. And so they "take knowledge of" him, Putin, as if he "had been with Jesus."[159] After all, they have fervently prayed for his ascendancy, and now their champion is set to rule and reign over Russia's resurrection; yes even to global dominion.

Belief drives boldness, and increased boldness undergirds and confirms ever-deepening belief. It should then come as no surprise that "Russia is once again flexing its muscles as an international power, after the decade of economic pain and political instability that followed the collapse of the Soviet Union in 1991."[160]

By 1995, "Russia's fury over its loss of sway" in the world, particularly in Eastern Europe, was becoming palpable. So great was the sense of loss of dominating power that Russian politicians were saying "that NATO expansion may prod Russia to seek a military alliance with China."[161] Only desperation for dominion would drive the once-proud Russians into the arms of their neighbor competitor for global dominion, each to use the other for temporary gain. Within a year, the world would witness "THE RUSSIAN BEAR: RISING AGAIN."[162]

*U.S. Today* reported an exultant Russian ultranationalist, Vladimir Zhirinovsky (a virulent anti-Semite and anti-American), predicting Russia would do away with "Western-style economic and democratic reforms." "He thundered, "No one will dictate his will to us.... We can and we will, by the year 1999... take over the remains of the former Communist Party of the Soviet Union."[163] The Forecast made clear, "Russia's apparent yearning for the past is not happening in a vacuum." "With the resurgence of Communism and the renewal of Russian nationalism, there will be an ever-growing need for petroleum to fuel its industrial enterprises." "The stage is being set for what could be the cataclysmic battle prophesied in the 38th chapter of Ezekiel."[164]

Enter Vladimir Putin. "Catch a rising czar" declared the feature in *U.S. News and World Report*, March 27, 2000. The question was posed, "Is Russia's next president a power freak, a reformer, or both?" Putin "has miraculously managed to unite Russians around a vague combination of reforms and tough leadership encapsulated in his ambiguous promise to establish a 'dictatorship of the law,'" but "hasn't talked much about basic democratic values." "He's a little man who has gained great power."[165] *TIME* called Putin, "THE SPY WHO CAME IN FROM THE CROWD," "... willing to play by the old rules in the name of new politics." Yet perhaps the most telling note sounded in *TIME*'s commentary is reflected in this striking statement.

> "Strong state" is the ambiguous phrase that reverberates most troublingly around Putin. The vast majority of Russians, sick and tired of the way things are, are perfectly ready to put faith in the state as their salvation.[166]

History was now poised to repeat itself. Just one year earlier, *U.S. News* had dramatically announced "Proud Russia on its knees."[167] And a year after Putin's rise to power, *The Atlantic*, in its cover story, announced "Russia Is Finished—The unstoppable descent into social catastrophe and strategic irrelevance."[168] These are the words Putin refused to accept. The Russian bear would rise and roar again.

Consider the crushing analysis of 2001 as Vladimir Putin began his ruthless drive for dominion. The *Atlantic Monthly* had stabbed the pride of Putin and his Russian comrades in the heart. The words cut to the quick. "The drama is coming to a close, and within a few decades Russia will concern the rest of the world no more than any Third World country with abundant resources, and impoverished people, and a corrupt government. In short, as a Great Power, Russia is finished."[169] But that was then.

## FROM POGROMS TO GOD'S PROMISE

As Russia's pomp and power waned, a window was opened as well as a door of opportunity. For millions of Jews long-enslaved in godless gulags by a godless government under the stifling dominion of Soviet Russia, life was little more than an excruciating marathon endurance contest. Yet with the fall of the Iron Curtain, hope sprang forth. The light of freedom pierced the darkness of god-hating dominion, and a million Jews seized the window of opportunity to flee to the homeland of Israel, for as has been so aptly said, "Home is where the heart is." The door of freedom flung open and the modern "Exodus" was begun, just as foretold by the ancient prophets.

> The days come, saith the LORD, that it shall no more be said, The LORD liveth, that brought up the children of Israel out of the land of Egypt;

> But, The LORD liveth, that brought up the children of Israel from the land of the north, and from all the lands whither he had driven them: and I will bring them again into their land that I gave unto their fathers (Jer. 16:14-15).

The prophet Isaiah also made clear God's end-time call to the scattered remnant of Abraham, Isaac and Jacob.

> Thus saith the LORD that created thee, O Jacob, and that formed thee, O Israel, Fear not: for I have redeemed thee...

> Fear not: for I am with thee: I will bring thy seed from the east, and gather them from the west;

I will say to the north, Give up; and to the south, Keep not back: bring my sons from afar, and my daughters from the ends of the earth (Isa. 43:1, 5-6).

Savage Russian pogroms had repeatedly wreaked havoc among the Jews for decades, but Russia, now eviscerated by economic havoc, returned her vitriolic anti-Semitism upon her own head. Devastation swept through the largest country on earth (in terms of land), spanning ten time zones. Her demise was deemed complete and her dominion doomed to the ash heap of history. But God's purposes will not be thwarted by man's short-sighted vision. Russia would rise again.

## The Rise of Russia

Russian angst over her ignominious deprivation of power exploded onto the world scene even as most in the western world still celebrated her demise. By the Spring of 2005, "Russia began a serious Middle East venture designed to reassert its influence."[170] The *Jerusalem Post* noted:

Russia's ambitions are growing to Soviet-era size. It wants to be involved in the international games that are now the recreation of the European Union and the United States.

By renewing political and military relations with countries the US has blackballed, the downsized former superpower aims to bring back the glory of its Soviet-era days when it played countries like chess pieces.[171]

Russian resurgence seemed to catch many by surprise, but the obvious conclusion by any open-eyed observer was that indeed, the Russian bear "was rising again." William Safire, in the *New York Times*, called it "Putin's 'Creeping Coup.'"[172] Another presciently proclaimed it "Emerging Shadows of the Hammer and Sickle."[173]

## "The Man Who Would Be Tsar"

The heart of national histories and the souls of nation states are being revealed in high definition as we hurtle toward the biblical demarcation of the last days of the end times. This is becoming glaringly true as the battle for *KING of the Mountain* nears the final conflict.

To gain proper perspective, we must step back to the turn of history's clock as we stepped into the third millennium AD. *NEWSWEEK* gave us a shockingly frank portrait of Vladimir Putin, revealing almost frighteningly the hard truth regarding "The Man Who Would Be Tsar," noting: "What the rise of Putin says about the Russian soul." Consider carefully…

> … he reveres the KGB, never resigned from the Communist Party, believes that snitches in the Soviet era were patriots and says a strong state is in Russia's "genetic code."

> Vladimir Putin's rise to the brink of the Russian presidency… has been so swift, and so unexpected, that Washington and the rest of the world have been caught flat-footed.[174]

Yet the West seemed to decide that nothing had changed. Nothing, however, could have been further from the truth. Putin's popularity soared. As *NEWSWEEK* so aptly stated, "He strikes just the right chords of nationalism, speaks to Russian pride and… backs up his words with action." "Putin is the Russian Everyman made good." He "never ran for office, and had never won a single vote." "He is like a leader of a street gang on whom you can rely." "Putin makes it clear that in his heart, he is comfortable with the use of force." "You have to hit first," he says, "and hit so hard that your opponent will not get to his feet." "Where else—and to what end—Putin might apply it in the future is what the world will soon find out."[175]

## DARK FORCES

The problem the world faces with Russia did not begin with Vladimir Putin. *TIME* put the matter in perspective as early as 1992. "The 20th century has dealt harshly with Russia: revolution, three wars, 60 million dead, a people enslaved by a 70-year experiment in ideology called *Communism*. Now Russia (in 1992) is in a critical juncture in its struggle to be reborn as a democracy." A *juncture* is an intersection in time, space or history where choices must be made and where destiny is determined. From Moscow, James Carney made clear for *TIME*'s readers the forces directing Russia's choices. He called them "The Dark Forces."[176]

> Whether the messenger is a top government official, a parliamentary leader, a member of an opposition party or an ordinary Russian with a gut instinct, the message is always the same: dark forces are at work devising a scheme to take power and install a dictatorship.[177]

The looming question presented in *TIME*'s cover story was—and still is—"CAN RUSSIA ESCAPE ITS PAST?" The invariable answer, borne on the broken wings of twenty more years of history, is a resounding "NO!" By

October, 2011, the *Los Angeles Times* sounded a global alarm… "Watch out for Putin and Russia." The conclusion: "Russia is entering rough waters, and the world will feel the turbulence."[178]

## BID TO DOMINATE THE WORLD

The troubling tale of increasing "turbulence" generated by Putin's Russia has been written on the trembling walls of history beginning with the turn of the third millennium. The Associated Press captured the drama in the headline, "Russia sees U.S. bid to dominate the world." Putin, the new acting president, unveiled Russia's new national security doctrine, "broadening the Kremlin's authority to use nuclear weapons and accusing the United States of trying to weaken Russia and become the world's dominant power."[179]

Viewpoint always sets the course of destiny. And it is a fascinating aspect of human psychology that we often see our own nefarious ways and intentions born out in the lives of others. We tend to project our own undisclosed and undesirable thoughts and intentions onto others so as to justify otherwise unjustifiable reactions. It was then of great interest when Russia's own paper, *PRAVDA*, carried the headline just eight years later— "USA believes Russia threatens its interests all over the world."[180] And of even greater interest was the bold lead-in to a troubling email message this author received from the UK earlier in 2008, bearing the words: "Russia's plans to invade and control the World."

A summary exploration of the dramatic developments between the years 2007 and 2012 reveals Russia's true objectives in pursuit of the elusive prize to be *KING of the Mountain*. In order to comprehend the greater panoply of Putin's purposes, it is necessary to rise above the two-dimensional into a multi-dimensional outlook, for indeed the craftiness of political chicanery, at nearly every juncture and on nearly every conceivable issue, exceeds in spades that which customarily meets the natural eye. The battle lines on this front are decidedly drawn. It is Putin vs. the Pope.

### COMMUNISM IS NOT DEAD… BUT SLEEPING

A massive resurrection is bringing about Russian resurgence. It appears that the "Bear" only went into hibernation with the dramatic "fall" of the Iron Curtain in 1989 and of the Soviet Union in 1991, led by so-called "democratic reformers" such as Mikhail Gorbachev and Boris Yeltsin. Consider with care the entry of Yeltsin in his *Midnight Diaries*, 2000.[181]

I was waiting for a new general to appear, unlike any other. Or rather, a general who was like the generals I read about in books when I was young. I was waiting… Time passed, and such a general appeared.

And soon after his arrival, it became obvious to our whole society how really courageous and highly professional our military people were. This 'general' was named Colonel Vladimir Putin.

The KGB has now gained the presidency as well as prime ministership of the rising "Bear." And the roar of the "Bear" can be heard across distant lands, even around the globe. But perhaps nowhere is the roar more clearly heard than in the ears of the papacy, as we shall see. Communism was thought dead, but is now rising as a global contender under mother Russia through the cunning of Colonel Vladimir Putin.

## MOSCOW'S REVIVING ARMS SALES

Hoping to revive its defense industry and recapture influence in the Middle East, North Africa and East Asia, Russia, by 2001, was strategically stepping up arms production and sales of weapons to foreign countries.

"Under Vladimir Putin, Moscow is attempting to reclaim the arms market that withered as Russia's military-industrial complex declined after the Soviet Union collapsed. China and India have been warmly wooed into Russia's conniving arms by massive arms sales. The balance have been dispersed to former "clients" of the Soviet Union to re-secure their allegiance to the resurrecting Russian empire… Algeria, Vietnam, Syria, Libya, yes, and especially Iran. These are countries, many of which are uniquely situated within the ambit of the prophet's warning, destined to invade Israel in "the latter days" (Ezek. 38-39).[182]

## MILITARY TOMBS TOUTED

Why, you might reasonably inquire, have military tombs become a high priority to Putin? Yet they are, and a strategic time-table has been set, as reported by the Russian paper *ITAR TASS*.[183]

"All military tombs in Russia will be put in order by 2015, the commander of the Russian Armed Forces Logistic Service and Deputy Defense Minister, General Vladimir Isakov, told reporters." But why should military tombs be of strategic import when the country still languishes in economic doldrums? And why the seemingly strategic date of 2015? Colonel Putin is both cunning and consummately dedicated to Russian dominion, and that global vision is directly connected to unsurpassed military dominance and national vision of military power and pride. While her economic power is fueled by petrol, Russia's "economy" of people motivation is rooted in military power and pride, which must be revived at all costs. Furthermore, the world should take serious notice of Putin's timetable. The year 2015 was not idly chosen by "the man who would be Tsar."

## RESURGENT RUSSIA SEES OIL AS A WEAPON

"A resurgent Russia has taken steps that some analysts consider using oil as a weapon. The question that experts and government officials ask is how the West should respond." Using oil as a political weapon "is a banal way to deal with dissenting countries Russia would like to keep in its orbit of influence…." The tone of relationship with the West, however, has shifted "from friendship to adversary."[184]

It is indeed fascinating that at this precise moment of history, Russia should have become the premier exporter of oil and gas around the globe.[185] Her entire economy and power is ultimately predicated on petrol. When the price of oil rises, Russia's economy is flush with cash for military expansion and global influence. As the price wanes or oil reserves deplete, Russia becomes existentially threatened. And when a bear, mothering her political cubs, feels threatened, the world of mother bear should take heed. This concern has driven Russia to further petroleum and gas alliances to sustain the unrestrainable drive for global domination.

Headlines tell the tale of strategic intent. The trend is incontrovertible.

### Gazprom plans to become global energy leader

Russia's energy giant Gazprom said it plans to become the world's largest energy company, the largest in the 21st century.[186]

### Russia looks for clout in pipeline talks

Russian President Vladimir Putin pushed for the construction of a web of pipelines that would cement Europe's dependence on Russia's energy supplies.[187]

### OPEC plans closer links with Russia to control half of the world's oil supplies

Closer ties between OPEC, whose 13 member states produce 40 percent of the world's oil supply, and Russia, will claim consumer countries, giving immense control over global prices.[188]

### Russian pipeline tightens grip on West's gas supply from Caspian

Russia took another step toward dominating the European energy market… to build a huge natural gas pipeline along the Caspian Sea. "Absolutely not in Europe's interest… very bad news for Europe."[189]

## RELIGION AND THE RISE OF RUSSIA

Few who strive for *KING of the Mountain* believe such dominion can be achieved without a religious component, however disingenuous it may be. And Putin's Russia is no exception. For Vladimir Putin, an emerging politically-motivated religious syncretism gives an entirely new perspective on the "sacred," except for all of the past and present global political and religious power-brokers who have similarly set their course to become *KING of the Mountain*. Religion is recognized as an inescapable requirement for any and all comers to realistic global conquest. For Putin's Russia, the ploy is threefold.

### THE MERGING OF CHURCH and STATE

The seventh millennium of human history burst upon a rapidly changing world, revealing the emergence of religious systems and renewed drawing to the fundamentals of ancient sacred practices. Russia, surprisingly, was no exception.

*The Associated Press* captured one of the most significant developments linking Russia's rise to Russia's religious roots that the Soviet era had sought to sever. The headline heralded: "Orthodox church edges closer to state."[190] "Orthodoxy, the bedrock of Russian society for centuries, suffered massively" during the 70 dark years of Soviet repression. "It is again the country's dominant faith, and while its leadership is officially apolitical, it [the Orthodox Church] has cultivated ties with today's Kremlin." "The church's pro-Russian message is welcome at a time when nationalist sentiment is rising...." "Many Russians have turned to Orthodoxy to fill the ideological vacuum left in the 1991 collapse of the Soviet Union." Orthodoxy has become the political step-stool to absolute power for Vladimir Putin.

> Even the purists aren't questioning why Russia's acting president attended church in the first place, despite his 15 years with the Soviet KGB, which mercilessly repressed religion and its followers for decades.

> Putin's perceived piety... reflects the increasingly viable role of the Orthodox Church in Russian politics—and in re-forging Russia's long-lost national identity.

> Few Russians will forget the image of the Orthodox Patriarch Alexy II, in his gold-and-white cape, presiding over Boris Yeltsin as he resigned and handed over Russia's helm to Putin in a Kremlin ceremony December 31, 1999.

## THE COURTING OF ISLAM

As the drama of Russia's rise unfolds before a startled Pope and the West, perhaps no development has been more obviously intentional in Putin's pursuit of global dominance than his unprecedented progress in choreographing the Islamic world into the Russian geopolitical camp. Neither time nor space allow us here to trace the trajectory and amazing geopolitical transformation that has quickly re-modeled the non-western world as we have known it for a century past. However, poignant headlines give us a window through which then astounding events can be quickly viewed.

Headline: ***Russia Courts the Muslim World***[191]

Vladimir Putin was the first head of a non-Muslim majority state to speak at the Organization of the Islamic Conference, a gathering of 57 Muslim states, in October 2003. That was a political and diplomatic feat...." "Putin stressed that 15% of the total population of the Russian Federation are Muslim, and that all the inhabitants of eight of the 21 autonomous republics are Muslim...."

Since then, Putin and other Russian leaders, including the foreign minister, Sergei Lavrov, claim Russia 'is, to some extent, part of the Muslim world.'

So Russia now claims to have privileged political relationship with the Arab and Muslim world and believes that... it has a historic vocation as a mediator between the western and Muslim worlds.

The purpose in seeking special ties with the Arab and Muslim world is related to Russia's foreign policy aim to 'reinforce multipolarity in the world'—to develop poles of resistance to US hegemony and unilateralism... taking advantage of the hostility to US foreign policy in the Arab and Muslim world.

The on-the-ground translation of these facts is twofold. First—Russia is "using" the Islamic world to buttress her own final and ultimate thrust for world domination. Second—the Muslim world is "using" Russia as a political and military power to advance the ultimate and final bid of Islam to rule the world under a global caliphate. Mark well, in this regard, the following report from *Moscow News* (moscnews.com).

Headline: ***Putin Calls Russia Defender of Islamic World***

In the words of Vladimir Putin, "Russia is the most reliable partner of the Islamic world and most faithful defender of its interests."

Russia has always been the most faithful, reliable and consistent defender of the interests of the Islamic world. [Russia is] one of the main pillars of the Islamic world in the struggle for rights (of Islamic states) in the international arena…

## THE COURTING OF ISRAEL

Historically, there has been little love lost in the relationship of Russia to either Israel in general or the Jews in particular. The vast exodus of Jews (persecuted for decades in the recurring Russia pogroms) at the collapse of the Soviet Union in 1991, clearly revealed no genuine affection or even tolerance in the womb of Mother Russia for the descendants of Isaac. Only the descendants of Ishmael were to be favored.

It was indeed a shock to Israeli sensibilities, then, that *ynetnews.com* should bear the headline June 25, 2012:

*Putin: Russia Wants Peace for Israel*[192]

Putin declared he wanted to boost "strategic ties" between the two countries, noting that Russia "has a national interest in guaranteeing peace and tranquility for Israel." Of notable interest, however, is that no such "peaceful" overtures were deemed desirable until a series of disclosures that Israel had made massive gas and oil discoveries rendering Israel free of dependence upon Russian gas and oil, thus also freeing Israel to export energy to many of Russia's "secure" markets throughout Europe.

Yet Putin's ingratiating religious courting of Israel took on unexpected proportions June 26, 2012, with this *Jerusalem Post* headline:

*Putin wishes us a rebuilt Temple.*[193]

Putin, in visiting the *Kotel* or Wailing Wall, was told of its importance and of the Temple that had been destroyed. Putin responded: "… this is exactly for what I came here, to pray that the Temple will be rebuilt. I wish that all your prayers be answered." Some might be tempted to ask… "Did Mr. Putin, as "Defender of the Islamic World," really hope for or expect Israel's prayers to be answered by unequivocally supporting Muslim violent objection to even a single Jew praying on the Temple Mount?

Is Putin sincere, or is he seeking to seduce Israel into a false sense of peace and security, only to be betrayed when the pivotal moment of opportunity comes? Since the majority of prophetic analysts seem secure in identifying Russia as the infamous Gog in the prophesied battle of Gog and Magog, drawing Russia's Islamic clientele into a calamitous confrontation with Israel "in the latter days," why the solicitous words of "the man who would be Tsar" at this unique moment in global developments? Is he, by means of an Islamic confederation, setting the stage to "take a spoil" as prophesied by Ezekiel, thus luring Israel into unjustified complacency? It would behoove us all to reacquaint ourselves and our leaders with the God of Abraham, Isaac and Jacob's viewpoint on these soon-forthcoming events recorded in Ezekiel 38 and 39.

**COURTING OF THE VATICAN**

As the Russian Orthodox Church unites with Putin's program for nationalistic resurrection of the Russian bear, historic tensions with the Vatican are becoming prominent, even palpable. However, for political purposes, Putin has made historical overtures toward the papacy while the Pope has made historical overtures to mend the thousand-year "Great Schism" between western Catholicism and Russian Orthodoxy. Each, in turn, seeks the favor deemed essential to consolidate political and religious power as the final confrontation for conquest as *KING of the Mountain* draws near. In order to comprehend the historical gravity of the conflict between the Russian bear and the Pope, we must explore the "myth" of *The Third Rome*.

## "THE THIRD ROME"

"Despite criticism from abroad, [Russian] Parliament's lower house overwhelmingly adopted a bill that would curb the influx of religious organizations that would proselytize in Russia," reported *The Associated Press*. The bill "enshrines Russia's Orthodox Church as the country's pre-eminent religion…." Supporters of the bill said, "Russia needs to protect itself from foreign sects and cults which have been coming in since the 1991 breakup of the Soviet Union." "The law protects the traditional Russian religion, Orthodoxy, so we believe it undoubtedly must be passed." "But critics say the Orthodox Church also is backing the measure as a way to prevent other Christians, such as Catholics and Protestants, from operating freely in Russia." The sheer magnitude of the measure, in the eyes of Russian leadership, was revealed in the Duma (lower house) voting 385:6 in favor of the bill and in the upper house, 137:0 for approval.[194] Such a bill may baffle the western world, particularly since the legislation singled out "Islam, Judaism and Buddhism" for "respect," (while pointedly rejecting Protestantism, but more particularly Catholicism), as proper for Russian promise and purpose. This can only be meaningfully understood in the context of what historians refer to as "the myth" of *The Third Rome*.

When what many may view as "myth" becomes, whether consciously or unconsciously, the words and matrix through which much of life and the very meaning of existence and purpose is interpreted, the facts and history underlying the so-called "myth" take on a defining and directive life of their own, leading to a destiny otherwise incomprehensible to the outside world. And so it is with the "myth" of *The Third Rome*. Indeed, the post-Soviet resurrection of Putin's Russia as well as the past 1000 years of Russian history, both religious and political, suddenly emerge into the sunlight, sweeping away the shadows that once obscured the role of Russia in these end times as we approach the final battle for *KING of the Mountain*. Inevitably, viewpoint determines destiny.

We now enter the broader Russian mind through the matrix of religious history which ultimately merged into a powerful partnership with the political for their respective mutual protection and pursuit of power.

Universal history, at least from a biblical viewpoint, was revealed through the Hebrew prophet Daniel as a succession of four great empires represented by the parts of the colossus in Nebuchadnezzar's troubling dream (Daniel 2, as further clarified in Daniel 7). These empires have been traditionally identified as Babylon, Persia, Greece and Rome. For much of the developing period of the Christian faith (a conviction that remains to the present day), Rome represented the ultimate kingdom of the Anti-Christ that would oppose the true Messianic kingdom to be ushered in by the Second Coming of Christ. Yet within Rome itself (with the transfer of title of "Pontifex Maximus" from Caesar to the Bishop of Rome), the developing papal-powered Rome was seen to be the present-day manifestation of the kingdom of God on earth through the "VICAR of Christ," the Pope. These two views had no overlap, but were (and are today) mutually exclusive. They cannot both be true.

History, however, has an interesting way of re-defining otherwise defining viewpoints. And so it is with the alleged "myth" of *The Third Rome*. We must therefore unfold the mystery of the "myth." After the union of Christianity and imperial Rome, consummated by Constantine the Great, the conception of a Roman-Christian empire was overthrown by the barbarians, and not restored until 800AD, with the coronation of Charlemagne...."[195]

With the dramatic weakening of the Rome of the West, Constantine built Constantinople in what is now Turkey, shifting the religious/spiritual weight and center of "Rome" to Byzantium. The primary purpose was to purify the Church which had become overtaken by a perceived ungodly merger of church and state in the form of "Caesar-papism." The very concept of the investiture of secular and spiritual power in the "Pontifex Maximus," (the Bishop of Rome—Pope who would reign supreme over what was deemed to be an apostasizing church), was considered anathema, thus the Rome of the East was translated into a "New Rome"—Constantinople.

The Eastern and Western Churches were increasingly estranged over doctrinal, theological and linguistic issues. There were serious disputes between Rome and Constantinople about Rome's assertion of papal primacy. "In 1054 Pope Leo IX and the patriarch of Constantinople, Michael Cerularius excommunicated each other. The event marked the final break between Eastern Orthodoxy and Roman Catholicism and came to be known as the Great Schism. The rift later widened and the churches have remained separate...." "After the schism, the Russian Orthodox Church gradually gathered strength." "The Russian state [over several centuries] grew more and more powerful and so did the Russian Orthodox Church," all as recorded by the *Russian Times*.[196] Thus the year 1054AD shook the world, separating Russia forever from the Western Christian world.

The term *Third Rome* refers to the doctrine that Russia, more specifically, Moscow, succeeded Rome and Byzantium Rome (Constantinople) as the ultimate center of true Christianity and of the "Roman Empire." The seeds of the concept were actually planted by Constantine when, upon moving the capital of the empire from Rome to Constantinople, he renamed the small town "New Rome," only later to be called "Constantinople." "Within decades after the capture of Constantinople by Mehmed II of the Ottoman Empire in 1453, some were nominating Moscow as the 'Third Rome,' or the 'New Rome.'"[197]

*Third Rome* thinking served to elevate Russia's conception of its place within the Orthodox Christian world, indeed within the entire world. So closely linked was Russia's identity of soul within the concept of Third Rome, that "in the 1510's Joseph of Volok, while claiming that the Orthodox Tsar is in power like unto God, asserted that any wavering from Orthodoxy would lead to the fall of Russia."[198]

It all began as somewhat of an apocalyptic moniker. Rome had fallen to Catholicism, Constantinople had fallen to the Muslims, and Moscow saw itself as the last stand against the heretics—both Muslims and Catholics. And so *The Third Rome* has become Moscow's "most compelling and enigmatic epithet." But it remains yet to be seen the vast impact for these end times, in "the latter days," of such a seemingly small seed planted centuries long past. The fruit of that seed, which has germinated for nearly a thousand years, is now ripe and ready to be tasted by an unsuspecting world, whose political and spiritual taste buds have been unprepared for the coming assault on global senses, particularly in the West. Perhaps only Pope John Paul II saw the conflict to come, unwittingly unleashing, under the aegis of Russian democracy, a resurrected *Third Rome* ready to assert its global rule as *KING of the Mountain*.

## TRANSLATION OF EMPIRE

The persistent mystery of "Rome" has assumed a "metaphysical reality" superseding geographical, political or cultural reality.[199] In a very real way in the historical imagination, Rome took on the aura of a Gentile surrogate for Jerusalem. It was "Rome," metaphysically imaged, that would largely define and determine the direction and destiny of the Gentile world, with the exception of Islam. For this reason, the shift of Christian centers from Rome to Constantinople effectively shifted the spiritual and political implications of "Rome" to Constantinople, and upon the fall of Constantinople, to Moscow. These shifts were of no mean consequence, both politically and spiritually, in the march of history to this pivotal moment. It has been referred to as the doctrine of *translation imperii* or "translation of empire."[200]

Rome's greatness, according to Virgil's *Aeneid*, was not only grounded on its political might. It was "the city of the gods." The Romans believed the city would never perish; hence it was "The Eternal City." Because it was "eternal," Rome was also deemed "universal," destined to "supersede the disorderly competition between nations and establish world peace."[201] This was the underlying conceptual force of the *Pax Romana*, and according to ancient Roman religion, the aim of the existence of the whole world. This would culminate in universal peace in the final phase of world history under a global "Roman" rule.

From where, however, does the very idea of Moscow as the *Third Rome* find its original nexus? That answer requires a journey back into the first half of the sixteenth century to meet an obscure Russian monk who wrote a series of letters to the grand prince of Moscow, Vassily, and to Ivan IV (Ivan the Terrible). In these letters, the monk, Filofei, explained that Rome had deviated from the true faith, adopting heresy. Rome, according to Filofei, had been "imprisoned by the devil." Thereafter, Constantinople, the second "Rome," had fallen both from doctrinal purity and by conquest of the Moslems. The world would do well to solemnly consider the echoing import of Filofei's crucial words to this pivotal moment in history, for their lingering gravity is now driving destiny.

> I would like to say a few words about the existing Orthodox empire of our most illustrious, exalted ruler. He is the only emperor in all the earth over the Christians, the governor of the holy, divine throne of the holy, ecumenical, apostolic church which in place of the churches of Rome and Constantinople is in the city of Moscow, protected by God. It alone shines over all the earth more radiantly than the sun. For know well, those who love Christ and those who

love God, that all Christian empires will perish and give way to the one kingdom of our ruler, in accord with the books of the prophet, which is the Russian empire. For two Romes have fallen, but the third stands, and there will never be a fourth.[202]

## THE GLOBAL IMPLICATIONS

The idea that Moscow is the Third Rome did not come out of the blue. The concept had already been developed by other Russian authors. It had a well-defined meaning both in Russia and in the wider Christian world. But it had immense implications, as well, both for Russia and the wider world. Woven increasingly, generation after generation, through Russian culture and consciousness was the conviction that Moscow had become the eternal "Rome" for the world.

It should take little imagination, then, to comprehend the driving, directive force such a deep-seated belief would bear upon the political role and destiny of Russia, only later to be seen as "the bear." When the "bear" roars, the world (to the subconscious mind of the Russian people) must listen. But to a man such as Vladimir Putin, who sees himself as the virtual incarnation of the historical Russian spirit and destiny, it becomes the mantel of personal and collective "divine" ordination to bring the declared role of Holy Mother Russia to her culmination as reigning *KING of the Mountain* in this closing hour of mankind's dominion on earth.

## THE GLOBAL RELIGIOUS IMPLICATIONS

It is profoundly challenging to distill fifteen hundred years of Russia's political and religious history so as to understand the vast implications for that which now is and will soon be confronting the peoples of this planet. Entanglement in excessive details would divert from our clear purpose. Much has been written concerning the concept of *Third Rome*, and the reader is directed to that body of material for further in-depth research.

It is fascinating that, "at the time of Prince Ivan III, Russian sources called their own nation the *New Israel*. Although the idea of Russia as the New Israel never became so popular or as influential as the idea of the *Third Rome*, nevertheless it actually never faded away. And even much later, Moscow was sometimes called the *New Jerusalem*.[203] One only modestly familiar with history might well see, then, the inherent conflict thus imposed by such belief in Russia's relationship with upstart America, in the West, whose Puritan and Pilgrim founders saw her also as a "New Israel," a Gentile "Promised Land," a vision that to this day remains the subconscious foundation of America's rapid rise to power and pervasive hope-filled promise to the world. Is it Russia's envy, deep-seated religious enterprise, or both that undergirds her seeming unrestrainable urge to dominate the West and oppose all that is "America?" After all, in the mind and heart of Putin's Russia, Russia has "real" roots. With such seeming overtly contrary and competing calls on national destiny, from Putin's view, can these powers co-exist on the near edge of the Second Coming of Christ?

## THE SAVIOR OF THE WORLD

But there remains yet another, perhaps stronger motivating force propelling Russia in this pivotal moment. In the last quarter of the nineteenth century, "Third Rome" came to be identified with the idea of a "Russian mission." One of the chief characteristics of the *Third Rome* concept is its absolute supremacy. Therefore, "Moscow as the newest Rome is above other countries. And as the supreme state, Russia is the holy Russia." Thus, Russia, as Third Rome, is "an instrument of God chosen by him for the fulfillment of his aims." For as the monk Filofei wrote, "all Christian realms will come to an end and will unite into the one single realm of our sovereign."[204]

This "burden of the Third Rome" is revealed in "the long tradition of Russian messianism which is rejuvenated after every cyclical decline of Russian political authority." For this reason, "modern All-Russian nationalism has become a new and dangerous chimera of economically and politically frustrated Russians."[205] The preview of the book *Russia's Rome: Imperial Visions, Messianic Dreams*, notes: "… the myth of Russia or the 'Third Rome' was resurrected to create a Rome-based discourse of Russian national identity that endured even as the empire of the tsars (Russian Caesars) declined and fell and a new state replaced it"[206]

"The doctrine of the Third Rome came to justify Russian imperial ambitions and to legitimize the idea that it was Russia's destiny to save and rule the world."[207] The fear of Russia's resurrecting "messianic imperialism"[208] not only pervades and provokes the West, but also strikes deeply into papal and Vatican ambitions in this final historical moment when history and prophecy converge in the battle for *KING of the Mountain*.

## THE BEAR VS. THE POPE

It is unfortunate that such a lengthy historical background was required to lay a proper foundation for comprehension of the brewing conflict between the Russian "bear" and the papacy as seated in the Vatican, but it could not be avoided. The late Pope John Paul II made the case.

"Everything Must Change!" That was the opening salvo of one of the most profound history-revealing books of our time… perhaps of all time... *THE KEYS OF THIS BLOOD*. Malachi Martin, a Vatican insider and author of the provocative work, made clear his piercing analysis in a single subtitle: "Pope John Paul II versus Russia and the West for control of the New World Order."[209]

"On October 14, 1978," observed Malachi, "a new era began for the Roman Catholic Church [Western catholicism] and its nearly one billion adherents around the world. And with it, the curtains were raised on the first act of the global competition that would end and a thousand years of history as completely as if a nuclear war had been fought. A drama that would leave no regions or nations or individuals as they had been before." On that momentous day, the cardinals of the Roman Catholic Church assembled in the Vatican from around the world and elected the 264th Pope of the Roman Catholic Church, Cardinal Karol Wojtyla of Krakow Poland, who adopted the name John Paul II.

John Paul II spoke on that day as to how he viewed human history: "The entire history of man is in fact persuaded by a tremendous struggle against the force of evil in the world...." He announced that day his overarching new principle of religion: for all Christians, yes, but for all mankind as well. "This Pope commits himself to Mary.... He commits the Roman Church to her as the token and principle of all the churches in the world in their universal unity" No pope had ever before spoken of such a "universal unity" of all churches.[210] But where would it lead? In what broader geopolitical context was it to be understood?

## THE MILLENNIUM ENDGAME

We get our first clue as Malachi Martin introduces the "Grand Design" of Pope John Paul II in his opening pages through a speech given by the pope-to-be on a visit to America in her bicentennial in 1976. Martin describes it as "one of the most prophetic speeches ever given."

> "We are now standing in the face of the greatest historical confrontation humanity has gone through." "... a test of two thousand years of culture and Christian civilization...." But he chided his listeners—"wide circles of American society and wide circles of the Christian community do not realize this fully...."[211]

"No one," noted Malachi Martin, "had any idea that he [the pope-to-be] was pointing to a competition he already saw on the horizon: a competition between the world's only three internationally-based power structures for truly global hegemony." "It is not too much to say, in fact, that the chosen purpose of John Paul's pontificate—the engine that drives his papal grand policy and that determines his day-to-day, year-by-year strategies—is to be victor in that competition."[212] It is, and was, a supreme competition to become *KING of the Mountain* in history's consummating contest for religious and geopolitical supremacy.

These consummate contenders as seen through the eyes of John Paul II are and were: (1) The Roman Catholic Church under its supreme leader, the Pope; (2) The Soviet Union, now having metamorphosized into the Russian Federation (now under its supreme "Tsar" or virtual Caesar—Vladimir Putin); and (3) An agglomeration of western democratic-capitalistic nations unified by Internationalists and Transnationalists dedicated to dissolving nation states—"the Western democratic alliance." As Malachi Martin noted: "There is one great similarity shared by all three of these geopolitical contenders. Each has in mind a particular grand design for one world governance."[213] Indeed, so definitive is the cleavage and distinction among the three that each realizes only one of them can ultimately be the victor in the millennium endgame.

Discussion of the arch competitors for a "New World Order" is not our purpose in this chapter and will therefore be reserved for more detailed exploration. For now, we must return to *The Third Rome*.

## THIRD ROME vs. FIRST ROME

The concept of Russia as the *Third Rome* has been woven so thoroughly and tightly into the fabric of Russian life, thinking, culture, religion and politics as to be virtually inextricable. In a sense, whether consciously or unconsciously, it defines what it means to be Russian. This the world can little comprehend, either in concept or consequence. But it is nevertheless real, circumscribing the world of politics and religion into a combined Russian state denominated within the Russian mind as "Holy Russia," regardless of its factual "holiness" of life.

It is this "nationalistic" view of messianism as Russian rule over others that is deeply rooted in the concept "Moscow, the Third Rome." It is also related to the "universalist" idea of redemption through Russian suffering, making Russia the spiritually and geopolitically redemptive state to ultimately rule the world as God's ultimate, end-time gift to mankind. If we look closely, we see a virtually identical vision for global rule expressed through fifteen hundred years of the Roman Catholic Church versus the Russian Orthodox Church. Each deems itself the sole and pure representative of Christianity, and thus mutually exclusive and irreconcilable.

No mistake was made when it was written: "Moscow became the third (and last) Rome. Along with the title *tsar* (caesar) and the claim that Orthodox Russia was the only remaining true Christian state, the doctrine of the *Third Rome* came to justify Russian imperial ambitions and to legitimize the idea that it was Russia's destiny to save the world."[214] We do well to remember the classic and crucial quote by Filofei fifteen centuries ago, a viewpoint not missed by the papacy of the Roman Catholic Church in this culminating moment when the *KING of the Mountain* shall be determined.

> So be aware of God and Christ, that all Christian empires have come to an end and are gathered together in the singular empire of our sovereign in accordance to the books of prophecy, and this is the Russian empire: because two Romes have fallen, and a third stands, and a fourth there shall not be.[215]

## POPE vs. PATRIARCH

The *Great Schism* between Roman Catholicism in the West and Constantine's "Rome" of the East—Constantinople—one thousand years ago resulted, in effect, in two "popes," one to rule each of the two competing "Christian" religious empires. That schism was so great that it continues to this troubling and tenuous moment of man's experience on earth. And it will soon most likely have an unexpected effect upon world affairs and destiny.

When Constantinople fell to the Turks, the Muscovites laid claim to be the final bosom of genuine Christian faith, hence, the *Third Rome*. All others were deemed to be heretics or apostates. For this reason, a new "pope" was deemed necessary to oversee the *Third Rome*, the first of which was anointed in 1589, as "Patriarch" of the Russian Orthodox Church. The Patriarch of the Russian Orthodoxy and Pope of western Catholicism were thus set, both by position and conviction, in direct—even notorious— opposition to one another. How would either gain historical ascendancy to fulfill their claimed mandate to govern among men across the seven seas and seven continents?

Furthermore, another important aspect of *Third Rome* was a new "eschatological dimension."[216] Since eschatology is the study, teaching and doctrine regarding the final hours of history known as "the end times," Moscow's role representing all of Russia and Russian Orthodoxy assumed proportions vastly more significant than understood by most historians and prognosticators, including the various presidents and prime ministers of the nations. Moscow was now "not only the most important city but it was chosen by God and in a way set apart from other places on earth. Moscow has a special religious function. It is in some ways closer to God. But that is not all. According to Filofei, Moscow is the Third Rome and 'the third stands, and there will never be a fourth.' Moscow is the last Rome...

the center of history and therefore its fulfillment. This means that Russia had to preserve its rich store of faith in purity in the last phase before the end of the world."[217]

Are we now living in that "last phase before the end of the world" as we know it? That is not a question to be lightly or cavalierly brushed aside. Perception is a person's or power's reality. It drives destiny.

According to Florovsky, this theological concept of history marching to its soon end was deeply rooted. In other words, "the world is approaching its end. The world exists only while Moscow exists. And Moscow exists only while it is the center of the Christian [Orthodox] world. If Moscow perishes or ceases to be this center, then it is the end of the world."[218] Such a vision woven tightly into the fabric of a pervasive Russian "exceptionalism" creates an inevitable, yet almost incomprehensible, conflict of immense proportions between the Pope of western Catholicism and the Patriarch of Russian Orthodoxy.

Yet the question is asked, "Will the 'Third Rome' Reunite With the 'First Rome'?"[219] Not surprisingly, Pope Benedict XVI embarked upon just such a mission as part of the continuation of John Paul II's monumental effort to bring all estranged branches of Christendom together with all other world religions under the protective global wings of the "Mother Church"... Roman Catholicism. On September 18, 2009, at the Pope's summer palace thirty miles outside Rome, a Russian Orthodox Archbishop, Hilarion Alfyev, met with Benedict XVI for almost two hours. It is said that this meeting may have marked a turning point in relations between the 'Third Rome' (Moscow) and the 'First Rome' (Rome) which have been divided since 1054 AD. The Russian Archbishop also met with Cardinal Walter Kasper, who suggested a future meeting in a "neutral" place. Meanwhile, the influence of the Russian Orthodox Church, in Russia itself, is growing under its new Patriarch Kirill of Moscow, arousing opposition from the old KGB forces. As one observer noted: "What is occurring... may have ramifications not only for the overcoming of the 'Great Schism,' but also for the cultural religious and political future of Russia, and of Europe as a whole."[220]

The historical, seemingly irreconcilable differences between *First Rome* and *Third Rome*, however, remain. *First Rome* remains in "apostasy" in the view of *Third Rome*. Furthermore, Filofei's famous prophecy remains... that Moscow, the *Third Rome*, is the last and final "Rome" to usher in the end of the age and the Second Coming of Jesus Christ as Messiah.

The complications of such a reconciliation, bringing *Third Rome* (Russia) back under the mothering wings of *First Rome*, loom larger than life in view of the almost incestuous relationship between the Russian

Orthodox Church and the Kremlin each for their respective benefit, the religious authenticating the political, and the political increasing the power, perks and position of the patriarchy. Although such a "papal-Caesar" relationship is generally denied, it nevertheless remains a vital, undergirding and operative force to be reckoned with in the battle for *KING of the Mountain*.

In contrast, the Pope of the *First Rome* has no such direct symbiotic relationship with a single political power. The Vatican, as a self-authenticated political state claiming ultimate global religious authority, must rely upon the political obeisance of the world's nation states to maintain and increase its dominion. This, in effect, also undergirds the choreography of the western world against the long-perceived, underlying historical thrust of Russia for global dominion as the ultimate "savior of the world." This historic and growing tension, given the pervasive sense that history is rapidly becoming a mere congruency and co-extension of biblical prophecy, is creating a disconcerting sense of urgency among the contestants to bring matters to a conclusive head because "time is short." We therefore conclude this fascinating exploration with a reversal of title. We shift from "The Bear vs. The Pope," to "The Pope vs. The Bear."

## THE POPE VS. THE BEAR

We have seen the long-persistent view over fifteen centuries of the Pope or papacy as a series of "Absolute Monarchs."[221] The word *absolute* means "absolute." An *absolute monarch* brooks no opposition. In view of nearly fifteen centuries of an opposing Third Rome, it takes little imagination to comprehend or grasp the potential magnitude of the enduring conflict between First Rome and Third Rome, if in fact we are approaching the culmination of this age as envisioned by a host of biblical prophets. No amount of airbrushing the sharp edges of the conflict by notions of political correct "tolerance," multiculturalism or religious pluralism will be efficacious to resolve the unresolvable claims of two religious/political powers claiming absolute global dominion and authority, each purporting to be "saviors of the world."

As we conclude our troubling trek through the thick underbrush of this historical conflict, we return briefly to a synopsis of the implications of *Third Rome* thinking, culminating with a striking view from the Vatican.

### THE ROOT OF THE CONTEST

Russian poets, Dimitri Merezhkovski and Viacheslav Ivanov, gave interpretive expression to the Russian mind and heart of the meaning of "Third Rome" early in the twentieth century. The former believed "Third

Rome" to be "part of a vain Muscovite dream of universal caesaro-papism," ending with "the emergence of a new Christian consciousness." The latter saw "Third Rome" as a symbol of Russia's mission "to unite mankind in Christian brotherhood, in a 'Rome of the spirit.' Nikolai Berdiaev identified "Third Rome" as an essential Russian messianism... that differentiated Russian people from all others and informed its world-historical mission." With the advent of the first history of the idea of "Third Rome" in 1914 just preceding the Bolshevik Revolution, I. Kirillov framed "Third Rome" as "organically embedded in the Russian mind" and that it now represented "a fundamental shift in the mentality of the Russian people that marked a new era in Russian history." He was convinced that "Third Rome" now "reflected the fact that the Russian nation had come to self-consciousness and assumed its world-historical mission as the divinely-chosen guardian of Orthodox [true] Christianity."[222]

*Third Rome* doctrine became a standard element in textbooks of Russian history. It might be said, *It was the leaven baked in Russian bread.* It permeated all things "Russian," and became "a synonym for Muscovite Russia." With the advent of Communism, then, "Third Rome" thinking catapulted the inbred concept into unexpected new and even explosive relevance. Berdiaev, who was expelled from the Soviet Union in 1923, explained that "Third Rome" was "the fundamental element in 'Russian religious psychology'," and "was the primary force behind Bolshevism." "The ancient Russian messianic idea goes on living," he said, "in the deep layers of the Russian people," and "rises out of the collective unconsciousness of the people's life...." Internationalist Communism, he concluded, was actually a "transmogrified 'Russian messianism'."[223]

For many observers of the expansionistic endeavors of the Soviet Union in its global dominion of Communism, it became understood that this was merely a reflection of the long-time Russian aspiration to be not only *Third Rome* but final and last "Rome." By the 1950's, Ukrainian scholars argued "that every moment in Russian history was informed by the 'messianic' doctrine of 'Third Rome'." "Third Rome remains alive and well today."[224]

## THE RESPONSE OF THE PAPACY

Germany's Chancellor, Helmut Kohl, made clear his view of Third Rome in 1984. He explained, as reported in *The New York Times*, that the Russian "drive for expansion" and the "belief that Mother Russia will bring salvation to the world" could be traced directly to the concept of "Moscow as the Third Rome...."[225]

This driving blend of "messianic" calling, coupling religion and political power in seamless connection with Russian culture as the *raison d'être* of the Russian people, did not escape the ever-watchful gaze of the Papacy of *First Rome*, that was as much concerned about political threats to papal power as it was to religious competition. "In the sixteenth century, the Papacy and Hapsburgs attempted to gain control over the Russians by denying the sovereignty of both their church and state. They insisted that only the Catholic Church and its secular arm, the Holy Roman Empire, were truly sovereign entities. In response, the Muscovites claimed that their realm was itself an empire, in fact *the* empire—the *Third Rome*. Armed with this official ideology, the Russians founded the patriarchate and crowned their grand prince 'tsar,' in effect creating their own Pope and Emperor."[226] The proverbial "line in the sand had been drawn for all remaining history.

Four centuries later, the contest had become crystal clear for John Paul II. As difficult as it may be with the rapid apostasization of the western world, as Pope he could finesse the West to preserve the power of *First Rome* by facilitating the growing globalism while diminishing Russia's influence through the demise of the Soviet Union as the engine driving global conquest through Communism. In the West, the European Union and America, the Pope would have to battle the assault of secularism as a major regional force.[227] But Russia, then expressed in the Soviet Union, was a much different and more threatening problem, for it represented through the very concept of *Third Rome* quest for global caesaro-papistic dominion. Who would be the remaining gladiator in Rome's battle for *KING of the Mountain*?

Unfortunately for John Paul II, fate pre-empted faith, and the time-table of destiny was determined. The "Third Secret" of the mysterious Fatima vision in 1917, a "prophetic" ultimatum, could neither be evaded nor avoided. It was a fateful timetable in which "Russia is the ratchet."[228] "That message predicts that a catastrophic change will shortly shatter any plans or designs that men may have established."[229]

John Paul II was a Pole, and the Poles had, for centuries "identified their national politics with the geo-religion of Roman Catholicism" and its two inextricably linked elements: the universalism of the Roman Pontiff, and the universal queenship of Mary, the Mother of Jesus." For John Paul II, Mary was a virtual "master"… "political reality, geopolitical reality." Since the Fatima message made clear that "World peace or world catastrophe was described in terms of Mary and of Russia," to John Paul's mind, "reform of his Roman Catholic institution was impossible outside the Fatima framework of events—as was world peace." John Paul "expected the beginning of the Fatima event to start where the millennium endgame started: in the area of Central and Eastern Europe," the very areas over which the Soviet Union (Russia) had sway in carrying out its Third Rome destiny.[230]

At least for geopolitical purposes, Mary was the master of global destiny in the eyes of the Pontiff. "Two-thirds plus one of the Vatican Conclave gave the world a Slavic Pope anointed under the seal of the human Mother of God." Not only did he dedicate his Polish homeland to Mary, but Russia in particular, animated by "belief in the geopolitical action and power of Mary as Queen of the world."[231] Marian devotion, he believed, would direct and determine destiny.

The geopolitical picture has been persuasively painted. Mary would become cover in the contest for papal supremacy and victory of *First Rome* over *Third Rome*, indeed over all comers. Karol Wojtyla, known to the world as Pope John Paul II, was "formed in the womb of Poland's proud and terrible history." A "symbiosis of religious devotion" developed between Poland's Cardinal Stefan Wyszynski and his protégé, Father Karol Wojtyla, leading to a unique agreement about destiny and "the geopolitical function of the Roman papacy."[232] As Malachi Martin noted: "Wyszynski spread the extra protective mantel of the preparations for the Marian devotional vow... always a part of those preparations was the explication of what this vow implied for Poland... for the Soviet Union... for Europe... for the society of nations as a whole, and for the Roman papacy as... 'the builder of the world' and 'the guardian of nations....'"[233]

Wyszynski persuaded Pope Paul VI to proclaim Mary as "Mother of the Church" on November 21, 1964, in front of the whole Council of Bishops of *First Rome*. The decision, declared Martin, "to so honor Mary had deep implications." The First Rome officials "transformed the already great importance of Mary from the merely devotional and purely religious to a geo-religious plane.... Mary was now, whether one liked it or not, recognized as a geopolitical element in Christian salvation [as now promoted by *First Rome*]. It was a capital point in the formation of a prepapal mind in Wojtyla [John Paul II]."[234]

By August, 1968, the "supernatural current" was let loose. Then Archbishop Wojtyla boldly declared, "Our temporal theology demands that we dedicate ourselves into the hands of the Holy Mother," which, in the words of a visiting newsman, "was reminding us Poles that, if we fulfill our destiny, it will be a European destiny, a worldwide destiny."[235]

Now, noted the Vatican insider, Malachi Martin, "the only other institutional organization that measured up to the Soviet Party—State [rooted in Russia] was the Roman Catholic Church." "Rarely in the long history of papal elections had the choice of a pope held such portentous consequences...."[236] And so it was that the twenty-five year papal reign of John

Paul II began in 1978, catapulting the human mother of Jesus into the consummate role of "mascot" and reigning Mother over *First Rome* in its bid to claim global dominion. Mary now stood as the open-armed intermediary between Christ as Messiah and mankind. Thus, the exaltation of Mary as the universal mother of *First Rome*, preempted the geopolitical claim of *Third Rome* as the final "Rome" destined (by Third Rome belief) to be "the savior of the world."

Lest one should respond protectively of *First Rome* in desiring to weight both the cause and consequence of the supreme exultation of Mary as primarily religious, it might be instructive to tune our thoughts in spiritual humility as well as in intellectual integrity to the observations of a Vatican insider in discussing "The Politics of the Papacy." It is noted: "There was one very constant characteristic of the Wyszynski—Wojtyla geopolitical outlook and program: the function of Mary, the Mother of Jesus." "It is difficult for the secularized minds of the West to realize that this official act of dedication to an invisible person—Mary—was meant not merely as an act of public piety and devotion, but explicitly as a geopolitical strategy...." It was this confidence in Mary [not Christ] that animated John Paul II, a "belief in the geopolitical action and power of Mary as Queen of the world."

From John Paul II's viewpoint, if Mary was "Queen of the World," and he, exercising papal supremacy as "Absolute monarch" of *First Rome*, had dedicated first Poland, then Russia, then the world to Mary, *First Rome* would emerge the global victor over not only *Third Rome* but over the peoples of the entire earth as *KING of the Mountain*.

Thus John Paul II was nearly terrified by the "Third Secret" of the Fatima visions of three young children allegedly with the Virgin Mary in 1917. Mary had purportedly given them explicit instructions regarding future geopolitical developments in our world, more particularly in the "Third Secret" regarding the end-time role of Russia. That "Third Secret" remained, under Vatican order, hidden in the Pope's private apartments. By 1980, John Paul II began to reveal the shocking nature of the final secret's contents, a foreboding confrontation between Russia and First Rome as well as between Russia and the western world.[237]

There is a reason why John Paul II, reputed by an ancient Catholic prophecy to be the next-to-last pope, travelled to 130 nations during his papacy, feverishly worked to bring down the Soviet Union, and strove to unite all religions of the world under the *First Rome* umbrella. For him, "World peace or world catastrophe was described in terms of Mary and of Russia."[238] This was the "georeligion of Roman Catholicism," tied inextricably to two elements; "the universalism of the Roman Pontiff, and the universal queenship of Mary, the Mother of Jesus."[239]

It is therefore clear that Russia and papal Rome remain on a collision course. John Paul II feared the fateful fallout of the fulfillment of the "Third Secret" of the Fatima vision. Regardless of the actual authenticity of Fatima, the Marian devotion and "Third Rome" beliefs, perception becomes reality and viewpoint always directs and determines destiny. *First Rome* and *Third Rome* will yet battle for supremacy as *KING of the Mountain.*

## DOES IT MAKE A DIFFERENCE?

It is said that *Knowledge is Power.* Yet it is only a partial truth. Knowledge without wisdom and purported "wisdom" without underlying truth can be profoundly dangerous. Indeed our world is being driven to the brink of inescapable conflagration and catastrophe without a biblical course correction. It is not *religion* but a reconciled *relationship* with the God of the Bible that provides the only future hope for a faith-starved planet that increasingly places its trust in charismatic personalities, political power, and geopolitical maneuvers and alliances, however "religious" they may purport to be.

Neither *First Rome* nor *Third Rome* will ultimately rule and reign as the consummate *KING of the Mountain,* completing this age in the millennium end-game. Christ alone, as "KING of kings and LORD of lords" will have the final word. Mary will give way to the Master. His will and His alone will stand. The rulers of this terrestrial planet will conspire, conceive, conjure and confederate in their desperate and final enterprises to rule the hearts and homes of men and to establish historically-elusive utopian empires. And in this cacophony of confusing voices, each of us, of whatever nation or persuasion, must make ultimate choices.

The contestants for *KING of the Mountain* will continue their climb and clamor to usurp the glory of their Creator, but you and I, each of us, must make eternal choices now, even in the face of the epic, end-time battle raging in our world. But what we do, the choices that we make, must be done quickly, for "the end of all things is at hand" (I Pet. 4:7)."

This is not a time to persist in embracing the false gods of the unholy trinity of multiculturalism, religious pluralism and political correctness. Rather, it is an urgent time, a precipitous moment, in which choices defining eternal destiny are being determined. As the Scriptures so pointedly warn: "Today if ye will hear his voice, Harden not your heart...." (Psa. 95:7-8, Heb. 3:7-19). "For the LORD is a great God and a great King above all gods" (Psa. 95:3).

*Chapter 18*

# PROBING THOUGHTS *for* PROPHETIC TIMES

1. Do you believe "God has appointed Vladimir Putin to Russia to prepare for the coming of Jesus Christ?" What do you think might be the global implications of such belief in the mind and heart of the Russian people?

2. Why do you suppose *TIME* magazine called the forces directing Russia's choices as "The Dark Forces?" Why might *TIME*'s cover story inquire "CAN RUSSIA ESCAPE ITS PAST?"

3. What facts of past and recent history reveal Russia's continuing desire and intent to dominate the world?

4. Why did Pope John Paul II see Russia as the preeminent global opponent to the Vatican?

5. Is it not fascinating that at this advanced moment in human history, the three premier global competitors for global dominion are also the three powers that, more than any others, merge church and state or religion and civil politics, i.e., Russia, Islam and the Vatican?

6. Why do you think Vladimir Putin declared Russia to be "Defender of the Islamic World?"

7. What is the end-time significance of the historical terms, *First Rome*, *Second Rome* and *Third Rome*?

8. Can you see how *First Rome* and *Third Rome* may well be in a no-holds-barred battle for supremacy as *KING of the Mountain*? Why did this particular contest consume Pope John Paul II? Why was he terrified by the "Third Secret" of the Fatima visions?

9. Does this contest of THE BEAR vs. THE POPE have any significance in your own life and choices? Why, or why not?

# Chapter 19

# THE DRAGON VS. THE EAGLE

———— ⬡ ————

*"China's rising star is sinister, strategic and has surreal implications in the mounting battle for KING of the Mountain."*

"THE JAWS OF THE DRAGON ARE OPEN." China has re-emerged center stage, on the global theatre." For the Christian Church in the world, on the near edge of an exploding 21st century, "the center of spiritual gravity is shifting from the United States to Asia."[240] For the United States, the message appears to be quite simple: "Move over," and "meet your new rival—the globe's newest superpower."[241]

## SINISTER STAR RISING

The picture has been poignantly painted and the colors are vivid. The Red Dragon is rising. Over the past two decades, his sinister star has risen well over the horizon and is rapidly approaching its zenith at high noon. The warnings have been clear and consistent, yet largely ignored, as China has flooded the globe with low-cost merchandise, enervating the financial nerves of the world, particularly the West. But the West has steadfastly ignored its purchase of temporary prosperity that has simultaneously funded the coffers of an emerging global power having every obvious intent of proclaiming world dominion. *TIME* called it, "DAWN OF A NEW DYNASTY,"[242] proposing a heretofore unthinkable question. "Already a commercial giant, China is aiming to be the world's next great power. Will that lead to a confrontation with the U.S.?"[243] The clearly-implied answer was and is a resounding "YES."

"Now China is turning that commercial might into real political muscle, striding onto the global stage and acting like a nation that very much intends to be the world's next great power." As one observer noted, "…after nearly 200 years of foreign humiliation, invasion, civil war, revolution and unspeakable horrors, China is preparing for a date with destiny."[244] That date with destiny rapidly approaches, indeed is knocking at the door of history. China's rising star is sinister, strategic and has surreal implications in the mounting battle for *KING of the Mountain*.

## AS THE EAGLE FALTERS...

The wings of the "Great Eagle," the United States of America, have suffered a moderate clipping over the past two decades. The glory of her majestic flight over the nations has become tarnished and her pursuit of a *Pax Americana* through exportation of democracy has met with open antagonism in a pervasively politically-correct world where multicultural-ism and religious pluralism reign blindingly supreme and where genuine biblical faith at home has fled the public domain in fear of offending a world increasingly driven by feelings.

"As the eagle falters, the dragon swoops in," noted a review of Joshua Kurlantzik's *Charm Offensive: How China's Soft Power is Transforming the World*. Although not pleasant to ponder, the observation is expressed that "those who raised pro-democracy banners in Tiananmen Square once looked to America's ideals with hope. No longer, it seems." Kurlantzik further notes in *Charm Offensive*, Beijing's ascension in soft power—defined loosely as diplomatic and cultural muscle—is not occurring in a vacuum. It is marching in lockstep as American soft power declines, sharply."[245]

It is and is becoming, in the words of Henry Kissinger, "A World We Have Not Known."[246] "Never before have so many structural changes in the international system occurred simultaneously." In 1997 Kissinger noted: "China will emerge as an incipient superpower." "China's vast market, reinforced by its growing military power, will, in the hands of determined leaders, provide a vehicle for growing political influence." And in reality, "China's foreign policy is not so much driven by communist ideology as by growing nationalism...."[247] It is a burgeoning nationalistic pride fueling a secular faith in political and military power increasingly asserting itself not only in the China Sea but across the seven seas and seven continents, driving inexorably toward a dreamed destiny of global dominion.

Even as Kissinger recorded his observation in *NEWSWEEK* (January 1997), countermanding observations, albeit warnings appeared in *U.S. News & World Report*. Ross Munro, co-author of *The Coming Conflict With China*, noted the rising voice of critics arguing that "China has become an adversary." "China identifies us [the U.S.] as the enemy," he exclaimed, "and it's time we recognized it."[248] "China's population is five times larger than that of the United States." "Its military is the largest in the world."[249]

It was therefore shocking to many that Bill Clinton, then U.S. President, would allow his presidential campaign and allegiances to be "purchased" by the Chinese, soliciting and joyously receiving vast sums from Chinese suitors seeking political and economic favors (including "Most favored Nation" status), rewarding such brazen bribery with unprecedented hospitality in the Lincoln Bedroom at the White House. Would the "Eagle" court the "Dragon," entering into a dance with destiny where each, seeking to exploit the other, would prostitute principle in the pursuit of power and prosperity?

## SOUNDING THE ALARM

In a somewhat cryptic column January 1, 2000, launching the 21st century and the seventh millennium, Jonathan Spence declared, "China has a chance to be the next century's dominant international player." He noted: "The last time there was a Chinese century was the 11th. During the 11th century, China was both the largest and the most successfully run country on earth." "…there is just a chance," said Spence, "that it will give its name to a century for the second time. Except perhaps for the Roman Empire at the height of its glory, that is not a feat any single state has been capable of before."[250]

The problem lies not in the pursuit of *prosperity,* but of *power.* When the world considers that "China's human resources are vast, but its natural resources are limited,"[251] it does not require a Harvard graduate to imagine, indeed comprehend, the lurking dangers to the free world, specifically to the West, in China's pursuit of natural resources, not only to drive the engine of prosperity but to advance the political and military power requisite for realizing the dream of dominion.

The attention-grabbing headline of *The New York Times* just a decade later made clear the ominous direction of Chinese destiny. The message could not be missed: "U.S. Alarmed by Harsh Tone of China's Military."[252] U.S. Defense Secretary Robert M. Gates had met his Chinese counterpart to prevent "mistrust, miscalculations and mistakes." The Pentagon was worried over the "increasingly tense relationship" with the Chinese military that viewed "the United States as the enemy," "bent on thwarting China's rise." One observer noted: "Unfortunately, the two militaries are locked in a classic security dilemma, whereby each side's supposedly defensive measures are taken as aggressive action by the other, triggering similar countermeasures in an inexorable cycle."

Such reciprocating moves in an environment of growing distrust are dangerous, but they are not occurring in an historical or prophetic vacuum. Neither are they without foundation in expressed Chinese intentions buttressed by growing economic power, nationalistic pride, and resurrecting vision for Chinese dominion in the budding "Chinese Century." By September 2011, the *WORLD AFFAIRS JOURNAL* asked a question shocking to American and western sensibilities—a question not to be taken lightly: "Is China Planning a Surprise Missile Attack?"[253] There was substance behind the question.

A retired Chinese general, Xu Guangyu, had revealed that his country might be planning a surprise missile attack on the United States. Commentator Gordon G. Chang made a troubling connection. "Unfortunately, Xu's hostile sentiment fits within a worrisome trend. Especially since the beginning of last year [2010], there has been a series of belligerent comments from China's generals, admirals and colonels, some talking about war with the U.S. in the near future." "Given the bellicose statements coming from some of China's military brass—along with China's well-documented aggressive behavior in the South China Sea—it is difficult to imagine how Western observers can deny China's intentions and the clashes that lie ahead."[254]

As if that were not enough, the *Washington Times* disclosed, "A Pentagon report has found that a multi-billion dollar Chinese telecommunications company that has been seeking to make inroads into the U.S. market has close ties to China's military, despite the company's denials." The Pentagon's annual report to Congress on China's military released August 2011 "identifies Huawei as a high-tech company linked to the People's Liberation Army." At issue is "widespread concern among U.S. military and intelligence agencies that Huawei's switches, chips and firmware contain 'back doors' that can give China's military the equivalent of listening posts all over the U.S. telecommunications infrastructure."[255]

Warning signs are not lacking. Tensions are mounting. *Reuters* reported a serious warning from China to the United States on September 4, 2012, not to get involved in disputes over oil-rich territorial waters in the South China Sea, where China has engaged in provocative confrontation against U.S. regional allies such as Japan and the Philippines. China also has made abundantly clear its intent to reclaim Taiwan. Yet all of China's military buildup and saber-rattling manifesting the resurrection of the Red Dragon remains a bit obscured and geopolitically disconnected until it finds its nexus in the Middle East, the biblical center of history and prophecy. Not surprisingly, China leads us back to the magnetic center of world conflict.

## MIDDLE EAST GAME-CHANGER

As far back as 1995, the "handwriting on the wall" with regard to China was becoming clear, drawing warnings. According to the August 27 issue of the *New York Times Magazine*, Red China had already emerged as a "real threat to world peace."[256] Another headline read, "China Emerges as Global Power" with a troubling byline, "The Red Chinese dragon is roaring like an emerging global power, but no one is listening."[257] China had already increased its published military budget from 1988 to 1995 by 75 percent, a vastly understated reality. As the *New York Times Magazine* noted, "It's not communism and it's not trade. It's military expansion fueled by growing nationalism—and no one is paying attention."

Warnings continued to grow while America fueled China's military machine by insatiable lust for low-priced Chinese goods. By 2001 we were again jolted by the looming threat of China. *U.S. News & World Report* declared, "China looms as the biggest factor in U.S. defense policy since the demise of the Soviet Union." "What makes China especially controversial is that Western intelligence agencies know so little about it." "The argument is about its significance."[258]

"China is preparing for conflict 'in every direction,'" China's defense minister, Liang Guanglie, boldly stated. Speaking in December 2010, Liang declared, "In the coming five years, our military will push forward preparations for military conflict in every strategic direction." "We may be living in peaceful times, but we can never forget war… or put the bayonets and guns away."[259] Alarm bells are going off not only with China's neighbors but globally. What does it all mean? When China's Ministry of National Defense warns of China's "war option,"[260] what is the world, particularly the western world, to conclude?

Suddenly we are taken to the Middle East. The South China Sea, threats to Taiwan, Japan and the U.S., are merely backdrops to a much bigger unfolding drama. China's landscape design is global, and the focal garden of its grand scape increasingly brings our attention to the Middle East. Perhaps this is why The *JERUSALEM POST* put forth a mind-boggling headline May 20, 2010—"Why China can be a game-changer in the ME."[261]

In his op/ed piece, Avrum Ehrlich declared, "China's role in resolving the Middle East stalemate is overlooked as if it didn't exist." "China's influence over Iran and the Arab world," he said, "is many times greater than that of the U.S. It has massive, unprecedented investments, hundreds of thousands of workers, engineers and professionals on the ground. China consumes and underwrites a huge percentage of the Middle East and Iranian Gross Domestic Product (GDP)." "Iranian and Arab world economies are dependent on China's continued engagement."[262]

But is China really interested in becoming a "game-changer" in the Middle East, either for peace or for the region's prosperity? Or is China only raping the resources of an energy-rich region to satisfy its insatiable appetite for energy necessary to drive the engines of global conquest? China may be flush with growing economic and military power, but has shown no heart-motivated propensity to provide for or protect others in some semi-utopian dream. Rather, China has dramatically demonstrated the Dragon's self-serving antics in the South China Sea together with its takeover of the western Panama Canal and its managerial invasion of the Arab and Iranian oil and gas spheres. Her goal is nothing less nor more than global dominion by the Red Dragon. Ehrlich's euphoric vision for China's eleemosynary (charitably-motivated) drive into the Middle East is destroyed by his own net observations: "At present, China is cherry-picking the oil, gas and resource deals while selling its goods to a captive market."[263]

## THE BIBLICAL GAME-CHANGER

China is and will be a "game-changer" in the Middle East and beyond. It would behoove the prognosticators, presidents and prime ministers of our world to pay particular attention to the Dragon as it grows ever-more powerful economically and militarily. Its voracious appetite is becoming insatiable. Its tail is lashing out ever-more-frequently toward any person or power perceived to block, slow or direct its progress from global dominion. But to fuel the engines of envy that drive the Dragon, oil and gas have become inseparable from nationalistic investment in "the Chinese Century" and Dragon-ion domination. Make no mistake. Explosive times loom just ahead as foretold by the ancient prophets and apostles of Yeshua the Messiah.

As it is written, men will cry "Peace, peace," yet "there is no peace" (Ezek. 13:16). Even purported "prophets" will be caught up in the euphoria of *Peace*. In the last century we were promised "Peace in our time." But that time never seems to become a reality, and will not until the "Prince of Peace" returns to rule and reign among men. Yet China presses on, determined to rule by a simulated "Sino" defined peace as the world surrenders progressively to the Dragon's will. Preferably for now, that surrender gains traction through economic engines and exploitation. But raw power will soon replace the more passive economic interchange with the intimidation of marching men.

These seemingly contrary forces are even now setting the stage for the world's greatest confrontation. The first seems peaceful and highly desirable, but the second promises activation of the world's greatest army to claim the ultimate prize. The Dragon must dispense with the Eagle while exploiting the Bear so as to overwhelm the Woman riding the Beast, confederating with the current guardians of Middle East oil and gas to grasp for earth's greatest "spoil" to be found among "the land that is brought back from the sword, and is gathered out of many people" (Ezek. 38:8).

We return, then, to "the land that is brought back from the sword," to the remnant Jews "gathered out of many people" by *Aliyah* over the two generations last past, to the burgeoning nation of Israel. China is there. And it is truly amazing! The Dragon is determined to secure its global destiny, even if it must basically humble itself to a "start-up" nation, leading Israel to a false faith in the Dragon's purportedly desirable intentions. Joseph Puder gives us insight in his article posted September 5, 2012, in *Daily Mailer, Front Page.*[264]

"When the Chinese Communist regime announced its latent Five-Year-Plan in 2011, it proclaimed to the world that China is no longer satisfied with being 'the world's factory,' and that it seeks to become one of the world's innovators. To do that, China's leaders realized that they must turn to the 'Start-up' nation, which is the Jewish state of Israel. The Chinese are fully cognizant of the fact that neither the Arabs nor Iran (which provides them with raw energy) can provide them with innovative technology."[265] Put succinctly, the Dragon will play peaceful until it permanently secures Middle East (Arab and Iranian) energy and Israeli technology deemed necessary to secure its destiny for global dominion. The stakes could not be higher, nor the pathway more disingenuously deceptive. Iridescent signposts should arise in the capitals of the world—"DANGER AHEAD!"

Israel's response to the Dragon's seduction spells "DANGER" both to Israel and the Eagle. Israel is being seduced into a place of political fornication that will produce a bastard son dedicated both to her destruction and to the destruction of the Eagle which heretofore has guarded the "Start-up Nation" with his global wings. Nevertheless, the stage is set.

China and Israel established diplomatic relations in 1992. They are now marking a generation of growing relationship. "China is Israel's third largest export market, with sales of everything from telecommunications and information technology to solar energy and agricultural equipment and pharmaceuticals. More than 1000 Israeli companies operate in China." "Wishing the Chinese people a Happy Year of the Dragon, Israel's Prime Minister Benjamin Netanyahu declared in March 2012: 'We are two ancient peoples whose values and traditions have left an indelible mark on humanity. But we are also two peoples embracing modernity; two dynamic civilizations transforming the world."[266]

"Transforming the world"… yes. But to what end does Christ seek such "transformation?" In celebrating the 20th anniversary of Sino-Israeli diplomatic relations on January 24, 2012, Prime Minister Netanyahu remarked: "The rise of modern China is one of the most important events of our time, as is the rise of modern Israel." "I believe that Israel and China can act together to ensure peace in the Middle East."[267] Indeed, what China *can* do will bear no biblical resemblance to what the Dragon *WILL* do.

Perhaps most telling was the report of the *Times of Israel* on August 15, 2012, declaring that "three Chinese warships are in Port of Haifa as part of a four-day goodwill visit marking 20 years of Sino-Israeli relations—the first time Chinese naval ships have ever docked in Israel."[268]

Why warships to celebrate the winning of the Chinese-Israeli heart? Without doubt, the Dragon is "very impressed with Israel's economy and believes it is a model." There is little question that "Israel has become an increasing object of interest for the Chinese...." Yet as Joseph Puder made plain, "What is still missing, however, are stronger political relations."[269] Do not expect such heart-felt relations any time soon, for the Dragon is merely developing economic, technological and military strength until the propitious moment when history and prophecy become congruent, and the Dragon reveals the true nature of "dragons" as our world enters the final confrontation in the battle for *KING of the Mountain*.

## "THE KINGS OF THE EAST"

It was an attention-grabbing headline for anyone remotely familiar with the always-fascinating yet little-understood book of Revelation, the culminating book of the *New Testament* in the *Bible*. The opening words of this famous, yet often frustrating, book declare it to be "The Revelation of Jesus Christ, which God gave unto him, to show unto his servants things which must shortly come to pass...." "Blessed is he that readeth, and they that hear the words of this prophecy, and keep the things that are written therein; for the time is at hand" (Rev. 1:1-3).

What time is it? What is the time that is "at hand?" What are those things that "must shortly come to pass?" And if those words were penned nearly 2000 years ago, what could the word *shortly* possibly mean? If these words of the *Apocalypse* (Revelation of Jesus Christ) are so important to hear and heed, why are they shrouded in such mystery? The answers to these questions and many others have been progressively revealed and the curtain will continue to be pulled back throughout this book as we approach the soon unveiling of the King of kings. But for now we must pursue the ploys of earthly kings increasingly reaching for their moment of preeminent earthly glory and global governance.

For these reasons, the words of the headline September 2012 in *World Net Daily* were particularly gripping: "'KINGS OF THE EAST' HAUNT U.S."[270] The six-page piece was a particularly insightful inspection of the interrelationship of the eastern nations and their rulers, notably: China, North and South Korea, Myanmar (formerly Burma), Russia, and their political and military juxtaposition with regard to the United States (the "Eagle"). The author described the triangulation of China, Burma and North Korea as a "three-headed snake," with Burma (Myanmar) holding "all of the cards" as between the Dragon and the Eagle (China and the U.S.).

From a purely geopolitical standpoint, the discussion was both troubling and perhaps terrifying. Yet it was the title that spoke most powerfully... "'The Kings of the East' Haunt U.S.". To gain perspective at this juncture, we would do well to visit the Book of Revelation, Chapter 16, beginning with the twelfth verse, in order to establish a biblical foothold on the climb with those seeking the summit as *KING of the Mountain*. Please read with deliberation and with a will to comprehend the disastrous direction upon which the rulers of this age have determined to set their course.

> And the sixth angel poured out his vial upon the great river Euphrates; and the water thereof was dried up, that the way of the kings of the east might be prepared (Rev. 16:12).

There again are those title words—"The Kings of the East." These are clearly biblical words and point to one of the most stupendous, yet ominous, events of biblical prophecy—an event known as "the Battle of Armageddon."

> And I saw three unclean spirits... they are the spirits of devils [demonic spirits], working miracles, which go forth unto the kings of the earth and of the whole world, to gather them to the battle of that great day of God Almighty.

> And he gathered them together into a placed called in the Hebrew tongue Armageddon.

> And the seventh angel poured out his vial into the air; and there came a great voice out of the temple of heaven, from the throne, saying, It is done (Rev. 16:13-17).

## THE RELEVANCE OF REVELATION

We dare not take these words lightly. They are a profound warning from a loving and merciful God who is "not willing that any should perish [spiritually], but that all should come to repentance" (II Pet. 3:9). Yet He warns, as a concerned Father, "the end of all things is at hand" (I Pet. 4:7) and that "the day of the Lord will come as a thief in the night" (II Pet. 3:10).

There is a reason why God, in His lovingkindness and patient mercy, prevails by the hand and heart of His prophets and apostles upon the minds and hearts of mankind in this final generation of human history, pleading that we would prepare the way of the Lord through humble repentance. The

God of Creation and Lord of Nations desires that none should be damned to eternal judgment (II Thess. 2:12), but that all should come to repentance, being reconciled with God, and having been thus reconciled with our Maker, enabled to be genuinely reconciled with our fellow man (II Cor. 5:17-20). This is the supreme relevance of all prophetic revelation (both Old and New Testament) and indeed, of the Book of Revelation itself. And such supreme relevance cannot be sidestepped without supreme consequence.

## THE WAY OF THE KINGS... OF THE EAST

We return now to the "kings of the east." Nowhere does the Bible either describe or delineate these "kings" nor their dominions. Yet they are plural, and in their plurality, obviously powerful.

While not giving us their names nor the countries they govern, the Scriptures do describe their designated route and destination in Revelation, Chapter 16. Their final intended destination is Har Megiddo (the hill or mountain of Megiddo), which is translated Armageddon, which is the assembly point of nations in the apocalyptic scene of "the great day of God Almighty."

Har Megiddo is most likely a reference to the ancient Tel or archeological mound at Megiddo which is under the shadow of the famous Mt. Carmel where the prophet Elijah dramatically confronted the four hundred prophets of Baal in the days of Ahab and Jezebel. Elijah there presented Israel with a historic choice between the gods of the nations or the God of Israel. His rhetorical question echoes down through the annals of time to our time: "How long will you halt between two opinions? if the LORD be God, follow Him: but if Baal, then follow him" (I Kings 18:21). Interestingly, Israel is, to this metamorphic moment, still confronted by Elijah's call to choose, having not yet truly and transformingly chosen.

This choice remains the fulcrum of Israel's destiny. Israel, indeed the world, is facing its "Elijah moment." As the nations gather at Armageddon in final, desperate pursuit of becoming *KING of the Mountain*, each will be making the choice of destiny. The nations, by gathering "against the LORD and His anointed [Israel]" in the Valley of Jezreel below Har Megiddo, will be declaring their final and decisive position as to whether or not they will submit to the God of Abraham Isaac and Jacob [Israel]. By collectively opposing Israel as God's chosen people and Jerusalem as the place where God chose to place His name, they, in effect and from God's viewpoint, shake their collective fist against God's Messiah, declaring: "We will not have this man reign over us."

Thus, Israel's only hope for survival will be the ultimate intervention of Yeshua Messiah to rule the nations as "Prince of Peace" and "Lord of lords" (Isa. 9:6-7; Rev. 19: 11-21). In her terrifying existential moment, the remnant of Israel and Judah will "look upon Him whom they have pierced" (Zech. 12:10) and embrace the long-rejected Messiah as Savior and Redeemer. "In that day shall there be a great mourning in Jerusalem, as the mourning of Hadadrimmon in the valley of Meggidon" (Zech. 12:11).

The "valley of Meggidon" is that vast valley, variously known throughout history as "the plain of Megiddo," "the Jezreel Valley," and "the valley of Esdraelon." It is one of history's famous battlefields, having witnessed major conflicts "from one fought by Tuthmosis III in 1468 BC to that of Lord Allenby of Megiddo in 1917 AD."[271] From 1917 to 1918, Lord Edmund Allenby of Britain led the Arab allies against the Ottoman Turks at the Battle at Megiddo, thus destroying the six-century rule of the Ottoman Empire, a dominion which Turkey now seeks to restore.

"The way of the kings of the East" is therefore the way that leads to the Valley of Megiddo—to Armageddon. We must then return to Revelation 16, verse 12, to gain further description of the "way" to be taken by the kings of the East. In this passage we are clearly warned that the "way" involves the drying up of the "great river Euphrates." This is the preparation necessary to facilitate the horrendous confrontation of the globe's great powers in their final, desperate grasp to become *KING of the Mountain*.

## THE EUPHRATES AND THE FUTURE

The Tigris and Euphrates Rivers defined the Fertile Crescent of ancient history. The Euphrates is the largest river in Western Asia, and is generally referred to as "the river" in the *Old Testament* or *Tanakh* (e.g. Deut. 11:24).[272] The source is in eastern Turkey and it flows to the Persian Gulf, a distance of 2000 kilometers or approximately 1240 miles. This ancient river, renowned throughout the history of man, divides the Middle East from the East and Far East. It is a major natural and strategic barrier for any significant land passage from the East to the Middle East. Thus, it stands in "the way of the kings of the east."

The Book of Revelation, however, declares unmistakably that the waters of this great river will be "dried up." Is that possible? When might that happen—and how? It would be wise to be sitting down and to be well-anchored before proceeding with the balance of this chapter, for prophecy and history are indeed becoming congruent.

Yet what might be the further significance of this great historic river leading back to the remotest edge of biblical time and man's sojourn on earth? Why is it so important in the drive for global dominion—in the struggle of nations and rulers to become *KING of the Mountain*? It is because the Euphrates River is the eastern boundary of the Promised Land—the land promised to Abraham, Isaac and Jacob.

> In the same day the LORD made a covenant with Abram, saying,
> Unto thy seed [Isaac and Jacob, etc.] have I given this land, from the
> river of Egypt unto the great river, the river Euphrates (Gen. 15:18).

The Euphrates is the biblical border of Israel in God's eyes. He gave
it to Israel, through Abraham, in anticipation of Israel's emergence into
history. This great river also forms the northeastern border of the *land of
promise*, for we read in II Samuel 8:3 that King David "… went to recover
his border at the river Euphrates." Thus, three great waters define and protect Israel's land and borders—the Euphrates on the east and northeast,
the "River of Egypt" on the south, and the "Great Sea" or Mediterranean
on the west. The nations will seek to breach these eternal barriers in their
final battle "against the LORD, and against His anointed" (Psa. 2:2).

It is necessary for the great river, the River Euphrates, to "dry up" so as
to provide access for the massive ground forces of the "kings of the east"
to invade the land of promise, to claim this Promised Land as their own. It
appears that now is the divinely-appointed time.

## THE DRYING OF THE EUPHRATES

On January 13, 1990, the *Indianapolis Star* carried the headline:
"Turkey will cut off flow of Euphrates for 1 month."[273] A huge reservoir
had been built by Turkey, and to fill the reservoir, Turkey would stop the
flow of the Euphrates for one month. With this dam, Turkey is now capable of controlling… indeed stopping… the Euphrates River at will.

Turkish control of the Euphrates became of greater significance in
light of the unexpected, yet region-revising, breakdown of Turkish/Syrian
relations in 2012. Turkey, in effect, holds the control lever over the very life
of Syria, military power notwithstanding, for the Euphrates is Syria's life
support. "Syria is drying up."[274]

"The immense Euphrates River, Syria's main source of water, is drying
up. The Turks are stopping its water in their territory, so that Syria and
Iraq are receiving a declining portion of the water. Within about 10 years,
the river is expected to dry up completely outside Turkish territory."[275] Fish
are already becoming extinct. Over 400,000 wells have run dry. If there is
no water, there is no agriculture. Political pressure is building. "Syria is
experiencing an economic holocaust." This then becomes a driving force
for Syria to regain dominion of the Golan Heights. "Syria has an existential
interest in getting its hands on the Sea of Galilee," which in turn places an
existential threat on Israel. The implications are vast and beyond the scope
of our discussion here. The Bible, as both history and prophecy, is true. It
not only touches us where we hurt but reveals the horrors coming upon

our world due to mankind's collective and persistent rebellion against the Creator's authority. It is, at the same time, both a book of hope and a herald of a global holocaust to come. Its purpose is to bring humanity, made in God's image, to a place of humble submission to His Word, will and ways so that we all, both Jew and Gentile, might receive the blessings of Abraham… through Jesus Christ, that we might receive the promise of the Spirit [the Holy Spirit] through faith" (Gal. 3:14). "And the scripture, fore-seeing that God would justify the nations through faith, preached before the gospel unto Abraham, saying, In thee shall all nations be blessed" (Gal. 3:8). But we must choose, and time is no longer on our side.

Snakes are now serious business along the Euphrates. The British headline of The *Independent* commanded the attention of any open-minded Bible scholar June 26, 2009: "As Iraq runs dry, a plague of snakes is unleashed."[276] In actuality, it was not Iraq but the Tigris and Euphrates rivers that were running dry, due to "an unprecedented fall in the water levels." The report was graphic. "Swarms of snakes are attacking people and cattle… as the Euphrates and Tigris rivers dry up and the reptiles lose their natural habitat…." "People are terrified and are leaving their homes…."

Just how serious is this decade-long development? "The plague of snakes is the latest result of an unprecedented fall in the level of water in the Euphrates and Tigris, the two rivers which for thousands of years have made life possible in the sun-baked plains of Mesopotamia." "The collapse of the water levels of the rivers has been swift, the amount of water in the Euphrates falling by three-quarters in less than a decade." In addition to the multiple dams blocking the flow, there has been a drought for several years with less than half the normal rainfall. "From Nineveh in the north to Ur of the Chaldees in the south… a buildup of salt in the soil is making much of the land barren and infertile. Meanwhile, the Saw Scaled Viper and the Desert Cobra are staging a command performance.[277]

## A Two-Hundred Million Man Army

"It's not just the Middle East. China's on the march," noted prominent historian, Niall Ferguson in *NEWSWEEK*, September 20, 2012. "Perhaps," he said, "we should all worry about a different kind of rage: the Chinese rage that takes the form of a hyperventilating nationalism."[278]

The record is both clear and convincing. China is and has been "on the march" for at least a quarter century, and that "march" looms ever-more ominous with every passing month. The "march" of China is manifest by every modern measurement, whether economic, technological, political or militarily. The Dragon's claws are grasping greedily for expanding dominion. Preliminary to military force is global economic expansion, technological triumph and ever-widening politically-persuasive power. Out of these spill dragonian military enterprises driven by increasingly hyperventilated nationalism. As one commentator observed, "Ever since President Richard Nixon entered into détente with the communist regime in China, America has doggedly assisted in the commercial and military buildup of the Marxist nation. Both Republican and Democratic administrations have mollycoddled the Red Chinese to the point that now they have grown big enough to cause serious harm."[279]

Whether Bill Clinton, George W. Bush, or Barack Obama—each president has refused to identify China as an adversary, choosing rather to call it a "trading partner." Thus the U.S. has been willing to sacrifice its safety on the altar of transitory economic success, knowingly and brazenly building China's now-formidable military apparatus. Détente may no longer be the destiny between the dragon and the Eagle. "China is preparing for war, and few notice."[280] As reported September 13, 2005, a Chinese dissident has unequivocally stated that "Beijing is planning nuclear war."[281]

"A GIANT IS STIRRING," declared the headline. "If the 20th century belonged to America, the 21st may belong to China." "The world has never seen so big a nation rise as far and as fast as China has in the past 20 years." "Americans and people around the globe can feel the effects of China's voracious appetite…."[282] What, however, are the effects of this unprecedented growth and devouring appetite of the Dragon? How might this connect with Revelation's infamous prophecy of Armageddon? Does it matter to mean citizens of our planet? And should it matter to Israel?

The plot-lines of biblical prophecy are relatively clear, yet many details remain undisclosed. Who are these "kings of the east" for whom the Euphrates River will dry up as they march toward Har Megiddo in central Israel? Are they rulers of a single surpassing nation, or are they representative of an aggregate of nations of the East who combine forces for history's ultimate military moment, hoping to divide the spoils of victory? We do not know these answers with specificity. Therefore, to attempt to answer them with certainty requires a level of speculation which would seriously compromise the solemnity sought to be conveyed in these pages. We must rely, then, upon what we clearly know from Scripture, and upon clear, undisputed facts "on the ground."

We turn, then, to the Book of Revelation, chapter 9, verses 13 to 16.

And the sixth angel sounded, and I heard a voice from… the altar which is before God, saying to the sixth angel…

Loose the four angels which are bound in the great river Euphrates. And the four angels were loosed… to slay the third party of men.

And the number of the army of the horsemen were two hundred thousand thousand… and out of their mouths issued fire and smoke and brimstone.

By these three was the third part of men killed, by the fire, and by the smoke, and by the brimstone, which issued out of their mouth.

Here is a picture of a level of carnage unprecedented in the annals of human warfare. Try to imagine—one third of the entire population of earth decimated in the thirteen months during which this campaign will be waged (Rev. 9:15). Though some may choose to differ, it would appear that this devastating force destroying perhaps in excess of two billion people is directly laid at the feet of diabolically-empowered and directed "kings of the east" who are destined to cross a dried-up Euphrates on their desperate enterprise to destroy other world powers gathering in the Jezreel Valley at the foot of Tel Megiddo.

The Scripture describes 200 million men in the combined fighting force of the "kings of the east." Such a force is so overwhelming to contemplate that some believe the description to be symbolic of "myriads of myriads" of warriors. If, however, we let the passage speak for itself, the number 200 million so dwarfs the historical records of great armies, world conquerors and current standing armies as to be almost inconceivable… except, that is, for a few inconvenient and little-known facts. These facts may be shocking, but are nevertheless true. This leads us back to China and the deafening roar of the Dragon. Consider for a moment some fascinating facts that may shed light upon numbers that otherwise may appear impossible.

1. China has a current population in excess of 1.3 billion people.

2. *TIME* magazine, May 21, 1965, contained these astounding words: "Red China passed the word that its 200 million-man (and woman) militia had gone into serious training. The mainland press screamed shrilly that units… were engaged in intensive bayonet and machine-gun drill: men and women in blue boiler suits marched briskly through Peking streets with rifles slung."

3. "Gendercide" has dramatically changed the demographics within China, creating a sense of male desperation. The cover of The *Economist* in March, 2010, asked the troubling question: "What happened to 100 million girls?"[283]

"It is no exaggeration to call this gendercide. Women are missing in their millions—aborted, killed, neglected to death." "For those who oppose abortion, this is mass murder." The culprit is China's "one-child" policy. If couples want two children but are allowed only one, they will sacrifice—kill… abort—unborn daughters in pursuit of a son. Now, both China and northern India have unnaturally large numbers of boys, but, as noted in *The Economist*, "few appreciate how bad the problem is, or that it is rising."[284]

In April 2009, the Pakistan *Daily Times* reported that selective abortions had resulted in an excess of 32 million males in China, that would result in "bitter fruit"—men actually having to physically fight for a bride.[285]

The problem is actually far more serious, having not only national but international ramifications. In "The ominous rise of Asia's bachelor generation," Niall Ferguson notes that the advent of ultrasound scanning has resulted in "scary implications" with the exportation of massive Chinese testosterone wedded to hyperventilated nationalism. At an excess now of over 100 million males, "Don't be surprised if, in the next generation, it takes the form of macho militarism and even imperialism," for "Men without women are about violence."[286]

From the Chinese military perspective, what is the value of a male life among so many that are already causing us trouble? What better way to resolve the problem but to render them "cannon fodder" in the final pursuit of Chinese glory in the battle for *KING of the Mountain*?

4. "China's already burgeoning military poses a significant security threat to Southeast Asia and beyond unless quickly counterbalanced by the U.S. and its allies, said several retired military officers at a Washington symposium" March 19, 2012. Admiral Koda, who was a senior fellow at the Harvard University Asia Center, stated, "The role of China's navy is much larger than that of the United States." Naval presence in Africa and South America is "a way to expand its global influence. That's the frontier for China."

China's political, economic and military expansion will be both "dramatic and traumatic," according to retired U.S. Navy admiral, Patrick M. Walsh. "This is not an ideology. This is a nation state coming in to direct contact and collision with a country that views itself as a civilization." Echoing the concern, Kook Jim Moon, chief executive of Saeilo Enterprises and Tongil Group, called on the U.S. and democratic nations worldwide to band together to keep China's military in check. "China has never used its power to benefit others," he warned. "This has been its history."[287]

Neither time nor space permit further documentary support for the gravity of this historical and prophetic moment as related to the vast, invading army that, in its scorched-earth policy, will annihilate everything and everyone in its path as it makes its way to Armageddon. Mercy will have no place in its mission.

## THE MESSAGE OF MEGIDDO

The much-touted or disputed "Clash of Civilizations" cannot be obfuscated or obliterated by massive prescriptive doses of political correctness, multiculturalism, and religious pluralism. Eventually, reality comes knocking at the door. And the sooner the increasingly God-denying West comes to grips with the truth that not all viewpoints are created equal, the greater will be the hope of divine intervention and protection in the unimaginable devastation soon to sweep this planet.

At root, the reeling of the nations in prophesied rage is not primarily a matter of politics, of economics or of military prowess. The root is global spiritual rebellion against the Creator, revealing an unprecedented tidal wave of violence and unrighteousness far beyond the contemplation of most mortals. Every poison and ungodly imagination of men's hearts will be spewed out with such vitriol that words will not suffice a totally inept media to describe it. No preconceived notions of a movie and media-exploited "Armageddon" could prepare the peoples of this planet for that which will soon destroy one-third of the world's inhabitants in fiery fury.

Israel will once again be the epicenter of this debacle. While miscellaneous, extraneous and parenthetical issues may serve as secondary international irritants, there is a reason why the world's power brokers are beating tracks to the Promised Land. Their individual and collective envy of Israel's chosenness by the Creator is more than those raging against the Lord of Nations can countenance. Resistance against a promised Messiah, who would reign supreme as King of kings and as Lord of lords is, quite simply, beyond the pale of raging impatience. Driven deeply into the reprobate psyche is the deceptive conviction: "We will be king;" "We need not that some divine interloper should encroach upon our domain and interfere with our plans and purposes;" "No, we will not have this man, Yeshua the Messiah, to reign over us."

It is not only the kings of the earth facing seemingly imponderable decisions in the inexorable march to Armageddon, but every denizen of this earthly domain faces an ultimate dilemma. Neither is Israel, nor are the Jewish people, safely removed, notwithstanding millennia of promises flowing from Abraham, Isaac and Jacob. For all, both Jew and Gentile, both the powerful and the poor, have come short of the glory of God, and must repent (Acts 17:30-31). Any genuine trust in these extraordinarily trying times is secured only by the salvation that is in Jesus the Christ, the Holy One of Israel, who once came as a suffering servant to save us from our sins, but who is soon coming again to judge us all in and for our sins. Today, if you will hear His voice, whether a part of the Orient or the Occident, do not harden your heart.

But for now, Armageddon is looming larger… alarmingly so. "Taking Megiddo is like capturing a thousand cities," remarked Pharaoh Thutmose III. Megiddo's tremendous value came from its strategic location as guardian of the most important pass through the Mt. Carmel range where Elijah once called upon the people to choose whom they would serve. Whoever held Megiddo in the ancient world controlled the traffic and trade, meaning both military and financial security.[288] Today, Megiddo looms not only as a controller of traffic and trade, but as the final arbiter of truth in the culminating course to determine who will be *KING of the Mountain*.

## RECONCILING THE IRRECONCILABLE

Facts are very stubborn things. Regardless of western paralysis in discerning truth and accepting facts due to the post-modern dogmas of political correctness, multiculturalism and religious pluralism, the on-the-ground realities of the Dragon's resurrection can no longer be either rationalized or ignored. The warnings have grown in intensity for two decades. The Dragon's dark shadow now hovers over the entire earth, from Asia to the Middle East, and from the South Pacific to North, South and Central America, where China now governs even the historic and strategic Panama Canal.

Both China and Russia, each for their own respective global objectives, have made unprecedented alliance to protect their positions in the Middle East, threatening the "Eagle" and Israel that any attack on Iran or Syria will be deemed "An Attack on their National Security." Russia's deputy prime minister, Dmitry Rogozin, has made this abundantly clear. A Chinese general has alleged that China would launch World War III if Iran is attacked. There is no doubt that oil is greasing the greed of the Dragon and other global powers in a desperate attempt to gain dominion, which will require further exploration in the chapter following.

The Dragon will brook no opposition. China's goals are irreconcilable with those of the leading powers of the West. Each has been using the other to facilitate their respective short and long-term objectives, but the Dragon's true intentions and global condition are no longer masked or camouflaged but have become frighteningly stark. On the normal, natural human plain of nature defined by mutually-beneficial economics, mutual human respect and military protection of borders, there remains no further foundation upon which the Eagle and the Dragon can coexist. The best of international politics, negotiations and diplomacy are incapable of bridging the gap created by irreconcilable goals. The world cannot reconcile the irreconcilable.

This understanding undoubtedly prompted China's late leader, Mao Tse Tung, to brag in his diary back in the 1960's that he could field an army of 200 million soldiers. Confirming the terrifying truth of this calculation was the 1999 *Fact Book* put out by the CIA, stating that China then had 198 million men of military age (15-49). By the year 2000, China exceeded the 200 million mark.[289] In a shocking twist, commentator Mark Steyn noted that China is intentionally seeking to bankrupt the "Eagle" through the debt-financing of America's economy, and that fully 80 percent of the Dragon's military buildup has been funded by interest paid on America's debt.[290] "Enter the Kings of the East into prophetic play."[291]

## YET ANOTHER "EVIL EMPIRE"

"Now another evil empire—China—is attracting attention;" wrote Marvin Olasky in a *WORLD* magazine column over two decades past.[292] Sinologists speculate about "the Chinese character," observed Olasky, but there is a universal truth summarized well by Whittaker Chambers: "Man without God is a beast, and never more beastly than when he is most intelligent about his beastliness." "Those who believe that education and markets tame man's aggressiveness," noted Olasky, "are ignoring the Bible and the evidence of all history. As China breaks out of poverty, it becomes more of a threat to its neighbors, not less."

As so aptly set forth by *WORLD* March 15, 1997, "Since Christ is the Lord of history and the destroyer of kings who do not honor Him, we know that even the days of China's tyrants are numbered. We cannot predict China's short-term future, but we know that Christ is the hope for both America and China, and that American diplomacy should do all it can to promote opportunities for Christianity to expand in China."[293]

"Chinese Christians are our friends; we should pray that God will protect them. The current Chinese leaders, from all appearances, are our enemies; we should pray that God will change their heart." "The United States needs to defend itself militarily, but all of us should remember that our only true *defense*, in the long run, is the *offense* of Christ."

*Chapter 19*

# PROBING THOUGHTS *for* PROPHETIC TIMES

1. What is the meaning or implication of the quote: "As the eagle falters, the dragon swoops in?"

2. How long has the West been warned of China's dangerous emergence as an "incipient superpower?" Has the West taken heed to the warnings, or blindly sacrificed security for temporary prosperity?

3. Why would the *JERUSALEM POST* call China a "game-changer" in the Middle East? Is that desirable… or dangerous? Why?

4. In what way will China become a Biblical "game-changer" in the Middle East and beyond?

5. What is the significance of the words "the kings of the East" as found in the Book of Revelation?

6. What role will the Euphrates River play in the future of Israel and the world?

7. Is it possible that China or a far-eastern confederation could actually field an army of 200 million men in the march toward Armageddon? How?

*Chapter 20*

# GOG AND MAGOG VS. GOD

——— ∞ ———

*"The imagery is graphic." "Thus saith the Lord,*
*I am against thee… and will put hooks in thy jaws…."*

THE BATTLE OF GOG AND MAGOG will be perhaps the most
decisive military confrontation ever recorded on this earthly plane in the
progression of human history to that time. The prophet Ezekiel has told us
in no uncertain terms that it will take place "in the latter years," and "in the
latter days" of our sojourn on this planet (Ezek. 38:8, 16). The prophet also
foretold a distinct confederation of nations which will "come like a storm,"
"like a cloud," to cover the land of Israel, precipitated by "an evil thought"
impelling them to "take a spoil" (Ezek. 38:9-12).

## GOG AND MAGOG VS. ARMAGEDDON

Before we proceed with the amazing, yet horrendous, import of the
Gog and Magog prophecy, we should, so as not to distract from the fateful focus, preliminarily discuss and dispense with a number of conflicting
ideas and opinions that could, for some, divert attention to details sending
the mind on endless "rabbit trails."

The first such concern relates to whether the battle of Armageddon, referenced only by name in Revelation 16:16, is the same battle described in explicit
detail by Ezekiel 38 and 39 as the battle of Gog and Magog. There are serious and sincere thinkers which take the position and argue persuasively that
these battles are one and the same. On the other hand, there are serious and
sincere students of prophecy who believe and argue persuasively that these
notorious battles are separate and distinct, that perhaps the Gog and Magog
struggle takes place at a time perhaps seven years before the ultimate battle of
Armageddon. Regardless of alleged depth of study and sincerity of opinion,
the reality is that no one can, with absolute certainty, declare to have the last
and final word on the issue. The absolute truth of the matter will, however, be

soon revealed. Furthermore, for purposes of the driving import of this writing, each battle, whether the same or distinctly different in time, nevertheless falls within the overall historic and spiritual battle for *KING of the Mountain*.

The second concern relates to the specific identity of Gog and Magog. Since there are no existing countries or people groups known by these names, sincere and substantial research, reasoning… and yes, speculation, are involved in ascertaining their identity. Regardless of their speculated or reasoned identity, the progressive congruency of history and prophecy will eventually prove the truth of the matter. Nevertheless, specific identification of Gog and Magog is not necessary for purposes of this writing, either to comprehend or consider the overarching epic, eternal and end-time battle for *KING of the Mountain*.

## SETTING THE STAGE

The stage must be properly set for this most infamous of battles. The ancient prophet Ezekiel, therefore, foretold the resurrection of the long-dispersed nations of Israel and Judah. His prophecy of the "valley of dry bones" coming to life is sufficiently well known as to have been put to music in a classic "Negro spiritual" in America's past. The consummation of this prophecy, which commands the entire 37th chapter of Ezekiel, declares:

And ye shall know that I am the LORD…

And shall put my spirit in you [Israel and Judah], and ye shall live, and I shall place you in your own land: then shall ye know that I the LORD have spoken it, and performed it, saith the LORD.

Behold, I will take the children of Israel from among the heathen [Gentile nations], whither they be gone, and I will gather them on every side, and bring them into their own land:

And I will make them one nation in the land upon the mountains of Israel; and one king shall be king to them all: and they shall be no more two nations, neither shall they be divided into two kingdoms any more at all.

And David my servant shall be king over them; and they shall have one shepherd…

And they shall dwell in the land that I have given unto Jacob my servant… even they, and their children's children for ever: and my servant David shall be their prince for ever.

And the heathen [Gentile nations] shall know that I the LORD do sanctify Israel, when my sanctuary shall be in the midst of them for evermore (Ezek. 37:14-28).

The stage is now set. After 2700 years of progressive dispersal by God for their spiritual rebellion, Israel and Judah (the long-divided tribes), are being reunited in the land promised over three thousand years earlier to Abraham, Isaac and Jacob. A national resurrection never before recorded or known to the mind of man has taken place. Joseph and Judah are drawn back to Jerusalem. And the nations are not happy. Each, in their own way, is seeking to quash the quickening of the dry bones of Israel, and to prevent David… their "prince for ever" … from taking the throne, not only as KING of the Jews, but as KING of kings and LORD of lords over the nations. But the nations need a self-deceiving rationale, a self-justification to destroy the resurrecting nation of Israel. They need a pretense to facilitate their unholy purpose.

## "HOOKS IN THEIR JAWS"

The imagery is graphic. To Gog and Magog, the chief prince of Meschech and Tubal, God instructed Ezekiel to prophesy: "Thus saith the Lord God; Behold, I am against thee… and I will turn thee back, and put hooks in thy jaws, and will bring thee forth, and all thine army… Persia, Ethiopia, and Libya with them… Gomer, and all his bands; the house of Togarmah of the north quarters… and many people with thee.

For what purpose are these nations confederated? When will this prophesied event take place? Where will it take place? And what conse-quence will flow from this end-time alliance? Ezekiel makes the plans and purposes quite plain, as well as the disastrous effects.

After Israel/Judah have "come into the land" that has been recovered from her occupying enemies, and after the physical descendants of Abraham, Isaac and Jacob have been largely "gathered out of many people [where they had been dispersed], and "brought forth out of the nations," this great con-federation will form. It will take place "in the latter years" wherein Israel/Judah have been regathered to their homeland and in "the latter days" of world history. It will occur when the regathered peoples find themselves, for the first time since their dispersion, in relative peace. And it will take place when the timing is ripe, from the perspective of the unholy alliance, to effec-tuate their unholy purpose. And that purpose, in substantial part, is "to take a spoil" and to destroy the nascent nation (Ezek. 38:8-12, 16).

## "AN EVIL THOUGHT"

It is a phrase common to historical literature. "The spoils of war," how-ever, contains a possible three-fold connotation. The first possible meaning of the word *spoil* may be to damage, ruin or destroy. A second meaning may refer to the incidental benefits or goods and property falling into the hands and possession of the victor in a conflict. The third possible meaning contains the implication of motivation. To *spoil*, in this sense, is better used as a verb than as a noun, since the *spoil* is obtained not by incident but by intent. The *spoil*, then, becomes the fruit of the intent to plunder or to take by force. The spoil is therefore the object and driving purpose of the conflict rather than being merely incidental to other motivating purposes. It is this third meaning that would seem to be clearly implied in Ezekiel's rather detailed prophecy.

The prophet notes that the attacking confederation and its leaders will "think an evil thought." While various peoples, cultures and nations may have varying nuances as to what may be deemed to be *evil*, the Scriptures seem to give a simple, yet principled understanding that can only be truly discerned by a true knowledge and understanding of the Bible itself, in its fullness.

This biblical understanding of that which is *evil* is perhaps best seen in the life of Moses and leading representatives of the twelve tribes of Israel, when, after forty years in the Wilderness after escaping the bondage of Egypt, they are preparing to enter the Promised Land. The entire account and the consequences of choice can be found in Numbers 13-14 in the Torah (the first five books of the Old Testament). This ancient biblical understanding of that which is *evil* has equally profound significance for all of us today as it had 3500 years ago. We must take a moment, then, to evaluate the facts, their connection to faith and their implication for our future. Here is the situation.

The Lord spoke to Moses, as leader of Israel, to appoint and send a ruling representative of each of the twelve tribes of Israel to "spy out the land of Canaan" which was the land, about 500 years earlier, promised to Abraham, and through him to Isaac (Gen. 17:17-21) and then to Jacob whose name was changed to "Israel." So important was this matter that the names of each of these tribal leaders is specified in the text with particularity. They were to investigate this "Promised Land," which God had already said he had given to them (Num. 13:2), for forty days and bring back a report.

This is where the trouble began. These twelve noted leaders of the twelve tribes delivered what, at best, was an equivocating report. While confirming that the land was, as promised, a lush land, ten of the twelve denied that the Children of Israel were able to take dominion of the land because of the "giants" in the land, for as they reported, "they are stronger than we" (Num. 13:31). This report, which was in fundamental disagreement with God's promise, was called "an evil report." Interestingly, (and as an aside) this is Israel's greatest problem to this very day, the unwillingness to trust God and to agree with His viewpoint.

The very essence of *evil* is to elevate one's viewpoint, opinion and conclusions over what the Creator God has spoken in His Word, the Bible. Such disagreement is profoundly dangerous both for individuals and for nations, affecting behavior. God calls both Israel and the nations to "Come now, and let us reason together…" (Isa. 1:18) so that all humanity, made in God's image, might come into blessed agreement with the Creator's word, will and ways. We refuse such a plea at our personal and collective peril, as proven by God's response to the arrogant and untrusting disagreement of the ten leaders who brought back "an evil report" that infected the people with a spirit of rebellion, costing them the "Promised Land." Those men that did bring up the evil report… died by the plague before the Lord" (Num. 14:37).

Why is this biblical understanding of *evil* relevant in the context of the Gog and Magog war? The supreme relevance is that God has clearly spoken regarding His eternal view of Israel, first declared to Abraham (Gen. 12:1-3, 15:1-18, 17:1-27, 18:1-18), confirmed in Isaac (Gen. 25:11, 26:24-29), and re-confirmed in Jacob—"Israel" (Gen. 28:1-15). When the kings, presidents, prime-ministers and potentates of this world, lifted up in pride, choose to invade the very providence of the God of Israel, for whatever reason and however justified it may appear, they are treading on exceedingly dangerous ground, setting themselves "against the Lord, and against his anointed" (Psa. 2:1-2). If one truly comprehends that God is "God," it defies all reason to comprehend how anyone could knowingly invite the catastrophic consequences of such an egregious defiance of the eternal, declared will of the Creator of all things. With that further insight of *evil* from God's viewpoint, we return, then, to the provocative move of the end-time confederacy to attack Israel to "take a spoil."

## "TO TAKE A SPOIL"

Ezekiel's prophecy of the Gog and Magog confederation and battle clearly indicates the motivating goal will be "to take a spoil." It is not the *spoil* that is "evil" but rather the *thought* regarding the taking of the spoil that is deemed "evil" in God's sight. The reason the thought driving this collective action is "evil" is that the spoil the confederacy seeks to acquire, from God's viewpoint, belongs to and is His blessing to Israel, the "apple of his eye" (Zech. 2:8). The spoil, seen by the unholy confederation as a consummate prize, will inure to the participating nations as a devastating curse. Notice is hereby given of the overwhelming scourge that will drown in devastation all who deign to trouble themselves with this "spoil," for God has spoken, "my fury shall come up in my face" (Ezek. 38:18).

But what is this "spoil?" What might be deemed so precious, so desirable, so needful as to risk open rebellion "against the Lord, and against His anointed" as well as the responsive retribution of other nations and coalitions? Some have theorized the spoil to be the vast mineral deposits in the Dead Sea. Others have considered the spoil to be the very land itself. Certainly the Dead Sea is rich in minerals. It is true that many nations seek dominion over the Promised Land so as to frustrate the promise and its purpose. Yet there would appear another "spoil" that would draw these nations into confederation like a magnet—that would be like "a hook in the jaw," drawing them lustfully into a divine net, unaware of and oblivious to the outpouring of holy fury that will descend upon them. That spoil is often referred to as "Black Gold," a euphemism for oil.

Gold may glisten with unequalled luster, but "Black Gold" is greedily sought by all global powers seeking dominion. *Black Gold* is the ultimate resource for which world leaders lust and will confederate and conspire to almost any length to obtain. For oil alone is deemed the quintessential commodity to protect and project power while providing for domestic prosperity. Oil is, therefore, the world's ultimate "spoil." But why confederate to attack Israel for this "spoil" when it appears, historically, that Israel (among all nations) has been uniquely deprived of this precious product of nature's bounty? We must reserve that discussion for the chapter following. Further insight, however, will be gleaned by a more detailed look at the Gog-Magog confederation and the nations that conspire to "take a spoil."

## THE "SECRET" CONFEDERATION

Many of the names of those nations set to "secretly" confederate and attack Israel are specifically set forth in the shocking prophecy of Ezekiel. Those nations or people groups identified with particularity are:

1. Gog—the land of Magog (chief prince of Meshech and Tubal);
2. Persia—(now Iran since 1935);
3. Ethiopia—(Ancient Cush—now Sudan);
4. Libya;
5. Gomer—and associated peoples/tribes;
6. House of Togarmah (in the north quarters); and
7. "Many people" with those specified.

There has been much scholarly research as well as popular reasoning and speculation concerning the specific identity of "Gog, the land of Magog," "Gomer," and the "house of Togarmah." We will neither resolve nor even attempt to resolve these identities with absolute particularity here. However, there is some general consensus that may assist our comprehension sufficient for our present purposes.

In general terms, the "Gog-Magog" identity finds its locus in what is now Russia—perhaps also the southern republics of the former U.S.S.R. The "house of Togarmah" is most generally connected with all or part of what is now Turkey. As to "Gomer," ideas of identity are less firm. Some look to Germany or countries of former Germanic influence; others look to portions of eastern Europe, including the span westward between western Turkey and Germany. In reality, the true identity will be revealed in the formation of this cataclysmic confederation and in the real-time effectuation of the "evil thought" that compels them to "take a spoil."

In truth, the confederation is neither "secret" nor select. Rather, it is "secret" only from the standpoint that it exists and will create an existential threat to Israel without further collective public pronouncement. And it will consolidate for this Gog-Magog enterprise "in the latter years," and "in the latter days" (Ezek. 38:8, 16)—our days. It is "select" only in that the confederate powers are linked by the common lust for oil. A brief review of the linking magnetism of oil in confederating these peoples and nations will help us comprehend the devastating solemnity of that which is now knocking at Israel's door and will result in solidifying further international alliances in the world's final press to become *KING of the Mountain*.

## RUSSIA

Russia is the lead force in this soon-to-be-seen confederation. Russia's role is sinister and deadly serious. Russia is also desperate. Vladimir Putin, in his quest to resurrect Russia as a global power, is convinced that his desperate enterprise will rise or fall on Russia's control of oil and gas. On August 23, 2006, the British *Financial Times* reported statistics from *MosNews* and OPEC, declaring: "RUSSIA OVERTAKES SAUDIA ARABIA AS WORLD'S LEADING OIL PRODUCER."[294] *Reuters* and CHBC.com confirmed the striking news.[295] The headlines then reveal the extent to which Russia aspires to dominate the world through oil and gas.

### "Russia, Algeria meet as gas OPEC plan gains ground."[296]

The presidents of Russia and Algeria, two of the biggest gas suppliers to Europe, met to discuss energy ties in a drive to create an OPEC-like gas cartel. Iran and Qatar have pushed for the idea. In 2005, Russia accounted for 45 percent of Europe's gas imports while Algeria's share was 21 percent.

### "Turning Up The Heat"[297]

"Gazprom is marching forward with its plan to become a global energy superpower. From Libya and Nigeria to Germany and Italy, Russia's gas monopoly is making shrewd moves." Gazprom, the world's largest gas company in terms of reserves, has power to project Russian political influence abroad. Gazprom intends to dominate by building new gas pipelines into Europe, Turkmenistan, Kazakhstan and China. Of particular interest is the chairmanship of Nord Stream, a new gas pipeline to Germany, by the former German Chancellor, Gerhard Schroeder.

### "Russia's gas weapon"[298]

Gazprom announced plans to take up to a 20 percent share of the U.S. gas market by moving into the United States. Gas is now one of Russia's three geopolitical weapons, the other two being oil and military arms.

### "Russia's energy giant flexes its muscles"[299]

"Gazprom's marriage of economic and political power is particularly threatening," declared The *Economist*. "It used to be tanks and submarines and missiles that we were frightened of, now it's banks and pipelines" as Russia consolidates its monopoly of gas imports into a virtual "gas dictatorship." The Kremlin and Gazprom are politically and economically incestuous, inviting grave concern in the West.

### "Russia's lethal gas weapon"[300]

Gazprom, the Russian oil and gas giant, which controls 20 percent of global gas production; has become "a decisive geo-economics actor," as "an agent of Moscow."

### "Putin's new secret weapon"[301]

"President Vladimir Putin came to the conclusion… that Russia was sitting on a secret weapon more powerful than all its military might."

### Putin's "ultimate weapon—control of worldwide energy sources"[302]

"If Russian plans are implemented… shrewd Putin will soon control more than 50% of the oil and gas reserves in the world."

### "Gazprom—New Russian Weapon"[303]

**"Oil, gas pipeline is the key element of Russia's incursion into Georgia"**[304]

"Vladimir Putin is perfectly willing to sacrifice the rule of law… to protect the Russian empire and the energy monopoly that sustains it."

**"Pipeline dreams entangle Russians and Europeans"**[305]

"Despite calls by the EU for more diversification to ensure energy security, the Europeans still look mostly to Russia for its energy." "As if blind to this, Europe has neglected to find new alternative gas sources." "The writing is already on the wall."

**"Russia's Israeli Oil Bond," Dr. Sam Vaknin**[306]

"Russia and Israel—erstwhile enemies—have agreed to make use of Israel's neglected oil pipeline, known as the Tipline." It is designed to carry nearly a million barrels per day, circumventing the Suez Canal. "Russia is emerging as a major oil supplier and serious challenge to the hegemony of Saudi Arabia and OPEC." (Note: This was reported in 2002. Ten years later, Israel had become near totally dependent on Russian oil and gas—except for historical and prophetically-significant revelations disclosed in the following chapter).

## IRAN/PERSIA

The ancient nation of Persia, referenced by name in Ezekiel's prophecy became *Iran* in 1935. With its capital at Tehran, it is now known as an *Islamic Republic*. Iran's flag, adopted in 1989 by the newly established Islamic revolutionary government of Ayatollah Khomeini, declares eleven times "Allah Akbar" (God is Great).

Britain and Russia competed for influence in the area. The discovery of oil in Southwest Iran led to the Russian and British division of the country in 1907. In a 1919 treaty, Iran (Persia) effectively became a British protectorate. In 1941 British and Soviet forces occupied Iran, but in 1943 Iran's independence was declared. In 1951, Iran's oil industry was nationalized. The shah fled the country, but soon returned with US backing and restored Western oil rights in 1953. Under the shah Iran increased defense spending to become the largest military power in the region. When Khomeini established an Islamic theocracy through the Islamic revolution in 1979, the oil industry was renationalized in a profoundly anti-western attitude.

Iran's prosperity is based on oil production. Oil accounts for 95 percent of its exports, and it is the world's fourth largest producer of crude oil. With this background, and given a modicum of understanding of the current geopolitical context, the headlines following should be sufficient to grasp the global significance of Iran.

### "Iran poses most dangerous threat to world order"[307]

Israel's Foreign Minister Avigdor Lieberman declared February 11, 2011, that "Iran poses the largest, most dangerous threat to the current world order."

### "Iran and Russia in secret nuclear pact"[308]

"An Iranian delegation travelled clandestinely to Russia to negotiate a secret, expanded nuclear pact between the two countries worth nearly $40 billion." (Note: While this pact related specifically to nuclear power rather than oil, its greatest motivational purpose for Russia was to secure its oil hegemony in the region and the world.)

### Investment in Iran oil sector will exceed $40b…"[309]

Iran's Oil Minister Rostam Qasemi declared October 30, 2012, that in spite of tough Western sanctions against the Islamic Republic, "… total investment made in the oil industry will jump to above USD 40 billion" within the twelve months concluding March 2013.

## LIBYA

Libya also is an ancient land known in early biblical times, having been specifically mentioned in Ezekiel's end-time prophecy of a last-days confederacy that would attack Israel to "take a spoil." Once again, we see oil being the chief identifying factor unifying the supreme interest of these stated countries (Ezek. 38).

Libya's discovery of oil in 1958 transformed Libya's economy. Oil was used to finance welfare services and to develop projects. Formerly one of the world's poorest countries, by 1997 it became Africa's richest in terms of GDP per capita. Oil accounts for over 95 percent of its exports.

## TOGARMAH

"While scholars have differed somewhat on the exact location of ancient Togarmah, it is always associated with a city or district with the boundaries of the modern nation of Turkey."[310] The term "Beth Togarmah" merely means "the house of Togarmah" or the people generally associated with living there. Whatever these people be, they come from "the north quarters" as related geographically to Israel. And modern Turkey is the large, heavily populated Islamic country enveloping the "north" of Israel, separating the Mediterranean from the Black Sea, with Iran (Persia) and Armenia immediately to the east and Russia and its former Soviet republics to the north. The Hebrew scholar, Gesenius, identified Togarmah as a northern nation known for its horses, located in ancient Armenia, which is largely now located in modern Turkey.[311] Prophetic fulfillment now catapults Turkey into global prominence.

Historically, Turkey was the center and capital of the Ottoman Empire and, under its current leadership, President Tayyip Erdogan, has global aspirations to resurrect the ancient Ottoman Empire with Turkey at the head of the entire Islamic world, and by Koranic implication, of the entire world. Interestingly, Turkey has not been endowed with significant oil and gas resources and so is almost entirely dependent upon Russian oil and gas. Yet Turkey is positioned as a strategic trajectory for oil and gas transportation. Furthermore, Turkey's neighbor to the immediate east is Iran (Persia), one of the world's most energy-endowed nations, which also happens to be Turkey's arch opposition and competition to reign supreme over the Islamic world—hence Iran's title—the "Islamic Republic." It is fascinating that each of these competing nations is heavily dependent upon the world's #1 oil exporting country and leading gas exporter—Russia. And therein lies the magnetic connection between the three in their latter-day attack upon Israel to "take a spoil."

Again, headlines reveal the globally-troubling changes in historic Turkish relationships. A massive geopolitical tectonic shift in Turkish alliances in the past ten years has set the biblically-prophetic stage for developments heretofore deemed impossible. Turkey and Russia have been nearly arch enemies, "primordial contenders" for dominion on the Caucasus and Black Sea.[312] Turkey has pursued membership in the EU persistently, and has been repeatedly denied. The U.S. and Turkey shared mutually warm alliance for over six decades, and Turkey was Israel's sole ally among Islamic nations. But all this has changed in an unprecedented upheaval which has taken global pundits and western politicians by surprise.

### "Russia and Turkey in the Middle East"[313]

"Turkey, until recently one of the most faithful allies of the USA, has progressively become a supporter of Moscow's interests in the Middle East." "No one could have predicted such a succession of events five years ago." "This is an alliance of Eurasian states: Russia—Turkey—Iran—Syria."

**"Turkey—Russia relations"**[314]

"For centuries, Turkey and Russia have been rivals for regional supremacy. Recently... cooperation rather than rivalry appears to dominate the ties."

**"Turkey: An ally no more"**[315]

"Outrageous assertions point to the profound change of orientation by Turkey's government—for six decades the West's closest Muslim ally...."

"As for the Israelis, this 'sudden and unexpected' shift shook to the core their military alignment with Turkey... 'a seriously worrying development.'"

**"Anti-Americanism hits new record in Turkey"**[316]

"The Turkish public dislikes the United States more than any other nation in the world...." "...only 9 percent of the Turkish people [out of a 47 country survey] have a favorable opinion of the US, 83 percent a negative view."

**"Turkey losing interest in EU"**[317]

"After years of having been refused-entry into the European Union [largely due to serious human rights violations], Turkey is losing interest and looking eastward...."

**"Turkey seeks restoration of Ottoman Empire"**[318]

"Ankara is looking to regain its historic ties in Central Asia with the idea of resurrecting what once was the grandeur of the Ottoman Empire...."

"Erdogan's ambitions are similar to those of Russian Prime Minister Vladimir Putin, the former KGB agent who wants to bring all the countries of the former Soviet Union back under the influence of modern Russia."

"Regional analysts say Turkish Prime Minister Erdogan seeks to re-establish Turkey's historical influence in the Turkic countries of Azerbaijan, Kazakhstan, Kyrgyzstan, Turkmenistan, and Uzbekistan... where it either ruled or dominated for centuries."

**"Turkish PM: Iran is Our Friend"**[319]

Prime Minister Erdogan declared that relations between Iran and Turkey are "very good," even as Israelis see Turkey overtly distancing itself from Israel, its historic ally.

**"The Rise of a Sinister Russo-Turkish Axis"**[320]

**"Turkey's military to military ties with Russia growing"**[321]

**"Turkey and Russia on the Rise"**[322]

"Both are clearly ascendant powers...." "Russia is moving aggressively to extend its influence throughout the former Soviet empire, while Turkey is rousing itself from 90 years of post-Ottoman isolation."

**"Presidents of Russia, Turkey adopt strategic declaration"**[323]

"This is a strategic document," said a Kremlin source." It will promote ties and enhance bilateral friendship and partnership." Indeed—for "Turkey receives about 65% of its gas from Russia...."

**"The New Turkey/Russia Axis"**[324]

"Just as Turkey is heir to the Ottomans, Russia is heir to the Byzantines, who ruled a largely peaceful Middle East for close to a millennium before the Turks." There is "a great new plan of creating a Middle East Union as a regional equivalent of the European Union," with Turkey leading up a "re-established Caliphate" with Albania, Jordan, Lebanon, Libya and Syria.

**"Turkey wants to revive Ottoman Empire"**[325]

**"Iran, Syria, Turkey Cementing Ties"**[326]

**"Turkey to help with Iranian gas exports"**[327]

"The Islamic state [Iran/Persia] is Turkey's second biggest gas supplier after Russia."

**"Turkey's change is of 'historical proportions'"**[328]

"The change in Turkey's orientation and its return to the Middle East is an event of historic magnitude," said Michael Oren, Israel's ambassador to the U.S.

## GOMER

The last of the listed nations or people groups specifically mentioned by name in the Ezekiel 38:39 prophecy of the last-days confederate attack on Israel is *Gomer*. Significant historical tracing provides insight as to this ancient people group.

Noah, as recorded in Genesis 5:32, had three sons—Shem, Ham and Japheth. The descendants of Japheth are most commonly identified with the Europeans—all gentiles—since only the Jews can directly trace their lineage, and all Jewish lineage is in the line of Shem. Gomer was the eldest son of Japheth, and was the father of Ashkenaz, Rephath and Togarmah. We have already met the Togarman-ites, traceable to ancient Armenia, and most commonly known today as Turkey. But what of the Gomer-ites? Who are they, and why does it matter?

The Jewish historian Josephus placed Gomer and the Gomer-ites in Anatolian Galatia, whom the Greeks call Galatians. The Christian writer Jerome (c. 390) seemed to agree generally with Josephus, broadly identifying Gomer with the Galatians (in Turkey), Gauls and Celts.

Interestingly, the Hebrew name *Gomer* is widely considered to refer to the Cimmerians who dwelt in the Eurasian Steppes and attacked the Assyrians, who called them *Gimmerai*. But according to tractate Yoma in the Hebrew Talmud, Gomer is the ancestor of the Gomermians or modern Germans. Furthermore, the identity of Gomer's son Ashkenaz has, to the Hebrew people and their descendants, been established as those peoples in middle Europe now known as Germany.

Since Togarmah, another of the three sons of Gomer, is clearly connected with modern Turkey, the astounding geopolitical realignments since the turn of the 7th millennium begin to take on great and discernible significance in the battle for *KING of the Mountain*, particularly in the Gog-Magog confederation to "take a spoil" from Israel in these "last days."

It is of growing interest to see the comparative similarities at this juncture of history and prophecy between Germany and Turkey. The historic enmities between these two descendants of Gomer and Russia are not only fading into relative obscurity, but overtures of increasing favor now are blossoming into new and almost shocking geopolitical and economic alliances. Again, the demand for oil and gas to feed their respective economics is creating a bond that just twenty years earlier could not be envisioned by global pundits.

As one history professor observed, "Both Germany and Russia Are Reinventing Their Pasts."[329] Each country, with recognized authoritarian traditions, increasingly seeks to advance national pride and power by re-envisioning their historic, horrific expressions of totalitarian/authoritarian pasts by selectively diminishing the horror and by re-casting these characteristics as the foundation of a new dynamic of hope. The introduction of the mutual economic bond of oil and gas virtually compels each country into the waiting arms of the other, a somewhat baffling bond considering that the hated Berlin Wall fell just a short generation ago.

Germany and Russia have thus "emerged from a long period of national humiliation and, in a way, subservient position toward the USA. In both instances, there is a new sense of stability in the minds of the countries' elite, and this required a new version of the past. In this construction of the past, subtle anti-Americanism is present." This so-called "subtle" anti-Americanism is, to any honest observer, also reflected in a less-than-subtle anti-Israel undercurrent just waiting for the propitious moment when the mutual bonding agent of oil and gas is deemed threatened, catapulting these sons of Gomer-Germany and Turkey—into a Russian rage to "take a spoil" from a resurrecting Israel.

The Gomer/Germany alliance with Russia has already been secured by the former German Chancellor, Gerhard Schroeder. In December 2005, Schroeder swapped his job with the German government for a job funded by the Russian government when he became board chairman for Nord Stream, a Russian-German gas pipeline that the Chancellor championed while in office. The *Washington Post* called it a "Sellout."[330]

Said the *Post*, "…it turns out that [Matthias Warning] the chief executive of the pipeline consortium is none other than a former East German secret police officer who was friendly with Vladimir Putin back when he was a KGB agent in East Germany. The Russian government chose a costly route under the Baltic Sea rather than a land route for the Nord Stream pipeline because "the Baltic Sea pipeline could allow Russia… to cut off gas to central Europe and the Baltic states while still delivering gas to Germany."[331] Yet Gerhard Schroeder touted the 745 mile pipeline controlled by the Russian Gazprom as Europe's only hope to become a major global geopolitical competitor. *United Press International (UPI)*, on October 9, 2012, put the matter most succinctly: "NORD STREAM touted as EU savior."[332]

## THE "GREAT GAME"

Oil would appear to be "the spoil." The inexhaustible thirst of Europe and the world for "black gold" and its sister, gas, is creating unprecedented, indeed shocking, alliances among nations just as foretold by the Hebrew prophet Ezekiel. And it should capture the attention of every thinking and thoughtful person that all of this prophetic fulfillment is taking place before our eyes in such a short time—our time. The players of the Gog-Magog prophesied confederacy are now aligned.

Europe and the world are truly "over a barrel." Europe cannot function now without the collective cooperation of Russia, Turkey and Germany. Iran dominates access to thirty percent of the world's oil flow through the Persian Gulf and is also one of the world's preeminent oil producers.

As one writer astutely observed, "... the current government in Russia is skillfully playing the board in "The Great Game" and hoping that no one notices its strategic efforts."[333] "Russia's plan to dominate energy markets" is undeniable. Yet in "the Great Game," the grease of Gazprom may soon grind the world in a confederate expression of Russian rage as the Russian Bear roars in revenge to protect its hegemony in the face of dramatic new developments in the Promised Land.

Ezekiel made clear that many other peoples/nations will be drawn into this *latter days* confederacy, in addition to those specifically named. But the prophet minced no words in declaring their total destruction. When the bodies of five-sixths of their collective forces lie still upon the mountains of Israel to be devoured by ravenous birds and beasts, the world will know that the final battle for *KING of the Mountain* is nearing its glorious culmination.

> For I have spoken it, saith the Lord GOD. And I will send a fire on Magog...

> So will I make my holy name known in the midst of my people Israel: and the heathen [nations] shall know that I am the LORD, the holy One of Israel (Ezek. 39:5-7).

*Chapter 20*

# PROBING THOUGHTS *for* PROPHETIC TIMES

1. Why do you think the prophet Ezekiel described God as being "against Gog and Magog?"

2. Do you find it fascinating that all the nations and people groups described 2500 years ago as confederating against Israel are all united either by Islam, Oil, or both today?

3. What is "an evil thought" from God's viewpoint as made clear in the Bible?

4. Do you have any reason to doubt that oil is the "spoil" referenced in Ezekiel 38? How does that become profoundly significant at this moment of history, both for Israel and the world?

5. After reading this chapter and those preceding, have you gained perhaps a greater respect and appreciation for biblical prophecy? Why… or why not?

# Chapter 21

# THE MAHDI VS. THE MESSIAH

———∞∞∞———

*"The world today is in a state described by sages*
*as Labor that precedes the coming of a Messiah."*

"THE COMING IS NEAR" declared a video produced by the Iranian government. This video, virtually unreported in the western world, says that all the signs are moving into place—that Iran will soon help usher in the end times.[334]

## RELIGION AND REVOLUTION

The theme is revolution, but revolution in Iran and the entire Islamic world is driven exclusively by religion, despite the naïve claims of western pundits and politicians of a purported hunger for democracy. Democracy, a political concept of fundamental freedom, is radically inconsistent with Koranic Islam, which mandates exclusive and inviolable adherence to and practice of Sharia law.

Islam, by its very nature, is the ultimate and inseparable melding of religion and all civil and governmental rules and relationships, in effect, a religious "dictatorship" mandating absolute submission by all in its sphere, either by voluntary submission or by force or threat of force. And Muslims anticipate their "messiah," called the *Mahdi*, who will lead them in the final conquest of earth, deposing all who deign to resist, ushering in a global Caliphate. It is the Islamic "apocalypse" or unveiling to be soon revealed in the end times.

While the western world, self-blinded and paralyzed by the trinitarian lordship of political correctness, multiculturalism and religious plural-ism, preaches the doctrine of democratic "salvation" to an "unbelieving" Muslim world, the global cause of Islam is advanced by deceptively—or blatantly—employing the tools of democracy to gain political power and cultural/religious acceptance in the God-forsaking West. But there is coming a moment of truth—a global explosion of Islamic reality—that is seen as necessary to usher in the return of the Mahdi or 12th Imam. It is called "The Coming."

The Iranian government sees the current advancing unrest in the Middle East as a sign that the Mahdi—Islamic messiah—is about to appear. "While the revolutionary movements gripping the Middle East have created uncertainty throughout the region," CBN News reports that "the video shows that the Iranian regime believes the chaos is divine proof that their ultimate victory is at hand." Titled *The Coming is Near*, the video produced by a group called "the Conductors of the Coming" in connection with the Basij, the Iranian paramilitary force, claims the Mahdi will lead the armies of Islam to victory over all non-Muslims in the last days.[335]

The video, approved at the highest levels of the Iranian government, claims Iran is destined to rise as a great power in the last days to help defeat America [the West] and Israel, and thus prepare the way for the return of the Mahdi. That time, the Iranians believe, is fast approaching—indeed at the very door. And it should be readily apparent to thoughtful observers that such religious fervor and conviction cannot and will not be ultimately compromised at a diplomatic table. Thus, the Iranian pursuit of nuclear capability is not truly a matter merely of geopolitical maneuvering but of a profound and unalterable commitment to intimidating power intended solely to impose the integrated rule of the religious government of Islam upon the entire world. Let the world be wary, for every man, woman and child soon faces the final choice of a "messiah."

## RIGHTEOUSNESS AND RELATIONSHIP

Contrast can produce color and variety but also conflict and vengeful animosity. Contrast can aid us in evaluating truth, yet it can also devolve into unabashed terror. Resolving contrast can lead to restored relationships and righteousness, yet also catapult individuals and people groups into unholy and unfettered rage. Thus presents the profound—yes even terrifying—dilemma faced by every denizen of this aging planet in these end times. It is a choice no man or woman, no politician, pastor, priest or pontificating pundit can escape. It is an ultimate question demanding each human inhabitant upon the face of the earth to profoundly ponder. The question is…

### WHO IS THE MESSIAH?

Both Jew and Gentile believers anticipate the "coming" of the Messiah. In the New Testament, the coming of the Messiah is described as the *parousia* or *appearing*. The physical descendants of Abraham, Isaac and Jacob have, to one degree or another, anticipated for millennia the first coming of a promised *Anointed One* or *Mashiach*...Messiah. The Messiah's coming has most often been described in the *Tanakh* or Old Testament as "the day of the LORD" (Isa. 13:6-13; Joel 1:15; 2:1-11). The New Testament writers, believing that Yeshua (Jesus) was indeed the promised Messiah, anticipate and look for the *Second Coming* of Christ (The Anointed One-Messiah). That *Second Coming* is referred to as the "blessed hope" of the Church (Titus 2:13).

The anticipated "coming" of the Messiah by Jews looks for a time of reconciliation of all things. It is seen as a time of redemption, a *buying back* of a destroyed planet and its inhabitants, both man and beast—the restoration of all things—bringing Shalom (peace, wholeness and completion) to all mankind. Preparation for that *coming* is largely made by doing good works (mitzvahs) so as to usher the world into the time of *tikkun olam* or the restoration of the world fit for the Messiah.

Christians and Messianic Jewish believers, on the other hand, believe that Jesus Christ was, indeed, the promised Anointed One, who was crucified and rose again after three days as prophesied and will soon return at a day and hour least expected to judge the earth in righteousness, requiring all who will receive His promised salvation to repent. Genuine repentance is initiated by heart conviction of one's sinful condition that separates humankind from God their Creator, followed by confession of sin and turning of both mind and heart to conform to God's Ways as described in His Word—the Bible. All who, by faith, receive Jesus Christ—the Messiah—the Holy One of Israel, and who repent and follow Him with a whole heart will be saved from eternal damnation.

## THE CONTRAST IS CRITICAL

Except for the paralyzing thought construction demanded by political correctness, religious pluralism and multiculturalism, the contrast between Allah and Jehovah, the Mahdi and the Messiah could not be clearer. Contrary to politically-correct perception and promise, the god of Islam and the God of the Bible could not be more radically dissimilar. Neither Muslims and Jews, nor Muslims and Christians worship the same God, for Allah—god of Islam—demands eradication of Jews and Christians as stated by the father of Islam, Mohammed, after having forsaken peaceful Mecca for violently-transformational Medina.

The contrast of purported "messiahs" is critical, both for each individual, for the nations and for our world, not to mention the eternal consequences. Again, *VIEWPOINT* will determine destiny.

Islam demands absolute submission to the religious government of the Mahdi, to be ushered in at the point of an unsatiated sword through creation of global chaos. Purported peace will be purchased, not by the sacrificial blood of the "infidels" (those who refuse to submit to Sharia under the Mahdi), but through self-destruction in the pursuit of martyrdom. It therefore leaves little to the informed imagination to comprehend the coming convulsive conflict as the serious followers of Mohammed strive to implement the prophet's mandate for Islam to rule the world, believing this to be the propitious moment to fulfill Islamic "prophecy." No purported peace will pacify such martyr-driven ideological commitment, thus global conflagration is inevitable to bring about the anticipated reign of the Mahdi over the planet. The epic, end-time, and eternal battle for *KING of the Mountain* is emerging even now from partial cover to open and unrestrainable conflict.

## THE MESSIAH FACTOR

Even as the Muslim world prepares to usher in "the coming" of the Mahdi, so the Jewish world is experiencing a rising expectation that both Jew and Gentile are now living in the *messianic age*, however one may define it. Many Lubavichers were convinced that the Rabbi Manachem Mendel Schneerson was the awaited Messiah. He is long dead, yet some expect his resurrection. A debate rages as to whether the late Lubavitcher Schneerson was merely a great Rebbe or future redeemer.[336]

Interestingly, a campaign began in the late 1970's with the slogan "We Want Moshiah Now." Of further interest is that the call for "Messiah" among the more fundamentalist Jewish groups corresponded in time with the publication of the phenomenally best-seller, *The Late Great Planet Earth* by Hal Lindsey, which enjoyed distribution primarily within the greater gentile Christian world. At the same time, the soul-gripping, heart-stirring film *A Thief in the Night* strikingly made its debut within the gentile Christian world. By 1992, as both the western world began to unravel at the seams and Israel and Islam emerged with increasing prominence, the Messiah movement among Jews also picked up steam declaring, "Prepare for the Coming of the Messiah."[337] At the same time, a series of dramatic full-size billboards appeared along a busy Southern California freeway announcing, "SWORD of the LORD coming Soon," followed by another… "PREPARE TO MEET THY GOD." These were placed, not by a church or religious group, but by a simple and unassuming man in his early 30's who invested his life savings to shout out a message that he said "the Lord burned on my heart."

The "Messiah Factor" has since mushroomed amazingly across the planet. By 2005, Russian Chief Rabbi Berel Lazar publically announced his conviction that the earth will soon see the coming of a Messiah to judge all mankind. "We know that he is very near at hand," he said. In explaining his assumptions, Rabbi Lazar noted: "The world today is in a state described by our sages as 'hevley mashiah,' that is, labor that precedes the coming of a Messiah." "We are living on the verge of history," he said. "It can be felt everywhere."[338]

Many purported "messiahs" have appeared and disappeared over the course of history. Several such have died within the generation last passed. But it is indeed fascinating that messianic expectations should weave their way into even the secular world.

Indeed politicians are now purported to bear the glorious mantle of "messiah." None has been more nobly endowed with the seductive promise of secular salvation than Barack Hussein Obama, often depicted with an angelic halo heralding his global entry to divine dominion. For any with eyes open, it is impossible to escape the aura of the "divine" cast by man and media over the putative 44th president of the United States of America.

For true Christian believers and undoubtedly serious physical descendants of Abraham, Isaac and Jacob, such blatant depiction of Barack Obama in messianic glory is tantamount to nothing less than outrageous blasphemy. A few illustrations of the sheer sacrilege of such messianic allusions is most likely necessary to dispel any doubt of the implications and not-so-hidden expectations of "salvation" for those who embrace the Obamafication cult of such idolatrous secular faith. *NEWSWEEK* sets the tone, declaring "America is desperate for a messiah."[339] Consider well these unvarnished quotes.

— "Our Lord and Savior, Barack Obama." These were the shocking words repeated twice by actor Jamie Foxx at the Soul Train Awards and broadcast boldly on BET (Black Entertainment Television) in 2012. The proclamation was followed by unrestrained and uproarious audience acclamation.

— "In a way Obama is standing above the country, above the world. He's sort of GOD." (*NEWSWEEK* editor Evan Thomas).

— "No one saw him coming... like Jesus being born in a manger." (Lawrence Carter, dean of the Martin Luther King Jr. International Chapel, *Chicago Tribune*, Dahlan Glanton, "Some See God's Will in Obama win," Nov. 29, 2008).

— "Obama: Son of Promise, Child of Hope." (The book title of Nikki Grimes spread across the cover image of Barack Obama surrounded by rays of light in the aura of Christ, Simon and Schuster 2008).

— "This was the moment when the rise of the oceans began to slow and our planet began to heal." (Barack Obama, Speech in St. Paul, MN, June 3, 2008).

— "This is bigger than Kennedy.... This is the New Testament." (MSNBC host Chris Matthews responding to the Obama presidential primary victory, Feb. 13, 2008).

— "He is not the Word made flesh, but the triumph of word over flesh...." (Ezra Klein).

— "He communicates God-like energy..." (Steve Davis, Charleston, SC).

— "We're here to evolve to a higher plane... he is an evolved leader... a Tongue dipped in the Unvarnished Truth." (Oprah Winfrey)

— "Is Obama a (or the) Messiah? (Claire Hoffman, newsweek.washing-tonpost.com/onfaith/undergod/2008/02/Obama_the_messiah.html), Feb. 18, 2008.

— "I'M ASKING YOU TO BELIEVE..." (Obama website 2008, included in a blog declaring 'OBAMA IS GOD').

— "Prophecy Fulfilled." (The heading of a poster depicting Barack Obama as Jesus Christ, Obama's face hovering over an open Bible. The poster was sold on the streets during the Democratic National Convention 2012 in Charlotte, NC).

— "Is Barack Obama the Messiah?" (Article heading in *abcnews*, Feb. 10, 2008).

— "Obama Greater than Jesus," (An editorial in the Danish newspaper *Politiken* Dec. 28, 2009, proclaiming Obama "the practical savior of our times.").

— "Yes, I just said it. Obama is my Jesus... I've officially been saved, and soon... the rest of the country will be too ... In the name of Obama." (Article by Associate editor of Smith College's *The Sophian* titled "I Will Follow Him," Sept. 18, 2008).

— When Obama talks "the Messiah is absolutely speaking." (Viewpoint of Louis Farrakhan speaking to the crowd at Nation of Islam Savior's Day, Feb. 24, 2008).

— "THE TRUTH." (A painting by Michael D'Artuono depicting Barack Obama as Jesus Christ, wearing a Crown of Thorns with arms out-stretched as if offering himself for global salvation. Since Jesus declared "I am the way, the truth and the life..." (John 14:6), the artist now bla-tantly attributes the ultimate title, "THE TRUTH" to America's puta-tive president. The notorious sacrilege has now been displayed in a college "Art Gallery").

It is truly troubling that, in officially removing God from its platform during America's 2012 presidential election campaign, the Democratic National Convention erected a stained-glass window backdrop so as to gloriously present in a church-like atmosphere their patron saint and pseudo messiah to millions of adoring worshipers. At the same time, a calendar was peddled on the streets proclaiming Barack Obama as deity, i.e., a photograph of Mr. Obama's purported birth certificate with the words "Heaven Sent," a photograph of Mr. Obama referencing the well-known John 3:16, stating, "For God so loved the world that He gave His only begotten Son..." and yet a further page depicting people with their hands reaching for Obama's back- with the words of Psalm 23, "The Lord is my Shepherd, I shall not want," thus declaring the political rising star to be not only "Savior" and "Heaven Sent" but also "The Truth" and ultimate and only trustworthy "Provider" for the peoples of this planet. It should therefore come as no surprise that *Der Spiegel*, Germany's widely-respected news magazine, should have presented a cover picture of Barack Obama July 2008, with the words "The MESSIAH FACTOR" emblazoned to capture the darkening conscience of an increasingly hope-less world.

"If Obama is the Messiah, it might explain why he has not presented an original birth certificate and why he lacks a valid US Social Security number," opined the *Israel Insider*. While the observation may have been facetious, the headline was not..."Palestinians... ask him [Obama] to be their Messiah."[340] The same sentiment echoes throughout Europe. A survey by the German Marshall Fund found Europe's approval rating of ninety percent for Barack Obama to be "unprecedented for any American president," then concluding, "People in the European Union and Turkey have fallen under the Obama spell" and that "Obamamania" continues to sweep Europe.[341]

Messianic fever and fervor is not receding but rather rising world-wide as clouds of global destruction hang ominously over the peoples and nations of our planet. None less than the Prince of Wales has been heralded as the winged hero "saving the world." A giant bronze statue of Prince Charles became the centerpiece of a remote Amazon town. The immortalizing statue clothed the Prince in a loin cloth and sported angelic wings. Although the Prince of Wales is destined by tradition to become "Defender of the Faith," he has already expressed his intentions to broaden the title to "Defender of Faiths," thus ingratiating himself as the global messianic figure for all religious persuasions. The inscription on the statue in Brazil honoring the winged Prince reads, "Savior of the World," in response to which the Prince remarked that he was "amazed" and "deeply touched." Prince Charles made clear he believes "My duty is to save the world: I was born for a purpose."[342] [343]

## MESSIANIC FERVOR IS GROWING

Anticipation of the Messiah is growing among professing Christian believers throughout the world, but perhaps most prominently in Third World countries where persecution and poverty are most acute. Unfortunately, prosperity does not pave the path to prophetic expectation. Notably, however, vision for the Messiah is now being increasingly voiced in Israel. "Zion Needs the Messiah" declared the *Arutz Sheva* (Israel National News) headline. "There is disillusionment" with various military and political leaders who "have failed to bring us redemption." "This disillusionment should increase our yearning for the spiritual leadership and vision of the Messiah…." "The belief in the coming of the Messiah is deeply embedded within the consciousness of the Jewish people… even the secular…." "We are therefore awaiting the arrival of the true Messiah…." "Even though He may tarry, we are not to lose hope."[344]

"Hope maketh not ashamed," wrote the Apostle Paul (Rom. 5:5). The Psalmist David declared prophetically, "My flesh shall rest in hope" (Psa. 16:9), hope in a coming Messiah but also in the resurrection of the just. And certainly, "If in this world only we have hope, we are most miserable" (I Cor. 15:19). The true expectation of believing hope for both Jew and Gentile Christian is in the soon-coming of the Messiah to rectify earth's wrongs, and to redeem the remnant of those who put their trust in Him, and to judge the world in righteousness (Psa. 96:13, Psa. 98:9, John 16:8).

This hope was shockingly catapulted down the prophetic track of time by one of Israel's most prominent rabbis. Shortly before he died, Yitzhak Kaduri wrote the name of the Messiah on a small note which he requested would remain sealed until one year after his death. When the note was opened, it revealed what many have known for centuries, yet many others (particularly Jews) have categorically rejected. This is the name Rabbi Kaduri wrote: "'Yehoshua', or Yeshua (Jesus), is the Messiah."[345] The secret note said, "He will lift the people and prove that his word and law are valid."

Jewish leaders and readers responded with questioning amazement— the ultra-orthodox with denying scorn. "So this means Rabbi Kaduri was a Christian?" they lamented. Yet two of Kaduri's followers in Jerusalem admitted that the note was authentic, but confusing for his followers. A few months before his passing at the age of 108, the Rabbi surprised his followers as he gave a message in his synagogue on Yom Kippur, the Day of Atonement, teaching how to recognize the Messiah. Kaduri's grandson, Rabbi Yosef Kaduri, said his grandfather spoke many times during his last days about the coming Messiah and redemption through Yeshua ben Joseph, Yeshua ben David, the promised Anointed One.

## WHO IS THE MESSIAH?

The question then lingers—How would we recognize the Messiah? Upon what authority will His authenticity be established? Will many be confused, deceived or even destroyed by a false hope in a counterfeit?

The conjunction of history and prophecy now makes plain that three primary choices are presented to the planet in which to invest ultimate hope. Jesus, Yeshua, who is called *Christ* or the *Anointed One;* the Mahdi or Third Imam—*Lord of the Age;* and the *Anti-Christ* who will present himself as the promised peacemaker of a New World Order. The Mahdi will be ushered in by coercion and conquest, the Anti-Christ (the "lawless one") will obtain dominion through godless democracy and conquest, and Yeshua Messiah-Christ will obtain authority and dominion through heart conviction and soul salvation. While all will promise peace, only one will ultimately deliver on the promise. All will compete for the crown as *KING of the Mountain,* but only one will ultimately reign. Two will be usurpers while only one will rule and reign under legitimate authority.

It is the Mahdi vs. Messiah… and the Antichrist. The world's destiny rides in the balance. The forces of each are coalescing for conquest. And each inhabitant of planet earth will decide destiny, both now and for eternity. "Multitudes, multitudes in the valley of decision: for the day of the LORD is near in the valley of decision" (Joel 3:14).

*Chapter 21*

# PROBING THOUGHTS *for* PROPHETIC TIMES

1. What role, if any, does the Islamic video *The Coming Is Near* produced by the Iranian government play in revealing messianic expectation as a major factor in the end-time (our time) battle for *KING of the Mountain*?

2. If, as politically-correct politicians are prone to say, Muslims worship the same god as Jews and Christians, how does one explain the Islamic mandate of the Koran and Hadith to kill all Christians and Jews as "infidels," wherever you find them?

3. Why do you suppose there has been an escalating expectation of a coming Messiah or of a messianic age among Jews (both religious and secular), Christians and Muslims since the 1970's? What does this burgeoning belief say about our times?

4. What explanation can you give to validate the amazing and blatant attribution of "messiahship" to Barack Obama? Or to Prince Charles, Prince of Wales?

5. What is the significance of a leading Jewish rabbi declaring Yeshua (Jesus) as being the Messiah?

6. Are you able to fathom how messianic expectation becomes a leading force in the ultimate battle for *KING of the Mountain*?

7. Everyone on the planet will choose a "Messiah." Whom will you choose, and on what basis—the Mahdi, the Anti-Christ of the New World Order, or Jesus Christ (Yeshua)?

*Part*

# III

# THE CONQUEST

NEARLY EVERY CONTEST ENDS IN CONQUEST of some sort, and so it is and will be with regard to the Eternal, Epic and End-Time Battle for *KING of the Mountain*.

The historic, prophesied and now end-time battle for *KING of the Mountain* is the "mother of all battles" and will determine both the ultimate rulership of this planet and define the destiny of the souls of men. No battle in recorded history approaches the surmounting danger, drama or destruction destined to spill out upon the nations and upon every human inhabitant of this mortal sphere.

In this final segment of *KING of the Mountain*, we look with greater specificity at the unfolding drama being enacted before us. It is real, it is certain and it will have unparalleled consequences.

We return first to Jerusalem so as to better understand the bloody battle ahead. It becomes not only the primary set in the unfolding drama but also stands as a metaphor for the momentous political and spiritual decisions at stake. "THE GREAT GAME" makes real the mystery of mind-challenging prophecy, leading finally to solving the "Mystery of History" and the "Mystery of the Mountain," the "Throne on the Mount" and the decision we must all make. Let the final curtain call of history commence.

*Chapter 22*

# THE BATTLE FOR JERUSALEM

———— ∞∞∞ ————

### *"Truly a dangerous war. At stake: Who will Rule and reign over planet Earth?"*

"THE FIGHT HAS BEGUN FOR JERUSALEM," declared Palestinian Authority Prime Minister Ahmed Qurei, "and it is a dangerous war."[346] That was August 2005. Five years later, the *Arutz Sheva* headline reaffirmed "THE BATTLE for JERUSALEM," noting, "so goes Jerusalem, so goes the peace process." This Opinion commentary in *israelnationalnews. com* plainly presented the controversy confronting the nations: "The focus on settlements or the 'occupation' has now taken a back seat to the focus on Jerusalem itself."[347]

## A BLOODY BATTLE AHEAD

The battle for Jerusalem will truly be "a dangerous war." No war in the history of mankind will have had more momentous impact. At stake is the final battle for *KING of the Mountain.* Who will rule and reign over planet Earth?

The Palestinian cause is a mere political and religious ploy to obscure the true objective. The purported compassion driving the nations to demand a "two-state" solution for the ultimate establishment of world peace has become a powerful diversion, providing "cover" for the nefarious purposes lurking in the global shadows, soon to be unleashed with a vengeance intent on victory in the ultimate and cataclysmic battle for Jerusalem. Until now, narrow and provincial perspectives have clouded vision as to the intended purposes of global powers, whether political, economic or religious. But gusty winds of war are now blowing, with gale force, driving away the clouds that once provided cover, revealing both motive and method in the passionate pursuit to become *KING of the Mountain.*

## The City of God

"God's City." That was the cover title for *U.S. News and World Report* December 18, 1995, citing Jerusalem's 3000 years of history, beginning with King David.[348] Indeed, "The history of Jerusalem is writ in stone," and "The Holy City's final political disposition remains one of the sorest points of Mideast peace negotiations."[349] While the city's history is quite clear, her future (from a political standpoint) is not. Yet her symbolic status is perfectly clear.

Jerusalem has become, in effect, the center of the world. He who would rule the world must reign in Jerusalem. Will it be the God of Abraham Isaac and Jacob, the God of Jacob (Israel) as revealed in and through Yeshua ben David (Jesus); Mohammed's Allah; the "Vicar of Christ" empowered by the Vatican; or an ascendant secular global cabal with its counterfeit messiah, elevating again the "Goddess of Reason" over the Creator? Prophecy will soon become history for "the City of God."

The real question looming over the fate of the "Holy City," then, is much greater than "Who will be *KING of the Mountain?*" but is rather, "Who is God?" or "Who will be God?" This battle on earth will be nothing other than a final playing out of the cosmic war historic in the heavenlies between God and His arch-enemy Satan, who is the ultimate enemy of your soul. The battle for the "City of God" is the symbolic battle for the souls of men. It is "winner take all." All other current conflicts are merely peripheral to the ultimate prize.

Until recently, Jerusalem has remained "too holy to handle," according to The *JERUSALEM POST*.[350] But unholy boldness is now brashly embracing the profane in desperate pursuit of the prize. As was stated in *Jerusalem Betrayed, Prophecy and Conspiracy Collide in the Holy City* (1997),

> The fuse has already been lit that ultimately will ignite the final conflagration around Jerusalem. The nations of the world are aligned for spiritual and physical warfare against the city of God.[351]

## God's Vortex

"There is a vortex over Jerusalem, and it is rapidly growing in intensity as we move unerringly toward the last chapter of this age," wrote the editor of *Zion's Fire* (2006). "It is God's vortex, and it is whirling out in a circular motion across the whole earth and drawing evil and wicked men and nations toward Jerusalem." "The nations think they are coming to fulfill their purposes. The reality is, God's vortex is drawing them there for His Judgment...."[352]

A *vortex* is a swirling mass, whether air or liquid. The faster it moves in its circular sphere, the greater its influence on the air or liquid around it, ever extending its impact. At the heart of the greatest storms known to man is such a vortex. The sheer volume and violence generated from the vortex is beyond the ultimate control of man and has devastating consequences. And so it is with the "Vortex Over Jerusalem."

Jerusalem was the capital of King David. It is written that the "Redeemer" of Israel, Messiah, yes "the Prince of Peace" shall return to rule "upon the throne of David" (Isa. 9:6-7). He will rule with true "judgment and justice" (Isa. 9:7). But Satan is determined that will not happen. He, throughout time, has sought to triumph over God's eternal purposes so as to make void the covenant of promised salvation for mankind through Jesus Christ, His "Anointed One." Lucifer lusts after God's glory. His ambition is to rule the earth. And the nations want to be free of divine restraint. Hence, since the dawn of history, Satan has opposed the Jewish people as well as Jerusalem, their capital.

"And now, at this hour of history, the heat is being turned up. Soon it will be hotter than Nebuchadnezzar's 'burning fiery furnace' (Dan. 3:20). Satan knows that the time of Christ's coming is fast approaching and that his time is running out."[353] Unfortunately, our world and its leaders are promoting unprecedented rebellion against God and, from their viewpoint, are winning. The epicenter of that rebellion is the "Holy City" where God chose to place His name (I Kings 14:21).

The raging spiritual war that drives external events renders it nearly impossible for the power-brokers of earth to "connect the dots" and to comprehend the dire consequences to be precipitated in their blinding rage. Tragically, most Jews and perhaps most professing Christians remain relatively clueless as to the unfolding disaster about to consume our planet.

"Everyone and everything will be drawn into the vortex of God. For some, it will be for deliverance—for others, it will be for judgment."[354] But make no mistake—Jesus Christ will rule the nations from Jerusalem.

## "A BURDENSOME STONE"

The warning of the Lord of nations through the ancient prophet, Zechariah, is being fulfilled daily in the decisions of the world's dictatorships and democracies. Jerusalem has become a "burdensome stone" and is becoming a "cup of trembling." In more modern terms, "push is coming to shove" in regards to Jerusalem.

It would behoove the so-called "better natures" of the world's leaders to heed the Lord's dire warning.

> Behold, I will make Jerusalem a cup of trembling unto all the people round about, when they shall be in siege both against Judah and against Jerusalem.

And in that day will I make Jerusalem a burdensome stone for all people: all that burden themselves with it shall be cut in pieces, though all the people of the earth be gathered together against it (Zech. 12:2-3).

But why Jerusalem? Why is Jerusalem so precious in the eyes of the God of Abraham, Isaac and Israel? It is a matter of the eye. Jerusalem is the "apple" of God's eye. It is of center focus because of His covenant with Abraham through Isaac and confirmed in Jacob. It is the earthly symbol portraying the eternal substance of God's redemptive plan for the inhabitants of earth, both Jew and Gentile, who will receive from the heart the salvation proffered through Yahweh's Messiah, Yeshua, who will rule and reign from the Mount in Jerusalem. "For thus saith the LORD of hosts;

Jerusalem shall be inhabited as towns without walls…

For I, saith the LORD, will be unto her as a wall of fire round about, and will be the glory in the midst of her.

For thus saith the LORD of hosts: he that toucheth you toucheth the apple of his eye.

And the LORD shall inherit Judah his portion in the holy land, and shall choose Jerusalem again" (Zech. 2:4-12).

Unfortunately, the nations will neither hear nor heed. Their collective rebellion and rage against the LORD and against His anointed (Israel) (Psa. 2:1-2) is culminating in catastrophe. The proverbial "handwriting is on the wall" of the world's powers. Their nationalized "good intentions" driving them to resist the Holy One of Israel will inur to grave destruction. Consider well!

In that day shall the LORD defend the inhabitants of Jerusalem…

And it shall come to pass in that day, that I will seek to destroy all the nations that come against Jerusalem (Zech. 12:8-9).

## ETERNAL CAPITAL VS. ETERNAL CONFLICT

Viewpoint always determines destiny. For this reason, the prophet Joel concluded his ancient warning to the world concerning the dividing of the land of Israel and of the city of Jerusalem with these seemingly strange words…

Multitudes, multitudes in the valley of decision: for the day of the
LORD is near in the valley of decision (Joel 3:14).

Consider further Yahweh's viewpoint (the God of Abraham, Isaac and
Israel). God leaves nothing to reasoning or imagination as to His viewpoint
concerning Israel and Jerusalem. It is this clear understanding that the nations
are now compelled either to accept or reject, and they reject at their peril.

The LORD shall roar out of Zion, and utter his voice from Jerusalem;
and the heavens and the earth shall shake: but the LORD will be the
hope of his people, and the strength of the children of Israel.

So shall ye know that I am the LORD your God dwelling in Zion,
my holy mountain: then shall Jerusalem be holy....

Judah shall dwell forever, and Jerusalem from generation to generation... for the LORD dwelleth in Zion (Joel 3:16-21).

With this biblical backdrop, we briefly review the growing rage of the
nations against Jerusalem juxtaposed with Israel's Bible-based view. In this
way we can clarify the conflict "on the ground" which is, at root, a spiritual
conflict. The nations are thus put on notice, for our Creator is a God of
"due process."

## EUROPEAN PLAN

Will the "baby" be divided so that both Jew and Gentile, Isaac and Ishmael,
can claim a piece of Jerusalem? The entire Gentile world has apparently made
such a decision. The headline December 2, 2009, read "Europe Moves to Divide
Jerusalem." Led by Sweden, 27 member states of the European Union were
preparing to recognize a portion of Jerusalem as the capital of a Palestinian
State. "This unprecedented campaign has united Israel's political parties as
never before." "The Europeans have become aggressively active in a desperate attempt to save the collapsing government of the Palestinian Authority."[355]
Benjamin Netanyahu, Israel's Prime Minister, made a major effort to
foil the Swedish plan to divide Jerusalem. Yet "Sweden, with the support
of Britain, Ireland, Belgium and a number of other countries," including
France, have persisted in promoting the "original formulation of the proposal calling for East Jerusalem to be the capital of the Palestinian State."[356]

## CANADIAN PROPOSAL

Canada formally unveiled a plan in May 2010, to "resolve the conflict over the future of Jerusalem's Old City." The proposal was released

after seven years of research and planning. It called for "a special regime" comprised of Israeli and Palestinian officials headed by "an effective and empowered third party" commissioner to oversee the contested Jewish, Muslim and Christian holy sites and described the Old City as "a microcosm" of the wider Israeli-Palestinian conflict.[357]

## VATICAN INTERVENTION

In February 2000, the Vatican and the Palestinian Authority signed an agreement for an "internationally guaranteed special status" for Jerusalem. During the visit by Pope John Paul II to Bethlehem that year, he announced that the Vatican had always recognized "Palestinian national rights to a homeland." In response, Rabbi Shlomo Aviner, Dean of Yeshivat Ateret Cohanim said that the Pope's goal was simply to obtain a foothold in Jerusalem for the Roman Catholic Church.[358]

The Jewish Sanhedrin, the restored and resurrected spiritual governing body of Israel, warned Israel's President, Shimon Peres, and incoming Prime Minister Benjamin Netanyahu against the Roman Catholic Church's agenda via the Vatican hiding behind diplomatic agreements. Over the course of many years, the Catholic Church has sought to gain possession and/or authority over sites such as Mt. Zion, the Old City of Jerusalem, the Sea of Galilee, and other traditional "Christian" venues. The main purpose for these efforts, as disclosed by *Israel National News*, has been to "rid the Temple Mount and the Old City of exclusive Jewish sovereignty" leaving Israel "bereft of respect for the spiritual and political essence of the nation." The extraordinary extent of Vatican intervention will be revealed in a later chapter.

## MUSLIM MANDATES

"First Jerusalem, Then We'll Take All Palestine." Those were the words of Abbas Zaki, the Palestinian Authority's Ambassador to Lebanon on Lebanese television. "We will talk politics;" said Zaki, "but our principles are clear." "Israel must pay a heavy price," he said. "We will drive them all out of Palestine."[359] This is not exactly an expression of desired peace, good faith or good will, but it is a clear statement of true Palestinian intentions when spoken in Arabic to an Arab-Muslim audience.

Four years later, June 2012, a prominent Egyptian cleric made an even more provocative proclamation in the course of Egypt's first "democratic" presidential election. According to Safwat Hagazy, "Egypt's new capital will be Jerusalem." The claim was made at a presidential rally for Mohammed Morsi, the Muslim Brotherhood candidate, and was aired on the Egyptian Al-Nas TV station. The world's leaders must carefully consider the true and uncompromising Islamic conviction regarding Jerusalem. Here are Hagazy's further words.

> We can see how the dream of the Islamic Caliphate is being realized. The United States of the Arabs will be restored, Allah willing. The Capital of the Caliphate... will be Jerusalem, Allah willing.[360]

Hagazy's speech called for "millions" of "shakeeds"—Muslim martyrs—to take Jerusalem.

> Our capital shall not be Cairo, Mecca or Medina. It shall be Jerusalem with God's will. Our chants shall be: 'millions of martyrs will march towards Jerusalem'... Yes, we will either pray in Jerusalem or we will be martyred there."[361]

According to some analysts, Hagazy's call for Jerusalem as the capital of the Islamic Caliphate speaks of Islamic apocalyptic writings and prophecy concerning Islam's messiah figure known as the "Mahdi." Egyptian authors of the book *Al-Mahdi and the End of Time* write: "Jerusalem will be the location of the rightly guided Caliphate and the center of Islamic rule, which will be headed by Imam al-Mahdi... That will abolish the leadership of the Jewish...."[362]

## EMBASSY ROW

The global rise, particularly driven by the western world, of multiculturalism, religious pluralism and political correctness has poisoned the minds of presidents, prime ministers, pastors, priests, and yes, even popes, impairing reason and promoting a perverse form of human pride. The "political correctness" which now defines, yes even dictates, the decisions of political, business and religious leaders throughout the world has declared a platform of determining beliefs entirely in opposition to the declared Word, Will and Ways of God as set forth in the Bible. Political correctness is thus driving destiny and producing decisions that define a world increasingly set against God and His anointed, "Israel and Yeshua (Jesus)." There exists no clearer evidence of this phenomenon than the "Embassy Row."

In June of 2012, the U.S. President Barack Obama, refused to observe a law passed by both the Senate and House of Representatives in 1995 stating that "Jerusalem should be recognized as the capital of the State of Israel and the United States Embassy in Israel should be established in Jerusalem no later than May 31, 1999." In reality, no U.S. president, Republican or Democrat, including Bill Clinton, George W. Bush and Barack Obama, has acted to comply with this law, citing security concerns continually impressed upon the President by the U.S. State Department, which has harbored and stirred perpetual animus toward Israel for at least seven decades. In truth, it was the U.S. State Department that sought desperately to politically intimidate President Harry S. Truman from recognizing the State of Israel in 1948.

New efforts have been initiated by six U.S. senators to put an end to the needed presidential confirmation to implement the Jerusalem Embassy Act of 1995. Over 80 senators were ultimately willing to sign on to the bill which, shockingly, was opposed by the Israeli government.[363]

Therefore the row over the embassy continues unabated. But that row is not limited to the United States. On August 16, 2006, Costa Rica announced it was moving its embassy from Jerusalem "to mend relations with the Arab nations." The next week on August 25, El Salvador became the last nation among the nations of the world to relocate its embassy from Jerusalem to Tel Aviv. Diplomatic sources said the decisions "were aimed at ending their diplomatic isolation in the Arab world."[364]

Once again, "political correctness" triumphed over biblical correctness, leaving the entire family of nations aligned, either openly or tacitly, against Israel and the city where God chose to place His name. Israel responded with regret, saying, "Jerusalem would remain Israel's eternal capital."[365] Interestingly, the God of Abraham, Isaac and Israel—the Lord of Nations—has spoken on the issue for those who care to concern themselves with His viewpoint.

> And in that day will I make Jerusalem a burdensome stone for all people: all that burden themselves with it shall be cut in pieces, though all the people of the earth be gathered against it.

> And it shall come to pass in that day, that I will seek to destroy all the nations that come against Jerusalem (Zech. 12:3, 9).

It would seem apparent on its face that to arrogate one's viewpoint over what the God of heaven and earth has declared in His sovereignty is to display a level of *chutzpah* beyond all reasonable human comprehension. Persisting in such pride will manifest the profound and painful truth that "*VIEWPOINT* determines destiny"[366]

## JERUSALEM SHOWDOWN NEARS

"When it comes to Jerusalem, we are ready to confront anyone... to assert our sovereignty," warned Benjamin Netanyahu in 1997. "If we do not stand up to threats over Jerusalem, we will not stand up to threats over anything."[367] That was sixteen years ago, and the Jerusalem "showdown" is no longer "near" but imminent. We must all take heed, for the "day of the Lord" is knocking at the door.

## EHUD BARAK'S BREACH

In June 2000, Prime Minister Ehud Barak vowed that Jerusalem "will never again be divided." "Jerusalem shall forever remain ours because it is in our souls," he said. "Only someone who has no sense of reality, who does not understand anything about Israel's yearning and the Jewish people's historical connection to Jerusalem for over 3000 years, would even consider making concessions over the city," he said. Yet, "I cannot and do not want to ignore the dark clouds gathering upon us,"[368] responded Jerusalem's then mayor Ehud Olmert. "On this Jerusalem Day," he warned, "Very soon you will be faced with decisions that affect the fate of this city. No decision that you have taken in your whole life was similar to the one you will be faced with. Everything you have done in your life… was but a preparation for this moment…."[369]

Just one month later, fear replaced the last vestiges of faith for Ehud Barak at the Camp David marathon negotiations convened by U.S. President Bill Clinton. Fortunately for Barak, his unprecedented offer of almost unending compromises was amazingly rejected by Yasser Arafat, shocking the world and revealing the true intentions of the Palestinian Authority, not for peace but for annihilation of Jewish presence. Clinton said of Barak, "He took a big risk."[370] Indeed he did, for he lost the trust of his countrymen. [371]

## ARIEL SHARON SUCCUMBS

Ariel Sharon became Israel's Prime Minister with a crushing electoral victory over Barak. The next day, at the Western Wall, Sharon sent an unmistakable signal to the world. "I am visiting the capital of the Jewish people for the past 3000 years," he said, "and the united and indivisible capital of Israel—with the Temple Mount at its center—for all eternity." With that he served notice that any proposal or offers his predecessor made regarding sharing sovereignty over the sacred city with the Palestinian Authority were henceforth null and void.[372] Shockingly, by 2005 the daring military hero-turned-premier dramatically reversed his hard-line positions and unilaterally withdrew Israel from Gaza. He launched a new centrist party, Kadima, and but for a massive stroke putting him in a permanent coma, it is generally believed he would have been re-elected in a landslide due to his radical shift in his earlier commitment to protect Jerusalem and the

West Bank at all costs., thus revealing also the increasingly weak stomach of peace-pommelled Israelis to endure incessant and redoubled global demands to sacrifice further land on the altar of world peace.

## EHUD OLMERT CAPITULATES

Even the military hero, Sharon, began to waffle as pressure mounted in the increasingly international squeeze upon Israel. Following the stroke, which, through continuing coma from which he has not yet recovered, rendered him unable to govern, Ehud Olmert took over as Prime Minister. As mayor of Jerusalem from 1993 to 2003, Olmert had repeatedly stated the capital city would never be divided, often dramatically pounding his hands against podiums to accentuate his pronouncements. But then he too felt the pressure and declared in March 2009, "There will be no peace if a significant part of Jerusalem is not the capital of the Palestinian state."[373]

The pressure intensified as political arms were twisted into virtual pretzels. The Jerusalem affairs adviser to Palestinian Authority Prime Minister Salaam Fayad confirmed in February 2008, in an interview with The *JERUSALEM POST*, that Jerusalem "is not only on the table, it's also under the table." He also stated that "negotiations are taking place both openly and secretly."[374]

## BENJAMIN NETANYAHU EXUDES BOLDNESS

The re-election of Benjamin Netanyahu as Prime Minister seemed to restore Israel's spine. In January 2010, the Prime Minister declared that Israel would never cede control of united Jerusalem nor retreat to the 1967 borders. The statement came after Egypt's foreign minister said that Netanyahu was ready to discuss making "Arab Jerusalem" the capital of a Palestinian state.[375] Three months later, Israel's Foreign Minister Avigdor Lieberman boldly stated, "Jerusalem is the eternal capital of the State of Israel and it will never be divided—neither directly nor indirectly." Quoting a speech made by former Prime Minister Menachem Begin, Lieberman said, "Today I stand before you in Jerusalem, and confirm Begin's words: the city will remain our capital and will never be divided."[376]

Two weeks following, *Arutz Sheva*—Israel National News—published a lengthy "Op-Ed" by Eli E. Hertz titled, "One Nation's Capital Forever."[377] World leaders would be well served to read this serious review of Jerusalem's history unadulterated by the political correctness of our day that persistently distorts and revises the facts of history to suit the vacillating fancies of politicians and self-appointed global "fathers." As Eli Hertz accurately claims: "Jerusalem and the Jewish people are so intertwined that telling the history of one is telling the history of the other." "Jerusalem," wrote historian Martin Gillent, is not a mere city. "It holds the central spiritual and physical place in history of the Jews as a people." "Throughout its long history, Jerusalem has served, and still serves, as the political capital of only one nation—the one belonging to the Jews." Yet, hidden in plain sight within the Hertz historical review is a reminding warning: "But the war for control of Jerusalem and its religious sites is not over."

## THE BUSH and OBAMA BETRAYAL

The progressive and increasingly persistent betrayal of United States pledges of unalterable support for Israel is not primarily a matter for partisan politics but of mind-altering political correctness that, like a virulent cancer, consumes all reason regardless of biblical persuasion. Witness first the reign of Bill Clinton who famously abandoned all reality "on the ground" by publically embracing Israel's Prime Minister, Yitzak Rabin, and his pledged terrorist opponent, Yasser Arafat, in a flagrant pursuit of personal pride under the aegis of world peace, claiming political authority by back-dropping the display with America's White House. The purported Oslo Accords produced nothing but further discord, setting the stage for the escalating battle for *KING of the Mountain*.

America's 42nd President, George W. Bush, pledged absolute and continuing support for Israel, yet famously stated that Islam was no problem either for Israel or America—that the real problem was "terrorism" and "extremism"—utterly ignoring the 4000 year open antagonism between the sons of Isaac and the sons of Ishmael. Then, with a politically-correct flourish, embellished with the personal claim of "Christian," declared decisively, yet deceptively, that "Muslims, Christians and Jews all worship the same God." The final years of his administration were dedicated to place his name in history, hell-bent with the persistent help of Secretary of State Condoleezza Rice to bring about a final Middle East peace accord by compelling Israel to divide the sacred land and Holy City once deeded by God to Abraham and confirmed 3000 years ago in King David and his son, Solomon. Again, the Palestinian hand, augmented by Muslim hopes, frustrated the endeavor, clearly revealing the true goal of pushing Israel into the sea and ushering in an Islamic Caliphate to rule and reign from the Mount in Jerusalem.

Then came Barack Hussein Obama. Never in the history of the United States of America has the world or Israel faced an American president who would deal with such a deceptive hand in resolute defiance of the God of Abraham, Isaac and Jacob while touting the title of "Christian" to obfuscate his devious and destructive decisions and intentions. Space does not here permit the catalogue of unbiblical demands and blatant deceptions perpetrated in a mere single term of office upon an Israeli government that

is continually told, "We are your best friend" and "We have your backs...."
"You can trust us." A few illustrations will have to suffice.

Mr. Obama's first foreign act upon assuming the U.S. presidency was
not to assure America's best ally and friend, Israel, of unswerving support,
but rather to ingratiate himself to the entire Islamic world, which has and
continues to repeatedly pronounce Israel's annihilation. His first stop was
in Turkey, which is striving to be the head of a new "Ottoman Empire" to
rule the Islamic world and thereby the entire globe by an Islamic Caliphate
to govern from Jerusalem. Consider Mr. Obama's words to craftily encourage the entire Muslim world as his first diplomatic act in the context of
never once visiting Israel during his first term, yet cavorting in surrounding Islamic nations threatening Israel's very existence.

Here are those words taken directly from the April 6, 2009, Press
Release of The White House, Office of the Press Secretary, as delivered by
Mr. Obama, in person to the Turkish Parliament.

> Let me say this as clearly as I can: The United States is not, and will
> never be, at war with Islam. In fact, our partnership with the Muslim
> world is critical.... I also want to be clear that America's relationship
> with the Muslim community, the Muslim world, cannot, and will
> not, just be based upon opposition to terrorism. We seek broader
> engagement based on mutual interest and mutual respect.

> We will convey our deep appreciation for the Islamic faith, which
> has done so much over the centuries to shape the world—includ-
> ing my own country.

His next stop was the world's oldest Islamic university in Egypt,
renowned as a premier center for teaching and exporting Muslim theology
and Sharia law throughout the earth, all under the banner of "education."
Again, Mr. Obama's words belie what lies in the heart.

Deception became apparent during his campaign for the presidency.
In order to capture the Jewish vote essential for his election, Mr. Obama, in
his first foreign policy speech after clinching the Democratic nomination,
made dramatic assurances to Israel. In a speech to the American Israel
Public Affair Committee (AIPAC), Obama declared:

> Let me be clear. Israel's security is sacrosanct. It is non-negotiable. Any
> agreement with the Palestinian people must preserve Israel's identity
> as a Jewish state, with secure, recognized and defensible borders.

> Jerusalem will remain the capital of Israel, and it must remain
> undivided.[378]

Enraged, Palestinian Authority Chairman Mahmoud Abbas responded, "We will not accept a Palestinian state without having Jerusalem as the capital."[379] Political chicanery was vividly exposed. Obama immediately backpedalled to protect Muslim favor. Israel's security and Jerusalem's sanctity could be readily sacrificed on the altar of political pragmatism… if indeed genuine security and sanctity had ever, for even a moment, manifested the Obama mind and mystique. The only thing that would ever be truly "clear," is that Obama, for whatever reasons (be they political, religious or both) owed a "debt" to the Muslim world.

The plot, however, continued to thicken as evident betrayal spilled out with "potentially damaging Election Day news." "The Obama campaign urged Palestinian officials to deny a report that the Democratic nominee confided to Palestinian leadership that he supports their right to a capital in eastern Jerusalem, according to a senior Palestinian official." The official said that "Obama advisers have engaged in a series of intense conversations in the last few hours asking that the office of President Mahmoud Abbas issue a denial." "Obama asked the Palestinians to keep the remarks secret," said the official. The headline says it all: "Obama makes Palestinians deny he promised Jerusalem."[380]

The next week, hundreds of prominent Israeli rabbis urged President-elect Barack Obama to "implement the will of God" by ensuring the entire state of Israel remains under Jewish sovereignty. The Rabbinical Congress for Peace, composed of more than 350 Israeli rabbinic leaders and over 850 rabbis from abroad, including the U.S., made clear, "The ruling of Jewish law forbids the surrender of any part of our Holy Land to Israel's neighbors…." "This ruling is anchored in God's eternal Torah…. We are therefore confident that you, Mr. President elect… will now do everything in your power to implement the will of God that the Promised Land that He expressly allocated to the Jewish People will remain under Jewish sovereignty."[381]

President-elect Obama, in preparing for transfer of power pending his inauguration, selected Rahm Emmanuel as his Chief of Staff. Perhaps he believed it would be easier to utilize a Jew to further the betrayal of the Jewish people, while purporting to embrace the Jews by placing one of their own in such a prestigious position. Mr. Obama had to be well aware of the celebrated caustic and profane mouth of Mr. Emmanuel, Senior Adviser to President Clinton for Policy and Strategy, who was one of the loudest voices for dividing Jerusalem during the Clinton Administration. Might a Jew be more effective in facilitating the division of Jerusalem than a Gentile?

The inauguration of Barack Obama catapulted the effort to divide the Promised Land and its eternal capital into high gear in his headlong pursuit of ultimate global governance. He fawned over the world while forsaking his own country and his chief ally and friend, Israel. Accolades of the planet's globalists, whether George Brown as Prime Minister of Britain or Henry Kissinger, former U.S. Secretary of State, have only exacerbated the fundamental, fraudulent betrayal. When a prime minister reports you to be "the hope and inspiration of the world"[382] and a former Secretary of State declares you to be the one to lead into the New World Order,[383] constitutional and covenantal loyalties become a casualty. When educators call you "My Jesus" and international magazines image "The Messiah Factor," it becomes increasingly apparent that "all the foundations of the earth are out of course" (Psa. 82:5).

It could not have been said more pointedly. "The recent appointments of Jews by U.S. President-Elect Barack Obama to his new administration should not be reassuring to the Jewish community in America or Israel." David Bedein, Bureau Chief of the Israel Resource News Agency, said that Obama's "Jewish appointees are not pro-Israel." "We are facing a situation," he lamented, "of Jews around the next president who are very, very antagonistic to any of Israel's settlement policies in Judea [where Jerusalem lies] and Samaria." "It was the Jewish servants of Pharaoh who hated Moses the most. They liked being in the palace of the king."[384]

By May of 2009, the direction of the new United States administration was abundantly clear and potentially catastrophic for America's "ally." This prompted Knesset speaker Reuven Rivlin to speak out a warning—that Israel "must take action now in order to make united Jerusalem a reality, and not merely a slogan." "If Jerusalem were to be divided in any way," he said, "the entire state of Israel would be at risk. If anyone were to give any part of this city away—G-d forbid—they would cause the collapse of the moral basis for our sovereignty elsewhere in the land."[385]

## "Fight For Jerusalem—Fight For Truth"

The anniversary of the Six Day War is the day that commemorates the miraculous liberation of the Old City of Jerusalem which is biblical Jerusalem. The war marked Israel's return to the Old City for the first time since having been driven out in 1948 and for the first time in 1899 years as sovereign rulers.

Israel had begged Jordan's King Hussein not to become involved in the attack by Egypt and Syria upon the Holy Land, but to no avail. Had Hussein listened, history may well have been different. Israel destroyed the Egyptian Air Force in a single day, miraculously beat back the assault of Syria and Jordan, taking over Jerusalem, Gaza, Judea, Samaria, the Sinai and the Golan Heights, the very land God had promised to Abraham, Isaac and Jacob as an everlasting covenant. Israel wept with Joy![386]

It is therefore fascinating that, to this day, most Palestinians and their leaders deny that there ever was a Jewish presence in Jerusalem and they "make preposterous allegations that the holy sites, including the Temple, were Zionist fabrications concocted to justify 'the Jewish colonialist enterprise.'" "To this day they persist in systematically destroying archeological evidence on the Temple Mount," as if one can truly erase history. As stated November 5, 2010, in The *JERUSALEM POST*, "We are faced with a determined campaign in which most of the world, including the Obama administration, is pressuring us to once again divide Jerusalem. Even Prime Minister Yitzhak Rabin, an architect of the Oslo Accords, on the eve of his assassination warned the Knesset that Jerusalem must remain united."[387]

Jerusalem Day, 2010, brought forth a telling statement from Israel's Prime Minister, Benjamin Netanyahu. In the face of oppressive and near dictatorial pressure from the United Nations, the European Union, Russia, and especially the United States State Department under Hillary Clinton and the Obama administration, Mr. Netanyahu cut to the core of the issue. "The struggle for Jerusalem is a struggle for truth," he said.[388] The truth is that Jerusalem is our lifeblood. We have an indissoluble connection to it. For three thousand years, we have never relinquished this connection. We didn't relinquish it when the temple was destroyed a second time." "No other nation has such a connection to its capital." Indeed, "The fight for Jerusalem is the fight for truth."[389]

## WORLD CAPITAL... OR ISRAEL'S CAPITAL?

Sometimes the most profound revelations can be found in mining letters to the editor. Never was this more true nor telling than the September 22, 2000, issue of The *JERUSALEM POST*. Consider well the implication of these few words.

> The PA National Assembly spokesperson has called Jerusalem to become the capital of the world. It is high time the world grants Jerusalem this title and function.

> NYC [New York City] is presently known as the capital of the world, with the UN and all the international institutions there.

> They could all be removed to Jerusalem. Just as this function worked in New York, it can work well in Jerusalem.[390]

In the same issue of The *JERUSALEM POST*, the Director of the Jerusalem Embassy Institute wrote:

### THE MOUNT IS OURS

The Jerusalem Embassy Act of 1995 clearly reflected our sovereign right to Jerusalem.

277

Jerusalem and the Temple Mount cannot be shared. They are our heritage and form the base of our spiritual sovereignty.

The Jerusalem Embassy Initiative of the Root and Branch Assoc. calls upon the nations of the world to recognize United Jerusalem as the eternal capital of the State of Israel, and to move their embassies in Israel to Jerusalem.[391]

## THE BATTLE LINES ARE DRAWN

The world is facing its "moment of truth" and is staging its final battle in "the valley of decision." Indeed, "the day of the LORD is near in the valley of decision" (Joel 3:14). Jerusalem is the prize. Just as the God of Creation—the God of Abraham, Isaac and Jacob—chose to place His name there, so the rebellious and arrogant power brokers of this earth are determined to place their names there. It will be the consummate spiritual battle of the ages fought in bloody array and deceptive chicanery on planet earth.

In June 2012, Members of the International Israel Allies Caucus Foundation met in Washington D.C. and called on the United States to "recognize Jerusalem as the undivided capital of Israel." Congressman Allen West asserted, "Jerusalem is the rightful capital of the Jewish people, and it should stay that way." "It should always be unified under one simple flag, that star of David, because that is David's city."[392] Congressman Dave Weldon agreed. "For us, the greatest country in the world, the United States of America, the greatest country the world has ever known, to be fearful of moving our embassy to Jerusalem… is a disgrace, and we need to do that and do that right now."[393]

Even more pointedly, Rabbi Benny Elon, President of the Israel Allies Caucus, cut to the heart of the matter. "They don't need Jerusalem," he said. "They just want to make sure that we, the Jews, do not have it."[394]

## A MOMENTOUS CHOICE

The world and its leaders, yes even each of us as citizens of this planet, face perhaps the choice of greatest moment in the history of mankind. It is a choice for destiny, not just of the physical destiny of Jerusalem but of our own spiritual destiny. It is the ultimate choice of our lifetime. Will we align ourselves individual and collectively with the clearly-expressed and historically-consistent viewpoint of God as Creator recorded in the Bible, or will we collectivize our rebellion in unfettered and diabolical tyranny "against the LORD and against His anointed" (Psa. 2:1-6)?

Prophecy will soon become history, and divine judgment awaits our decision. It is the final battle for *KING of the Mountain*.

*Chapter 22*

# PROBING THOUGHTS *for* PROPHETIC TIMES

1. Why do you think the battle for *KING of the Mountain* is encapsulated in "The Battle for Jerusalem?"

2. Why have all nations of our world withdrawn their embassies from Jerusalem, or, as with the United States of America, refused to place their embassy there (even though a 1995 resolution of Congress required it)?

3. Can you see how the various geopolitical and religious powers of earth are each conniving or confederating to rule the world from the Temple Mount in Jerusalem?

4. Is there any way to resolve this escalating conflict over Jerusalem other than for world leaders (and their peoples) to accept and conform to the precise words of the Bible expressing the unchanging viewpoint of God as Creator toward Jerusalem?

5. What consequences, if any, will be incurred by our world and its peoples if they collectively persist in defying God's sovereign selection of Jerusalem?

# Chapter 23

# THE GREAT GAME
# BLACK GOLD AND GLOBAL
# GOVERNANCE

———∽∾∾———

*"The reality is that the nation that controls
the world's energy supply controls the world."*

GLOBAL GOVERNANCE IS THE GOAL driving the economic, political and military machinations of the leading nations and confederations, often supported by religious persuasion. But there is one essential that binds their respective goals and lubricates the engines of their lust for power, and that is oil. Politically-correct voices may cry for "alternative energy," but, in reality, oil remains the indispensable energy source making the wheels of the world turn. In order to viscerally comprehend the sheer magnitude of this matter, we must look briefly at the issue through the eyes (viewpoint) of the primary players in this epic battle for *KING of the Mountain*.

### "OIL PRESSURE RISING"

Regardless of the banal observations and reporting of world events through standard media outlets, oil lies at the very heart of national, regional and global decisions, including international alliances. And, as The *Economist* reported February 24, 2011, "Oil pressure is rising."[395] Oil prices have surged dramatically with the demise of Middle East dictators and the rise of the Muslim Brotherhood-dominated "Arab Spring." The region provides 35 percent of the world's oil, and the big concern to observing nations is that spreading unrest will drive prices shockingly higher.

However, what is not commonly known is that as of 2009, Russia became the world's greatest exporter of oil, overtaking Saudi Arabia. OPEC's share of production has diminished from 51 percent in the mid

1970's to about 40 percent now. Further, demand for oil is rising globally at a blistering pace.[396] Yet by September 2010, we were greeted with a shocking headline: "U.S. military warns about a massive oil shortage by 2015."[397] According to this report, "The world will run out of oil surpluses by 2012, with severe shortages following as little as three years later...." The US Joint Forces command warned—"... as early as 2015 the shortfall in output could reach nearly 10 million barrels per day." "One should not forget that the Great Depression spawned a number of totalitarian regimes that sought economic prosperity for their nations by ruthless conquest."[398]

Perhaps mind-numbing to most, the very year such massive oil shortages were projected by the US military, *Israel National News* announced: "US expert Predicts 'Oil and Gas Rush' to Israel."[399] Yet why such an announcement, and why now? Might this prediction actually bring ancient prophecy and history into congruency as our world heads inexorably toward the Gog and Magog/Armageddon scenarios?

## DAWN OF A NEW OIL ERA

The world's demand for oil is not diminishing but accelerating dramatically. The projected pattern is not merely troubling but terrifying to transparent thinkers globally. The implications are not hard to imagine, at least in general terms, but are vastly underrated and under-reported for popular consumption. The enormity of potential catastrophic consequences, however, has not escaped the conniving and incontinent aspirations of corporate and governmental power brokers seeking not only to protect positions but to advance power in hot pursuit of global control of black gold and its energy cousin, gas.

In 2005, columnist Robert J. Samuelson wrote of "The Dawn of a New Oil Era."[400] He asked, "Have we entered a period when, owing to consistently strong demand and chronically scarce supplies, prices have moved permanently higher?" "Higher oil demand," he noted, "has now strained the global production system to its limits." At that time, oil prices had surged and hovered around $50 per barrel. Within twelve months of his writing, those prices had skyrocketed to nearly $110 per barrel, dropping back over twenty percent amid global economic uncertainty and recession to around $85 to $88 per barrel, and then quickly resurged to $98 per barrel.

Radical fluctuations in black gold could be tracked in the price of gold itself. "Anything could now happen to oil," observed Samuelson. That is even truer than most oil barons, economists, presidents and prime ministers could conjure in their wildest imaginations, for it is not prognosticators and politicians but biblical prophecy that will ultimately direct and determine the course and consequence of history.

## BLACK GOLD AND BIBLE PROPHECY

"Oil markets do undergo seismic shifts," wrote economist Samuelson.[401] The radical degree of those "shifts" could never have been foreseen beyond five years in the future in 2005. Within eight years oil prices doubled. The West, particularly the US and Canada, foresee vast new and almost unlimited production capability through technological advances in extraction coupled with discovery of new sources and rising prices rendering more costly extraction feasible, thus potentially and provocatively reducing demand from Middle East providers. Vast new sources in various republics of the former Soviet Union also present alternatives to traditional Middle East providers.

Truly honest observers can, indeed, see "seismic shifts," and seismic activity always results in troubling, even terrifying shaking for those in proximity to the powerfully-shifting tectonic plates. Now, however, while the various "seismic" developments shifting the ground for global oil consumers and providers may appear to be merely natural and periodic upheavals, they should more accurately be discerned as prophetic. For oil will truly lubricate the engines of earth's presidents, prime ministers and global moguls in their final pursuit to become *KING of the Mountain*.

Mesopotamia is the cradle of civilization and the place from which all of Abraham's descendants originate. It is also the location of most of the world's known hydrocarbons. Though never specifically mentioned in the most recognized prophetic passages of the Bible, "oil is inextricably linked to most, if not all of the major nation-players of endtime events," wrote investment economist Wilfred J. Hahn in his illuminating article, "Endtime Nexus: Prophesied Oil Crisis."[402] "Oil is a main reason the Western world has become fixated on affairs of the Middle East, which possesses the huge energy resources needed to serve as Europe's oil tanker and as America's supplier of last resort. For example, as early as the 1950's, the US began to cozy up to Saudi Arabia,"[403] thus creating otherwise strange bedfellows indeed, each prostituting primary and glaringly opposite political positions in order to facilitate the flow of Western-craved energy and Wasabi-craved funds needed to bring the world to their knees before Mohammed and his Mahdi.

Perspective in this unfolding of oil-lubricated prophecy is essential in order to comprehend "The Great Game" now being played out on the not-so-sporting oil and gas fields of this small planet. Consider the historical timing and development of oil-based tribulation now troubling the increasingly terrified leaders around the world. Israel was founded (re-born) on May 14, 1948, after 2000 years of Roman-driven diaspora. To date, no proven oil reserves of meaningful size have been tapped in

Israel. Yet its archenemies have reaped untold wealth since that time from a never-ending flow of black gold. At the same time, Israel's potential protectors—the world's largest nations'—are enslaved to a continuing supply of cheap oil. In 1948—the same year Israel was re-founded—America for the first time became a net importer of oil.

Most of the emerging global organizations and institutions were also birthed in the same decade. The International Monetary Fund was conceived at the July 1944 Bretton Woods conference as was the World Bank. The United Nations was founded in 1945. These were committed to rapid economic growth and global prosperity perceived to be the salvation of the world. The world's dependence on oil exploded even as the consumer era of the West increased demand for oil five-fold, ushering in "the golden age of oil."[404] China has now joined the chase in the play-for-keeps "Great Game" being played out in the boardrooms of oil conglomerates and the smoke-filled rooms of lusting political leaders.

Yet the majority of the world's operational oil reserves lie strategically (or prophetically) in the Muslim lands of the Middle East, Asia and Africa. Non-Muslim demand for oil increasingly fuels the goal of the Islamic faith to rule the world as the final *KING of the Mountain*.

## "HOSTAGE TO OIL"

Even as investment economist Wilfred J. Hahn was warning of the biblically-prophetic nature of oil, a further geopolitical warning issued in a nine page feature in *U.S. News and World Report* titled: "Hostage To OIL." "As goes oil, so goes the economy," the article lamented. "Now, because the world slurps up nearly every drop it produces and grows thirstier by the day, the tiniest sniffle in Saudi Arabia or Russia sends financial markets into a fever and brings aches and pains to the world's economies." "When supply and demand are tightly matched, as they are now, we're subject to an oil shock," said Federal Reserve Governor Edward Gramlich.[405]

The same issue of *U.S. News & World Report* declared, "Wherever you look on the oil scene, you have political and economic problems." Leo Drollas, chief economist at the Centre for Global Energy Studies in London, further noted: "This is probably the most dangerous period we've gone through since World War II."[406] Furthermore, "oil riches encourage corruption." Oil, says a senior U.S. official, "becomes a narcotic." And for U.S. and western economies, "terrorist groups have determined oil to be their Achilles heel," according to Gal Luft, executive director of the Institute for the Analysis of Global Security," but "the Middle East is the core zone of risk."[407]

As investment economist Wilfred Hahn noted, "many energy experts expect that a major oil crisis is inevitable" before the end of the year 2015.

He further concludes, "The facts suggest that the world will face a major oil crisis of endtime significance."[408] For that reason, we must interpret the growing intensity of "The Great Game" and its global players of even greater significance than economic, geopolitical or military consequences.

## THE GAME GETS SERIOUS

*Forbes*, one of America's leading business magazines, was blunt as the year 2012 came to a tumultuous conclusion: "Nobody wants to lose: Peak oil is dead, the Great Game is back."[409] In a complete reversal of geopolitical and economic outlook, *Forbes* focused on the seeming increasing availability and discovery of hydrocarbons rather than on their coming to a "peak" with ever-decreasing reserves. Such a reversal is nothing short of dramatic for market economics as the price of oil may not surge to stratospheric levels in the near future as prophesied by pundits. Thus, the economic pressure on Islamic nations and Russia, so dependent upon ever-higher oil prices and "inexhaustible" reserves, raises and redistributes the nature and objects of energy-based global threats. Hence, "The Great Game lives on...."[410]

"Geopolitics is not called *The Great Game* without reason," wrote Charles Hugh Smith in his article, "The Great Game: Geopolitics and Oil."[411] "The Great Game is afoot, and no matter how we may disapprove of the Global Empire, we would do well not to discount the cards it alone holds." "The game of dominating the world's resources, nation-states and alliances, is like a combination of chess and [other games played simultaneously], with the threat of military conquest or defeat always hovering over the statecraft and financial game." For now, "There is only one nation-state which can project hard power: the U.S." "Until the U.S. loses its currency hegemony, it can outbid any other great power for any resource." "...the U.S. will pursue Oil and Empire until the U.S. economy and dollar are no longer able to support an Empire."

In order to gain both geopolitical and prophetic perspective at this juncture, it should not be forgotten that the global enemies of the United States are the global enemies of Israel, and likewise, the enemies of Israel are co-extensively the enemies of the U.S. The nation-states and alliances engaged in The Great Game are intensely aware of this fact and await the precise and propitious moment to make their strategic moves so as to become *KING of the Mountain* by dispossessing other would-be "kings."

"Welcome to Pipelineistan." "Oil Pipelines are the 'New Great Game', warned Pepe Escobar."[412] "What happens on the immense battlefield for the control of Eurasia will provide the ultimate plotline in the tumultuous rush towards a new, polycentric world order, also known as the New Great

Game." "Forget the mainstream media's obsession with al-Qaeda…or that 'war on terror'…. These are diversions compared to the high-stakes, hardcore geopolitical game that flows along the pipelines of the planet." "…what flows where and to whom may turn out to be the most important question on the planet."

"A global showdown is in the works." "History is in the making," noted the report of Global Research.[413] The world is now at "the Historical Crossroads of the 21st Century." "The haunting spectre of a major war hangs over the Middle East. Russia and Iran are the nations with the largest natural gas reserves in the world and are the #1 and #3 exporters in the world. Russia and Iran control the export of Central Asian energy to global markets and exercise control and influence through Syria and Turkey over energy corridors to and through the European continent.

"The 'Great Game' Enters the Mediterranean," reported Global Research.[414] It is the developing story of "Gas, Oil, War and Geo-Politics." "The strategic course of Eurasia and global energy reserves hangs in the balance." "Iran, Russia and China have already been long in the process of courting the Arab Sheikhdoms of the Persian Gulf." "The ultimate aim of Russo-Iranian energy cooperation will be the establishment of a north-south energy corridor from the Baltic Sea to the Persian Gulf with the Caspian Sea at its mid-axis. An east-west corridor from the Caspian Sea, Iran, and Central Asia to India and China will also be linked to this." Thus "…consolidating Russo-Iranian control over international energy security."

Anticipating these strategic moves, twenty years earlier *NEWSWEEK* reported, "The Game Gets Serious." "The Great Game," it was observed, "it's already underway."[415] The *Economist* graphically described it on its cover as a game of "Blood and oil."[416] The title "Great Game" is a term that originates from the struggle between Britain and Czarist Russia to control a vast geographic area that not only included Tibet, the Indian sub-continent, and Central Asia, but also the Caucasus and Iran. The term was immortalized by the 1901 publishing of Rudyard Kipling's novel *Kim*. Now, "A contemporary version of the 'Great Game' is being played once again for control of roughly the same geographic stretch, but with more players and greater intensity." "The 'Great Game' has also taken new dimensions and has entered the Mediterranean." "…this contest has been playing itself out violently," with "intentional and dangerous rivalries."[417]

In order to understand the immense prophetic gravity of this "Great Game," we must make our way to Israel, the epicenter of endtime prophecy as played out on the rapidly-increasing yet closing pages of history.

## OIL AND ISRAEL'S EXISTENCE

"If oil reaches a certain price, the world will no longer want Israel to exist," warned Eugene Kandel, head of Israel's National Economic Council addressing the Israel Energy and Business Convention in October 2010. Alluding to forecasts of the price of oil escalating even to $200 per barrel, Kandel said, "If we don't do something, [the world's largest] countries will be dependent on countries unfriendly to us."[418] While the comment to some may seem extreme, the geopolitical reality of the growing global attitude toward Israel, whether in East or West, reveals a current level of animus toward the nascent State of Israel of either restrained or open contempt. But for overwhelming public support from the United States Congress, Israel is nearing complete isolation in a world frantically playing the "Great Game" for hegemony of the world's energy supply. Neither grace nor gratitude flows from the capitals of their world toward the prophetically-resurrected nation declared in Scripture to be the "apple" of God's eye (Deut. 32:10, Zech. 2:8). What does this mean? What are the prophetic implications of Israel being increasingly held hostage to world powers over a barrel of oil? The answers to these questions are now setting the course of world destiny, whether or not foreseen by famous pundits and politicians.

The late Golda Meir, fourth prime minister of the State of Israel once humorously noted: "If Moses had turned right instead of left when he led his people out of the Sinai desert, the Jews would have had the oil; and the Arabs would have ended up with the oranges."[419] That was her humorously painful lament over Israel's apparent energy deficiency while her energy-rich Arab/Islamic neighbors, ever designing her destruction, command 25 percent of the world's known oil and gas reserves. These nations adroitly use oil as a weapon as does their Russian benefactor, creating a geopolitical pressure cooker now nearing a regional explosion triggering an international tsunami of grave and destiny-determining consequences.

The world oil shock of 1973 gave us a window of revelation into the vast implications of oil hegemony and its power to manipulate economies and drive political policy among the nations. The Yom Kippur War, launched by Israel's surrounding neighbors to effectuate her annihilation from among the nations of earth, triggered a massive energy crisis. But why did this happen? Was it merely the result of market fluctuations and "adjustments?" A resounding "NO!" The sole cause was the angry response of Arab members of (OPEC) the Organization of Petroleum Exporting Countries, to all then—allies of Israel (Western Europe and the United States) that had supported Israel and enabled her to defend herself. The resulting Arab oil embargo caused world oil prices to quadruple. Arab fury forced gasoline rationing and long gas lines in the U.S. and abroad.[420] It also triggered the massive inflation in the United States in the latter 1970's, resulting in interest rates soaring to 21 percent. If the western world was then so instantly shaken, what might be expected in this decade if the balance of energy hegemony should suddenly be disturbed? How might destiny be affected... or determined?

## HEADLINES REVEAL ISRAEL'S HOPE

There is perhaps no better way to summarily disclose the history-making developments over the past few years in the geopolitically-charged arena of oil and gas than through a series of rather eye-popping headlines related to Israel. These have captured the attention of the world, in particular Russia and its Arab-Islamic oil and gas compatriots, all of which are silently and surreptitiously exploring response. Try for a few moments to digest the potential implications.

**"Oil reserves found in Israel could change power structure in the region."** (Sept. 1, 2010)[421]

"In a major development that could alter the situation in the Middle East, large oil reserves have been discovered in Israel while a second firm believes the Bible lists the location of oil fields...." The companies referenced are Givot Olam Oil and Zion Oil and Gas. John Brown, Zion Oil's founder, says he believes the Bible discloses generally where oil is located and has been drilling accordingly. "Imagine if Israel becomes a huge oil producer," said Brown. "The discovery of oil would change the dynamics of the Middle East." "You have these Arab states that threaten boycotts and throw their oil weight around to get countries to pressure Israel." But if Israel has substantial oil, "there will be no more placating anyone...."

**"U.S. Expert Predicts 'Oil and Gas Rush' to Israel."** (April 11, 2010).[422]

A U.S. energy expert, Fred Zeidman, said that "it is very likely that international firms will join the exploration efforts on Israeli territory...." "Two of Israel's largest financial groups... have also entered the sector." Referencing gas discoveries by Noble Energy, Zeidman said there will be a "crazy rush." "Around the world as Noble goes to a place, many other companies follow in its wake. The prospects are amazing." "The U.S. Geological Survey estimates 122 trillion cubit feet of undiscovered but recoverable gas in the

Levant Basic Province in the eastern Mediterranean region." "Its gas resources are bigger than anything we have assessed in the United States." "The Levant Basin Province also holds an estimated 1.7 billion barrels of oil, that can be recovered with existing technology."

**"Israel bids to end global oil dependency by 2020."** (Sept. 2010)[423]

**"Israel's Coast May Be Gold Mine of Oil..."** (June 2011)[424]

"Israel may have the last laugh to the old joke that 'Moses took the wrong turn in the desert'... said Israeli oil expert Dr. Yaakov Mimran, outgoing Petroleum Supervisor." "Oil shale deposits cover 15 percent of the country... one of the largest oil reserves in the world."

**"Natural Gas Bonanza for Israel, Possible Oil Bonanza as Well."** (June 2010) [425]

"A survey of the natural gas field off the shore of Haifa... has been discovered to be even greater than previously thought." Yitzchak Teshuva, controlling shareholder who developed the field, said, "We have turned Israel into a great energy power."

**"Oil Well Compared to 'Giving of the Torah'."** (Aug. 2010)[426]

Tuvia Luskin, chief geologist for Givot Olam, exulted over the company's new drilling site near Rosh Ha'Ayin that finally produced black gold after years of unsuccessful drilling. He declared, "Meged 5 is an event like the giving of the Torah"—the first five books of the Bible.

**"Leviathan Oil Field Could Sustain Israel For Decades."** (Aug. 2010)[427]

"All big oil and gas fields have geopolitical significance, but we haven't seen a big oil find in recent years that could matter more than the Leviathan field in the Mediterranean Sea off of Israel." "Leviathan could hold upwards of 4.3 billion barrels of oil." "This is hugely important for Israel... almost completely reliant on imported oil... and could have enough oil to satisfy Israel for more than two decades."

## ISRAEL'S HOPE—MIDDLE EAST HORROR

So great is the significance of the recent discoveries of major oil and gas fields and reserves in the Mediterranean Sea just off the coast of Israel that the *Jerusalem Post* announced December 12, 2012: "Israel introduces stamps picturing gas reserves."[428] The stamp features a drilling rig at sea. "One of the ways in which the state records a seminal event in history," said Israel's Energy and Water Minister Uzi Landau, "is by means of issuing a postage stamp."

While Israel rejoices in new-found energy freedom and a fantastic economic future, the nations heretofore having secured what they believed was near absolute hegemony over the flow of oil and gas are privately infuriated and publically exasperated. This level of reactionary contempt and overflowing anger for such an unexpected geopolitical disruption to their well-choreographed dominion over global energy resources upon which their economics rely for survival is almost impossible to contain. And this enraged fury is issuing from the very nations foreseen by the prophet Ezekiel as the latter-days confederation that will attack Israel "to take a spoil" (Ezek. 38:1-12). Once again, the headlines reveal the hyper-ventilated and growing animosity toward Israel.

**"Erdogan drives toward armed clash with Israel. Oil and gas at stake."** (Sept. 2011)[429]

"Turkish Prime Minister Tayyip Erdogan coolly moved his country step by provocative step towards an armed clash with Israel—not just over the Palestinian issue, but because he covets the gas and oil resources of the eastern Mediterranean opposite Israel's shores." "… he has plumped for seizing eastern Mediterranean natural resources to elevate Turkey's standing [among Arab powers]. Not only will he snatch the treasure out of Israel's hands, but will challenge his country's traditional rival Greece whose military ties with Israel are growing stronger." "Erdogan is counting on President Barack Obama's backing in a military clash with Israel."

**"Israel painted as bad guy to speed Lebanese drilling."** (November 2011)[430]

"…an energy policy expert said that Lebanese claims to Israeli exploratory territory may be fueled by a need to position Israel as the 'bad guy' in order to get its own laws passed faster." "The Lebanese are claiming sovereignty over areas that are claimed by Israel and to which exploration rights have already been granted to various companies by the Israeli government."

**"We will defend gas fields."** (June 2010)[431]

"Israel is ready to defend with force the recently discovered natural gas fields off its Mediterranean coast," warned Infrastructure minister Uzi Landau. "We will not hesitate to use our force and strength to protect not only the rule of law but the international maritime law."

**"Putin Eyes Lebanon's Energy Sources."** (December 2010)[432]

"It appears that Putin has got his sights set on some of the energy stores recently discovered in Israel." What does he want? According to DEBKA, "Moscow could help Lebanon place itself on the map of oil and gas fields and pipelines in the eastern Mediterranean. But to exploit its oil and gas wealth under the sea, Lebanon needed Russia as energy partner and provider of funds, equipment and skilled labor." "… this certainly sounds like the potential Northern Invasion in the making [as foretold by the prophet Ezekiel—Ezek. 38-39]." "… here is a case where Putin is obviously up to something."

"It certainly appears that Putin has his eyes on the prize of energy reserves in Lebanon. Since he is so anxious to get his fingers on those reserves, it will bring him much closer to Israel, where oil has been discovered as well." Since Russia has large energy reserves, "one can only wonder why Russia would need to look elsewhere. The reality is that the nation that controls the world's energy supply, controls the world." "If the prices are starting to fall into place that will eventually turn into the Northern Invasion spoken of by Ezekiel, it means we are much closer to the end than we may realize."

## "GUSHER FROM GOD"

The date was April 6, 2005. *Reuters* news service issued a report distributed by *MSNBC News* titled, "Texas oilman seeks gusher from God in Israel."[433] Referred to as "BREAKING NEWS," the brief article began: "A Texas oilman is using his Bible as a guide to finding oil in the Holy Land." Is the 32 year old vision of John Brown, a born-again evangelical Christian, a mere "pipe dream?" He is convinced "NOT," and he has therefore invested a generation of time, talent and resources in the conviction, based upon several biblical passages, that the God of Israel has reserved for the descendants of Jacob an end-time blessing beyond all heretofore-imagined expectations.

*NEWSWEEK* also devoted a full page to the story of John Brown's faith in a final outpouring of God's blessing on the seed of Abraham and Isaac. The June 13, 2005, issue spoke of the oilman's vision as "grounded in theology but supported by science." Said Brown, "I believe God deposited the vision of oil for Israel in my heart." Brown has not been deterred by the failure of speculators over the decades to turn up significant deposits of oil. On the contrary, he formed Zion Oil and Gas in the year 2000, and veteran geologists working on the venture, including a former Exxon project manager, say their data seem to conform with Brown's vision. Can you embrace "A Vision of Oil in the Holy Land?"[434]

Just three years before the NEWSWEEK and REUTERS articles broke, United Press International (UPI) released a report by Dr. Sam Vaknin titled "Russia's Israeli Oil Bond."[435] Given the rapidly-changing face of the energy world and resources as we have reviewed herein, the observations of Dr. Vaknin in 2002 are of considerable import for the future—indeed for the playing out of Biblical prophecy in the realm of petroleum. Here are the then-salient facts.

"Last week (Oct/Nov 2002) Russia and Israel—erstwhile bitter Cold War enemies—have agreed to make use of Israel's neglected oil pipeline, known as the Tipline. The conduit, an Iranian-Israeli joint venture completed in 1968—is designed to carry close to a million barrels per day, circumventing the Suez Canal.

According to Stratfor, the Strategic Forecasting consultancy, tankers bearing Russian crude from the Black Sea port of Novorossiysk would unload at Israel's Mediterranean port of Ashkelon. After that, the oil would traverse the Tipline to Israel's Red Sea port at Eilat, where it would be reloaded onto tankers for shipment to Asia.

Russia is emerging as a major oil supplier and serious challenge to the hegemony of Saudia Arabia and OPEC. Even the USA increasingly taps the Russian market for crude and derivatives.

Israel has no commercial fossil fuel resources of its own. [Therefore] The deal with Russia is a godsend.

We must think this through with truthful solemnity. How will Russia respond to an Israeli "Gusher from God" that renders Russian fossil fuels devoid of fame, fortune or facilitation for Israel's economy, maintenance and development? Will Israel still feel Russia's 2002 Tipline agreement to be "a godsend?" ... or an engine of enslavement? We get a glimpse of immediate repercussions in Russia's summary cessation of advancing its highly-anticipated gas pipeline to Israel upon the announcement that several major gas discoveries were confirmed just off Israel's coast.

It should become shockingly apparent that should John Brown's vision become a reality, that should Zion Oil and Gas, Givot Olam, or any or all of the companies invested in the biblically-based and scientifically-supported promise of petroleum in Israel come to a glorious soon fulfillment, that Russia and her Middle East energy cohorts will face both economic crisis and power erosion of enormous proportions. As Zion Oil's founder so aptly stated, "Finding oil will give Israel a huge strategic advantage. It will change the political and economic structure of the region overnight."[436]

## PIPE-DREAM OR PROPHETIC DRAMA

"Petroleum prophecies." That was the title of The *JERUSALEM POST, UPFRONT* cover story, sporting an oil drilling rig jutting up into the Israeli sky December 7, 2007. The subtitle summarized John Brown's story: "Using the Bible as a treasure map, an American born-again Christian has founded Zion Oil and Gas Company in a serious multimillion-dollar quest to strike oil here." "John Brown is waiting for a miracle. Expecting one, in fact." "It's all there, he says, laid out in the First Book of Kings, chapter 8, in an overlooked part of Solomon's prayer upon the dedication of the Temple:

> Also a gentile, who is not of **your** people Israel, but will come from a distant land, for **your** name's sake... and will come and pray toward this Temple—may **you** hear from heaven, the foundation of **your** abode, and act according to all that the gentile calls out to **you**, so that all the people of the world may know **your** name....

"The purpose of Brown's company, Zion Oil and Gas, is to find the oil so that Israel can benefit economically, strategically and prophetically." Brown says, "It's all part of God's plan." But Brown is not alone. The *Associated Press*, in September 2004, reported on the extraordinary venture of an ultra-Orthodox Jew, Tovia Luskin. He formed Givot Olam Petroleum Co. to pursue his biblically-based conviction that the God of Abraham, Isaac and Jacob had promised vast blessing and prosperity for Israel in the latter days—blessing by barrels and prosperity by petroleum. "Givot Olam, he says, means 'eternal hills' and is taken from Deuteronomy 33, in which Moses promises Joseph 'the choicest gifts of heaven above, and of the deep that couches beneath." "Its meaning is very profound," said Luskin. The subtitle to the Associated Press's report says it all: "It may be a long shot. But armed with surveys and divine belief, one geologist says the crude is there."[437]

*USA Today* joined the choir, announcing Zion's pursuit of "the blessings of the deep that lieth under..." (Gen. 49:25), and "let Asher dip his foot in oil..." as prophesied in Deuteronomy 33:24. Zion's then geologist,

Stephen Pierce, and drilling manager, Stacy Cude, with decades of oil experience and successful discoveries under their belt for major producers such as Shell and Superior, have said "there is science to support their faith in the project." The skeptics "are going to have a hard time once the oil comes," predicted Zion's founder, John Brown.[438]

"A Sea of Oil?" That was the provocative question headlining The *Jerusalem Report* feature just a year earlier in April 2004. Said Michael Gardosh, researcher at the Israeli government's Geophysical Institute, "It's there, we just need to figure out how to get to it." "The problem is, we don't really know how oil moves underground." "The entire state of Israel is so small, there could be oil anywhere, flowing beneath our feet."[439]

"Drilling for oil takes a lot of faith—and a lot of money too." "Shortage of cash," observed geologist Michael Gardosh, "is the main reason why Israel has not seen a major petroleum strike." "No major companies with a lot of cash and time have invested here."[440]

We must again ask the probing... and for some provocative... question. "Is this a 'pipe dream' or a 'prophetic drama'?" Is Zion's and Givot Olam's pursuit of "blessings of the deep that lieth under" merely a "High Stakes Gamble" as noted in The *Jerusalem Report*,[441] or is this a legitimate and persistent pursuit of genuine biblical prophecy to be brought to fruition only at the precise moment of history ordained by the God of Abraham, Isaac and Jacob? And will the fulfillment of such a dramatic end-time hope for Israel trigger global horror through the unrestrained envy of the nations Ezekiel foretold would confederate together to attack Israel in "the latter days" so as to "take a spoil" (Ezek. 38)?

## WHY DOES IT MATTER?

Is all of this discussion regarding *The Great Game*, that consumes the minds, hearts and geopolitical aspirations of petroleum experts, presidents and prime ministers at this moment of history, of any overarching or grander significance than mere maneuvering on the ground in the machinations of business as usual? If so, what is that significance? And should it matter to you?

The *Great Game* being played out on the international chessboard is of supreme significance on many levels. If it were not, it would not command the attention of the world's capitals, financial moguls and foreign ministers. It is a deadly serious game, dramatic and profoundly dangerous as it plays out on the world stage. It is perceived by presidents, prime ministers and corporate giants as an ultimate game—a game to determine not only the provision of energy but of world power—indeed the power to rule the world as *KING of the Mountain*. For he who controls the oil and gas is deemed he who will dictate the destiny of the planet and its peoples.

While this "game" may be most prominently played out in the world of geologists and geopolitics, its driving substance is far more sinister and serious. In reality, the hidden yet hard truth underlying this *Great Game* is neither political nor financial, nor even a justifiable desire for energy to drive the wheels of modern civilization. The overarching motivational force churning the energy engines of world players is spiritual. It is directly linked to biblical prophecy and is, perhaps shockingly, a direct fulfillment of prophecy, setting the world stage for the FINAL ACT of history as we know it, culminating in the *parousia* (appearance) of Jesus Christ, the Mashiach, the Holy One of Israel, who will "judge the earth in righteousness and the people with His truth" (Psa. 96:13; Psa. 98:9; Acts 17:31).

Israel is, and has always been, the locus and ultimate focus of the rebellion of the nations against the God of Creation, the Lord of Abraham, Isaac and Jacob. Whether such rebellion is manifested through Pharaoh, Babylon, Persia, Germany, Rome, the United Nations, the Muslim Brotherhood, the Organization of Petroleum Exporting Countries (OPEC) or the U.S. State Department the ancient and progressive animus toward the people God called "the apple of my eye" not only persists but now incarnates itself in the global grasp for petroleum. Israel again becomes the final focus of the world's angst against the God who now commands everyone, whether Jew or Gentile, to repent and embrace Jesus Christ—Yeshua HaMashiach as Savior and Lord. That ultimate *Tipping Point* of truth has now arrived. All peoples, tongues and nations must now choose whom they will serve. Oil will now, in a quasi-spiritual sense, lubricate the direction of that choice, and ultimately determine the track of destiny.

Consider again. "All Arab countries, which are mostly populated by offshoots of Abraham's rejected son, Ishmael, also happen to be dramatically Islamic. There is not one exception. What's more, Arabic countries surround the nation of Israel. Investment economist Wilfred Hahn inquires, "With respect to world energy supplies, what is the probability that the 22-member League of Arab Nations today [as of April 2006] alone accounts for fully 75 percent of oil found underneath predominantly Islamic countries?" Yet Israel, though located in the Middle East, to date has no clearly identifiable, recoverable flow of "black gold." Furthermore, asks Hahn, "Would it be surprising to discover that there is only one other top-10 oil-rich country in the world that is not predominantly Islamic?"[442] That happens to be Russia (20 percent Islamic) which has become the world's largest oil exporter and possesses one of the largest natural gas reserves of any country. And we must not forget Iran [Persia], also one of the top ten oil producers, and although not Arab, as with Turkey, totally Islamic.

"Considering this unlikely confluence of facts... we pose the questions again: What would be the probability that the world's supply of energy would be so connected to Islam?" "Crucially, what is the likelihood that the factors surrounding oil today would end up aligning so tightly with a biblical, prophetic perspective," particularly when the primary petroleum players are the very nations and people groups delineated in Ezekiel's prophecy 2500 years ago, declaring that these confederated countries would attack Israel "in the latter days" in order to "take a spoil" (Ezek. 38-39)?[443]

Once again, the motivational machinations of the oil and gas players of *The Great Game* are many. These include the inexorable pursuit of dominion and power, preservation and creation of geopolitical alliances, regional security, insuring practical and permanent access to energy resources as well as pride in the never-ending battle to become *KING of the Mountain*. Ultimately, however, it will be the pursuit of power and dominion coupled with perceived economic threat that will, under a unifying hatred for Israel, collectivize the nations and peoples delineated by the prophet Ezekiel to attack Israel in these "latter days" to "take a spoil."

We do well to consider the implications, whether geopolitical, economic or spiritual. Just as the recent discovery of massive natural gas fields off the coast of Israel have shaken the gas providers of the Middle East (especially Russia), the soon discovery of similarly massive and available oil in Israel will totally upend and re-configure the Middle East and geopolitics within a fortnight. Israel will not only become totally independent of the political and economic pressure of Russia and her Middle-Eastern cohorts but will be positioned to be an exporter to Europe and others heretofore dependent upon Russia's oil and gas largess and the paralyzing control of the Arab/Islamic energy-rich nations. Russia's Putin will become apoplectic. Iran, Saudi Arabia, Iraq, Libya and other oil giants will tremble. Their respective and collective oil and gas hegemony will collapse as will prices upon which their entire economies depend. The "handwriting" of history and biblical prophecy is already "on the wall."

## THE WORLD TREMBLES

The "trembling" over the future among Russia and her Islamic oil and gas cohorts has suddenly and shockingly now become global. The *EU Times* shook the world March 11, 2013, with the headline: "World Trembles As US Becomes Greatest Energy Nation in History." According to a startling report prepared by Russia's Energy Minister for President Putin, "the United States is preparing to overturn the entire global economic system as it nears becoming the greatest energy producing nation in all of human history."

Just five years ago, no one could have conceived of such a report. The unprecedented, unexpected and unbelievable among the world's pundits, politicians and prognosticators is rapidly and continuously supporting a new proposition. That new proposition is that biblical prophecies that heretofore seemed to defy current realities suddenly re-define reality, re-establishing time and again the dependable authority of the Bible and its prescient import in our time. Its words must therefore be reclaimed from the dusty archives of modern memory so as to help us as we otherwise grope in the dark for answers and direction.

The Russian report referenced an announcement by the United States Energy Information Agency that the US has catapulted past Saudi Arabia as the world's biggest fuel producer and will overtake Russia in gas production by 2015 and Saudi Arabia in oil production by 2017, all of this despite the continuous efforts by the Obama Administration to block oil and gas production on federal lands.

Surprisingly, global fears raised by the nations as the United States becomes history's greatest energy powerhouse include the European Union, Canada, Nigeria and the OPEC nations. It is a revelation driven largely by hydro-fracking to recover America's "largest known deposits of oil shale in the world." Russia's Energy Minister, Alexander Novaks, reports that "the United States has become the largest fossil fuel energy producer our world has ever seen," and that "United States global geopolitical positions regarding foreign relations and economics cannot be fully understood without knowing these US energy facts."

How then might we comprehend the gravity and significance of this "game-changing" revelation in light of the increasing congruence of history in the making and biblical prophecy? Re-consider first the shocking revelation of Israel's massive gas and soon oil discoveries to the geopolitical sensibilities of Russia, Iran, Libya, Germany, Turkey as well as other Islamic/energy-driven nations. These are the nation groups specifically set forth in Ezekiel's prophecy that will attack Israel "in the latter days" to "take a spoil." Now add to this volatile mix the explosive revelation that the US, Israel's only "friend" among the nations capable of and committed to her defense, has dominion over the world's greatest energy resources. The believed Russian/Islamic hegemony over world energy depended upon for their respective and collective agendas in world domination and Israel's destruction have suddenly disappeared, thus threatening entire economies and their abilities to project power in their carefully-crafted designs to become KING of the Mountain.

Since Iran (Persia) has provocatively and persistently declared Israel "the little Satan" and America "the Great Satan," little is left to the imagination so as to comprehend the soon destructive coalition/confederation of these affected nations against Israel, but even the more so against America as Israel's only reliable protector. Indeed, "the world trembles" and "the handwriting is on the wall."

## THE "HANDWRITING IS ON THE WALL"

Yet we must seek to fathom the overarching spiritual/faith implications above all, for it is these that will (in an ultimate sense) truly define and determine the destiny of nations—indeed of every person on the planet, whether Jew or Gentile. All will face the final and faith-dependent judgment seat of Christ at the "great white throne" (Rev. 20:11-15). Before that final judgment, Yeshua HaMashiach—Jesus Christ, will return to this earth in consummate power and great glory, from whose presence the kings of the earth will flee. He will "tread the winepress of the fierceness of the wrath of Almighty God," and will "smite the nations." His name is called "Faithful and True, and in righteousness he doth judge and make war" (Rev. 20:11-15, Matt. 24:29-31; Rev. 19:11-15). "Every eye shall behold Him" when He comes "with the shout of the archangel and the trump of God"… "the last trump." "They also which pierced him: and all kindreds of the earth shall wail because of him" because they have rejected the "only begotten Son of God, full of grace and truth" (Rev. 1:7; I Thess. 4:16-18; John 1:14). They refused to "Behold the Lamb of God, which taketh away the sin of the world," "for there is no other name given under heaven whereby we must be saved" (John 1:29; Acts 4:10-12).

It is entirely possible—indeed likely—that one would respond to this last paragraph with a measure of incredulity, as if it were a non-sequitur to all that preceded. Let us, therefore, establish the necessary connection. The Bible and its contents is a message of the entirety, from the Torah (first five books) through the balance of the Tanakh (entire Old Covenant/Testament) and continuing on to the fulfillment of the promises, principles and prophecies of the "Old Covenant" in the "New Covenant/Testament" as revealed in Yeshua, the "Anointed One," the Holy One of Israel and his apostles. That record of roughly four thousand years entered the period called "the last days" which began two thousand years ago with the time of Israel's "visitation" by Yeshua the Messiah (Jesus) through His birth, death, resurrection and ascension followed by the pouring out of His Holy Spirit upon His followers (them that obey Him—Acts 5:32) on the Feast of Shavuot or "Pentecost" (Luke 19:44; Acts 2:1-21).

These things, despite the record of history and amazingly-fulfilled prophecy, the majority of Jews and Gentiles have continuously refused either to believe or receive. Now we come to "the latter days" of the "last days" that began two thousand years ago. Prophecy—those prophecies remaining yet unfilled—will soon be history. Their fulfillment, as revealed both historically and in "on-the-ground" reality throughout this book, is occurring in high-definition technicolor before our very eyes—if we have both the will and heart to see the obvious, thus making possible the profound biblical and spiritual connections.

The confluence of world events, the world's growing dependence upon the premier energy sources of oil and gas, the rebirth of Israel during this same period, the seeming controlling hegemony of these resources by the very nations and peoples prophesied 2500 years ago who will attack Israel "in the latter days" to "take a spoil," all point to the final and ultimate end and purpose for which God's revelation to man was given through the Scriptures.

There is an end to world events as we know them. That end is rushing in upon all the inhabitants of earth. The world's pursuit of and addiction to oil and gas are the on-the-ground geopolitical and economic vehicles by and through which the nations will come to a final face-off with the Lord of Nations who is the God of Abraham, Isaac and Jacob. No act of the United Nations, the Quartet of Nations, the New World Order, OPEC or any other confederation of power will change the ultimate spiritual reality with which the power brokers of this age will soon come into open and devastating conflict. Who will be KING? With whom does ultimate authority lie, both in this life and in the life to come?

Biblical prophecy provides a vivid vehicle to assist the wandering and willful mind of mortal man to come to grips with overarching realities beyond his short-focused perceptions. Any person or power genuinely seeking truth over selfish pursuits and blinding lust for power will, at the heart, be briefly drawn to seriously consider the implications of prophecies extending back four thousand years that have been progressively, and now nearly entirely, fulfilled and recorded in the annals of history. The events of the nearly seventy years last passed should, to a perceptive heart, provide substantial and even life-changing re-orientation toward matters of true moment. Questions such as "Why am I here?" "What is life's purpose?" and "Where does it all end?" should emerge at least in our subconscious and trouble the frayed edges of our conscious mind.

Indeed, it is Bible prophecy that puts a frame around life, helping to bring focus to the picture God has sought to paint for each of us to become part of His glorious plan for eternal destiny. The "handwriting is truly on the wall." It is Bible prophecy that for four thousand years has progressively and pointedly authenticated the authority and trust-worthiness of the Word of God as revealed in and through the Scriptures to bring all who will to "the knowledge of the truth" (I Tim. 2:4). Yeshua the Messiah, Jesus Christ, declared, "I am the truth. No one comes to the Father, but by me" (John 14:6). But what do you say? What does your life say? What do your decisions say?

We see then that the issues before us rise dramatically and profoundly above mundane geopolitical machinations to supremely more important considerations of eternal destiny. Who is God? Who is Jesus, Yeshua HaMashiach? Does He have legitimate authority? And if so, am I willing to submit to His authority? These are life and globe-shaking questions thrust upon us with ever-increasing intensity as biblical prophecy explodes in violent fulfillment before us now, nearly every day. Who will be king? Who will be *KING of the Mountain?*

*Chapter 23*

# PROBING THOUGHTS *for* PROPHETIC TIMES

1. Is it happenstance that the very nations and people groups prophesied by Ezekiel 38-39 over 2500 years ago have emerged both as Israel's greatest enemies and as the locus of the world's oil and gas reserves? Will these nations, as prophesied, attack Israel in "the latter days?" And what do you suppose "the spoil" they seek to be, warranting such a high-risk attack? What does Ezekiel 39 describe as the devastating consequences of such an invasion?

2. Which country took over the title of "the world's greatest oil exporter" in 2009?

3. Can you see how Vladimir Putin's recent proclamation that "Russia is the guardian of the Islamic world" might play in the battle for petroleum power in our world? What affect might that have if Israel were to suddenly experience a gusher of near inexhaustible oil?

4. As "push comes to shove" in the "Great Game" of power politics in pursuit of petroleum, what consideration should we give to the spiritual forces engaged in fomenting this end-time face-off? Is the real issue properly framed as the nations vs. Israel, or more perceptively and precisely labeled, "The Nations vs. The God of Israel?"

5. Where is your thinking as it relates to the also-prophesied Second Coming of Jesus Christ—Yeshua Ha Mashiach? Are you prepared for that event?

*Chapter 24*

# THE LOOMING BATTLE

————— ⌘ —————

***"The 'mystery of the Mountain' must be
discerned if we are to unravel the mystery of history."***

THE CONFLUENCE OF HISTORY AND PROPHECY in our time have placed every person, prelate and power broker of this planet in a position of consummate choice both for personal and global destiny. There is no escape. The choices and decisions each will now make, both great and small, will lead inexorably toward a final and irreversible decision as to who will rule and reign as *KING of the Mountain*. There will be no exceptions. The heart and mind of every man and mogul of earth will soon be irrevocably fixed. How we choose to conclude the message and meaning of history teetering over the fulcrum of Bible prophecy will reveal the hidden mystery of man's history.

## THE MYSTERY OF HISTORY

Mysteries are intriguing to the human mind precisely because they challenge us to discern a deeper, darker or even dramatic revelation lurking within facts and circumstances that otherwise appear straightforward or obvious at first glance when observed superficially. For this reason, the publication genre of "mystery" demands shelf-space in a bookstore seldom matched by other publishing genres. That which is not fully or generally understood is an enigma, demanding to be probed and precisely evaluated to uncover the true meaning and ultimate implications. The deeper the mystery, the more strongly it draws us to pierce the seemingly imperceptible so that we might find a measure of peace in the resolution of the matter. Such is the seeming "mystery" of history.

The mystery of history cries to be comprehended, not just by patched-together theories but by some profound revelation of a reality that transcends human wisdom chained to the limitations of our two or three-planed viewpoints on this terrestrial globe. Is history only to be understood as a series of lineal occurrences along the plane or passage of time, or is there greater import to these occurrences that, when more fully comprehended, would bring us to an "Aha" moment, revealing a message that would direct our thinking from the bondage of the temporal to the burgeoning hope of the eternal? Our willingness to honestly answer that question will determine our destiny, either of horror or of hope. The mystery of the "Mountain" must be discerned if we are to unravel the mystery of history.

## THE MYSTERY OF THE MOUNTAIN

Mountains throughout the world, on every continent, are enshrouded with a sense of mystery, usually connected with the surrounding human culture. So it is with God's "Mountain," the place where the Creator chose to place His name (Isa. 27:13; II Chron. 3:1, 6:6; Psa. 2:6). As a matter of fact, from God's viewpoint, that chosen mountain at Jerusalem otherwise known as Mount Moriah or The Temple Mount is the epicenter of all history. That means that history cannot be properly understood absent this unique nugget of truth, the key piece of the puzzle. Neither the trajectory of history nor its meaning can be comprehended without reference to The Mount of God. Jerusalem, the "Holy City," supporting the escarpment of the Temple Mount, must be embraced with open heart and hands if an individual or the nations are to be blessed by the God of history—for in the final analysis, history is HIS-STORY written in and through the lives of those created in His image.

The painful reality of this spiritual fact of history has been born out through the patterns of historical events painted in the great, yet ephemeral kingdoms of this earth—Babylon, Egypt, Greece, Persia, Rome—yes, even Germany, and now the Islamic world and the uniting gentile nations. The collective pain meted upon these historical powers for their egregious treatment of "the apple of God's eye" over millennia past will soon pale in comparison to the outpouring of His wrath in these last days upon those who refuse to learn either from history or biblical prophecy.

The "Mystery of the Mountain" will soon explode violently upon the closing pages of history as the fullness of the mystery is revealed, yet rejected, by a rebellious majority who, in absolute defiance and desperation, will seek to become the final *KING of the Mountain*. Make sure your chariot wheels are well-oiled and your horses well-fed, ye rulers of earth, for the looming battle will soon begin and great will be the carnage thereof.

## THE LOOMING BATTLE

The final battle of the ages is rapidly approaching, and there will be no ultimate escape. "For when they [world leaders] shall say, Peace and safety;

then sudden destruction cometh upon them, as travail upon a woman with child; and they shall not escape" (I Thess. 5:3). For those familiar with the prophesied plan of the God of Abraham, Isaac and Jacob know well "that the day of the Lord so cometh as a thief" (I Thess. 5:4).

Those who have "prepared the way of the Lord" in their lives through genuine repentance, obedience in righteousness and reconciliation with God through Yeshua the Messiah will not be taken unawares, nor will they be "shaken in mind, or be troubled," for they will know that "the day of Christ is at hand" (II Thess. 2:2) and they will "comfort one another with these words" (I Thess. 4:18, 5:11). They will be diligent to "be found of Him [Yeshua the Christ] in peace, without spot and blameless" (II Pet. 3:14).

Furthermore, because of the eternal hope that lies in the heart of this remnant people, whether Jew or Gentile, they will "present their bodies as a living sacrifice, holy and acceptable unto God." They will not "be conformed to this world," but will "be transformed by the renewing of their minds, that they may prove what is that good, and acceptable, and perfect will of God" (Rom. 12:1-2). "Denying ungodliness and worldly lusts," they will "live soberly, righteously, and godly in this present world; looking for that blessed hope, and the glorious appearance of the great God and our Saviour, Jesus Christ" (Titus 2:12-13). And "every man that hath this hope in him will purify himself even as he [Yeshua-Christ] is pure" (I John 3:3).

Yet the terrifying battle for *KING of the Mountain* lies straight ahead. The prophecies of old, fulfilled continuously through the ages to this poignant and precipitous moment, make clear the trajectory of mankind's historic (and soon to be horrific) battle against the God of Creation, played out for permanent status to forever depose and destroy any claim Yeshua the Messiah may have to become "KING of kings" on this terrestrial ball. The confrontation will be grand in its global scope, yet gory beyond human comprehension. To be forewarned is to be forearmed. Humanity's only hope is to humbly submit to the Creator of all things, falling now upon the only rock of salvation, lest that Rock fall upon us and we be crushed in the brightness of Messiah's glory when He returns to judge the earth in righteousness, for "who shall be able to stand when he appeareth" (Mal. 3:1-2; Rev. 6:15-17)?

## AN EPIC, ETERNAL, ENDTIME BATTLE

The great kings and potentates of our planet have all, in some way, sought to rule and reign over kingdoms and realms greater and more glorious than those before them. Their consuming passion, whatever the cost in men and money, was to take dominion over the earth as they then knew it. That goal has not diminished but rather has accelerated, soon to become manifest to all inhabitants of earth who will be caught up in the ultimate battle of history.

The battle soon to break forth upon the planet is *Epic* in nature. It has been an extended battle throughout humankind's sojourn on earth, only now to reveal its true intensity and over-arching gravity. It is a continuing dramatic story, a thread that, when traced through time reveals truth about life and history not otherwise apparent to the casual eye. It remains epic because it transcends every age, surpassing all other stories in scope, size and significance.

Furthermore, the looming battle is *Eternal*. It transcends not only every age but time itself, for it preceded mans' time on earth, having begun in the heavenlies, and will culminate in either eternal bliss or eternal torment. It is, in truth, the continuing and consummate display of Satan's welcomed dominion among the sons of men leading those who would defy their Creator, both now and throughout time, to eternal destruction and damnation.

Finally, the battle unfolding before us is an *Endtime* battle. The preparations for this battle are drawing the nations with demonic magnetism toward global conflict unprecedented in the annals of history, just as foretold by biblical bards and prophets of times past. This drama, soon to conclude the final ACT of history, will reveal who truly is and will be *KING of the Mountain*.

## RESURRECTION OF THE EMPIRES

From the age of Babylon's glory to this present age which is spawning a "Babylonian" New World Order, the great historical powers of earth have, mysteriously and seemingly miraculously, raised their heads for global and regional recognition. They have, as it were, been resurrected from the sands of time where they lay buried, bursting once again upon the world stage for their final grasp at glory. Each has emerged, in whole or in part, from the hidden and long-forgotten cocoons protectively enveloping the remnants of great powers long passed into a modern metamorphosis so as to assume their respective place among the world's powers in the final battle for *KING of the Mountain*. A brief review is in order.

### THE BAYLONIAN EMPIRE

It was at Babylon that humankind first notoriously betrayed allegiance to and trust in the Creator after the purging removal of unrighteous men from the earth by God through a global flood in the days of Noah. Within just one generation thereafter, Noah's son, Cush, begat Nimrod who "began to be a mighty one in the earth," and "the beginning of his kingdom was

Babel" (Gen. 10:8-10). Although God the Creator, by divine decree, had determined that Noah's descendants should disperse and "replenish the earth" as God had first instructed Adam (Gen. 1:28; Gen. 9:1-2), thus causing the nations to be divided (Gen. 10:32), Nimrod had other ideas.

Since "the whole earth was of one language, and of one speech" at that time, the peoples, under Nimrod's godless yet visionary leadership, determined to defy the Creator's command and to unify rather than to disperse. Thus, the first "New World Order" was born with intention to "build us a tower, whose top may reach unto heaven; and let us make us a name, lest we be scattered abroad upon the face of the whole earth" (Gen. 11:1-4).

The Lord, however, was not pleased at their provocative act, asserting the collective power of man's political will against the declared purposes of God. "And the Lord said, Behold, the people is one, and they have all one language… and now nothing shall be restrained from them, which they have imagined to do." Therefore the Lord "confounded their language, that they may not understand one another's speech," and "the Lord scattered them abroad from thence upon the face of all the earth: and they left off to build the city. Therefore is the name of it called Babel; because the Lord did there confound the language of all the earth" and the Lord did "scatter them abroad upon the face of all the earth" (Gen. 11:6-9).

Thus Babylon was born and became a universal symbol of mankind's historic and perpetual effort to supplant God's spiritual governance with man's secular government, de-constructing God while deifying man. The net effect, proven repeatedly throughout history, has been the elevation of mans' collective viewpoints over the clearly proclaimed viewpoint of the Creator, always resulting ultimately in chaos and destruction. The collective defiant decisions of humankind against the declared will of God have repeatedly caused the God of Creation to lift His beneficent protective and providing hand, thus opening the floodgate of His wrath in judgment "against all ungodliness and unrighteousness of men, who hold the truth in unrighteousness" (Rom. 1:18). "When they knew God," they refused to glorify Him 'as God'…." Invariably, humankind has "become vain in their imaginations, and their foolish heart was darkened. Professing themselves to be wise, they became fools…" (Rom. 1:21-22).

Because of this "Babylonian" spirit of collectivized rebellion against both the will and ways of the Creator, "God gave them up [over and over throughout history] to uncleanness through the lusts of their own hearts, to dishonor their own bodies between themselves." They "changed the truth of God into a lie, and worshipped and served the creature [man, animals and nature] more than the Creator…." "For this cause, God gave them up [repeatedly] unto vile affections" and "a reprobate mind" (Rom. 1:26-28).

Thus, the "civilization" of history, once deemed glorious, degenerated progressively into diabolical behavior, degenerate practice and destructive chaos. The "Babylonian" rebellion became so overwhelming against the authority of God that they (and we) became "filled with all unrighteousness" (Rom. 1:29). "Who knowing the judgment of God, that they which commit such things are worthy of death, not only do the same, but have pleasure in them that do them," (i.e., support, approve, wink at, legalize, promote, accept, embrace, etc.).

This "Babylonian" spirit has metastasized through the ages, becoming ever-more sophisticated and universalized, so that it now presents itself as dogma through the high priests of our creation-worshipping endtime religion and its unholy trinity—political correctness, multiculturalism and religious pluralism.

Indeed "Babylon" is alive and well, both geopolitically and spiritually. Modern Iraq is the site of ancient Babylon from which God ordered Abraham to flee on his faith journey to the Promised Land (Gen. 12:1-7). God's spirit and the spirit of Babylon were fundamentally inconsistent. For the four thousand years last passed, God has continuously called those who would truly trust Him out of Babylon, and has pronounced judgment upon all who embrace her proud and pernicious ways, from the days of Isaiah the prophet to the final days of the apocalypse.

Isaiah warned of "The burden of Babylon," foretelling of the destruction of not only physical Babylon but of the entire inhabitants of earth who embraced her spirit and ways in these end days (Isa. 13:1-22). The description should cause to shudder those who refuse to humble themselves to conform to the Word, Will and Ways of the God of Abraham, Isaac and Jacob.

> Howl ye; for the day of the LORD is at hand; it shall come as a destruction from the Almighty. Therefore shall all hands be faint, and every man's heart shall melt; and they shall be afraid: pangs and sorrows shall take hold of them; they shall be in pain as a woman that travaileth....
>
> Behold, the day of the LORD cometh.... And He shall destroy the sinners thereof out of the land.
>
> And I will punish the world for their evil, and the wicked for their iniquity; and I will cause the arrogancy of the proud to cease...
>
> And Babylon, the glory of the kingdoms, the beauty of the Chaldees' excellency, shall be as when God overthrew Sodom and Gomorrah (Isa. 13:6-19).

The warning of God's judgment upon Babylon is both physical/geo-political and spiritual. It is both site oriented and spirit oriented. The *Apocalypse* (Book of Revelation) speaks poignantly of God's purposes and Babylon's defilement of those purposes, as an angel cries out, "Babylon the great is fallen... for all nations have drunk of the wine of her fornication...." Therefore, "Come out of her, my people... for her sins have reached unto heaven, and God hath remembered her iniquities" (Rev. 18:1-4).

The picture is both powerful and prophetic. There will be no exit from the calamitous judgment soon to fall, with the sole exception of those who, in humble repentance, repudiate the iniquitous spirit of Babylon and turn, in faith, to embrace Jesus Christ, Yeshua the Messiah, in joyful obedience to His will—and His alone. Judgment will be swift and complete, "for in one hour is thy judgment come" (Rev. 18:10).

The final battle for *KING of the Mountain* is even now unfolding as the kings of the earth set themselves, in the spirit of Babylon, against the Lord and against His anointed, thinking vainly that they shall prevail. They fornicate with Babylon as the world's queen, saying to themselves "How much she hath glorified herself... for she saith in her heart, I sit a queen, and am no widow, and shall see no sorrow," yet "she shall be utterly burned with fire: for strong is the Lord God who judgeth her." "And the kings of the earth, who have committed fornication and lived deliciously with her, shall bewail her, and lament for her, when they shall see the smoke of her burning... saying alas, alas, that great city Babylon... for in one hour is thy judgment come" (Rev. 18:7-10).

From God's viewpoint, however, Babylon must not be seen as a mere geopolitical entity or as a mere site on the globe. For He warns more specif-ically of "MYSTERY BABYLON" which He calls "THE GREAT MOTHER OF HARLOTS" which is full of earth's abominations (Rev. 17:5). This "MOTHER OF HARLOTS" is further described as "the great whore" that sits upon many waters," with whom the kings of the earth have commit-ted fornication" (Rev. 17:1-2). This Babylonish whore is further depicted as "a woman sitting upon a scarlet coloured beast, full of names of blas-phemy, having seven heads and ten horns "and the woman was arrayed in purple and scarlet color, and decked with gold... having a golden cup in her hand full of abominations and filthiness of her fornication" (Rev. 17:3-4). This woman, depicting a powerful, unifying religion in these end days that seeks, in the same spirit as the ancient builders of the Tower of Babel, to unify the world, will be the religious "whore" that will assist the kings of the earth in forming and promoting to global acceptance their final world enterprise to save the world without God's proffered savior, Yeshua the Christ.

This "MOTHER OF HARLOTS" will bring the religions of the world under her mothering skirts, thus prostituting her supposed "Christian" purity and prophetic call on the lust-filled altar of political power. And when her prostitution for power has brought the final beast empire upon which she rides to ultimate power, she will (as with most prostitutes) be cast away and destroyed by the very kings of the earth over which she sought to reign as queen (Rev. 17:7-18). As it is written, "Come out of her, my people, that ye be not partakers with her sins…" (Rev. 18:4).

## THE EGYPTIAN EMPIRE

The phoenix of ancient Egypt has arisen from the ash heap of history in her final bid to reclaim earthly glory. The so-called "Arab Spring" gave rise to a shocking resurgence of Egyptian power as Egypt claims dominance over the Arab/Islamic world, choreographing the conquest of and uniting of the pan-Arab world under the once-outlawed Muslim Brotherhood. Yet, the Bible's focus on Egypt is not geopolitical but spiritual. Egypt, from God's viewpoint, became a perpetual snare to Israel's trust in the God of Abraham, Isaac and Jacob. It therefore became a metaphor for Israel's persistent love affair with the pagan ways of Egypt as exemplified by the then-ruling Pharaoh in the days of Moses, Israel's "great deliverer."

When Pharaoh was confronted by Moses to "Let my people go" from the bondage of Egyptian slavery, his response became a timeless expression of the rebel attitude of earth's rulers and citizens toward the God of Creation and of history that echoes ever-more-powerfully to this present hour. "Who is the Lord, that I should obey his voice?" bellowed Pharaoh in exuberant pride (Exod. 5:2). And the stories of that defiant and arrogant spirit can yet be heard throughout the world's halls of power, gaining strength even as the kings of the earth increasingly rage against the Lord and His anointed (Psa. 2:1-2) so as to prevent the Holy One of Israel, as KING of kings, from taking His throne both on the Temple Mount and in the hearts of men.

The spirit of Egypt represents an engine of distrust waging perpetual war against the God of Truth as set forth in the Bible. Egypt is mentioned 611 times, and over 400 times the words "OUT of Egypt" or similar phrases can be found from the book of *Genesis* to the *Apocalypse* of Revelation. The pervasive theme of the redemption story is that all who would be saved from Satan's house of bondage as followers of Creator God, the God of Jacob, must first come "OUT of Egypt" and refuse to return in mind or heart to place their trust in her worldly and pagan ways. Significantly, very few Israelites that God delivered from "the iron furnace" of Egypt were permitted to enter the Promised Land because, while God took them out of Egypt, He could not get the spirit of Egypt out of them (Numb. 14).

The prophets continually warned Israel to abandon their false trust in earthly power. "Woe to them that go down into Egypt for help…and trust in chariots; they look not unto the Holy One of Israel, neither seek the Lord," cried Isaiah (Isa. 31:1). "Therefore shall the strength of Pharaoh be your shame, and the trust in the shadow of Egypt your confusion" (Isa. 30:1-3).

This paralyzing spirit of Egypt has commandeered Christians and Jews, destroying genuine faith and shifting trust to ever-growing government and the "pharaohs" of this age. It is this trust-defying spirit that underlies Israel's present fear, compelling many to clamor to give up God-deeded land in the false pursuit of ever-elusive peace rather than to trust the promises of God secured in Abraham, Isaac and Jacob. Most professing Christians in the western world have long since succumbed to the spirit of Egypt. The increasing antipathy toward the word "obey" within the church, from pulpit to pew, reveals how pervasively those who purport to be followers of Christ identify with Pharaoh's self-exalted retort: "Who is the Lord that I should obey his voice?" (Note: The reader is here referred to the author's previous and more complete treatment of this issue in *OUT of EGYPT*, Elijah Books, ©2006).

The call to come "OUT of Egypt" throughout the Scriptures is a call, not to the pagans, but to those who profess to be followers of the God of the Bible. For it is seldom remembered that the greater problem was not in physically leaving Egypt but rather in leaving the trust-destroying spirit of Egypt behind. It was the persistent embracing of the spirit of Egypt that cost all but Joshua and Caleb the Promised Land, and will yet cost a rebellious majority their desired eternal destiny. For it is written, "Now all these things happened unto them for our examples: and they are written for our admonition, upon whom the ends of the world are come. Wherefore, let him that thinketh he standeth take heed lest he fall" (I Cor. 10:1-12).

Trust in the God of Truth and in His only begotten Son, Jesus Christ the righteous, unadulterated by false trusts in the governors, systems and governments of this age, is, and has always been, the true test that defines the *eclessia* or "called-out" ones who will share in God's eternal kingdom. Trust is always proven in and through faith-driven obedience to God's Word (John 14:15, 21, 23-24; I John 5:2-3).

"Come out of her my people" is the continuing call, both as to the spirit of Babylon and as to the spirit of Egypt, to all who will walk worthy of God's salvation and favor. The decision to leave "Egypt" and "Babylon" is a decision to enthrone Yeshua Messiah, Jesus Christ, as KING of kings upon the throne of your life.

## THE PERSIAN EMPIRE

The ancient world power known historically as Medo-Persia has similarly, as with Babylon and Egypt, risen from the desert sands of antiquity to claim power and dominion in our present world. Persia was transformed into the Islamic Republic of Iran in 1935, and even now she seeks ruling dominion over the entire Islamic world, and through collectivized Islam, over the larger Judeo-Christian world, indeed over all of the planet by means of Sharia law.

## THE OTTOMAN EMPIRE

We have also, since 1922, watched in amazement as the seemingly defunct and once-glorious Ottoman Empire that ruled and gained dominion over much of the then-known world for 500 years has now "reincarnated" itself as modern Turkey. It is Turkey that is progressively and aggressively emerging under Erdogan to assert a neo-Ottoman Empire over the Islamic World, and by means of Koranic authority, over the entire globe. The Turks and the Iranians (Persians and Ottomans) as competing Muslim yet non-Arab nations, now face potentially calamitous confrontation in their respective maneuverings to become *KING of the Mountain.*

## THE ROMAN EMPIRE

The great Roman Empire never truly died, yet as a secular power it became diluted and dispersed throughout the western world for over fifteen hundred years. The power and authority of the Caesars as *pontifex maximus* was ultimately transferred to the Bishop of Rome—the Pontiff—the Pope—as the reigning Pontifex Maximus, thus merging secular and spiritual authority in the "Vicar of Christ" as a substitute "Christ returned to earth," with all the power and earthly glory attendant thereto in the long-absence of "the Word made flesh" who declared Himself to be "the WAY, the TRUTH and the LIFE" (John 1:14; John 1:6). Thus the "Holy Father" on earth replaced God the Father; the world's leaders make obeisance to "His Holiness" while spurning the holy God of Creation; and Rome reveals itself to not be dead but very much alive.

The Rome that once appeared dead when Napoleon imprisoned Pope Pius VII in July 1809, is now taking its prophetic place in the long-anticipated and geopolitical battle to place the Pontifex Maximus upon his papal throne on the "Holy Mount" in Jerusalem. Thus the long-lost Holy Roman Empire envisioned by Charlemagne in AD800 with the Pope merging the church with the power of the state by crowning the emperor is, even now, in this propitious moment of history, positioning itself to crown the soon-to-be presented "emperor" of the New World Order. Shockingly, the Vicar of Christ and the Anti-Christ of Scripture will soon conceptually embrace a revived Holy Roman Empire. This purportedly "holy" empire will survive only so long as politically necessary to securely ensconce man's final utopian government in the minds and hearts of earth's inhabitants, after which the pseudo-spiritual institution which was progressively prostituted to secure power, will be summarily destroyed, and that without remedy (Rev. 17:9-18). The final great "beast" empire will no longer tolerate the burden of the "great whore" seeking transport to power on the back of the beast (Rev. 17:1-8, 17-18). The counterfeit christ (Anti-Christ) will brook no competition nor opposition in the final battle for *KING of the Mountain*.

## THE RUSSIAN EMPIRE

The Russian Empire, once grand and glorious, progressively lost its patina. Yet the vision of Russian grandeur and glory was preserved over fifteen hundred years by means of the "Third Rome" imagery. This imagery, invested deeply in the Russian imagination and psyche for centuries, emerged visibly from time to time, even through the Bolshevik Revolution in 1917 that gave birth to the vision to save the world through the spread of Soviet communism throughout the world.

With the demise of the Soviet Union in 1989-1991, all pride and longed-for power on the world scene seemed forever crushed—that is until the mysterious rise of Vladimir Putin. Russia, once again, now seeks to impress its "Third Rome" mark upon world history, feverishly choreographing former Soviet client states as well as new energy-oriented nations into its lustful arms, declaring even that "Russia is the guardian of the Islamic world." The inevitable conflict of "Third Rome" and the Vatican's "First Rome" will soon intensify in the final geopolitical positioning to claim the world's throne as *KING of the Mountain*.

## THE AMERICAN "EMPIRE"

"Empire" has not been a term commonly used in description of the United States of America, that is until the last generation. The most-used and recent phrase to depict and allude to the United States of America as "empire" is the Latin phrase *Pax Americana*. This phrase has been adapted from the historic phrase *Pax Romana*, most assuredly referencing the Roman Empire as the agent of worldwide peace, albeit under the iron fist of the Caesars and the persuasive presence and power of the Roman legions.

Is America truly, from a prophetic perspective, a "re-incarnation" or "re-iteration" of the famed and never-totally-destroyed Roman Empire? There is no direct scriptural passage to confirm with precision or particularity such a conclusion. We have only historical similarities through which to secure any level of direct comparison. These include:

- A Roman-type government;
- A Romanesque Capitol;
- A Roman/English legal system;
- A Greco/Roman way of thinking;
- A global foot imprint of Roman/American ways;
- An economy that has followed the same pattern of profligate spending as Rome;
- A moral degeneration effecting the same pattern characteristic of Rome's heyday of prosperity;
- A culture increasingly attacked and undermined by numerous outside influences, i.e., enculturation with values radically inconsistent with historic American values; terrorist plots; and internal uprisings from those increasingly dependent upon the empire's dole;
- A level of sexual promiscuity and debauchery increasingly characteristic of Rome in its prosperous prime; and
- A global spread of American forces increasingly unsustainable to secure the *Pax Americana.*

These alone should serve as dire warning to the sole superpower currently reigning over the planet, particularly if we are now in those last days of which the Bible speaks so soberly. Furthermore, since America per se finds no specific reference in the Bible, yet Rome is identified as the last great ruling empire before the prophesied Second Coming of Jesus Christ, two primary conclusions might be drawn. Either America will suddenly diminish or be destroyed from inside corruption or outside conquest— or—America will be absorbed or amalgamated into the resurrected European (Roman) Empire through economic and military expansion of the European Union and the Mediterranean Union, which was perhaps presciently described as reinstating "the footprint of the ancient Roman Empire."

Of salutary note is that as America's trust in the God who "made and preserved us a nation" has waned dramatically with the rise of national prosperity, so the trust of Americans has been increasingly (yes, dramatically) reposed in the power of Roman-like government that, in the days of yore, sought to stamp out the rise of the KING of kings—the king Messiah—causing the Jewish leaders to traitorously conspire with Rome— calling for Pilate's crucifixion of "The KING of the Jews" while the High Priest and Sanhedrin cried, "We have no king but Caesar" (John 19:1-22).

History, indeed, has a strange way of repeating itself. Caesar gains more and more power and authority while a nation, claiming to be "Under God," relegates their "KING" to the ash heap of history. Yet the great epic, eternal and endtime battle for *KING of the Mountain* has not yet concluded, but lies even now at the very door of destiny.

## THE GLOBAL EMPIRE

The world was one under Nimrod in the days of Babel. The world was one under Pharaoh in the days of Egypt. The world was one under Darius, Ahasuarus (Xerxes), and Cyrus in the days of Persia. The world was one under Alexander the Great and the cultural spread of Hellenism throughout the then-known world. The world became one under the *Pax Romana* of the Roman Republic and under the reigns of the deified Caesars. The world became progressively unified under Charlemagne's Holy Roman Empire and the decided shift of Rome's domination from earthly secular empire to a joint papal enterprise investing the Bishop of Rome with the mantel of *Pontifex Maximus.*

Suleiman the Great sought to make the world one in Mohammed through the Ottoman Empire. Constantine, through Constantinople, sought to reclaim unity under the cross through "Second Rome." The British sought and nearly gained global dominion, for "the sun never set on the British Empire." Russia, for fifteen hundred years, sought to effectuate the vision of *Third Rome* and thereby "save the world," eventually reposing its hopes in the spread of communism to not less than one-third of the earth.

Germany, through Hitler; Italy, through Mussolini; Japan, through Hiroshito; and China, through Mao; as well as many lesser players—all have sought global dominion; and those dreams have not fully died but lay dormant. Practitioners of the NEW AGE and its eclectic religious vision of global unity now combine forces with the United Nations and even the World Council of Churches to usher in the final utopian vision of a One World Order in this "Age of Aquarius" where "peace and understanding" will abound in a revolutionary new state of "global consciousness." This is our world. The planet has been and is being extraordinarily prepared for receiving a pontificating and powerful "peacemaker" in whom the peoples will repose their trust for temporal salvation and deliverance.

The ancient prophet Daniel spoke rather precisely of this man in whom the world will repose its trust to ostensibly "save us from ourselves." It will happen, he said, "in the latter time..." (Dan. 8:23). He is described as the "little horn" that shall receive delegated authority and power from 'ten horns" or world leaders (perhaps regional governments) and will be the "King" or ultimate governmental head of the "fourth beast" empire described as "dreadful and terrible." He will "make war with the saints" and "shall devour the whole earth, tread it down and break it in pieces" (Dan. 7:1-28; 8:23-27).

Thus, our world is now primed and positioned for the last great Luciferic enterprise destined to rule the world in defiance of the Creator and dedicated to the destruction and annihilation of all who purport to embrace the "KING" whom the Creator has chosen to place "upon His holy hill" (Psa. 2:6). It will be a no-holds-barred battle for *KING of the Mountain*. It is epic, endtime and of eternal consequence.

## THE WAITING "WATERLOO"

Just as Napoleon "met his Waterloo" in defeat of his enterprise to rule the world for France, so the demonically enterprising Anti-Christ heading earth's final effort to globalize against God will meet his demise at the Second Coming of Yeshua the Christ as KING of kings. All hell, however, will break forth in global horror before heaven's hand will bring deliverance and true peace. For "a time, times and the dividing of time (3 ½ years), the demonic despot who gains power through flattery will exercise his will. He will seek to "destroy the mighty and the holy people" and through his crafty policies, he will temporarily prosper in ever-palpable pride. Through the pretended pursuit of peace, he "shall destroy many "and shall ultimately stand up blasphemously against KING Messiah himself (Dan. 8:23-25).

## A TRUE GLOBAL DOMINION

There will be a global dominion. The extensive historical journey we have followed has enabled all who read with an honest heart to be deeply troubled in mind and perhaps convicted in spirit. The epic battle we have witnessed is now an endtime battle—a battle being staged for its final fury in our time. And it is a battle that will, when all is said and done, determine the eternal hope of many and the eternal horror of most.

The prophet Daniel not only witnessed the intensity of the final global battle but also the shocking outcome of the outrageous outpouring of mankind's unrestrained wickedness when untempered by the spirit of truth and the laws of God. Chaos does not begin to describe the cataclysmic carnage.

Yet Daniel saw "one like the Son of man come with the clouds of heaven... and there was given to him (Yeshua the Messiah, Jesus the Christ) dominion, and glory, and a kingdom, that all people, nations, and languages, should serve him: his dominion is an everlasting dominion, which shall not pass away, and his kingdom that which shall not be destroyed" (Dan. 7:13-14).

Furthermore, "the kingdom and dominion, and the greatness of the kingdom under the whole heaven, shall be given to the people of the saints of the most High, whose kingdom is an everlasting kingdom, and all dominions shall serve and obey him." This is "the end of the matter" (Dan. 7:27-28).

Yet one final battle remains. It is a battle not waged with traditional or asymmetric engines of war, nor is it pursued for control of oil or geopolitical power. It is, in glaring reality, the ultimate battle of the ages. It is a conflict of such enormous consequence that the combined and collective forces of human history meet on the beckoning plains of biblical prophecy to determine for all time the destiny of the souls of men. The spirit of every person on this mortal plane becomes the conclusive spoil as the ultimate and most glorious created being of time short of eternity makes his final bid to become "KING of the Mountain" over your life, in brazen defiance of the Creator Himself. Dare we peer into the future soon to become the eternal past?

*Chapter 24*

# PROBING THOUGHTS *for* PROPHETIC TIMES

1. How would you define or describe "The Mystery of History?" Do you believe history is merely composed of a series of disjointed and meaningless developments, or do you think there are identifiable threads that have woven into the tapestry of man's sojourn on the planet an emerging picture that provides understanding of a Divine hand at work? Does it matter?

2. Can you now see how the nations and empires marching throughout recorded history have inevitably sought to become *KING of the Mountain*, either geopolitically, spiritually or both?

3. Do you not find it fascinating that each of many historical and ancient empires have, over the past seventy-five years, resurrected from obscurity to claim power in this time when history and prophecy are rapidly converging into congruency? And is it not amazing that Israel should be re-born during this same period of time? What is the connection?

4. Will our world ultimately be defined by geopolitical dominion or by spiritual dominion? Who will ultimately reign as *KING of the Mountain?* Who will rule and reign on the throne of your life?

*Chapter 25*

# THE MOUNTAIN AND THE THRONE

*"The geopolitical stakes have never been higher. Yet they pale in the presence of the spiritual stakes that echo into eternity."*

A THRONE IS THE SEAT OF ULTIMATE POWER AND AUTHORITY. While a throne may physically present itself as an ornate and grand chair elevated upon a dais, its true significance is its symbolic place and purpose, declaring to all in its proximity that they are in the presence of sovereign and exclusive dominion. That dominion may be exercised under a monarch or king, an emperor or even a dictator.

## THRONES SPEAK

The throne speaks. It speaks of exclusive sovereignty, demanding allegiance, deference and obedience to the word, ways and will of the one who sits upon the throne.

So great is the "speaking" and the symbolic power of the throne that reference is often made not to the name of the person or power occupying the throne but rather merely to "the throne," not as a chair but as the repository of current power and authority ruling over the affairs of the subjects of the realm. The throne, by implication, references a citizenry or subjects who have either voluntarily or coercively been placed under the reigning king, emperor or dictator. Just as "thrones" have come and gone with the political kingdoms of this world throughout history, so there are spiritual kingdoms with commanding thrones that have demanded obeisance and increasingly assert power over the souls of men and women.

Those spiritual "thrones" are being consolidated. In the same fashion as the nations and political powers of our world have been progressively consolidating into a singular global order, so too have the spiritual "thrones" been unifying into what New Agers refer to as the new "global consciousness"

319

toward a One-World religion. The pattern is perfectly clear and demands our careful attention as the battle for *KING of the Mountain* accelerates toward the people's choice of thrones, both political and spiritual.

Of a truth, thrones speak, and they speak loudly. They have both a commanding and a beckoning voice. Yet in the end, when the helix of history abuts the end of time as we know it, only one timeless throne will remain and will reign over the kings of the earth and the remnant peoples that then populate the planet.

## POLITICAL AND SPIRITUAL THRONES

As the helix of history has wound its way across the sands of time to our time; great political empires have come and gone, leaving traces of their respective thrones in our collective memories. Yet, as has been so aptly said, "The only thing we learn from history is that we don't learn from history." Furthermore, "Those who don't learn from history are doomed to repeat it." And we are about to witness history repeated "on steroids."

VIEWPOINT DETERMINES DESTINY! The eyes through which we view the panoply of history determine the lessons, occurrences, observances and conclusions we ultimately claim to be "history". With great vigor—even vitriol—revered historians and renowned prognosticators have prevailed upon their respective publics to embrace their view of history's defining decisions, moments and implications—even "future shock." Yet precious few have given but a cynical or sarcastic glance to the biblical perspective that purports to be "God's Word" as confirmed not only by recorded signs and wonders but by four thousand years of increasingly and precisely-fulfilled prophecy.

Ponder the possibility. If, in reality, the biblical viewpoint of history is true, culminating in Satan's effort to usurp the Throne of Creator God by deceptively gaining dominion over the souls of men over the ages, rejection or defiance of that view leads us even now to the precipice of destruction. And we therefore, as blind men, now cast our collective hope and dependence upon increasingly godless men and government for our undeserved "salvation." Any desired destiny we may have anticipated, whether temporal or eternal, thus unravels before our pained and panicking eyes. The hope that should have reigned eternal has vanished—and is now vanishing—before our unbelieving eyes and hardened hearts, all because we refused to embrace the viewpoint of the God of history revealed in Yeshua Messiah—Jesus the Christ.

Perhaps the clearest and most meaningful way to comprehend the vast details of what we call *history* is to view man's sojourn on terra firma as the ever-recurring and oft-changing effort of our species –humankind—to set up both governmental and spiritual thrones so as to rule our lives without allowing our Creator to govern in our lives. The great empires of the past have all sought to deify men while denigrating or defying the Creator as He reveals Himself both in the natural order of creation and through Scripture. The same picture emerges in and through the various religions of the world, where man and animals become revered as gods while the Creator is shelved as an irrelevance.

It is fascinating that this pattern of deifying men and creation while denigrating God has persisted and presented itself as prevailing "wisdom" to this precipitous moment when the entire planet and its peoples lie in unprecedented peril. Yet we praise politicians, priests and a raft of spiritual charlatans who offer new thrones, both political and spiritual, upon which we can repose our hopes as the horrors of god-less-ness sweep our world. It is as if we revel in a perpetual "game of thrones."

## GLOBAL SALVATION

From Nimrod's Tower of Babel to the promised and now-emerging New World Order, mankind has sought to set himself upon the "throne" for global salvation and dominion. Charlemagne's "Holy Roman Empire" is now re-emerging as an end-time "Holy Roman Empire," as Pope John Paul II and Pope Benedict XVI sought vigorously to bring all the world's religions under the comforting wing of the Vatican. This pontifical plan will continue under Pope Francis to undergird history's grand scheme to unite the world in submission to man's ultimate utopian throne, co-ruled by the soon-to-be political savior and the Vicar of Christ, each plotting to ultimately depose the other so as to reign as regent over the globe.

This battle for earth's grandest throne is set in dramatic and eternal contradiction to the eternal throne of God, as it is written, "Thy throne, O God, is for ever and ever: the scepter of thy kingdom is a right scepter" (Psa. 45:6; Heb. 1:8). The temporal thrones of men and the eternal throne of God are soon destined to clash with calamitous consequences. That unprecedented clash will come even as man seeks to establish his global throne, under the authority of Satan, upon God's Holy Mountain, in open defiance of the Savior of the World—Yeshua the Messiah.

As we have earlier seen, "The kings of the earth set themselves, and the rulers take counsel together, against the LORD, and against his anointed…." Yet, says the Lord, "have I set my king upon my holy hill of Zion." Therefore, "Be wise now therefore, O ye kings: be instructed, ye judges of the earth. Serve the LORD with fear, and rejoice with trembling." "Blessed are all they that put their trust in him" (Psa. 2:1-12).

# KING OF THE MOUNTAIN

It is said that "history repeats itself," and after four thousand years since Abraham first set foot on Mount Moriah, the cycle of history returns us to "the place of which God told him" (Gen. 22:3)—the very place where Abraham, by faith, told Isaac his son, "God will provide himself a lamb" (Gen. 22:8). It is the place, also known as Mt. Zion, where King David chose to establish his kingdom 3000 years ago (II Sam. 5:7, I Kings 8:1) and of whom God spoke: "I will establish his throne forever" (I Chron. 17:12).

David reigned thirty-three years in Jerusalem (I Chron. 29:26-27). And upon his death, his son Solomon "began to build the house of the Lord in Mount Moriah, where the Lord appeared unto David his father…" (II Chron. 3:1). At the dedication of the Temple, the glory of God filled the place as "the house of God" (II Chron. 5:13-14, and Solomon, declaring the prophetic word of the Lord in consecration; made clear for all time:

> I have chosen Jerusalem, that my name might be there; and have chosen David to be over my people Israel (II Chron. 6:6).

Thus, God's kingdom on earth was forever established in David, at Jerusalem, on the Temple Mount—Mt. Zion. Yet "Israel rebelled against the house of David"—Yeshua the Messiah—whom Isaiah had prophesied would rule and reign "upon the throne of David… even for ever" (Isa. 9:6-7; Matt. 15:22, 20:30; Rom. 1:3-4; Rev. 22:16). He, Yeshua the Messiah, "came unto his own [Israel and Judah], and his own received him not. But as many as received him [whether Jew or Gentile], to them he gave power/authority to become the sons of God, even to them who believe on his name" (John 1:11-12). When Yeshua was publically presented and acknowledged, even by a godless Roman governor, to be the "KING of the Jews," their ruling Sanhedrin and chief priests cried "Crucify him, crucify him" for "We have no king but Caesar" (John 19:3-6). And Pilate proclaimed, "Thine own nation and the chief priests have delivered thee unto me…" (John 18:35).

And so the eternal "Lamb of God, which taketh away the sins of the world" (John 1:29) was offered by his own people on Mount Moriah as the requisite "lamb without blemish" to be crucified by the collective will of Jew and Gentile to destroy the "Lamb of glory," "the Word made flesh," "the glory as of the only begotten of the Father, full of grace and truth" (John 1:14). Jew and Gentile had become complicit in dethroning God's anointed King so as to protect and preserve their own "game of thrones" for power, perks and position. They did Satan's deceptive business for him. Yet when Christ cried out from the cross "It is finished" (John 19:30), the end times were just beginning.

The King God had ordained from the beginning to rule and reign over the hearts of men rose again. The grave could not hold God's promised *governor*, for it is written, "Of the increase of his government and peace there shall be no end, upon the throne of David..." (Isa. 9:7). The scriptures have clearly promised that "this same Jesus, which is taken up from you into heaven, shall so come in like manner as you have seem him go into heaven" (Acts 1:11). And when He returns, He shall reign as "KING of KINGS, and LORD of LORDS" (Rev. 19:16).

> At that time they shall call Jerusalem the throne of the LORD; and all the nations [that remain] shall be gathered unto it, to the name of the LORD to Jerusalem: neither shall they walk any more after the imagination of their evil heart (Jer. 3:17).

## THRONE OF THRONES

The KING of kings will sit upon the THRONE of thrones upon the Holy Mount of Jerusalem. The "great trumpet shall be blown" and the outcasts of earth who refuse to bow to the treacherous thrones of ungodly men "shall worship the LORD in the holy mount at Jerusalem (Isa 27:13). Every other mountain and throne "shall be made low: and the crooked shall be made straight... And the glory of the LORD shall be revealed, and all flesh shall see it together: for the mouth of the LORD hath spoken it" (Isa. 40:4-5). "The voice of him that crieth in the wilderness, Prepare ye the way of the LORD [both Jew and Gentile], make straight in the desert [of your life and of this barren and brazen world] a highway for our God" (Isa. 40:3).

"Every knee [both Jew and Gentile] shall bow... and every tongue shall confess that Jesus Christ [Yeshua the Messiah] is Lord, to the glory of God the Father" (Phil. 2:10-11). "The LORD sitteth upon his throne, high and lifted up" and the angels also cry "Holy, holy, holy is the LORD of hosts: the whole earth is full of his glory" (Isa. 6:1-3).

"Here ye now, O house of David [Israel and Judah]," is it a small thing that ye have rejected and wearied God? "Therefore, the LORD himself [hath given you] a sign; Behold a virgin conceived, and bore a son, and his name was called Immanuel [God with us—the Word made flesh like unto our brethren]" (Isa. 7:13-14). "He was and is despised and rejected of men... and we esteemed him not" (Isa. 53:3), even though He was "bruised [crucified and beaten] for our iniquities" (Isa. 53:5).

"Thus saith the Lord, The heaven is my throne, and the earth is my footstool: where is the house that ye build unto me? and where is the place of my rest?" "...but to this man will I look, even to him that is poor and of a contrite spirit, and trembleth at my [the KING of king's] word" (Isa. 66:1-2). "He who blesseth himself in the earth shall bless himself in the God of truth" (Isa. 65:16) and shall embrace with joy and salvation the Lord of glory, Jesus Christ the righteous, who declared, "I am the way, the truth, and the life: no man cometh unto the Father, but by me" (John 14:5-7).

## THRONE OF JUDGMENT

The throne is the ultimate symbol of power and authority and therefore stands as the revered and feared seat of final judgment in any kingdom. When a king or monarch is righteous, righteous judgment is expected. When the legitimate authority of the throne is disrespected or disregarded through blatant lawlessness or rebellion, any genuine expectation of merciful justice loses meaning and is replaced by a new reality—terror of the throne.

The history of mankind is replete with unrighteous judgment by unrighteous rulers who dispense terror because they love not truth but rather seek increasing dominion through the terror of the throne. No love is lost between such rulers and their terrified subjects. They are tyrants. And tyrants are notorious, not only for their tirades against their subjects and other competing thrones, but against the very God of Creation who rightly has authority over all those created in His image. The tension between godless tyrants, including those purportedly raised up democratically, and the Supreme Potentate of creation, the Creator God, is growing and coming to its final expression as "the kings of the earth set themselves, and the rulers take counsel together, against the LORD, and against his anointed" (Psa. 2:2).

The ultimate moment of historical truth is at hand. The Judge of the universe is preparing to render judgment. And His judgment will be sure, righteous, true... and final. History has been HIS story, and that epic account is rapidly coming to a holy and just end.

"The LORD reigneth; let the earth rejoice," declared the Psalmist. "Righteousness and judgment are the habitation of his throne" (Psa. 97:1-2). "Say among the nations that the LORD reigneth: ...he shall judge the people righteously" (Psa. 96:10), "for he cometh to judge the earth: with righteousness shall he judge the world, and the people with equity" (Psa 98:9). Therefore, "Exalt the LORD our God, and worship at his holy hill [Jerusalem, Mt. Zion, the Temple Mount]; for the LORD our God is holy" (Psa. 99:9).

## USURPING THE THRONE ON THE MOUNT

Judgment is coming and is sure. As it was prophesied. "Behold, the Lord cometh with ten thousands of his saints, to execute judgment upon all, and to convince all that are ungodly among them of their ungodly deeds…" (Jude vs 14-15). Yet, amazingly, that final judgment shall not come until Satan's final effort to usurp the Throne on the Mount of God has played out in the greatest deceptive exhibition of spiritual *chutzpah* ever conceived in the demonically-directed mind of man since Judas betrayed Jesus the Messiah by dipping his hand of purported commitment in the symbolic Passover blood and body of Yeshua in the upper room of the Last Supper, deceiving even Jesus' closest followers (Matt. 26: 17-29).

The scenario surreptitiously emerging in these end times is breathtakingly brazen. The Vatican now seeks to vanquish all competitors for governance of the Mount of God. Rome, ensconced throughout antiquity on the Seven Hills upon which it was built, is no longer satisfied with dominion on the Aventine, Caelian, Capitoline, Esquiline, Palatine, Quirinal and Viminal hills. Only the Temple Mount will suffice—the place of ultimate and consummate world dominion. Will this then be the power linked in partnership with the New World Order, through which Satan's final bid to supplant the Creator God's claim to that Holy Mount shall be accomplished or attempted?

Let it here be acknowledged the tremendous conflict such a demonically-conceived concept might have upon the lives and minds of those who look to the Roman Catholic Church and her Pontifex Maximus (the Pope)—or any man—for ultimate spiritual truth and eternal hope. It must be clearly understood that our individual and collective commitment (whether Catholic, Protestant or otherwise) must be to Christ and Christ alone rather than to any man—even the "Vicar of Christ"—who not only purports to be "head of the Church" but also the "Absolute Monarch" of a governmental system known as The Vatican.

With this caveat in mind, let us consider prayerfully this "Late Breaking News," published January 2, 2013, by *Arutz Sheva, Israel National News*, in an article by Giulio Meotti. The gravamen of this shocking piece must, of necessity, be here distilled as to the salient facts. You may wish, at this moment, to fasten your proverbial seatbelt in light of the global gravity of this disclosure.

"Israel seems to have sold Jerusalem to the Vatican" is the subtitle. "An historic agreement has been drafted between Israel and the Vatican. The Israeli authorities have granted the Pope an official seat… on Mount Zion in Jerusalem, where David and Solomon, kings of Israel, are believed to be buried—[and upon which Mount they also reigned as the earthly forerunners of the Christ of God who would come in the flesh and ultimately govern upon the throne of David (Isa. 9:6-7)].

"This is an enormous issue…." "…the agreement, expected to be ratified in June 2013, gives the Pope a 'special authority' over the room where the Last Supper is believed to have taken place on Mt. Zion," thus allowing the Pope to sit in the place of Christ so as to exercise global dominion. "The Catholic Church has long wanted control over part of the area on Mt. Zion...." Yet that is not all. "The Church has long been working to reduce Jewish rights in Jerusalem and in the Old City. Now after the Muslim Waqf authority expelled Christians from the Temple Mount and turned it into a mosque, it's the turn of the Vatican to lay its hands on the Jewish Jerusalem."

A brief trek through this Pontifical process reveals that the Vatican will resort to virtually any means to accomplish this end-time objective. For the most part, it seems to pass under both the spiritual and geopolitical radar so as to gain little Israeli or global attention. For instance, "The Custody of the Holy Land, the Franciscan order which, with Vatican approval, is in charge of the holy sites, campaigns with the Arabs against Israel." The very week this article appeared, "the Vatican in its official documents began referring to the 'State of Palestine.'" Indeed, "Sovereignty over Mt. Zion is politics, not only religion." It is about power—ultimate earthly power—over the souls of men.

The half has not yet been told. "The Vatican is also asking that Israel hand over to the Vatican's control dozens of sites, 19 in Judea and Samaria and 28 in Jerusalem"... even the "Mount of Olives." "The Vatican wants the Jews out of the Old City [biblical Jerusalem]...." Furthermore, "The Vatican and the Palestinian Liberation Organization exposed a common position in the Basic Agreement of February 15, 2000... signed by Vatican officials and the PLO—an organization dedicated to the mass-deportation of Israel's Jews." That memorandum made plain—"the Catholic Church [Vatican] wants Israel relinquishing sovereignty at the Western Wall and the Temple Mount."

## OF TEMPLES AND THRONES

It is imperative that no politician, prime minister, president, pastor nor pope miss the eternal point and grave significance of the epic, eternal, and now endtime battle for *KING of the Mountain*. This historic geopolitical and spiritual conflict that has coursed through the annals of time has, in some fashion, touched every human inhabitant of this terrestrial ball, whether rich or poor, Jew or Gentile, bond or free. It has been probative of the human heart and will soon prove the sovereign of every soul.

Every man and woman is given by the Creator God a free will to choose whom he or she will serve. While there may be many earthly kings and potentates commanding allegiance, there remain only two ultimate masters, each ready to take the throne on the mount of your heart and mind. Which one will rule and reign will determine your destiny. Will it be—the god of this world—the Deceiver—the Lawless One who comes ultimately and seductively to "steal, kill and destroy" or will it be the One who "came to save His people from their sin" and "to seek and save those that are lost?" Will it be Satan who has been seductively competing for lordship over the lives of men since Adam so as to declare himself "King of the Mountain," or will it be the Creator of all things who in the fullness of time sent forth Yeshua, His only begotten Son, that whosoever would believe on Him should not perish but have everlasting life?"

Time is now merging inexorably into eternity. And the final words of prophecy are being inscribed in the final pages of human history. The time to choose who will reign as sovereign ruler of your life can no longer be dismissed or delayed. It is time to choose.

The Epic, Eternal and End-time Battle for *KING of the Mountain* has been played out throughout time in real time, and will ultimate conclude in our time. This battle has manifested itself tangibly throughout time as we have known it, from the Tower of Babel to the pressing New World Order. Satan, the enemy of your soul, is determined to ensconce his pseudo-savior, a counterfeit "Christ," a usurper upon the throne of David on the Temple Mount, so as to vicariously proclaim himself "god" in the flesh. Yet in reality, the more pressing problem is not the Temple Mount but the high place of your life—your heart.

The six-thousand year battle for *KING of the Mountain* has been a dramatic metaphor for God's eternal message, to the Jew first but also to we Gentiles. Yeshua the Messiah, born of a Jewish virgin, came unto His own, but His own "received Him not." But as many as would receive Him [both then and now] to them He gave authority to become the sons of God, even to them that believe on His name" (John 1:11-12)—both Jew and Gentile who, by faith, would confess their sin and walk in humble obedience to His Word, His Will and His Ways.

Every person on this planet will elect a king. In the end, there are only two choices on the spiritual ballot. Satan, the historic arch-enemy of your soul and of the Creator, promises that each person can become his own "king" and need not submit to the Word, Will and Ways of God. Yet God remains "God." He desires that none should eternally perish by choosing the Deceiver's lordship, but rather that all should come to repentance and reconciliation with God through Jesus the Messiah (II Pet. 3:9).

The final battle for *KING of the Mountain* is at hand. We must all choose. The battle is raging for the souls of men and women. There is no time to lose. While the battle for *KING of the Mountain* progresses toward geopolitical culmination; the spiritual battle is even more intense.

In order for a third temple to arise in the Temple Mount, massive geopolitical and spiritual compromise will be required, resulting in Israel's desperate covenant of proffered peace by a false "messiah." Israel, as a state, will prostitute herself on the altar of promised peace presented by a counterfeit "peacemaker" who will masquerade as messiah (Isa. 28:14-18; Dan. 8:23-25, 9:26-27). The consequences will be devastating. God calls it "a covenant with death" (Isa. 28:15). So great will be that treasonous decision against the God of Abraham, Isaac and Jacob that God himself shall disannul it, calling it an "agreement with hell" (Isa. 28:18).

Fortunately for both Jew and Gentile, however, "the Most High dwelleth not in temples made with hands, as saith the prophets. Heaven is my throne, and earth is my footstool" (Acts 7:48-49, Isa. 66:1). The Temple is but a temporal symbol of the heart of man where God, by His Spirit, chooses to dwell upon our invitation. As it is written, "ye are the temple of the living God; as God hath said, I will dwell in them, and walk in them; and I will be their God, and they shall be my people" (II Cor. 6:16).

Who will then sit upon the throne? Who will be *KING of the Mountain*? Who will reign supreme in your life, upon the "mount" of the "temple" of your heart? Will it be Yeshua the Messiah, Jesus the Christ, the Holy One of Israel, the Lamb of God who takes away the sin of the world through our humble submission to His supreme authority in heaven and earth, or will it be Satan's messianic counterfeit invested "after the working of Satan with all power and signs and lying wonders—with all deceivableness of unrighteousness…" (II Thess. 2:8-10)?

## THE VALLEY OF DECISION

The geopolitical stakes are high and have never been higher. Our world teeters on the precipice of power. It is demonic power versus Divine power. Yet as profound as the geopolitical stakes may be, they pale in the presence of the spiritual stakes that echo into eternity.

"Multitudes, multitudes are in the valley of decision: for the day of the LORD is near in the valley of decision" (Joel 3:14).

"The LORD also shall roar out of Zion, and utter His voice in Jerusalem; and the heavens and the earth shall shake: but the LORD will be the hope of His people…. So shall ye know that I am the LORD your God dwelling in Zion, my holy mountain…" (Joel 3:16).

"Be wise now therefore, O ye kings: be instructed, ye judges of the earth. Serve the LORD [Christ, the Messiah] with fear and rejoice with trembling." "Blessed are all they that put their trust in Him" (Psa. 2:10-12).

Though "The kings of the earth set themselves, and the rulers take counsel together against the Lord, and against His anointed… Yet have I [the LORD God of Creation] set my king upon my holy hill of Zion" (Psa. 2:2, 6). And He has "a name written, KING OF KINGS, AND LORD OF LORDS" (Rev. 19:16). "Surely," He hath said, "I come quickly" (Rev. 22:20).

*Chapter 25*

# PROBING THOUGHTS *for* PROPHETIC TIMES

1. In what ways do thrones "speak" into our lives?

2. Could it be that the entire panoply of human history can only be fully understood as the continuing spiritual battle for the "throne" of everyman's life?

3. Can you see how the current global thrust toward a New World Order is merely the culmination of mankind's collective and historic effort to circumvent God's rule that began at the Tower of Babel?

4. Why do you suppose the Tower of Babel is a well-established symbol adopted by the European Union, coupled with the "Woman Riding the Beast?" Is this not a blatant declaration by those confederating together to usurp the throne or rulership of God in a culminating cause of self-salvation?

5. When and why will Jerusalem be called "the throne of the Lord (Jer. 3:17)?

6. Who is and will be "KING of kings and LORD of lords?" If your answer is Jesus Christ, Yeshua HaMashiach, is he truly KING and Lord of your own life? What evidence in your life reveals that ultimate of all relationships?

7. If Yeshua, Jesus, is not your true Lord and KING, who is... and on what authority?

8. In what ways, through allegiance, attitude or behavior, have you perhaps de-throned Christ as KING and Lord even while claiming Him as "savior?"

9. Are you prepared to enter these final prophesied cataclysmic days of human history without committing your life now to Yeshua, Jesus the Messiah, to whom the Bible declares every knee will soon bow as *KING of the Mountain*? Are you willing at this moment to bow humbly before Him in brokenness of heart, to confess and repent of

your sins and to be "born again" by receiving His forgiveness purchased for you at the cross, by simple faith?

10. Do you have a confident hope that when the nations and peoples of our planet are brought to final judgment before the KING of kings that you will be found righteous and be welcomed without fear into His holy presence?

"Seek the LORD while he may be found, call upon him while he is near:

Let the wicked forsake his way, and the unrighteous man his thoughts: and let him return unto the LORD, and he will have mercy upon him; and to our God, for he will abundantly pardon" (Isa. 55:6-7).

# Endnotes

1. "Is Temple Mount God's Time Bomb?" *World Net Daily*, August 15, 2008, discussing "Temple at the Center of Time" by David Flynn.

2. Ibid.

3. "Time for a New Temple?", Richard N. Ostling, *TIME*, Oct. 16, 1989, p. 64-65.

4. "64% of Israelis Want Temple Rebuilt," *WND.com*, Aug. 1, 2009.

5. "Seculars Want Temple…," Hillel Fendel, *Arutz Sheva.com*, Aug. 8, 2008.

6. "Is It Time for the Temple?", Thomas Ice, *Midnight Call*, Sept. 2005, pp. 20-22.

7. Ibid.

8. Op. it., "Time for a New Temple?," Richard N. Ostling, *TIME*, Oct. 16, 1989, p. 65.

9. "3rd Temple Cornerstone… History is Made;" *sabbathcovenant.com*, referencing *israel-nationalnews.com*, Aug. 6, 2003.

10. "A Cornerstone For The Third Temple at Sukkoth," *templemountfaithful.org/suk98*.

11. "A Cornerstone For The Third Temple at Sukkot," templemountfaithful.org/*suk98*.

12. "The Temple Mount Faithful Presents the Cornerstone…," by The Temple Mount Faithful, May 28, 2008, *his-forever.com/tmf_presents_cornerstone.htm*.

13. "The Cornerstone for the Third Temple Weighing 13 Tons Was Carried by the Temple Mount and Land of Israel Faithful Movement on Her 'Jerusalem Day' March, 21 May 2009," *templemountfaithful.org/Events/jerusalemDay2009-2.htm*.

14. "Prof. Weiss at rightest event: Build Third Temple immediately," ynetnews.com, Oct. 25, 2009.

15. "Model Altar of Unhewn Stones Completed at Temple Institute," Gil Ronen, *Arutz Sheva, israelnationalnews.com*, Dec. 25, 2009.

16. "Temple Institute to Build Sacrificial Altar on Tisha B'Av," Yehuda Lev Kay, *Arutz Sheva, israelnationalnews.com*, July 29, 2009.

17. "Temple Institute Announces: High Priest's Crown is Ready," Hillel Fendel, *israelnation-alnews.com*, Dec. 2007.

18. "Biblical Robe Produced For Use by High Priest in Holy Temple," Ezra HaLevi, Arutz *Sheva, israelnationalnews.com*, Dec. 20, 2005.

19. Ibid.

20. Ibid.

21. "Third Temple Preparations Begin With Priestly Garb," Danielle Kubes, The *JERUSALEM POST, jpost.com*, July 1, 2008.

22. "West Papua Delegation Donates Gold For Jerusalem Holy Temple," Ezra HaLevi, *Arutz Sheva, israelnationalnews.com*, Oct. 7, 2007.

23. Ibid.

24. "Let My Temple Artifacts Go! The Temple Is About To Be Rebuilt," cephas-*library.com/prophecy…*, Feb. 1, 2003.

25. A cornerstone for 3rd Temple?," Julie Foster, worldnetdaily.com, Sept. 26, 2001.

26. "Temple Institute in Jerusalem has Spent Approximately 27 Million Dollars on Preparations for the Rebuilding of the Temple," *signsofthelastdays.com*, Nov. 27, 2009.

27. "Sanhedrin Launched in Tiberias," Arutz *Sheva, israelnationalnews.com*, Oct. 13, 2004.

28. "Revived Sanhedrin discusses Temple," commentary by Hal Lindsey, *worldnetdaily.com*, Feb. 17, 2005.

29. "What? Muslim leader wants Temple rebuilt," *worldnetdaily.com*, Aug. 8, 2009.

30. "Moslem Sheikh Abdul Hadi Palazzi visits the Temple Institute," templeinstitute.org, June 12, 2010.

31. "The world needs the Temple," Ariel Jerozolimski, THE *INTERNATIONAL JERUSALEM POST*, July 13-19, 2007.

32. Ibid.

33. "Sacred Red Heifers Prepared… in Mississippi," Terry Duschinski, *Charisma*, April 1997, p. 21.

34. George Bush Sr., Speech on September 11, 1990, in National Archives.

35. "Blair says, 'Let us reorder this world'," Michael White, *The Guardian*, October 3, 2001.

36. Charles Crismier, *Renewing the Soul of America* (Richmond, Virginia; Elijah Books, 2002), p. 351-364).

37. William J. Federer (ed.), *America's God and Country*, (Coppell, Texas, FAME Publishing, Inc., 1994), p. 204-205.

38. Henry Morris, *Steeling the Mind of America*, (New Leaf Press, June 1995), p. 218-219.

39. Jeremy Rifkin, "The New Europe Shapes Its Version of Dream," *Richmond Times Dispatch*, November 7, 2004, p. E-1, from *The Washington Post.*

40. "The Messiah Factor"—"Der Messias Faktor," *Der Spiegel*, Spiegel online, July 2008, cover story.

41. "Who Runs The World?" Wrestling for Influence," *The Economist*, internet edition, July 7, 2008, p.3.

42. Jerome Rifkin, "New Europe Shapes Its Version of Dream," *Richmond Times Dispatch*, November 7, 2004, p. E-1, from *The Washington Post.*

43. Jerome R. Corsi, "Bush OK's 'integration' with European Union," *worldnetdaily.com*, May 8, 2007.

44. Jerome R. Corsi, "7-year plan aligns with Europe's economy," *worldnetdaily.com*, January 16, 2008.

45. Ian Traynor, "love tops agenda as Sarkozy launches Mediterranean Union," *The Guardian, guardian.co.uk*, July 14, 2008.

46. Benita Ferrero-Waldner, "The Secret of Europe's Success," *Haaretz Israel News, haaretz. com*, May 9, 2007.

47. Kobi Nachomi, "The Sanhedrin's peace initiative," *ynetnews.com*, May 6, 2007.

48. Steve Watson, "Euro Globalists: Anyone Who Resists EU Is a Terrorist," *New Interviews, prisonplanet.com*, June 18, 2007.

49. Gary H. Kah, *The New World Religion* (Noblesville, Indiana: Hope International Publishing, Inc., 1998), p. 199.

50. Ibid, p. 202.

51. Ibid, p. 209.

52. Ibid, p. 203.

53. Ibid, p. 204.

54. Ibid, p. 63.

55. Ibid, p. 65.

56. Ibid, p. 65.

57. Ibid, p. 65.

58. Ibid, p. 206

59. Ibid, p. 206

60. Ibid, p. 216.

61. James A. Beverly, "Smorgasborg Spirituality," *Christianity Today*, January 10, 2000, p. 30.

62. "One World Religion on its way?, *worldnetdaily.com*, June 14, 2005.

63. Ibid.

64. John Dart, "Ecumenism's new basis: testimony," *Christian Century*, August 21, 2007, p. 12.

65. Ibid.

66. Ibid, p. 13.

67. Julian Borger, "Moscow signals place in new world order," *Guardian Unlimited, guardian.co.uk*, April 11, 2007.

68. "Putin Calls Russia Defender of Islamic World," *Mos News, mosnews.com*, December 12, 2005.

69. "Timing not right for papal visit to Russia," *totalcatholic.com*, July 9, 2008.

70. Malachi Martin, *The Keys of This Blood*, "Forces of the 'New Order.'" (New York, New York; Touchstone, 1990), p. 370-371.

71. Ibid, p. 489-490.

72. "Pope Calls for a new world order," *CNN News* release from VATICAN CITY, January 1, 2004.

73. Deb Richmann, "Bush says US wants partnership with Europe," *BRIETBART.COM*, released from Associated Press, June 12, 2008.

74. Fareed Zakania, "The Post-American World," cover story, *NEWSWEEK.COM*, May 12, 2008, p. 24-31.

75. Ian Traynor, "Love tops agenda as Sarkosy launches Mediterranean Union," *The Guardian, guardian.co.uk*, July 14, 2008.

76. "Union for the Mediterranean," *Wikipedia, Wikipedia.com*, July 14, 2008.

77. Ian Traynor, "Love tops agenda as Sarkosy launches Mediterranean Union," *The Guardian, guardian.co.uk*, July 14, 2008.

78. Will Durant, *Caesar and Christ, The Story of Civilization Part III*, (New York, Simon and Schuster, 1944), p. 618-619.

79. Ibid.

80. Nigel Rogers, *Roman Empire* (New York; Metro Books, Anness Publicity Ltd., 2008), p. 415.

81. Will Durant, *Caesar and Christ*, p. 656.

82. Ibid.

83. John Julius Norwich, *Absolute Monarchs: A History of the Papacy* (New York; Random House, 2011), p. 57.

84. Ibid, p. 58.

85. Ibid, p. 61.

86. Nigel Rogers, *Roman Empire*, p. 13.

87. Alan Franklin, *EU-Final World Empire*, (Oklahoma City, OK; Hearthstone Publishing, 2002), p. 44.

88. "Chief Rabbi Asks Dalai Lama to Help Set Up Religious UN in Jerusalem," *Arutz Sheva, israelnationalnews.com*, February 19, 2006.

89. Alan Franklin, *EU-Final World Empire*, pp. 48-50.

90. "Rome," *The Catholic Encyclopedia,* Thomas Nelson, 1976.

91. Ibid.

92. R.W. Southern, "Western Society and the Church of the Middle Ages," Vol. 2, *Pelican History of the Church Series*, (Penguin Books, 1970), pp.24-25.

93. John Julius Norwich, *Absolute Monarchy: A History of the Papacy* (New York; Random House, 2011).

94. Alan Franklin, *EU-Final World Empire*, pp. 37-38.

95. Ibid, p. 39.

96. "Blair: I'll dedicate the rest of my life to uniting the world's religions," *dailymail.co.uk*, May 29, 2008.

97. James Macintyre, "Religion is the new politics...," *The Independent*, May 31, 2008.

98. Michael Elliott, "Tony Blair's Leap of Faith," *TIME*, June 9, 2008.

99. David Van Brima, "The Global Ambition of Rick Warren," *TIME*, August 18, 2008, cover story pp. 37-42.

100. Ruth Gledhill, "Churches back plan to unite under Pope," *timesonline.co.uk*, February 19, 2007.

101. Ibid.

102. Robert Broderich, ed, *The Catholic Encyclopedia*, Thomas Nelson, 1976, pp. 103-104.

103. John A. Hardon, S.J., *Pocket Catholic Dictionary*, Image Books—Doubleday, 1985, p. 99.

104. Dave Hunt, *A Woman Rides the Beast* (Eugene, Oregon; Harvest House, 1994), chapter 6.

105. John Julius Norwich, *Absolute Monarchs: A History of the Papacy* (New York: Random House, 2011), p. 51.

106. Ibid, p. 52

107. "Islam Is A Good Force, Says Prime Minister Tony Blair," *MIDNIGHT CALL*, July 1999, quoting *The TIMES*, Feb. 23, 1999.

108. Ibid.

109. Mark A. Gabriel Ph. D, (former professor of Islamic history at Al-Azhar University, Cairo, Egypt), *ISLAM and TERRORISM*, (Lake Mary, Florida; Charisma House, 2002), p. 48).

110. Ibid, p. 33.

111. Ibid, p. 28.

112. Ibid, p. 28.

113. Ibid, p. 37.

114. Ibid, p. 31.

115. Ibid, p. 30.

116. Ibid, p. 30.

117. Ibid, p. 30.

118. Ibid, p. 31.

119. Ibid, p. 31.

120. Ibid, p.39.

121. Ibid, p. 39.

122. "Al-Aqsa Sheikh—Jerusalem will be Muslim Forever," Elad Benari, *Arutz Sheva, israelnationalnews.com*, July 20, 2012.

123. "Vatican, Israel joust over Jerusalem site," Edmund Sanders, *Los Angeles Times, latimes.com*, Dec. 24, 2009.

124. "Al-Aqsa Sheik: Jerusalem will be Muslim Forever," Elad Benari, *Arutz Sheva, israelnationalnews.com*, July 20, 2012.

125. "A WORLD CAPITAL," Aharon Goldberg in a letter to the editor of The *JERUSALEM POST*, September 22, 2000, p. 21.

126. "IRAN: THERE WILL BE WAR—AND WE'LL WIN," Reza Kahlili, *wnd.com*, June 30, 2012.

127. "MUSLIMS: 'WIPE CHRISTIANITY FROM FACE OF EARTH'," Michael Carl, *wnd.com*, July 7, 2012.

128. "IRAN LEADER: WE MUST PREP FOR 'END OF TIMES'," Reza Kahlili, *wnd.com*, July 8, 2012.

129. "AYATOLLAH: KILL ALL JEWS, ANNIHILATE ISRAEL," Reza Kahlili, *wnd.com*, February 5, 2012.

130. Ibid.

131. Ibid.

132. "The Eternal City… one life is not enough," RomanHomes.com, 2012.

133. Ibid.

134. Ibid.

135. Ibid.

136. Ibid.

137. *The Bible*. The Book of Daniel, chapters 2 and 7.

138. "The Eternal City… one life is not enough," RomanHomes.com, 2012.

139. "Rome, the Eternal City," *BestCatholic.com/rome*, July 31, 2012.

140. "God's City," Richard Z. Chesnoff, *U.S. News and World Report*, Dec. 18, 1995, cover story pp. 62-70.

141. "One Nation's Capital Forever," Eli Hertz, *Arutz Sheva, israelnationalnews.com*, May 12, 2010.

142. Ibid.

143. "Vatican Plants To Establish Jerusalem As The Capital of the World," TOPIC, translated from the German, *Postfach* 1544, D57206, Kreuztal, Germany, March 1998, p. 5; As reported in *Midnight Call*, June 1998, p. 27.

144. "Expose: The Vatican Wants to Lay Its Hands on Jerusalem," Giulio Meotti, Italy; *Arutz Sheva, israelnationalnews.com*, December 15, 2011.

145. Ibid.

146. "Vatican demands Temple Mount to be placed under Pope rule," *YourJewishnews.com/Arutz7*, December 15, 2011.

147. Ibid.

148. "Israel's Control of Mt. Zion in Danger," Hillel Fendel, *Arutz Sheva, israelnationalnews.com*, April 26, 2009.

149. Ibid.

150. Ibid.

151. "Peres Presses for Cave-in to Vatican," Hillel Fendel, *Arutz Sheva, israelnationalnews.com*, May 4, 2009.

152. "Peres wants to hand over Christian sites in Israel to Vatican," Jack Khoury, *Haaretz.com*, May 4, 2009.

153. Op-Ed: "Exclusive: A Seat for the Pope at King David's Tomb." By Giulio Meotti. *Arutz Sheva*, israelnationalnews.com. February 1, 2013.

154. "A Russian Sect Honors Putin as Saint," Benjamin Bidder in Bolshaya Elnya, Russia, *SPEIGEL ONLINE*, Sept. 29, 2011.

155. Ibid.

156. Ibid.

157. Ibid.

158. Ibid.

159. *The Bible*, Acts 4:13.

160. "Country profile: Russia," *BBC News, bbc.co.uk*, February 5, 2008.

161. "Russia's fury over its loss of sway," Alan Cooperman and Jeff Trimble, *U.S. News and World Report*, Sept. 25, 1995.

162. "THE RUSSIAN BEAR: RISING AGAIN," Paul Malin, Ph.D., *The Forecast*, March 1996.

163. Ibid.

164. Ibid.

165. "Catch a rising czar," Christian Caryl, *U.S. News and World Report*, March 27, 2000, p. 32-35.

166. "THE SPY WHO CAME IN FROM THE CROWD," Johanna McGeary (Moscow), *TIME*, April 3, 2000, pp. 53-61.

167. "Proud Russia on its knees," Mortimer B. Zuckerman, *U.S. News and World Report*, February 8, 1999, pp. 30-36.

168. "Russia Is Finished," Jeffrey Taylor, *The Atlantic*, May 2001, cover story, pp 35-52.

169. Ibid, p. 35.

170. "Emerging Shadows of the Hammer and Sickle," Elwood McQuaid, *Israel My Glory*, May-June 2005, pp. 8-10.

171. "Analysis: Russia's ambitions growing," The *Jerusalem Post*, January 27, 2005.

172. "Putin's 'Creeping Coup'," William Safire, *New York Times*, as reprinted in the *Richmond Times Dispatch*, February 10, 2004, p. A13.

173. Op. it., "Emerging Shadows of the Hammer and Sickle," p. 8.

174. "The Man Who Would Be Tsar," Bill Powell and Yevgenia Albats, *NEWSWEEK*, March 27, 2000, pp. 40-42.

175. Ibid.

176. "The Winter of DISCONTENT," *TIME*, Special Report on the "New Russia," Dec. 7, 1992.

177. "THE DARK FORCES," James Carney, *TIME*, Dec. 7, 1992, p. 38-39.

178. "Watch out for Putin, and Russia," Leon Aron, *latimes.com*, October 3, 2011.

179. "Russia sees U.S. bid to dominate the world," *The Associated Press*, as reported in *RICHMOND TIMES DISPATCH*, Jan. 15, 2000, p. A1.

180. "USA believes Russia threatens its interests all over the world." http://english.pravda.ru/world/americas/18-12-2008/106846-usa_russia-0/#

181. Boris Yeltsin, *Midnight Diaries 2000*, as reported in *The McAlvany Intelligence Advisor*, Phoenix, Arizona, July 2001.

182. "Moscow Is Aiming To Regain Position in World Arms Sales," *Philadelphia Inquirer*, March 6, 2001, p. A3, as reported in *MIDNIGHT CALL*, August 2001.

183. "All military tombs in Russia to be put in order by 2015," *Itar-Tass.com*, August 1, 2008.

184. "Resurgent Russia Sees Oil as a Weapon," Brian Padden, *Voice of America, voanews.com*, Jan. 18, 2008.

185. "Russia overtakes Saudi Arabia as world's largest oil and fuel exporter," *TMC net, tmcnet.com*, May 26, 2007.

186. "Gazprom plans to become global energy leader," *RIA Novosti* as reported in en.rian.ru/business/20070403/63006530, April 4, 2007.

187. "Russia looks for clout in pipeline talks," Vladimir Isachenkov, *Business Week* as reported from *Associated Press*, Jan. 18, 2008.

188. "OPEC plans closer links with Russia to control half of the world's oil supplies," Robin Pagnamenta and Angela Jameson, *TimesOnline.co.uk*, Sept. 12, 2008.

189. "Russian pipeline tightens grip on West's gas supply from Caspian," Jim Heintz, *THE SCOTSMAN*, *thescotsman.scotsman.com*, Dec. 21, 2007.

190. "Orthodox church edges closer to state," *Associated Press*, as reported in *Richmond Times Dispatch*, January 22, 2000, p. A4.

191. "How Russia Courts the Muslim World," Jacques Levesque, *MiddleEastOnline.com*, December 29, 2008.

192. "Putin: Russia wants peace for Israel," Attila Somfalvi, *ynetnews.com*, June 25, 2012.

193. "Putin wishes us a rebuilt temple," *blogs.jpost.com/content/putin-wishes-us-rebuilt-temple*. Discussing Russian language conversation between Putin and recent Russian immigrant to Israel during Putin's visit to the Kotel. The Article originally reported in Hebrew on *bhol.co.il*, June26, 2012.

194. "Russia passes religion bill…," *The Associated Press*, as reported in *The Richmond Times Dispatch*, Sept. 20, 1997, p. A3.

195. "MOSCOW THE THIRD ROME: Sources of the Doctrine," by Dimitri Stremooukhoff, *j.stor.org/discover/10.2307/2847182*

196. "Moscow becomes 'third Rome'," *Russian Times*, *rt.com/news/prime-time*, July 18, 2008.

197. "Third Rome," from *Wikipedia*—Russian claims.

198. "Third Rome," from *encyclopedia.com*; as taken from *Encyclopedia of Russian History*; Goldfrank, David M.; 2004.

199. "The Concept of the Third Rome and Its Political Implications" by Alan Laats, (Cambridge University Press, 1997), p. 98 http://www.ksk.edu.ee/wp-content/uploads/2011/03/KVUOA_Toimetised_12-Laats.pdf

200. Ibid, p. 101.

201. Ibid, p. 99. Reference—John Meyendorff, Byzantium and the Rise of Russia (New York: St. Vladimir's Seminary Press), 1989, p. 11.

202. Ibid, p. 98.

203. Ibid, pp. 104-105.

204. Ibid, p. 108.

205. "Burden of the Third Rome," an abstract from *Islam and Christian-Muslim Relations*, Vol. 9, Issue 2, 1998, Taylor & Francis Online, *tandfonline.com/doi/abs/10.1080/09596419808721148*.

206. Judith E. Kalb, *Russia's Rome:* Imperial Visions, Messianic Dreams, 1890-1940, (University of Wisconsin Press) 2008, quotes taken from book preview by Google e Book.

207. "Third Rome," *Encyclopedia Britannica Online*, July 31, 2012.

208. "*Moscow, the Third Rome*": The Origins and Transformations of a "Pivotal Moment," Franz Steiner Verlag GmbH, Stuttgart, 2001, as provided by an essay by Marshall Poe, University of Iowa, *ir.uiowa.edu/history_pubs/21*.

209. Malachi Martin, *THE KEYS OF THIS BLOOD*. (New York, New York, TOUCHSTONE of Simon & Schuster Inc, 1990), Cover title and Subtitle.

210. Ibid, p. 68.

211. Ibid, p. 16.

212. Ibid, p. 16-17.

213. Ibid, p. 18.

214. "Third Rome," *Encyclopedia Britannica Online*, July 31, 2012.

215. Op. Cit., "Moscow, the Third Rome, p. 4.

216. Op. Cit., "The Concept of the Third Rome and Its Political Implications," p. 109.

217. Ibid.

218. Ibid, p. 110.

219. "WILL THE 'THIRD ROME' REUNITE WITH THE 'FIRST ROME'?" Robert Moynihan, *ZENIT*—The World Seen From Rome, *zenith.org*, Sept. 21, 2009.

220. Ibid.

221. John Julius Norwich, *ABSOLUTE MONARCHS*—A History of the Papacy, (New York; Random House, 2011).

222. Op. Cit., "Moscow, the Third Rome: The Origins and Transformations of a Pivotal Moment," pp. 12-13.

223. Ibid, pp. 13-14.

224. Ibid, pp. 15-16.

225. Ibid, p. 17, referencing *The New York Times*, Sept. 16, 1984.

226. Ibid, p. 15.

227. Op. cit., Malachi Martin, THE KEYS OF THIS BLOOD, p. 631.

228. Op. cit., Malachi Martin, THE KEYS OF THIS BLOOD, p. 631.

229. Ibid, p. 656.

230. Ibid, p. 654-655.

231. Ibid, p. 622.

232. Ibid, p. 578.

233. Ibid, p. 592.

234. Ibid, p. 592.

235. Ibid, p. 595.

236. Ibid, p. 602.

237. Ibid, p. 83.

238. Ibid, p. 655.

239. Ibid, p. 654.

240. Joseph Lam with William Bray, *China: The Last Superpower*, (Green Forest, AR, New Leaf Press, 1996), p. 17, 19.

241. Ibid, p. 22.

242. "CHINA-DAWN OF A NEW DYNASTY," *TIME Magazine*, January 22, 2007, Cover.

243. "THE CHINESE CENTURY," by Michael Elliott, *TIME Magazine*, January 22, 2007, p.

244. Ibid.

245. Ibid.

246. "A World We Have Not Known," Henry Kissinger, *NEWSWEEK*, January 27, 1997, p. 74.

247. Ibid, p. 74, 77.

248. "The year of the hawk?" by William J. Holstein, *U.S. News & World Report*, April 7, 1997, p. 45.

249. Ibid, p. 46.

250. "A 'New Era' Rises in the East," Jonathan Spence, *NEWSWEEK*, January 1, 2000, p. 38-40.

251. Ibid, p. 40.

252. "U.S. Alarmed by Harsh Tone of China's Military," Michael Wines, *The New York Times, nytimes.com*, October 12, 2010.

253. "Is China Planning a Surprise Missile Attack?" by Gordon G. Chang, *WORLD AFFAIRS JOURNAL, worldaffairsjournal.org*, September 2, 2011.

254. Ibid.

255. "Pentagon fears listening posts from China," Eli Lake, *The Washington Times, washing-tontimes.com/news/2011/sep/1/pentagon-fears-listening-posts-from-china/*, Sept. 2, 2011.

256. "China Emerges as Global Power," Mike Blair, *SPOTLIGHT*, Sept. 11, 1995, quoting *New York Times Magazine.*

257. Ibid.

258. "CHINA—How big a threat?" by Richard J. Newman and Kevin Whitelaw, *U.S. News & World Report*, July 23, 2001, pp. 30-32.

259. "Chin preparing for armed conflict 'in every direction'," Peter Foster, *The Telegraph, telegraph.co.uk/news...*, Dec. 30, 2010.

260. "Ministry warns of China war option," Lo Tien-Pin, *TAIPEI TIMES, taipeitimes.com/News...*, Sept. 2, 2011.

261. "Why China can be a game-changer in the ME," Avrum Ehrlich, The *JERUSALEM POST, jpost.com*, May 20, 2010.

262. Ibid.

263. Ibid.

264. "The Growing Chinese—Israel Relationship," Joseph Puder, *DAILY MAILER—FrontPagemag.com*, Sept. 5, 2012.

265. Ibid.

266. Ibid.

267. Ibid.

268. Ibid.

269. Ibid.

270. "'KINGS OF THE EAST' HAUNT U.S.," Anthony C. Lobaido, *WND.com*, September 2012.

271. Robert H. Mounce, *THE BOOK OF REVELATION (The New International Commentary on the New Testament)*, (Grand Rapids, MI; William B. Eerdmans Publishing Co., Revised Ed. 997), p. 301.

272. *The Illustrated Bible Dictionary* (Wheaton, IL; Tyndale House Publishers, 1980), pp. 485-486.

273. "Turkey Will Cut Off Flow of Euphrates for One Month," headline from the *Indianapolis Star*, January 13, 1990. As referenced in *Endtime* Magazine, vol. 15/ no. 3, May/June 2005, "Euphrates River to be Dried Up" article.

274. "Syria is drying up," Guy Bechor, *YNETnews.com*, August 3, 2009.

275. Ibid.

276. "As Iraq runs dry, a plague of snakes is unleashed," The *INDEPENDENT, independent.co.uk*, June 26, 2009. Story also reported in *Christian Life, zimbio.com/Christian+Life/articles...*

277. Ibid.

278. "All the Asian Rage," by Niall Ferguson, *NEWSWEEK*, September 24, 2012.

279. "CHINA PREPARING FOR WAR AND FEW NOTICE," Chuck Baldwin, *NewsWithViews.com*, September 23, 2005.

280. Ibid.

281. Ibid. Referencing a *WorldNetDaily.com* report dated September 13, 2005.

282. "A giant stirring," Tim Johnson, *Knight Ridder Newspaper* as printed in *Richmond Times Dispatch*, July 18, 2005, p. A-1.

283. "GENDERCIDE—What happened to 100 million girls?" *The Economist*, March 6-12, 2010, Cover story, p. 13.

284. Ibid.

285. "Selective abortions result in 32 m excess males in China," Pakistan *Daily Times*, April 10, 2009, dailytimes.com.pk.

286. "Men Without Women—The ominous rise of Asia's bachelor generation," Niall Ferguson, *NEWSWEEK*, March 14, 2011, p. 15, thedailybeast.com.

287. "Retired military officers call for curbing China's power," Sean Lengell, The *Washington Times*, March 19, 2012.

288. "Taking Megiddo is like capturing a thousand cities," Wayne Stiles, The *JERUSALEM POST*, jpost.com, April 21, 2011.

289. "32 Countdown Evens Towards the Last 7 Years of the Apocalypse," buzzardhut.net/index/htm/ProphecyRapture.htm.

290. "The Two Hundred Million Man Army from the East All Paid for by U.S. debt interest payments," thejosephplan.org, April 2012, quoting from raptureready.com

291. "Enter the Kings of the East into prophetic play," the-end-time.blogspot.com, June 23, 2012.

292. "Evangelism or disaster," Marvin Olasky, *WORLD*, March 15, 1997, p. 30.

293. Ibid.

294. "RUSSIA OVERTAKES SAUDIA ARABIA AS WORLD'S LEADING OIL PRODUCER," *Capitol Hill Prayer Partners* (Aug. 25, 2006) quoting *Mos News* and *Financial Times* report of Aug. 23, 2006.

295. "Russia Becomes World's Top Oil Producer—For Now," CNBC.com (Oct. 14, 2009), quoting *Reuters*, Oct. 2, 2009.

296. "Russia, Algeria meet as gas OPEC plan gains ground," *afp.google.com*, Feb. 21, 2008.

297. "Turning Up The Heat," Steve LeVine, *Russia—BEYOND THE HEADLINES*, rbth.rg.ru/articles/gazprom, Feb. 27, 2008.

298. "Russia's gas weapon," Ziba Norman, *International Herald Tribune*, iht.come/articles, Dec. 20, 2005.

299. "Russia's energy giant flexes its muscles," Duncan Bartlett, *BBC News*, news.bbc.co.uk, Feb. 24, 2008.

300. "Russia's lethal gas weapon," Federico Bordonaro, *Asia Times*, atimes.com, Jan. 4, 2006.

301. "Putin's new secret weapon," Tom McGhie, *thisismoney.co.uk*, Nov. 23, 2006.

302. "Rosneft and Gazprom ready to give Putin his ultimate weapon…," Sonia Joshi, *india-daily.com*, Sept. 30, 2006.

303. "Gazprom—New Russian Weapon," *Kommersant*, kommersant.com, Jan. 30, 2008.

304. "Oil, gas pipeline is the key element of Russia's incursion into Georgia," Steven Pearlstein, The *Washington Post*, as reported in The *Salt Lake Tribune*, Aug. 17, 2008.

305. "Pipeline dreams entangle Russians and Europeans," Judy Dempsey, *International Herald Tribune*, iht.com, Dec. 26, 2008.

306. "Russia's Israeli Oil Bond, Dr. Sam Vaknin, *samvak.tripod.comd*/brief-russia-israel, Nov. 4, 2002, also published by *United Press International* (UPI).

307. "Iran poses most dangerous threat to world order," *Haaretz.com*, Feb. 11, 2011.

308. "Report: Iran and Russia in secret nuclear pact," *WND.com*, Nov. 7, 2011.

309. "Investment in Iran oil sector will exceed $40b…," *PRESSTV.com*, Oct. 30, 2012.

310. Mark Hitchcock, *After the Empire: Bible Prophecy in Light of the Fall of the Soviet Union* (Wheaton, IL: Tyndale House Publishers, 1994), p. 64).

311. Ibid, p. 63-64.

312. "Russia-Turkey: The New Eurasian Allieance…," Asim Oku, *Axisglobe.com*, March 5, 2005.

313. "Russia and Turkey in the Middle East," Asim Oku, *Axisglobe.com*, March 5, 2005.

314. "Turkey—Russia relations," *EvrActiv.com*, January 12, 2005.

315. "Turkey: An ally no more," Daniel Piper, *Jerusalem Post*, online edition, jpost.com, October 27, 2009.

316. "Anti-Americanism hits new record in Turkey," *Todayszaman.com*, June 30, 2007.

317. "Turkey losing interest in EU," Joseph Farah's G-2 Bulletin, *WND.com*, June 29, 2009.

318. "Turkey seeks restoration of Ottoman Empire," Joseph Farah's G-2 Bulletin, *WND.com*, Oct. 23, 2009.

319. "Turkish PM: Iran is Our Friend," *Arutz Sheva*, israelnationalnews.com, Oct. 26, 2009, quoting from "Iran is our friend, says Turkish PM Recejp Tayyip Erdogan," *The Guardian*, Oct. 26, 2009.

320. "The Rise of a Sinister Russo-Turkish Axis," Dr. Muhammad Shamsaddin Megalommatis, *American Chronicle*, americanchronicle.com, June 28, 2007.

321. "Turkey's military to military ties with Russia growing," The *Journal of Turkish Weekly*, turkishweekly.net, June 18, 2007.

322. "Turkey and Russia on the Rise," Reva Bhalla, Lauren Goodrich and Peter Zeihan, *STRATFOR*, stratfor.com, March 17, 2009.

323. "Presidents of Russia, Turkey adapt strategic declarations, *NOVOSTI*, Russian News and Information Agency, en.rian.ru/Russia, Feb. 13, 2009.

324. "The New Turkey/Russia Axis," Eric Walberg, *WORLD BULLETIN*, worldbulletin.net/news, Oct. 3, 2010.

325. "Turkey wants to revive Ottoman Empire," *Pravda.ru*, Sept. 16, 2011.

326. "Iran, Syria, Turkey Cementing Ties," Hillel Fendel, *Arutz Sheva*, israelnationalnews.com, May 3, 2010.

327. "Turkey to help with Iranian gas exports," Doron Peskin, *Ynetnews.com*, July 29, 2010.

328. "Oren: Turkey's change is of 'historical proportions'," The *INTERNATIONAL JERUSALEM POST*, jpost.com, June 25- July 1, 2010.

329. "Both Germany and Russia Are Reinventing Their Pasts," Dr. Dmitry Shlopentokh, associate professor of history at Indiana University South Bend USA, *hnn.us*/articles/47367, Feb. 18, 2008.

330. "Gerhard Schroeder's Sellout," *TheWashingtonPost.com*, Dec. 13, 2005.

331. Ibid.

332. "Nord Stream touted as EU savior," *United Press International*, upi.com, Oct. 9, 2012.

333. "Smoking gun—Russia's plan to dominate energy markets," by Rod Adams, http://atomicinsights.com/2012/09/smoking-gun-russias-plan-to-dominate-energy-markets.html

334. "Iranian Video Says Mahdi is 'Near'," Erick Stakelbeck, *CBN NEWS*, cbn.com/cbnnews/world, March 28, 2011.

335. Ibid.

336. "Messiah Where?", Herb Keinon, The *JERUSALEM POST INTERNATIONAL EDITION*, August 30, 1997, p. 20-22.

337. Ibid.

338. "Chief Rabbi Sees Imminent Coming of Messiah," *World Net Daily.com*, August 12, 2005.

339. "Wanted: a New Messiah," Andrew Romano, *NEWSWEEK*, Oct. 3, 2011, p. 8.

340. "Palestinians massage Obama's ego, ask him to be their Messiah," *Israel Insider*, israelinsider.com, May 12, 2010.

341. "Europe and the American Messiah," Mario Del Pero, *Europressresearch*, europressresearch.eu, Nov. 2011.

342. "My duty is to save the world: Prince Charles…," Fay Schlesinger, *MAIL ONLINE*, dailymail.co.uk/news, July 30, 2010.

343. "Prince Charles 'the winged hero'.", *BBC News*, news.bbc.co.uk/2/hi/Americas, March 6, 2002.

344. "Zion Needs the Messiah," Yosef Ben Shlomo Hakohen, *Arutz Sheva* (Israel National News), israelnationalnews.com, March 1, 2009.

345. "Rabbi Reveals Name of Messiah," *israeltoday.co.il*, April 30, 2007.

346. "Qurei: Fight Has Begun for Jerusalem," Ezra HaLevi, *Arutz Sheva, israelnationalnews.com*, Aug. 14, 2005.

347. "The Battle for Jerusalem," Ted Belman, *Arutz Sheva, israelnationalnews.com*, March 19, 2010.

348. "God's City," Richard Z. Chesnoff, in Jerusalem, *U.S. News and World Report*, December 18, 1995, cover story, pp. 60-70.

349. Ibid, p. 70

350. "Earthly Jerusalem," The *JERUSALEM POST* (North American Edition), Nov. 26, 1999, pp. 1, 8.

351. Mike Evans, *Jerusalem Betrayed, Prophecy and Conspiracy Collide in the Holy City*, from excerpted portion in *Charisma*, April 1997, p. 91.

352. "God's Vortex Over Jerusalem," Marvin Rosenthal, *Zion's Fire*, Sept./Oct. 2006, Cover Story, pp. 6-14.

353. Ibid, p. 9.

354. Ibid, p. 14.

355. "Europe Moves to Divide Jerusalem," *onejerusalem.org*, Dec.2, 2009.

356. "Netanyahu makes final push to foil Swedish plan to divide Jerusalem," Barak Ravid, *haaretz.com*, Dec. 6, 2009.

357. "Canada unveils proposal to resolve conflict over Jerusalem," *haaretz.com*, May 10, 2010.

358. "Warning Issued Not to Sign With Vatican," Hillel Fendel, *Arutz Sheva, israelnationalnews.com*, Mar. 30, 2009.

359. "PA Ambassador: 'First Jerusalem, Then We'll Take All Palestine'," Hillel Fendell, *Arutz Sheva, israelnationalnews.com*, April 14, 2008.

360. "MUSLIM CLERIC: JERUSALEM TO BE EGYPT'S CAPITOL," Joel Richardson, WND.com, June 8, 2012.

361. Ibid.

362. Ibid.

363. "Congressman to Barkat: US Embassy should move to J'lem," The *JERUSALEM POST* Online Edition, Nov. 10, 2009.

364. El Salvador to move embassy from J'lem," Herb Keinon, The *International JERUSALEM POST*, Sept. 1-7, 2006.

365. Ibid.

366. "*VIEWPOINT* determines destiny," the defining bottom line for human and world opinion as repeatedly stated on the radio broadcast, *VIEWPOINT* heard worldwide, saveus.org/viewpoint.

367. "Jerusalem Showdown Nears," Associated Press as presented in *Richmond Times Dispatch*, March 18, 1997, p. A7.

368. "Jerusalem will never be divided," Etgar Lefkovits, The *JERUSALEM POST*, June 9, 2000, p. 3.

369. Ibid.

370. "Mideast talks fall through," New York times News Service as reported in *Richmond Times Dispatch*, July 26, 2000, p. A-1 and A-6.

371. Talks changed everything," Lee Houstador, Los Angeles Times/Washington Post News Service, as reported in *Richmond Times Dispatch*, July 26, 2000, p. A-6.

372. "Sharon: No concessions: Jerusalem united for all eternity" Los Angeles Times/ Washington Post News Service as reported in *Richmond Times Dispatch*, Feb. 8, 2001, p. A-4.

373. "Olmert: Divide Israel's capital," Aaron Klein, *worldnetdaily.com*, March 9, 2009.

374. "PA: Jerusalem is on the table—and under the table," The *International JERUSALEM POST*, February 15-21, 2008, p. 6.

375. "Netanyahu: Israel will never share Jerusalem with Palestinians," Barak Ravid, *Haaretz. com*, Jan. 12, 2010.

376. "Lieberman: Jerusalem is our eternal capital, it will never be divided," Barak Ravid, *Haaretz.com*, April 21, 2010.

377. "One Nation's Capital Forever," Eli E. Hertz, *Arutz Sheva, israelnationalnews.com*, May 12, 2010.

378. "Abbas slams Obama for saying Jerusalem to stay Israel's undivided capital," *Haaretz. com*, June 6, 2008.

379. "Arab Anger Forces Obama to Backtrack on Jerusalem," Hana Levi Julian, *Arutz Sheva, israelnationalnews.com*, June 6, 2008.

380. "Obama makes Palestinians deny he promised Jerusalem," Aaron Klein, *worldnetdaily. com*, Nov. 4, 2008.

381. "Rabbis call on Obama to 'implement will of God'," Aaron Klein, *worldnetdaily.com*, Nov. 10, 2008.

382. "Rabbis call on Obama 'to implement will of God'," Aaron Klein, *worldnetdaily.com*, Nov. 10, 2008.

383. "Kissinger: Obama Primed to Create 'New World Order'," Drew Zahn. http://www.wnd. com/2009/01/85442/.

384. "Jews Around the Next President," Tamar Yonah, *Arutz Sheva, israelnationalnews.com*, Nov. 11, 2008.

385. "Rivlin: Make 'United Jerusalem' a Reality," Maayana Miskin, *Arutz Sheva, israelnationalnews.com*, May 15, 2009.

386. "Jerusalem's Reunification: Back in Time to 1967," Hillel Fendel, *Arutz Sheva, israelnationalnews.com*, May 31, 2011.

387. "Rejoice on Jerusalem Day," Isi Liebler, *TheJERUSALEMPost.com*, May 12, 2010.

388. "Netanyahu: Struggle for Jerusalem is a struggle for truth," Yair Ettinger, *Haaretz.com*, May 16, 2010.

389. "Fight for Jerusalem—fight for truth," *TheJERUSALEMPost.com*, May 12, 2010.

390. "A WORLD CAPITAL," Aharon Goldberg's letter to the editor, The *JERUALEM POST*, Sept. 22, 2000, p. 21.

391. Op. Cit, "THE MOUNT IS OURS," Rebecca Weinberger's letter to the editor, The *JERUSALEM POST*, Sept. 22, 2000, p. 21.

392. "Israel Allies to U.S.: Recognize Jerusalem as Undivided Capital," Rachel Hirshfeld, *Arutz Sheva, israelnationalnews.com*, June 8, 2012.

393. Ibid.

394. Ibid.

395. "Oil pressure rising," www.economist.com/node/18233452, February 24, 2011, from the print edition of The *Economist*.

396. Ibid.

397. "US military warns about massive oil shortages by 2015," David Gutierrez, www.*naturalnews.com*/029642_oil_shortage_military.html, Sept. 2, 2010

398. Ibid.

399. "US Expert Predicts 'Oil and Gas Rush' to Israel," by Gil Ronen, *Arutz Sheva*, www.IsraelNationalNews.com/News/News.aspx/136960#.UPR-kmdJah8, 4/11/2010.

400. "The Dawn of a New Oil Era," Robert J. Samuelson, *NEWSWEEK*, April 4, 2005, p. 37.

401. Ibid.

402. "Endtime Nexus: Prophesied Oil Crisis," Wilfred J. Hahn, *Midnight Call*, April 2004, p. 27.

403. Ibid, p. 29.

404. Ibid, p. 29.

405. "Hostage to OIL," Marianne Lavelle, *U.S. News & World Report*, January 10, 2005, pp. 42-50.

406. "Trouble Spots," Thomas Omstead, *U.S. News & World Report*, January 10, 2005, pp. 50-52.

407. Ibid.

408. "Endtime Nexus: Prophesied Oil Crisis," Wilfred J. Hahn, *Midnight Call*, April 2004, p. 30-31.

409. "Peak Oil Off: Great Game On," Matthew Hulbert, *Forbes*, forbes.com, April 19, 2012, referenced elsewhere on Internet Dec. 18, 2012.

410. Ibid.

411. "The Great Game: Geopolitics and Oil," Charles Hugh Smith, *oftwominds.com*/blogoct10/great-game10-10, Oct. 19, 2010.

412. "Oil Pipelines Are The 'New Great Game'," Pepe Escobar, *huffingtonpost.com*, first posted April 24, 2009—updated May 25, 2011.

413. "The 'Great Game' Enters the Mediterranean: Gas, Oil, War, and Geo-Politics," Mahdi Darius Nazemroava, Global Research report, *globalresearch.ca*/the-great-game..., Oct. 14, 2007; reprinted on the Internet elsewhere Dec. 18, 2012.

414. Ibid.

415. "The Game Gets Serious," Bill Powell and Steve LeVine, *NEWSWEEK*, Nov. 24, 1997, pp. 48-49.

416. "Blood and Oil," cover—The *Economist*, Feb. 26- March 4, 2011.

417. Op. cit. "The 'Great Game' Enters the Mediterranean...."

418. "If oil hits a certain price, world will no longer want Israel to exist," Avi Bar-Eli, *Haaretz.com*, Oct. 19, 2010.

419. "Eye On the Middle East," Steve Herzog, *Israel My Glory*, Nov/Dec. 2011.

420. "1973 oil crisis," *Wikipedia* (Distillation of the world-shaking drama of the Arab world's response to the western world's aid to Israel in protecting her against the surprise attack of Arab nations against Israel on Yom Kippur, 1973. An article well worth current consideration). Jan. 24, 2005.

421. "Oil reserves found in Israel could change power structure in region," Jack Minor, *greeleygazette.com*/press, Sept. 1, 2010.

422. "U.S. Expert Predicts 'Oil and Gas Rush' to Israel," Gil Rosen, *Arutz Sheva*, israelnationalnews.com, April 11, 2010.

423. "Israel bids to end global oil dependency by 2020," Avi Bar-Eli, *Haaretz.com*, Sept. 19, 2010.

424. "Israel's Coast May Be Gold Mine of Oil…," Tzvi Ben Gedalyahu, *Arutz Sheva*, israelnationalnews.com, June 1, 2011.

425. "Natural Gas Bonanza for Israel, Possible Oil Field as Well," Maayana Miskin, *Arutz Sheva*, israelnationalnews.com, June 3, 2010.

426. "Meged 5 Oil Well Compared to 'Giving of the Torah,'" Chana Ya'ar and Chezky Ezra, *Arutz Sheva*, israelnationalnews.com, Aug. 24, 2010.

427. "Leviathan Oil Field Could Sustain Israel For Decades," Christopher Helman, *Forbes.com*, Aug. 30, 2010.

428. "Israel introduces stamp picturing gas reserves," Sharon Udasin, The *Jerusalem Post*, jpost.com, December 12, 2012.

429. "Erdogan drives toward armed clash with Israel. Oil and gas at stake," *DEBKAfile*, debka.com/article/21282/Erdogan-drives-toward-armed-clash-with-Israel-Oil-and-gas-at-stake, Sept. 9, 2011.

430. "Israel painted as bad guy to speed Lebanese drilling," Sharon Udasin, The *Jerusalem Post*, jpost.com, Nov. 7, 2011.

431. "Landau: We will defend gas fields," The *Jerusalem Post*, jpost.com, June 24, 2010.

432. "Putin Eyes Lebanon's Energy Sources," studygrowknowblog.com/2010/12/09/from-the-file-putin-eyes-lebanons-energy-sources/, reporting on *DEBKAfile* article "Moscow, Ankara move in on Lebanon's offshore energy potential," debka.com/article/20435/Moscow-Ankara-move-in-on-Lebanon-s-offshore-energy-potential, Dec. 8, 2010.

433. "Texas oilman seeks gusher from God in Israel," *Reuters* report as released by *MSNBC News*, msn.com, April 6, 2005.

434. "A Vision of Oil in the Holy Land," Dan Ephron, *NEWSWEEK*, June 13, 2005, p. 10.

435. "Russia's Israeli Oil Bond," Dr. Sam Vaknin, *United Press International* and *samvak.tripod.com*/brief-russia-israel101, November 4, 2002.

436. Op. cit., "A Vision of Oil in the Holy Land"

437. "Israeli Oil?," Peter Enave for The *Associated Press*, as published in The *Wall Street Journal*, Sunday, pp. E 3-6, Sept. 12, 2004.

438. "His mission: Seek and ye shall find oil," Leah Krauss, *USA Today*, usatoday.com, May 18, 2005.

439. "A Sea of Oil?" Rena Rossner, The *Jerusalem Report*, April 19, 2004, pp. 30, 32.

440. "High Stakes Gamble," Rena Rossner, The *Jerusalem Report*, April 19, 2004, p. 31.

441. Ibid.

442. Final Combustion: Oil, Islam and the Christian West," Wilfred Hahn, *Midnight Call*, April 2006, pp. 28-35.

443. Ibid, p. 33.

# ABOUT THE AUTHOR

FOR A VETERAN TRIAL ATTORNEY to be referred to as "a prophet for our time" is indeed unusual, but many who have heard Charles Crismier's daily radio broadcast, *VIEWPOINT*, believe just that. Now, in *KING of the Mountain*, his words, full of "passion and conviction," provide clear insight and direction in an increasingly chaotic, dangerous and deceptive world.

Crismier speaks from an unusual breadth of experience. After nine years as a public school teacher, he spent twenty years as a trial attorney, pleading causes before judge and jury. As a pastor's son, also serving in pastoral roles for 30 years, Crismier has been involved with ten distinct Protestant denominations–both mainline and otherwise, together with other independent and charismatic groups from coast to coast–providing an enviable insider's view of American Christianity and life as well as unique insight into world events.

Deeply troubled by the direction of America, Israel, the Church and our world, this attorney left his Southern California law practice in 1992 to form SAVE AMERICA Ministries and was awarded the Valley Forge Freedom Foundation award for his contribution to the cause of "Rebuilding the Foundations of Faith and Freedom." "Chuck probes the heart and conscience with both a rare combination of insight, directness, urgency and compassion, and a message that desperately needs to be heard and heeded before it is too late."

From the birthplace of America–Richmond, Virginia–this attorney speaks provocatively and prophetically on daily national radio as "a Voice to the Church," declaring "Vision for the Nation" in America's greatest crisis hour, *preparing the way of the Lord* for history's final hour. That passion now pleads persuasively with the peoples, presidents, prime ministers, pundits and proclaimed religious leaders of our world in *KING of the Mountain*.

Charles Crismier can be contacted by writing or calling:

PO Box 70879
Richmond VA 23255
(804) 754-1822
crismier@saveus.org

or
visit his website:
www.saveus.org

## Other Life-Changing Books by Charles Crismier

### OUT of EGYPT
*Building End-time Trust for End-time Trials.*

Liberating... yet sobering. If Abraham, Moses, Israel, and...yes, Jesus had to "come out Egypt," how about us? The words "out of Egypt" or similar words appear over 400 times from Genesis to Revelation. Why has this theme been mentioned perhaps more than any other in the entire Bible? You will read... and re-read this book!

**$ 17**

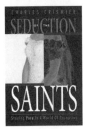

### SEDUCTION of the SAINTS
*Staying Pure in a World of Deception*

"Take heed that no man deceive you," declared Jesus just before his cruci-fixion. His words were chilling! They cast a frame around life and eternity. In the final moments of his life on earth, Jesus chose to leave the disciples, with whom he had invested his life and ministry, a penetrating and haunt-ing warning they would never forget...a warning that echoes through the centuries to all his disciples preparing for the end of the age.

**$ 18**

### The POWER of HOSPITALITY
*An Open Heart, Open Hand and Open Home Will Change Your World*

The Apostle Paul reminds that ALL who claim Christ as savior must, as a demonstration of their faith, be "given to hospitality." Pastors and leaders are to be "lovers of hospitality" as a condition of leadership. And Peter said, "The end of all things is at hand,... therefore use hospitality." Here is life-changing inspiration... PRACTICAL, PERSONAL and PROPHETIC.

**$ 16**

### The SECRET of the LORD
*The Hidden Truth That Defines Your Destiny*

God has a secret. It is a life-changing, destiny-determining "secret." It is a "secret" because the Bible says it is. It is God's secret because He has declared it to be "secret." Yet it is a secret God desires to disclose to all who will seek it, unlocking all of the covenantal blessings and promises of God, both on earth and for eternity.

**$ 16**

### RENEWING the SOUL of AMERICA
*One Person at a Time...Beginning With You*

In this compelling and insightful book by Charles Crismier, you will be inspired and challenged as an American and a patriot as you experience a candid look into the true American dream, reminding us that America's soul can be renewed...one person at a time...beginning with you.

**$18**

**Find them ALL at saveus.org
or call SAVE AMERICA Ministries 1 (800) SAVEUSA**